UNDERSTANDING INTERNATIONAL RELATIONS

Also by Chris Brown

International Relations Theory: New Normative Approaches

Political Restructuring in Europe (editor)

International Relations in Political Thought (editor with Terry Nardin and N. J. Rengger)

Sovereignty, Rights and Justice

Understanding International Relations

Fourth Edition

**Chris Brown
and
Kirsten Ainley**

First edition 1997
Second edition 2001
Third edition 2005
Fourth edition 2009

Published by
PALGRAVE MACMILLAN

Palgrave Macmillan in the UK is an imprint of Macmillan Publishers Limited,
registered in England, company number 785998, of Houndmills, Basingstoke,
Hampshire RG21 6XS.

Palgrave Macmillan in the US is a division of St Martin's Press LLC,
175 Fifth Avenue, New York, NY 10010.

Palgrave Macmillan is the global academic imprint of the above companies
and has companies and representatives throughout the world.

Palgrave® and Macmillan® are registered trademarks in the United States,
the United Kingdom, Europe and other countries

ISBN-13: 978-0-230-21310-4   hardback
ISBN-10: 0-230-21310-3   hardback
ISBN-13: 978-0-230-21311-1   paperback
ISBN-10: 0-230-21311-1   paperback

This book is printed on paper suitable for recycling and made from fully
managed and sustained forest sources. Logging, pulping and manufacturing
processes are expected to conform to the environmental regulations of the
country of origin.

A catalogue record for this book is available from the British Library.

A catalog record for this book is available from the Library of Congress.

10 9 8 7 6 5 4 3 2 1
18 17 16 15 14 13 12 11 10 09

Printed and bound in China

Contents

Preface to the Fourth Edition

The structure of this, the fourth edition of *Understanding International Relations,* follows that established in the third edition. Chapter 12 is wholly new, and reflects the changes that have taken place over the last four years and, especially, that are likely to take place in the future, in particular the re-emergence of something that looks a little like a multi-polar world. The serious possible consequences of the downturn in the world economy are also examined. Chapter 4 has been recast substantially around the agency–structure debate, and Chapter 11 has been revised extensively to take into account the fast-moving story of the International Criminal Court. All other chapters have been revised and updated, as have the suggestions for further reading, which are now orientated somewhat more towards the use of journals, since so much journal literature is now widely available on line.

The previous edition of *Understanding International Relations* was dominated by 9/11 and the issue of American power, but no such clear-cut organizing theme can be discerned in this edition. The unsatisfactory outcome of the Iraq War of 2003 – unsatisfactory being something of an understatement here – and the general sense within the United States that the country is on the wrong path has put debates about an American Empire on the back burner; if anything, the tendency now is to underestimate US power. The reawakening of Russian nationalism on the back of its oil and natural gas revenues, and the remarkable growth of the Chinese economy has led some to see the emergence of a new balance of power in the world, but this is clearly premature, and in any event, the present downturn in the world economy is likely to affect both these powers as severely as it does their more established rivals. Meanwhile, growth in what used to be called the South has been generally very substantial, but with the 'bottom billion' left behind and with few options for catching up. All this adds up to a world where it is not easy to summarise its main features. Our hope is that, as events unfold, readers of this book will find that the theories described here help them to make sense of the puzzle.

We are grateful to Joe Hoover and Marjo Koivisto for their work as our research assistants on bibliographical matters, and for their comments on the text, and to Joe for updating the 'Further Reading' sections of each chapter so assiduously. Thanks also to Amnon Aran, George Lawson and Brian Mabee for their comments and suggestions on particular chapters, and to Steven Kennedy and Stephen Wenham at Palgrave Macmillan; as always Steven has been relentless, but unfailingly positive, and Stephen has helped us with what is, we think, the best cover the book has had!

In order to save space, the prefaces to previous editions have not been included this time, and so we would like to conclude by thanking all the individuals who read the manuscript or contributed to earlier editions, and those students on courses at Kent, Southampton and LSE who have acted as guinea pigs for so much of what follows.

CHRIS BROWN
KIRSTEN AINLEY

London School of Economics and Political Science

List of Abbreviations

BIAs	bilateral immunity agreements
BWS	Bretton Woods System
CAP	Common Agricultural Policy
CEDAW	Convention on the Elimination of All Forms of Discrimination Against Women
CFCs	chlorofluorocarbons
ECLA	Economic Commission for Latin America
EDU	European Defence Union
FPA	foreign policy analysis
GATT	General Agreement on Tariffs and Trade
GSP	Generalized System of Preferences
ICC	International Criminal Court
ICRC	International Committee of the Red Cross
ICTR	International Criminal Tribunal for Rwanda
ICTY	International Criminal Tribunal for the former Yugoslavia
IGOs	intergovernmental organizations
IMF	International Monetary Fund
IPC	Integrated Programme for Commodities
IPE	international political economy
IR	International Relations
IRBM	Intermediate Range Ballistic Missiles
ISI	import substitution industrialization
IT	information technology
ITO	International Trade Organization
KLA	Kosovo Liberation Army
LIEO	liberal international economic order
MFA	Multi-Fibre Arrangement
MNC	multinational corporation
MSF	Médecins Sans Frontières
NATO	North Atlantic Treaty Organization
NGOs	non-governmental organizations
NICs	newly industrializing countries
NIEO	New International Economic Order
OECD	Organisation for Economic Co-operation and Development
R&D	research and development
RAM	Rational Actor Model
SRF	Soviet Rocket Forces

UN	United Nations
UNCED	United Nations Conference on Environment and Development
UNCTAD	United Nations Conference on Trade and Development
VERs	voluntary export restraints
WMD	weapons of mass destruction
WTO	World Trade Organization

Chapter 1

Introduction: Defining International Relations

This book is an introduction to the discipline of International Relations; 'International Relations' (with initial capitals – here frequently shortened to IR) is the study of 'international relations' (lower case) –the use of upper and lower case in this way has become conventional and will be employed throughout this book. But what are 'international relations'? A survey of the field suggests that a number of different definitions are employed. For some, international relations means the *diplomatic–strategic* relations of *states,* and the characteristic focus of IR is on issues of war and peace, conflict and co-operation. Others see international relations as being about *cross-border transactions* of all kinds, political, economic and social, and IR is as likely to study trade negotiations or the operation of non-state institutions such as Amnesty International as it is conventional peace talks or the workings of the United Nations (UN). Again, and with increasing frequency in the twenty-first century, some focus on *globalization* – studying, for example, world communication, transport and financial systems, global business corporations and the putative emergence of a global society. These conceptions obviously bear some family resemblances, but nevertheless, each has quite distinct features. Which definition we adopt will have real consequences for the rest of our study, and thus will be more than simply a matter of convenience.

The reason definitions matter in this way is because 'international relations' do not have any kind of essential existence in the real world of the sort that could define an academic discipline. Instead, there is a continual interplay between the 'real world' and the world of knowledge. The latter is, of course, shaped by the former, but this is not simply a one-way relationship. How we understand and interpret the world is partly dependent on how we define the world we are trying to understand and interpret. Since it is always likely to be the case that any definition we adopt will be controversial, this presents a problem that cannot be glossed over. Some of the difficulties we face here are shared by the social sciences as a whole, while others are specific to International Relations. The arguments are often not easy to grasp, but the student who understands what the problem is here will have gone a long way towards comprehending how the social sciences function and why IR theory is a such complex and difficult, but ultimately very rewarding, subject for study.

It is generally true of the social sciences that their subject-matter is not self-defining in the way that is often the case in the natural sciences. An example may help to make this clear. Consider a textbook entitled *Introductory Myrmecology*. This will, on page 1, define its terms by explaining that myrmecology is the study of ants, which is unproblematic because we know what an 'ant' is. The classificatory scheme that produces the category 'ant' is well understood and more or less universally accepted by the relevant scientific community; anyone who tried to broaden that category in a dramatic way would not be taken seriously. There is a scientific consensus on the matter. Ants do not label themselves as such; the description 'ant' is given to them by scientists, but since everyone whose opinion counts is of one mind in this matter, we need have no worries about forgetting that this is so. We can, in effect, treat ants as though they did, indeed, define themselves as such. By contrast, there are virtually no areas of the social sciences where this kind of universal consensus can be relied upon to define a field. Perhaps the nearest equivalent is found in economics, where the majority of economists do agree on the basics of what an 'economy' is, and therefore what their discipline actually studies – however, it is noteworthy that even here in the social science that most forcefully asserts its claim to be a 'real' science, there are a number of dissidents who want to define their subject-matter in a different way from that approved of by the majority. These dissidents – 'political economists' for example, or 'Marxist economists' – are successfully marginalized by the majority, but they survive and continue to press their case in a way that somebody who tried to contest the definition of an ant would not.

In the case of most of the other social sciences, even the incomplete level of consensus achieved by the economists does not exist. Thus, for example, in political science the very nature of *politics* is heavily contested: is 'politics' something associated solely with government and the state? We often talk about university politics or student politics – is this a legitimate extension of the idea of politics? What of the politics of the family? Much Western political thinking rests on a distinction between the public realm and private life – but feminists and others have argued that 'the personal is the political'. This latter point illustrates a general feature of definitional problems in the social sciences – they are not politically innocent. The feminist critique of traditional definitions of politics is that their emphasis on public life hid from view the oppressions that took place (and still take place) behind closed doors in patriarchal institutions such as the traditional family, with its inequalities of power and a division of labour that disadvantages women. Such critiques make a more general point; conventional definitions in most of the social sciences tend to privilege an account of the world that reflects the interests of those who are dominant within a particular area. There are no politically neutral ways of describing 'politics' or 'economics' – though this does not mean that we cannot agree among ourselves to use a particular definition for the sake of convenience.

What does this tell us about how to go about defining international relations/International Relations? Two things. First, we have to accept that if we can find a definition it will be a matter of convention; there is no equivalent to an actual ant here – 'international relations' does not define the field of 'International Relations'; rather, scholars and practitioners of the subject provide the definition. It should be noted that this is not to endorse the post-structuralist position that there is 'nothing beyond the text'; needless to say, there is indeed a real world, with real people acting in it – the point is that which actions we take to be the subject matter of International Relations is not something that is self-evident, but rather requires a contribution from the analyst. Second, while it may make sense for us to start with the conventional, traditional definition of the subject, we should be aware that this definition is sure to embody a particular account of the field – and that the way it does this is unlikely to be politically neutral. Instead, what we can expect is a definition of the field which, while purporting to be objective – simply reflecting 'the way things are' – is actually going to be, perhaps unconsciously, partisan and contentious. It follows that, having started with the conventional account, we shall have to examine its hidden agenda before moving to alternative definitions; which, of course, will in turn have their own hidden agendas.

There can be little doubt that the conventional definition of the field is that given first in the opening paragraph of this chapter, namely that IR is the study of the relations of states, and that those relations are understood primarily in *diplomatic, military* and *strategic* terms – this is certainly the way in which diplomats, historians and most scholars of IR have defined the subject. The relevant unit is the *state*, not the *nation*; most states may nowadays aspire to be nation-states, but it is the possession of statehood rather than nationhood that is central – indeed, the term 'interstate' would be more accurate than 'international' were it not for the fact that this is the term used in the United States to describe relations between, say, California and Arizona. Thus the United Kingdom fits more easily into the conventional account of international relations than Scotland, or Canada than Quebec, even though Scotland and Quebec are more unambiguously 'nations' than either the United Kingdom or Canada. The distinguishing feature of the state is *sovereignty*. This is a difficult term, but at its root is the idea of legal autonomy. Sovereign states are sovereign because no higher body has the *right* to issue orders to them. In practice, some states may have the *ability* to influence the behaviour of other states, but this influence is a matter of power not authority (see Chapter 5 below).

To put the matter differently, the conventional account of international relations stresses the fact that the relationship between states is one of *anarchy*.

Anarchy in this context does not necessarily mean lawlessness and chaos; rather, it means the absence of a formal system of government. There is in international relations no formal centre of authoritative decision-making such as exists, in principle at least, within the state. This is why stress is placed traditionally on diplomacy and strategy; while the term 'international politics' is often used loosely in this context, international relations are not really political, because, again for traditional reasons, politics is about authority and government, and there is no international authority in the conventional sense of the term. Instead of looking to influence government to act on their behalf, participants in international relations are obliged to look after their own interests and pursue them by employing their own resources – we live in, as the jargon has it, a *self-help* system. Because it is a self-help system, *security* is the overriding concern of states; and *diplomacy,* the exercise of influence, exists in a context where force is, at the very least, a possibility. The possibility that force might be exercised is what makes the state – which actually possesses and disposes of armed force – the key international actor. Other bodies are secondary to the state, and the myriad of other activities that take place across state boundaries, economic, social, cultural and so on, are equally secondary to the diplomatic–strategic relations of states.

What is wrong with this *state-centric* (an ugly but useful piece of jargon) definition of the subject? Placed in context, nothing very much. There is indeed a world that works like this, in which diplomats and soldiers are the key actors, and there are parts of the world where it would be very unwise of any state not to be continually conscious of security issues – in the Middle Eastern 'Arc of Conflict', for example. Moreover, it is striking that even those states that feel most secure can find themselves suddenly engaged in military conflict for reasons that could not have been predicted in advance. Few predicted in January 1982 that Britain and Argentina would go to war over the Falklands/Malvinas later that year, for example; or, in January 1990, that an Iraqi invasion of Kuwait would lead to a major war in the Gulf in 1990–1, but it is the nature of the international system that it throws up this kind of surprise.

For all that, physical violence and overt conflict are nowhere near as central to international relations as the traditional description of the subject would suggest. Most countries, most of the time, live at peace with their neighbours and the world at large. Transactions take place across borders – movements of people, goods, money, information and ideas – in a peaceful, routine way. We take it for granted that a letter posted in Britain or Australia to Brazil, the United States or South Africa will be delivered. Using the internet we can order a book or a CD from another country, confident that our credit card will be recognized and honoured. A cursory examination of the nearest kitchen, wardrobe or hi-fi rack will reveal goods from all around the world. We plan our holidays abroad without more than a passing thought about the formalities of border crossing. What is truly remarkable is that we no longer find all this remarkable – at least not within the countries of the advanced industrial world. These developments seem, at least on the surface, to be very positive, but there are other things that happen across borders nowadays that are less welcome, such as problems of pollution and environmental degradation, the drugs and arms trade, international terrorism and other international crimes – these factors pose threats to our security, although not in quite the same way as war and violent conflict.

What implication does this have for a description of the discipline of International Relations? There are several possibilities here. We might well decide to remain committed to a state-centric view of the discipline, but abandon, or weaken, the assumption that the external policy of the state is dominated by questions of (physical) security. On this account, states remain the central actors in international relations. They control, or at least try to control, the borders over which transactions take place, and they claim, sometimes successfully, to regulate the international activities of their citizens. They issue passports and visas, make treaties with each other with the intention of managing trade flows and matters of copyright and crime, and set up international institutions in the hope of controlling world finance or preventing environmental disasters. In short, national diplomacy goes on much as in the traditional model, but without the assumption that force and violence are its central concerns. Most of the time, 'economic statecraft' is just as important as the traditional concerns of foreign-policy management – even if it tends to be conducted by the ministry responsible for trade or finance rather than external affairs.

A problem with this account of the world of international relations is hinted at by the number of qualifications in the above paragraph. States do indeed try to do all these things, but often they do not succeed. Too many of these cross-border activities are in the hands of private organizations such as international firms, or take place on terrain where it is notoriously difficult for states to act effectively, such as international capital markets. Often, the resources possessed by non-state actors – non-governmental organizations (NGOs) – are greater than those of at least some of the states that are attempting to regulate them. Moreover, the institutions that states set up to help them manage this world of *complex interdependence* tend to develop a life of their own, so that bodies such as the International Monetary Fund (IMF) or the World Trade Organization (WTO) end up out of the control of even the strongest of the states that originally made them. Frequently, states are obliged to engage in a form of diplomacy with these actors, recognizing them as real players in the game rather than simply as instruments or as part of the stakes for which the game is played. For this reason, some think the focus of the discipline should be on cross-border transactions in general, and the ways in which states and non-state actors relate to each other. States may still be, much of the time, the dominant actors, but this is a pragmatic judgement rather than a matter of principle and, in any event, they must always acknowledge that on many issues other players are in the game. International relations is a complex, issue-sensitive affair in which the interdependence of states and societies is as striking a feature as their independence.

For a diplomat of the 1900s this would have seemed a very radical view of the world, but in fact it stands squarely on the shoulders of the older, traditional conception of the discipline; the underlying premise is that separate national societies are relating to each other just as they always have done, but on a wider range of issues. Other conceptions of international relations are genuinely more radical in their implications. Theorists of *globalization,* while still for the most part conscious of the continued importance of states, refuse to place them at the centre of things. Instead their focus is on global political, social and, in particular, economic transactions, and on the new technologies that have created the internet, the twenty-four-hour stock market and an increasingly tightly integrated global system. Rather than beginning with national states and working towards the global, these writers start with the global and bring the state into play only when it is appropriate to do so.

The more extreme advocates of globalization clearly overstate their case – the idea that we live in a 'borderless world' (Ohmae 1990) is ridiculous – but more careful analysts can no longer be dismissed by traditional scholars of IR. The more interesting issues nowadays revolve around the *politics* of globalization; are these new global trends reinforcing or undermining the existing divide in the world between rich and poor? Is globalization another name for global capitalism, or, perhaps, in the cultural realm, Americanization? One radical approach to International Relations – sometimes called *structuralism* or *centre–periphery analysis* – has always stressed the existence of global forces, a world structure in which dominant interests/classes largely – but not entirely – located in the advanced industrial world, dominate and exploit the rest of the world, using economic, political and military means to this end. From this neo-Marxist viewpoint, rather than a world of states and national societies, we have a stratified global system in which class dominates class on the world stage, and the conventional division of the world into national societies is the product of a kind of false consciousness that leads individuals who make up these allegedly-separate societies to think of themselves as having common interests thereby, as opposed to their real interests, which reflect their class positions. Clearly, this vision of the world has much in common with that of globalization, though many advocates of the latter have a more positive view of the process, but 'structuralist' ideas have also fed into the somewhat confused ideology of many of the new radical opponents of globalization who have made their presence felt at recent WTO meetings. One further consideration; what is sometimes referred to as the first globalization took place at the end of the nineteenth century, but collapsed with the outbreak of war in 1914 – will the second globalization end in the same way, perhaps a casualty of the events of 9/11 and the subsequent 'war on terror'?

These issues will be returned to at various points later in this book, but by now it ought to be clear why defining International Relations is a tricky business, and why no simple definition is, or could be, or should be, widely adopted. Each of the positions discussed above has a particular take on the world, each reflects a partial understanding of the world, and if any one of these positions were to be allowed to generate a definition of the field it would be placed in a privileged position that it had not earned. If, for example, a traditional definition of International Relations as the study of states, security and war is adopted, then issues of complex interdependence and globalization are marginalized, and those who wish to focus on these approaches are made to seem unwilling to address the real agenda. And yet it is precisely the question of what *is* the real agenda that has not been addressed. On the basis that there must be some kind of limiting principle if we are to study anything at all, we might agree that International Relations is the study of cross-border transactions in general, and thus leave open the nature of these transactions, but even this will not really do, since it presumes the importance of political boundaries, which some radical theorists of globalization deny. Definition is simply not possible yet – in a sense, the whole of the rest of this book is an extended definition of international relations. However, before we can approach these matters of substance we must first address another contentious issue, namely the nature of 'theory' in International Relations.

Perspectives and theories

This is a 'theoretical' introduction to International Relations. We have already seen the difficulty involved in defining the latter term – can we do any better with 'theory'? As always, there are both simple and complicated definitions of theory, but on this occasion simple is best – unlike defining 'international relations', where simplicity is misleading. Theory, at its simplest, is reflective thought. We engage in theorizing when we think in depth and in an abstract way about something. Why should we do this? Simply because we sometimes find ourselves asking questions we are not able to answer without reflection, without abstract thought. Sometimes the question we are posing is about how things work, or *why things happen*. Sometimes the question is about *what we should do,* either in the sense of what action is instrumental to bringing about a particular kind of result or in the sense of what action is morally right. Sometimes the question is about *what something or other means,* how it is to be interpreted. Different kinds of theory are engaged here, but the root idea is the same – we turn to theory when the answer to a question that is, for one reason or another, important to us is not clear. Of course, sometimes when the answer is apparently clear it may be wrong, but we shall not be aware of this until something happens to draw our attention to the possibility that a mistake has been made.

Most of the time things *are* clear – or at least it is convenient for us to live as though they are. There are many questions we do not try to answer theoretically – though in principle we could – because we regard the answer as being obvious, and life is too short to spend a great deal of time thinking in depth and abstractly about things that are obvious. Instead, very sensibly, we concentrate on questions where the answer is not obvious, or, better, seems actually to be counter-intuitive. To extend an example used in a brief discussion of the role of theory by Susan Strange, we tend not to waste too much time asking ourselves why people characteristically run *out* of a burning building (Strange 1988: 11). If we wanted to theorize this, we could; a theoretical explanation would refer to phenomena such as the effect of fire on human tissue and smoke on human lungs, the desire of humans to avoid pain and death, and so on. The point is that this is all pretty obvious, and there is no need to make a meal of it. On the other hand, if we wish to explain why people might run *into* a burning building, some kind of theorizing may be necessary. Again, the answer might be readily to hand – they may be members of a firefighting service who have contracted to do this sort of thing under certain circumstances – or it might not. It might be the case, for example, that the person running into the building was a private individual attempting a rescue. In such circumstances we might well wish to think in some depth about the circumstances under which one person would risk his or her life for another – asking ourselves how common this kind of altruism is, whether it is usually kin-related and so on. It is interesting that even this simple example is capable of generating a number of different kinds of theory – examples might include explanatory theory, normative theory, interpretative theory. However, rather than follow up this artificial example, it would be better to move to an example central to the discipline; an example of a difficult question which, Strange suggests, only slightly overstating her case, is the formative question for our discipline – namely: why do states go to war with one another?

In the nineteenth century there was not a great deal of theorizing on the causes of war in general, because most people thought that the causes of war, at least in the international system of that era, were obvious. Historical studies of particular wars might discuss the cause of the war in question, but only as a prelude to an account of the course of the war, not as a major focus. It was taken for granted that states went to war for gain, or in self-defence because they were attacked by some other state acting for gain. A premise of the system was that wars were initiated by states that hoped to be the victors, and hoped to reap benefits in excess of potential losses. War was sometimes a rational choice for states, and a legitimate choice too, because a majority of international lawyers believed that the right to declare war without any external approval was inherent in the nature of sovereignty. Wars were what states did; sometimes successfully, sometimes not. The self-evidence of this interpretation seemed supported by the historical record of nineteenth-century wars – successful diplomatists such as Bismarck, and imperialists such as Rhodes, fought wars of conquest which did, indeed, seem to bring results.

Now, if war is initiated on the basis of a simple cost–benefit analysis, it follows that if potential costs rise disproportionately to potential benefits, then there should be fewer wars – indeed, there should be none at all if costs were to rise very steeply while benefits stayed steady or actually fell. In the early years of the twentieth century, it seemed that just such a transformation was taking place. For modern industrial societies, the benefits from conquest seem trivial by comparison with the costs that war would bring – large-scale death and destruction made possible by new weapons, the collapse of an interdependent world economy, political instability and turmoil. This was a commonplace of the early years of the century, well caught by a best-seller of the day, Norman Angell's *The Great Illusion* (Angell 1909). It seemed obvious that war would no longer be a profitable enterprise. Moreover, these economic realities were reinforced by increasing moral disquiet over the idea that states had a right to go to war whenever they wanted to.

Then came 1914, and the greatest war the European system had seen for 300 years inaugurated a century of warfare. Of course, Angell had been absolutely correct. War was indeed disastrous to its initiators, and to many others too. Millions died pointlessly, regimes fell, economic chaos prevailed, and the seeds of a new war were sown. How could something so obviously and predictably counter-productive happen? Twentieth-century theorizing about international relations begins here. Something seemed to be wrong with the 'obvious' answer, and early students of international relations felt the need to think more deeply about the causes of war in order to answer a question that previously had not been thought not to demand a great deal of theoretical consideration. A vast literature was produced on the causes of the First World War, stimulated by the 'war-guilt' clause of the Treaty of Versailles, which attributed blame solely to Germany. More generally, over the twentieth century and beyond a number of theories of the causes of war have been elaborated, ranging from the role of special interests to the psychological profile of particular countries or leaders. At the end of the day, it may be the case that such work in fact vindicates the 'common sense' of the 1900s by showing, for example, that both sides believed themselves to be acting defensively rather than deliberately initiating a war – indeed, the dominance of rational choice theory in, especially American, political science today means that cost–benefit accounts of war are as privileged today as they were in the nineteenth century – but the point is that nowadays this is a conclusion based on theory (a version of the 'security dilemma' – see Chapter 5 below) rather than common sense, even though it confirms the latter.

Remaining with this example, we can see that there are various kinds of theory, various different circumstances in which abstract reflection is required. There are *explanatory* theories, which attempt to explain why, and under what circumstances, wars happen; and *normative* or *prescriptive* theories, which try to tell us what our attitude to war ought to be – whether, for example, we should volunteer to participate in a conflict or conscientiously object to it; to this pairing we can add theories that *interpret* events, attempting to give meaning to them – something that the carnage of the First World War seemed especially to require. In principle, these kinds of theories are interrelated – we cannot explain an occurrence without simultaneously interpreting it and orientating ourselves towards it – although, in practice, it may often be convenient for us to adopt the working practice of taking them in isolation.

As well as there being different kinds of theory, it is also the case that each kind of theory comes in a plurality of versions – there always seem to be different, competing accounts of why something happened, or what we should do, or what it means. There is rarely one single answer. Authorities differ; each offers apparently compelling reasons why their account is right, but each offers a *different* set of compelling reasons. Some students of International Relations find this rather scandalous, largely because it contradicts what our society regards as the most important exemplar of theory, the model of the natural sciences. In subjects such as physics and biology, students have 'proper' textbooks telling them what is right and what is wrong in no uncertain terms. Obviously, there are major debates within these subjects, but these are conducted at a rarefied level – textbooks generally convey the consensus prevalent among those who are qualified to have an opinion. Out-of-date theories are simply not taught, and advanced controversies are reserved for the professionals. As we have seen even in as basic a matter as the definition of the subject, this is not true in International Relations. Authoritative figures dispute with one another in public in what seems to be a very undignified way, and no idea ever really dies – though some do get close to the point where resuscitation is difficult.

Is this a matter for concern? Partly, this will depend on why we have so many theories. It might be the case that we have many competing theories because none of them is in reality very satisfactory. In the case, for example, of the causes of war, there are theories that lay stress on the personality characteristics of leaders, or on the political characteristics of regimes, or on the anarchical character of the international system. Each seems to explain some aspects of war, but not others. We might well feel that we do not really want to have so many theories in this case, but that we cannot afford to discard any of them because we are not sure which (if any) is right. Since any reduction in the number of theories might eliminate the correct answer (assuming that there *is* one correct answer), we have to keep them all in play. We cannot simply kill off the wrong answer, because we do not know which one *is* the wrong answer.

If this were the only way of looking at the multiplicity of theories and perspectives in International Relations, then the discipline would be in rather poor shape. However, it should be noted that, even from this pessimistic account of the discipline, it does not follow that there are no rules of discourse or that any single argument is as good as any other. The various competing theories of the causes of war each has its own account of what a good argument looks like, and the number of perspectives available, although multiple, is not infinite. There are some bad arguments, and a plurality of theories does not cover all possibilities, or validate all positions.

However, and in any event, it is possible to put another, rather less depressing, colouring on the existence of a plurality of theories. It may simply be the case that International Relations is not the sort of academic discipline where we should expect or welcome consensus and the absence of competing accounts of the world. In the first place, in International Relations, as in other branches of political science, we are dealing with ideas and concepts that are 'essentially contestable' because they have political implications. As we have seen above, in the natural sciences it is often possible to 'stipulate' a definition; that is, to employ a definition of a concept that will be accepted because it is clearly set out in advance. In politics, this is much more difficult – and some would say impossible. As we have seen, even the attempt to stipulate a definition of the subject-matter of the discipline, International Relations itself, runs into difficulties. If we attempt to stipulate a definition of a key concept such as *power* we run into even greater problems. We might describe power in operation along the lines of the popular formulation that 'A has power over B to the extent that A can get B to do what A wants B to do', and for certain purposes this might work, but we would be open to the objection that this does not cover, for example, structural power – the ability to shape issues in such a way that outcomes are restricted before they reach the point of decision. What is crucial here is that this is not simply an intellectual objection to this stipulated definition. It is also a political objection. The people, groups or classes who hold structural power in a society may well be different from the people, groups or classes who hold the kind of relational power envisaged in our definition, and by defining power in this way the power of the former group will be overlooked (to their considerable advantage).

This is a case in favour of pluralism in theory that applies to political science in general, but there is a further point that applies with particular force to the study of International Relations. One of the reasons why International Relations is an interesting field of study is because it attempts to produce theory on the widest canvas available to us – not simply a theory of politics in one country or continent, but a theory of global relations. This means that any worthwhile theory of international relations is going to have to be able to work with a multiplicity of cultures, with the aim of providing an account of the world that is not ethnocentric. What this involves in practice is the ability to keep in play a number of competing conceptions of how things are. We have to understand that politics often seems very different in the Middle East from the way it seems in Western Europe or Latin America. Even within these broad cultures there are significant differences that block understanding.

It may be helpful to illustrate this point with a couple of examples; first, as we shall see in Chapter 2, one of the formative diplomatic experiences of the century was the sequence of disasters that befell the international order in the run-up to the Second World War. In fact, so formative were these calamities that, some seventy years later, 'appeasement' is still a term of abuse, and new dictators are routinely compared to Hitler and Mussolini. How do we account for these disasters? Incompetence played a role, but it is also clear that a major factor was that the leaders of Britain and France thought that their view of the world was shared by all leaders, including Hitler, when in fact it was not. The most striking example of this phenomenon is supplied by the Soviet Union under Stalin, because, as is often forgotten, in this case appeasement of Hitler continued long after the outbreak of war had demonstrated the failure of this strategy in the West. Why did Stalin think that appeasement would work for him when it had failed for Chamberlain?

The answer seems to be that Stalin believed National Socialist Germany to be a capitalist state, and, as a good Leninist, he believed that the behaviour of capitalist states was driven by material needs – in particular, at this time, the need for raw materials to pursue the war. Between mid-1939 and mid-1941, Stalin acted on this belief, appeasing Hitler by helping him to pursue his war against Britain and France. He believed this would prevent Hitler from attacking the Soviet Union; since Hitler was getting what he really wanted from the USSR without war, to engage in war would be irrational, especially in the context of an unfinished war in the West. As perhaps twenty million Soviet citizens discovered, this perception was a mistake. Stalin's logic had been impeccable, but Hitler was marching to a different drum. Hitler's vision of the future was of the vast Eurasian plains populated by 'Aryans', which meant that the Slavs, Jews and other alleged undesirables who currently lived there simply had to be 'eliminated' – killed or driven into Asia. Moreover, Hitler wished to achieve this himself, and since it seems he believed (correctly as it happens) that he was destined to die relatively young, he was not prepared to wait until the end of the war with Britain before undertaking the conquest of Russia. Stalin seems genuinely to have been unable to grasp that this bizarre and evil concoction of ideas could have been seriously held by Hitler; even after the start of Operation Barbarossa – the German invasion of the Soviet Union. Stalin initially instructed his troops not to resist, on the principle that this could not be a real invasion, but must be a 'provocation' (Weinberg 1994: 186–205). We should be wary of drawing too many conclusions from such an

extreme example of miscalculation, but the basic point is that Stalin's theoretical account of the world led him badly astray because it was monolithic
rather than pluralist. He was wedded to the idea that there was always *one*
right answer, *one* right strategy; what let him down was his unwillingness to
grasp that alternative conceptions of the world might be equally powerful in
the minds of other decision-makers.

Consider, for a second and more recent example, the various different
readings of US foreign policy to be found nowadays. In the USA, while there
are many differences of opinion on foreign policy issues, most Americans,
and certainly nearly all prominent Democrat and Republican politicians,
agree in characterizing US policy towards the rest of the world as essentially
benign in intent. America protects its interests in the world, but it also sees
itself as promoting democracy and human rights, which are taken to be
universally desired; in promoting these goals, the USA is simply acting in the
global interest. Sometimes, and perhaps too frequently, mistakes are made
and the USA certainly does not always live up to its own values – the human
rights violations in Abu Ghraib prison in Iraq come to mind – but the USA
basically means well, even when things go wrong. America is a 'city on a
hill'; an example to the rest of the world. Given this perspective – a version
of what is sometimes known as 'American exceptionalism' – Americans find
it difficult to understand why their attempts to be helpful in the world are
so often misunderstood, and why their policies are misinterpreted as being
self-serving and imperialistic. The obvious answer is that those states that
oppose US policy are either behaving irresponsibly or, worse, are rogue
regimes.

In truth, of course, there is nothing particularly surprising about the fact
that peoples and governments want to define their own approaches to world
affairs, and defend their own interests, and there is no guarantee that these
definitions or interests will coincide with those of the USA. Disagreement on
such matters is part of the normal give and take of world politics, but rather
too many Americans today interpret the world through such a narrow
ideational frame that any opposition comes to be defined as essentially wrong-
headed or worse. Ironically, this attitude promotes anti-Americanism, which
is often set off not by the overt pursuit of American interests by American
governments, but by the reluctance to admit that this is what is happening, the
cloaking of interest in the language of altruism. There are echoes here of attitudes towards Britain in the days of British power – *Perfidious Albion's* reputation was based on a not dissimilar unwillingness to admit that the British
power served British interests. Continental diplomatists such as Bismarck
were not irritated by a Palmerston or a Disraeli – both unapologetic wielders
of British power – but by the liberal Gladstone, whose every foreign policy
move was covered by a miasma of moralizing rhetoric and appeals to the
interests of 'Europe'.

In fact, while the underlying attitude remains, events since 2001 have understandably instilled a certain degree of scepticism in many Americans, and a greater willingness to admit that the USA can sometimes get things badly wrong. Occasionally this tips into a kind of 'reverse American exceptionalism' which blames the American government – or sometimes the American people – for everything that goes wrong in the world. This attitude is often exemplified by radical Americans such as Noam Chomsky or (from the sublime to the ridiculous) Michael Moore, but also by figures such as John Pilger and Harold Pinter, who have become so convinced of the absolute evil represented by the USA that whenever anything bad happens it has to be interpreted to show that, essentially, America is to blame; conversely, whenever the USA does something that looks, on the face of it, to be a good thing, this cannot really be the case. Apart from leading to absurd arguments – the US-supported Australian intervention in East Timor in 1999 being designed to preserve Indonesia for exploitation by world capitalism being a personal favourite – this position is also profoundly patronizing, assuming as it does that national leaders elsewhere in the world would be unable to do wrong unless their alleged US puppet-masters pulled the strings. Alternatively, it leads to a frame of mind that excuses brutalities when they are committed by leaders who are reliably anti-American; the opposition by some parts of the left to intervention to prevent the genocide in Darfur on the grounds that this would be an act of imperialism comes to mind, or perhaps Michael Moore's lyrical scene in *Fahrenheit 911* of children playing happily in Saddam's Iraq until the arrival of the Americans.

The key point about American exceptionalism in both its positive and negative versions is not that it can lead to morally vacuous or obnoxious positions, though this is true, but that it presents a distorted view of the world. Theories that close down debates and attempt to impose a single view on the world will almost always mislead. In the recent documentary film *The Fog of War*, Robert McNamara states as his first rule for a successful war 'empathize with your enemy' – one might make this the first rule for a successful peace as well. In short, if we are to be successful theorists of IR, we must resist the tendency to define success in terms of simple models; instead, we must be prepared to live with quite high levels of ambiguity – if you want black and white, buy an old television, don't be an IR theorist.

On the face of it, this may seem to suggest that the study of International Relations is likely to be a frustrating business. On the contrary, the need for this kind of openness to ambiguity is a reflection of both the importance and the intrinsic interest of the subject. As students of international relations, we have a grandstand seat for some of the most exciting developments of our age, both in the 'real world' and in the social sciences. We are well placed to observe and comprehend what is sure to be one of the key themes of the twenty-first century, the working out of the clash between global social and economic forces on the one hand, and local cultures and political jurisdictions on the other. International Relations could be more than just an academic discourse; it could provide one of the most important languages for the peoples of the world to use in order to come to some understanding of what is happening to them. The danger is that this language will be impoverished by too ready a willingness to close down debates and reach premature conclusions, by too firm a commitment to one particular way of looking at the world – especially since that way is likely to be that of the advanced industrial countries, the rich and powerful West.

Conclusion

The aim of this chapter has been to discourage the notion that the theory of International Relations can be studied via an initial stipulative definition, the implications of which are then teased out and examined at length. Instead, the process is, or should be, almost exactly the other way around. What is required is that we explore the world of international relations from a number of different perspectives, taking each one seriously while we are examining it, but refusing to allow any single account to structure the whole, denying a privileged position to any one theory or set of theories. If, at the end of the day, we are still interested in definitions, we shall then be in a position to construct one, and in so doing identify ourselves with a particular theory or paradigm. Perhaps, instead, we shall find that this kind of identification does not help, and we shall resist the tendency to enrol in any particular theoretical army. Either way, this is a decision that ought to come at the end, rather than the beginning, of a course of intellectual study.

Still, it is necessary to start somewhere – and just as there are no innocent definitions, so there are no innocent starting-points. The approach adopted here will be to begin with the recent, twentieth-century history of theorizing of international relations, and with the theories that have underpinned this history. This starting-point could be said to privilege a rather conventional conception of the field, but in order to introduce new ideas it is necessary to have some grasp of the tradition against which the new defines itself. In any event, the approach here, in the first five chapters, will be to begin with traditional, 'common-sense' perspectives on international relations before opening up the field in the second half of the book.

Further reading

Full bibliographical details of works cited are contained in the main Bibliography after Chapter 12.

Walter Carlsnaes, Thomas Risse and Beth Simmons (eds), *Handbook of International Relations* (2004), is a very useful collection of original essays that help to define the field. Ira Katznelson and Helen Milner (eds), *Political Science: The State of the Discipline* (2002), does the same for political science as a whole, with good essays on our sub-field. The special issue of *International Organization* (1998) on the state of the discipline, edited by Peter Katzenstein, Robert Keohane and Stephen Krasner and published *as Exploration and Contestation in the Study of World* Politics (1999), is a good mainstream collection on different theoretical perspectives. The *Millennium* special issue on 'The Theory of the International Today' (2007b) is an excellent and diverse collection probing at the limits of IR as a discipline.

Readings for the different conceptions of international relations described above will be provided in detail in the individual chapters devoted to them in the rest of this book. For the moment, it may be helpful to identify a small number of texts that set out the relevant differences quite clearly. Tim Dunne *et al.* (eds), (2007) *International Relations Theories: Discipline and Diversity*, is a good, up-to-date collection that uses case studies to illustrate varied IR theories. Jennifer Sterling-Folker's *Making Sense of International Relations Theory* (2006) applies various theories to Kosovo, as a common case study. Robert Jackson and Georg Sorensen's *Introduction to International Relations: Theories and Approaches*, 3rd edn (2006) is excellent. Richard Little and Michael Smith (eds), *Perspectives on World Politics: A Reader*, 3rd edn (2006), is still a good collection of essays organized around state-centric, transnationalist and structuralist approaches. Paul Viotti and Mark Kauppi, *International Relations Theory* (1999), is organized on similar lines, providing brief extracts from important authors as well as a very extensive commentary. Scott Burchill *et al.*, *Theories of International Relations*, 4thd edn (2009), is a collection of original essays on each of the major theories. Michael Doyle, *Ways of War and Peace* (1997) is an outstanding general study. Of the big US textbooks, Charles Kegley and Eugene Wittkopf, *World Politics: Trend and Transformation* (2004) is the most sensitive to theoretical pluralism. Each of these books is listed above in its most recent incarnation: second-hand copies of earlier editions are still valuable.

William C. Olson and A. J. R. Groom, *International Relations Then and Now* (1992), gives an overview of the history of the discipline that is more conventional than Brian Schmidt's *The Political Discourse of Anarchy* (1998). In contrast, Steve Smith, Ken Booth and Marysia Zalewski (eds) *International Theory: Positivism and Beyond* (1996) is a very rewarding but more difficult collection of essays celebrating the range of approaches current in the field, and particularly interesting on methodological and epistemological issues, as is Booth and Smith, *International Relations Theory Today* (1995). John MacMillan and Andrew Linklater (eds) *Boundaries in Question* (1995) is an accessible collection on similar lines. A. J. R. Groom and Margot Light (eds) *Contemporary International Relations: A Guide* to *Theory* (1994) is a collection of bibliographical essays on different approaches and sub-fields, wider in scope than Katzenstein *et al.*, but rather dated. A recent *Millennium* exchange between Schmidt and Smith on theoretical pluralism in IR (2008) is a useful introduction to the issue.

A basic introduction to the philosophy of the natural sciences is A. F. Chalmers, *What Is This Thing Called Science?*, 3rd edn (1999). More advanced debates over 'paradigms' and 'research programmes' – of considerable relevance to the social sciences – can be followed in the essays collected in Imre Lakatos and Alan Musgrave (eds), *Criticism and the Growth of Knowledge* (1965/2008). Martin Hollis, *The Philosophy of the Social Sciences* (1995), is a good introduction to its subject, but students of International Relations have the benefit of his *Explaining and Understanding International Relations* (1991), co-authored with Steve Smith, which is the best survey of methodological and philosophical issues in the field, though not without its critics – see, for example, Hidemi Suganami, 'Agents, Structures, Narratives' (1999). Kathryn Dean *et al.* (eds), *Realism, Philosophy and Social Science* (2006), is a useful introduction to 'scientific realism' and 'critical realism' as emerging perspectives in IR and the social sciences.

The view that the social sciences can be studied in the same way as the natural sciences is often termed 'positivism', and positivists draw a sharp distinction between 'positive' and 'normative' theory – a classic statement of this position is by the economist Milton Friedman in his book *Essays in Positive Economics* (1966). A firm rebuttal of this distinction is offered by Mervyn Frost, *Ethics in International Relations* (1996), especially ch. 2, while the more general position that most key concepts in politics are 'essentially contested' is put by William Connolly in *The Terms of Political Discourse*, 3rd edn (1993). The essays in Smith, Booth and Zalewski (1996) and Booth and Smith (1994) (see above) are largely anti-positivist in orientation, in stark contrast to the current, rational choice-orientated orthodoxy examined in Chapter 3 below; the latter is probably best described as neo-positivist – Gary King, Robert Keohane and Sidney Verba (KKV), *Designing Social Enquiry: Scientific Inference in Qualitative Research* (1994) is the bible for this kind of research.

Michael Nicholson, *Causes and Consequences in International Relations: A Conceptual Survey* (1996), demonstrates that not all sophisticated positivists are realists. Chris Brown, *International Relations Theory: New Normative Approaches* (1992a), is a survey of normative theories of international relations; more up to date are Brown's *Sovereignty, Rights and Justice* (2002) and Molly Cochran's *Normative Theory in International Relations* (2000); Mark Neufeld, *The Restructuring of International Relations Theory* (1995) is a good brief introduction to 'critical' international theory, and Richard Wyn Jones's excellent *Security, Strategy and Critical Theory* (1999) has a wider range than its title would suggest. The latter's collection *Critical Theory and World Politics* (2001) is equally good. Jim George, *Discourses of Global Politics: A Critical (Re)Introduction to International Relations* (1994), covers so-called 'postmodern' approaches to the field: Jenny Edkins, *Poststructuralism and International Relations* (1999), is equally good, and more recent. A relatively accessible, albeit controversial, introduction to constructivism is Alexander Wendt, *Social Theory of International Politics* (1999).

Chapter 2

The Development of International Relations Theory in the Twentieth Century

Introduction

Wherever different territorially-based political orders coexist in the same social world, some form of international relations is to be found – even though the term itself was not coined until the end of the eighteenth century (Bentham 1789/1960: 426). The academic study of International Relations, on the other hand, existed only in embryo before the First World War. In the second half of the nineteenth century, when the social sciences as we know them today began to be differentiated, when 'economics' emerged out of political economy as an allegedly scientific field of study, and when 'sociology' and 'politics' and 'social theory' came to be seen as addressing different agendas – a position that would have surprised Jean-Jacques Rousseau, Adam Smith or Immanuel Kant – 'International Relations' remained unidentified as a discrete focus for study. Instead, what we nowadays think of as International Relations was for the most part seen as simply one facet of a number of other disciplines (history, international law, economics, political theory) although, as Brian Schmidt has demonstrated, political scientists addressed the field rather more systematically than had previously been thought to be the case (Schmidt 1998).

Pace Schmidt, it was not until the slaughter of 1914–18 persuaded a number of influential thinkers and philanthropists that new ways of thinking about international relations were required that the field of IR emerged. These philanthropists saw it as essential to *theorize* international relations, to move our level of understanding of the subject above that provided by an education in 'current affairs', and in setting this goal they established a concern with theory that has dominated the new discipline – perhaps to its disadvantage – ever since. Certainly, IR has always been a theoretically conscious social science, though this is often denied by the purveyors of new learning, which is, it might well be argued, a little too concerned with its own history, a little too self-referential. It has become customary to write of the history of IR theory in terms of a series of rather grandly titled 'great debates' between meta-theoretical positions such as *realism* and *idealism,* or *positivism* and *constructivism,* but it is by no means clear that this is a helpful way of characterizing the past of the discipline – rather, it may encourage a tendency to navel-gazing.

There is a broader issue here, which concerns the origins of IR theory. To simplify matters, has theory developed in response to events/changes in the real world (as has been the conventional belief), or is the process of theory development internal to the discourse, a product of the dynamics within a particular community, as revisionist disciplinary historians such as Schmidt suggest? Common sense suggests that both processes are involved. It is certainly the case that theories are never abandoned until a replacement is available, but, equally, it would go against the record to suggest that the international history of the twentieth century was not implicated in theory development – perhaps more to the point, the separation between a real world and a world of theory is, as was argued in Chapter 1, a little artificial. In any event, in this and the next chapter, the story of attempts to understand IR will be told with only a minimal number of references to the great debates, and the question of the origins of theory will be left open, with references made to both the above positions where appropriate; instead, in this chapter, a historical sketch of the conceptual development of the subject will be offered, while in the next, the currently dominant approach and its main critics will be examined.

Liberal internationalism and the origins of the discipline

The destruction on the battlefields of 1914–18 produced a sequence of reactions. The first response of many was to assign personal responsibility for the carnage – in Britain and France, the German Kaiser was widely blamed, and 'Hang the Kaiser' became a popular cry, although after the war no serious attempt was made to reclaim him from his exile in the Netherlands. Even during the conflict, more thoughtful people quickly came to the conclusion that this was an inadequate response to the causes of war. While Germany might bear a greater responsibility than some other countries, there was something about the system of international relations that was culpable, and a variety of different thinkers, politicians and philanthropists gave thought to ways of changing the system to prevent a recurrence. Most of these individuals were American or British (and, in fact, the discipline of International Relations remains to this day largely a product of the English-speaking world, though, happily, this may not be the case for much longer). The dominant mood in France was for revenge against Germany, while in Russia the Bolshevik Revolution of 1917 posed a challenge to the very idea of international relations. In Germany, the ideas of British and American thinkers were eagerly adopted at the hour of the country's defeat, which led to widespread disillusion when these ideas were realized only imperfectly at the Versailles Peace Conference in 1919. Britain and America were the homes of new thought, partly because these two countries were less devastated by the war than others had been, and were thereby perhaps more willing to look beyond the immediate issues, but also because the anarchic nature of world politics seemed particularly unfortunate to those nurtured by the liberal traditions of the two English-speaking powers. Given this latter point, the new thinking that was produced in Britain and America is summarized conveniently as 'liberal internationalism' – the adaptation of broadly liberal political principles to the management of the international system.

In Britain, liberal internationalist ideas were developed by the Fabians and radical liberals through bodies such as the Union for Democratic Control; but while there was some sympathy for these ideas by the government of the day, the general Foreign Office line was a more traditionalist one. Their account of what went wrong in 1914 stressed the failure of diplomacy, and in particular the slowness of the Great Powers in mobilizing an international conference on the problems of the Balkans, rather than any systemic failure. However, if British liberal internationalism was largely unofficial, in the United States these ideas were espoused by the president himself, Woodrow Wilson, and set out in the Fourteen Points speech of January 1918, in which America's war aims were specified. Liberal internationalism offered a two-part diagnosis of what went wrong in 1914, and a corresponding two-part prescription for avoiding similar disasters in the future.

The first element of this diagnosis and prescription concerned *domestic politics*. A firm liberal belief was that the 'people' do not want war; war comes about because the people are led into it by militarists or autocrats, or because their legitimate aspirations to nationhood are blocked by undemocratic, multinational or imperial systems. An obvious answer here is to promote *democratic political systems*; that is, liberal-democratic, constitutional regimes, and the principle of *national self-determination*. The rationale is that, if all regimes were national and liberal-democratic, there would be no wars.

This belief links to the second component of liberal internationalism – its critique of pre-1914 *international institutional structures*. The basic thesis here was that the anarchic pre-1914 system of international relations undermined the prospects for peace. Secret diplomacy led to an alliance system that committed nations to courses of action that had not been sanctioned by Parliaments or Assemblies (hence the title of the Union for Democratic Control). There was no mechanism in 1914 to prevent war, apart from the 'balance of power' – a notion that was associated with unprincipled power-politics. What was deemed necessary was the establishment of new principles of international relations, such as 'open covenants openly arrived at', but, most of all, a new institutional structure for international relations – a *League of Nations*.

The aim of a League of Nations would be to provide the security that nations attempted, unsuccessfully, to find under the old, balance-of-power, system. The balance of power was based on private commitments of assistance made by specific parties; the League would provide public assurances of security backed by the collective will of all nations – hence the term 'collective security'. The basic principle would be 'one for all and all for one'. Each country would guarantee the security of every other country, and thus there would be no need for nations to resort to expedients such as military alliances or the balance of power. Law would replace war as the underlying principle of the system.

These two packages of reforms – to domestic and institutional structures – were liberal in two senses of the word. In political terms, they were liberal in so far as they embodied the belief that *constitutional government and the rule of law* were principles of universal applicability both to all domestic regimes and to the international system as such. But they were also liberal in a more philosophical sense, in so far as they relied quite heavily on the assumption of an underlying *harmony of real interests*. The basic premise of virtually all this thought was that while it might sometimes appear that there were circumstances where interests clashed, in fact, once the real interests of the people were made manifest it would be clear that such circumstances were the product of distortions introduced either by the malice of special interests, or by simple ignorance. Thus, while liberal internationalists could hardly deny that in 1914 war was popular with the people, they could, and did, deny that this popularity was based on a rational appraisal of the situation. From the liberal view, international politics are no more based on a 'zero-sum' game than are international economics; national interests are always reconcilable.

The liberal belief in a natural harmony of interests led as a matter of course to a belief in the value of education. Education was seen as a means of combating the ignorance that is the main cause of a failure to see interests as harmonious, and thereby can be found one of the origins of International Relations as an academic discipline. Thus, in Britain, philanthropists such as David Davies, founder of the Woodrow Wilson Chair of International Politics at University College Wales, Aberystwyth – the first such chair to be established in the world – and Montague Burton, whose eponymous chairs of International Relations are to be found at Oxford and the London School of Economics, believed that by promoting the study of international relations they would also be promoting the cause of peace. The systematic study of international relations would lead to increased support for international law and the League of Nations. Thus it was that liberal internationalism became the first orthodoxy of the new discipline – but, even then, by no means all scholars of International Relations subscribed to it; international historians, for example, were particularly sceptical.

The peace settlement of 1919 represented a partial embodiment of liberal internationalist thinking. The principle of national self-determination was promoted, but only in Europe – and even there it was abused rather too frequently when it was the rights of Germans or Hungarians that were in question. The Versailles Treaty was dictated to the Germans, rather than negotiated with them, even though the Kaiser had been overthrown at the end of the war and a liberal-democratic republic established in Germany. Germany was held to be responsible for the war, and deemed liable to meet its costs; the allies very sensibly did not put a figure on this notional sum, hoping to decide the matter in a calmer atmosphere later, but the issue of German reparations was to be a running sore during the inter-war years. A League of Nations was established, incorporating the principle of collective security, but it was tied to the Versailles Treaty and thus associated with what the Germans regarded as an unjust status quo – a judgement soon shared by much liberal opinion after the publication of John Maynard Keynes' *The Economic Consequences of the Peace* which attacked the motives of the allies and portrayed the new Germany as the victim of outmoded thinking (Keynes 1919). The United States Senate refused to join the League as constituted by the Treaty, and, initially, neither Germany nor Russia was allowed to join. The unfortunate truth was that liberal internationalist ideas were not dominant in the minds of any statesmen other than Wilson – and Wilson, by then a sick man, was unable to sell these ideas to his fellow-countrymen, partly because he had allowed opposition leaders of the Senate no part in the negotiation of the peace. This was a mistake that Franklin Roosevelt learnt from and did not repeat a generation later.

For all that, the 1919 peace settlement was by no means as harsh as might have been expected, and in the 1920s it seemed quite plausible that the undoubted defects of Versailles would be corrected by the harmonious actions of the major powers. The Locarno Treaties of 1926 confirmed symbolically the western borders of Germany, and, more importantly, re-established more-or-less amicable relationships between the leading powers, a process helped by changes of personnel at the top. Gustav Stresemann in Germany, Aristide Briand in France, and Austen Chamberlain (followed by Arthur Henderson) in Britain seemed committed to peaceful solutions to Europe's problems. A symbolic high point was reached at the Treaty of Paris in 1928 – the so-called Kellogg–Briand Pact, in which a proposal to mark 150 years of US–French friendship by the signature of a non-aggression pact became transformed into a general treaty to abolish war, thereby closing the legal loopholes that the sharp-eyed had found in the Covenant of the League of Nations. Virtually all countries signed this Treaty – albeit usually with legal reservations – which, a cynic might remark, is one of the reasons why virtually all wars started since 1928 have been wars of 'self-defence'.

In short, as the 1930s dawned it seemed at least possible that a new and better system of international relations might be emerging. As no one needs to be told, this possibility did not materialize: the 1930s saw economic collapse; the rise of the dictators; a series of acts of aggression in Asia, Africa and Europe; an inability of the League powers led by Britain and France to develop a coherent policy in response to these events; and, finally, the global war that the peace settlement of 1919 had been designed to prevent. Clearly, these events were catastrophic in the 'real world', but they were equally damaging in the world of ideas. Indeed, the two worlds, as always, were inter-woven – it was the inability of decision-makers and intellectuals to think sensibly about these events that, at least in part, explained their inability to produce effective policy. The apparent inability of liberal internationalists to cope with these events suggested the need for a new conceptual apparatus, or perhaps for the rediscovery of some older ideas.

The 'realist' critique of liberal internationalism

Returning to the root ideas of liberal internationalism, it is easy to identify the problems this approach faced in the 1930s. In 1919, liberal internationalists believed that 'the people' had a real interest in and desire for peace, and that democratic regimes would, if given the chance, allow these interests and desires to dominate. The enemy of peace, on this account, was the kind of militarist, authoritarian, autocratic, anti-democratic regime that had, allegedly, dominated Germany, Austria-Hungary and Russia in 1914. Now, some of the crises of the 1930s were caused by this kind of regime – Japanese militarism in Manchuria and China, and 'Francoism' in the Spanish Civil War fit the bill quite well – but most were not. Hitler's Germany and Mussolini's Italy were not traditional military autocracies; rather, they were regimes that had come to power by quasi-democratic means and remained in power by the mobilization of popular support. There were no elections in Germany after 1933, but what evidence exists suggests that the National Socialists had clear majority support well into the war, perhaps even to its very end.

Moreover, these regimes, despite being popularly supported, actually glorified war. The rhetoric of fascism and national socialism stressed the virtues of armed struggle and its importance in building the nation. And, of course, the stated ends of these regimes – turning the Mediterranean into an Italian lake; or depopulating Eastern Europe of Slavs, Jews and other alleged inferiors and repopulating it with 'Aryans' – could not be achieved by any means other than war. Although Hitler still maintained in his public orations that he was compelled to resort to force by the obstinate and malicious behaviour of the enemies of the *Volk*, it was quite clear that this was nonsense – unless a reluctance to commit suicide is deemed to be a sign of obstinacy. The fact that

Nazism remained a popular force in spite of this posture – and perhaps, in some cases, because of it – dealt a terrible blow to liberal thinking.

The consequences of this blow were felt in particular with respect to support for the League of Nations and the rule of law. The basic premise of liberal internationalism was that the force of world opinion would buttress the League of Nations, and that no state would be able to act against this force. The point of collective security under the League was to prevent wars, not to fight them. The League's cumbersome procedures would act as a brake to prevent a nation that had, as it were, temporarily taken leave of its senses from acting rashly – international disputes would be solved peacefully because that was what the people *really* wanted. The behaviour of Hitler and Mussolini made it clear that, in this context at least, these ideas were simply wrong. The liberal internationalist slogan was 'law not war' – but it became clear, as the 1930s progressed, that the only way in which 'law' could be maintained was by 'war'.

An inability to understand this basic point bedevilled liberal thought in the 1930s. Well-meaning people simultaneously pledged full support for the League *and* never again to fight a war, without any apparent awareness that the second pledge undermined the first. When the British and French governments attempted to resolve the crisis caused by Italy's invasion of Ethiopia by supporting the Hoare–Laval Pact, which was seen as rewarding the aggressor, public opinion was outraged. Hoare was forced to resign, and the last real chance to prevent Mussolini from falling under Hitler's influence was lost. The public wanted the League to act, but the British government held, almost certainly correctly, that the public would not support a war, and therefore ensured that the sanctions that were introduced would not bring Italy to its knees. The 'appeasement' policy of Britain and France (and, as is often forgotten, of the United States and the USSR) posed a real dilemma for many liberal internationalists. They did not know whether to praise figures like Chamberlain for avoiding war, or condemn them for condoning breaches of international legality and betraying the weak. They usually resolved this dilemma by doing both.

What this seemed to suggest to many was that there were flaws in the root ideas of liberal internationalism, its account of how the world worked, and, in particular, its account of the mainsprings of human conduct. Gradually, new ideas emerged – or, perhaps more accurately, re-emerged, since many of them would have been familiar to pre-1914 thinkers. Perhaps the deepest thinker on these matters in the 1930s was the radical American theologian and critic, Reinhold Niebuhr. Niebuhr's message is conveyed in abbreviated form in the title of his 1932 book, *Moral Man and Immoral Society*; his point was that liberals wildly exaggerated the capacity of collectivities of humans to behave in ways that were truly moral (Niebuhr 1932). Niebuhr held that 'men' had the capacity to be good, but that this capacity was always in conflict with the sinful, acquisitive and aggressive drives that are also present in human nature. These drives are given full scope in society, and it is unrealistic to think that they can be harnessed to the goal of international peace and understanding in bodies such as the League of Nations.

These are powerful ideas that resonate later, but the intense Christian spirit with which they are infused – and the pacifism to which, initially at least, they gave rise in Niebuhr – limited their influence in the 1930s. Instead, the most influential critique of liberal internationalism came from a very different source, E. H. Carr, the quasi-Marxist historian, journalist and, in the late 1930s, Woodrow Wilson Professor of International Politics. Carr produced a number of studies in the 1930s, the most famous of which was published in 1939 – *The Twenty Years Crisis* (Carr 1939/2001). This book performed the crucial task of providing a new vocabulary for International Relations theory. Liberal internationalism is renamed 'utopianism' (later writers sometimes use 'idealism') and contrasted with Carr's approach, which is termed 'realism'. Carr's central point is that the liberal doctrine of the harmony of interests glosses over the real conflict that is to be found in international relations, which is between the 'haves' and the 'have-nots'. A central feature of the world is scarcity – there are not enough of the good things of life to go around. Those who have them want to keep them, and therefore promote 'law and order' policies, attempting to outlaw the use of violence. The 'have-nots', on the other hand, have no such respect for the law, and neither is it reasonable that they should, because it is the law that keeps them where they are, which is under the thumb of the 'haves'.

Politics has to be based on an understanding of this situation. It is utopian to suggest that the have-nots can be brought to realize that they ought to behave legally and morally. It is realistic to recognize that the essential conflict between haves and have-nots must be managed rather than wished away. It is utopian to imagine that international bodies such as the League of Nations can have real power. Realists work with the world as it really is, utopians as they wish it to be. In fact, as Ken Booth has demonstrated, Carr wished to preserve some element of utopian thought, but, none the less, realism was his dominant mode (Booth 1991b). The power of words here is very great – the way in which 'realism', a political doctrine that might be right or wrong, becomes associated with 'realistic', which is a quality of judgement most people want to possess, is critically important to its success.

Carr's position reveals its quasi-Marxist origins, and its debt to Karl Mannheim's sociology of knowledge, in its stress on material scarcity, and its insistence that law and morality serve the interests of dominant groups (Mannheim 1936/1960). On the other hand, the fact that the 'have-nots' of the 1930s were, on his account, Hitler's Germany and Mussolini's Italy, suggests that Carr's Marxism was laced with a degree of power-worship – an impression also conveyed by his monumental *A History of Soviet Russia*

(1978), which is often regarded as being rather too generous in its judgement of Stalin. The first edition of *The Twenty Years Crisis* contained favourable judgements of appeasement that Carr thought prudent to tone down in the second edition (Fox 1985). None the less, Carr made a number of effective points. It was indeed the case that the League of Nations and the idea of collective security was tied up with the peace settlement of 1919, and therefore could be seen as defending the status quo. Equally, the leading status-quo nations, Britain and France, had not built up their position in the world by strict adherence to the rule of law, however much the British might wish to tell themselves that they had acquired their empire in a fit of absentmindedness. But, above all, it was the policy failure of liberal internationalism as outlined above that gave Carr's ideas such salience and credence. As is often the way, a new theory is called into being by the failure of an old theory.

In any event, realism seemed to offer a more coherent and accurate account of the world than the liberal ideas it critiqued, and it formed the basis for the 'post-war synthesis', which is the subject of the next section of this chapter. However, before leaving the original version of liberal internationalism behind, there are a few general points that can be made. First, it is becoming clear that the liberal account of the origins of the First World War was faulty at a number of points, two of which still have considerable significance. The modern historiography of the origins of the war suggests that the gut feeling of Allied public opinion at the time (that Germany started the war as a deliberate act of policy) was rather more to the point than the more refined view of liberal intellectuals to the effect that no one was to blame. Of greater significance is the second point, which is that Germany in 1914 was not the militarist autocracy that some liberals took it to be. In reality, it was a constitutional state, governed by the rule of law, and with a government that was responsible to parliament as well as to the emperor. Certainly, it was not a 'democracy' – but then no country *was* in 1914; even the widest franchises (in the United States and France) excluded women from the vote. What this suggested was that the liberal view that constitutional, liberal-democratic regimes are less likely to engage in war than other types of regime required a great deal of refinement (which it received towards the end of the twentieth century in the form of the Democratic Peace thesis, discussed in Chapters 4 and 10 below).

A second point that is worth making here is that some of the criticisms of liberal internationalism – including some made above – take too little notice of the unique quality of the threat posed to international order in the 1930s. To put the matter bluntly, we must hope that it was rather unusual for the leaders of two of the most powerful countries in the world – Germany and the USSR – to be certifiable madmen. The lunatic nature of Hitler's plans to replant the world with true Aryans makes him an exceptional character to be a leader of any kind of state, let alone a Great Power – it is this latter point that makes comparison with figures such as Saddam Hussein or Slobodan Milošević misleading. The Munich analogy has been applied repeatedly since 1945, and 'appeaser' is still one of the worst insults that can be thrown at a diplomat, but all the dictators the world has thrown up since then – Nasser, Castro, Hussein – have been mere shadows of the real thing, not so much because of their personalities but because of their lack of access to the sinews of world power. Judging a set of ideas by their capacity to cope with a Hitler or a Stalin seems to set far too high a standard.

In a similar vein, it is striking how much of liberal internationalism has survived its defeat at the hands of realism. The 'settled norms' of the contemporary international order are still essentially those of 1919 – national self-determination, non-aggression and respect for international law combined with support for the principles of sovereignty. The United Nations is, in effect, a revision and rebranding of the League of Nations, even if it was convenient to gloss over this in 1945. Liberal internationalism is, without doubt, an incoherent and flawed doctrine, and we are still attempting to cope with its contradictions – in particular its belief that nationalism and democracy are compatible notions – but it is, none the less, a remarkably resilient doctrine, possibly because the values it represents seem to be widely shared by the peoples of the world.

The post-war synthesis

After 1945, realism became the dominant theory of International Relations, offering a conception of the world that seemed to define the 'common sense' of the subject. Most practising diplomats had always held views on international relations that were more or less realist; they were now joined by academics, as the discipline of International Relations expanded on broadly realist lines, and by opinion-makers more generally, as the leader writers and columnists of influential newspapers and journals came increasingly to work from the same general perspective. To a striking extent, realism remains to this day the dominant theory of International Relations. Most of the rest of this book will be an account of the struggles between realism and its critics, and if the latter have been increasingly effective over the years, it is difficult to deny the fact that realism still, in one form or another, provides the dominant mode of discourse in the discipline. Paradoxically, this dominance explains why this section on the realist post-war synthesis can be quite brief: while there are interesting things to be said about this period, most of the substantive theories developed in these years remain current and will be discussed in later chapters.

Although Carr remained influential, the post-war dominance of realism owed more to the work of other writers – Carr himself was switching his attention at this time, from International Relations towards Soviet history. In Britain, Martin Wight was an important figure, though his Chatham House pamphlet on *Power Politics* (1946/1978) is, despite its title, only dubiously realist in inspiration. In the United States, Niebuhr remained influential, as did the geopolitician, Nicholas Spykman (Spykman 1942), and the diplomat George Kennan (Kennan 1952). However, the key realist of the period was Hans J. Morgenthau, a German-Jewish émigré to the United States in the 1930s, who published a series of books in the 1940s and 1950s The most influential of these was *Politics Among Nations: The Struggle for Power and Peace,* a book that was to become the standard textbook on International Relations for a generation or more (Morgenthau 1948).

There were two major differences between Morgenthau and Carr. In the first place, Morgenthau, influenced partly by figures such as Niebuhr, and partly by his own experiences in the 1930s, saw the mainspring of realism as lying not in scarcity, a product of the human *condition*, but in sin, a product of human *nature*. The aggressive, power-seeking nature of states stems from the imperfect human material of which they are constructed. It could well be argued that this shift was a mistake. Unless explicitly defended on theological grounds, themselves dubious to many theorists, it leads towards psycho-sociological explanations for social behaviour, which are rarely satisfactory (although the renewed interest in socio-biology in recent years may yet provide some support for Morgenthau). Even among theologians there would be a reluctance to defend the version of original sin that seems to underlie much of Morgenthau's work – a strange foundation, since Morgenthau's Judaic heritage did not commit him to this stance. Morgenthau's second difference from Carr was equally suspect on intellectual grounds, but nevertheless was the key to the success of *Politics Among Nations*. Morgenthau systematized realism. His book is full of lists – the six principles of political realism, the three foreign policy strategies open to states and so on. This made it a very successful textbook, but at the cost of a significant coarsening of the realist position. By contrast, Carr's *The Twenty Years' Crisis* is a complex, nuanced book, open to a variety of different readings. The same is true of some of Morgenthau's other works, but most of the complexity in *Politics Among Nations* is provided by accident, as a result of some rather loose formulations, rather than by design. However, a simple guide to realism was what was required in 1948. Twenty years later, Hedley Bull commented that the United States had become the dominant power in the world without needing to develop a deep knowledge of the kind of statecraft practised in Europe; now they had this need, and American realism provided them with a 'crib to the European diplomatic tradition' (Bull, in Porter 1969: 39). This is patronizing, but broadly true.

Morgenthau's account of realism (at least the account given in *Politics Among Nations*) can be boiled down to one basic proposition about international relations, which is that international relations is about *states* pursuing *interests* defined in terms of *power*. This simple formula opens up in all sorts of ways, and the different component terms will be discussed at length below. A few comments to situate these later discussions may be helpful here. First, according to Morgenthau, the *state* is the key actor in international relations. Other bodies, such as international organizations (governmental and non-governmental), economic enterprises, pressure groups, even individuals, may, in certain circumstances, exercise influence and act independently of states, but the state is the key actor because the state is the institution through which all these other bodies operate, the institution that regulates these other bodies and decides the terms under which they can act. As we shall see in later chapters, it is a moot point whether this position will hold in the twenty-first century, but, for the moment, it should simply be noted that the claim is *not* that the state is the *only* actor but that it is the *most significant* actor; it is important not to 'win' arguments against realism by burning straw people.

Stress on *interests* conveys two notions: first, that states have interests; and second that state interests dominate state behaviour. The idea that states (nations) have interests could be problematic – can an institution rather than a person have interests in any meaningful sense? The realist position is that states are like 'persons', capable of possessing interests, and thus that the 'national interest' is not simply a shorthand term for the interests of whatever group controls the administrative structure of the state. States behave in accordance with these interests and not in response to abstract principles (such as collective security) or a desire to act altruistically. States never sacrifice themselves; they are essentially egoists. This seems straightforward, but could in fact easily become tautological. Suppose states define a system of collective security as being in their interest, and act to support such a system even when their own material interests are not directly threatened by an aggressor – would this be egoistical behaviour? Clearly, pinning down the idea of the national interest and using it in the analysis of foreign policy poses real problems, as we shall see in Chapter 4 below.

National interests may be complex and difficult to identify in concrete terms, but the realist proposition is that a degree of simplicity can be introduced by assuming that whatever else states seek, they seek *power* in order to achieve other goals. The need for power stems from the anarchical nature of the international system. There is no authoritative system of decision-making in international relations; states are obliged to look after themselves in what has become known as a 'self-help' system. Power is a complex notion; we can think of power as 'capability' – the physical force necessary to achieve a particular goal – but capability is always cashed out in a behavioural relationship. The possession of assets has political meaning only in relation to the assets possessed by others – although skill in deploying one's assets counts for something. One of the problems here is that, while measuring assets is not too difficult, measuring power in a relationship can be very tricky indeed.

We shall return to each of these points in the chapters that follow. For the moment, one further general point is worth making, namely that it is not always clear what *kind* of theory realism is. Morgenthau obviously thinks of it as *descriptive* and *explanatory* – describing how the world is, explaining how it works; but there are also clear *prescriptive* elements here – he is telling statesmen how they *should* behave, what they *should* do. Moreover, there is a critical edge to his doctrines. One of the points about the notion of the 'national interest' is that it can be employed to criticize the behaviour of a particular government. These different kinds of theory sit uneasily together. When Morgenthau attended 'teach-ins' at American universities in the early 1960s in order to protest that the Vietnam War was against the national interests of the United States, he was highly irritated by the tactics of State Department spokespersons who would quote back at him citations from his writings of the 1940s. Of course, he was right to think that they were missing the point – that the reasons why the national interest might call for engagement in European security in the 1940s had little bearing on the reasons why the national interest might call for disengagement in Vietnam in the 1960s. However, the young men and women from the State Department also had a point – *Politics Among Nations* is, at times, a very confusing text, purporting, inaccurately, to be simply an account of how things are, while in fact, and inevitably, containing a very strong lead on how they should be.

Before leaving Morgenthau behind, it is worth mentioning that he, and several other thinkers usually characterized as in the same camp, such as John Herz, produced many ideas that nowadays would not be considered characteristically realist. In the 1950s, as the thermonuclear revolution got under way, Morgenthau and Herz separately came to the conclusion that the nation-state was irreparably undermined by this new technology. Herz' classic paper on 'the rise and demise of the territorial state' presented this argument very clearly, and Campbell Craig has demonstrated that, for Morgenthau, the necessity of world government was not an aberrant thought, but rather a logical consequence of the development of what are now called 'weapons of mass destruction' (Herz 1956; Craig 2003). The centenary of Morgenthau's birth in 2004 has been the occasion for a serious rethink of the importance of this complex scholar, and it is a great pity that for the general IR student he is still best known for what was, in some respects, his worst book.

International Relations and the behavioural sciences

Morgenthau's text contains a great many 'laws of politics'; that is to say, generalizations that are held to apply very widely, perhaps universally. This seems to imply endorsement of the 'covering law' model of explanation, whereby something is deemed to have been explained when its occurrence can be accounted for under some general law. Such theorizing is in keeping with the aspiration of realism to make a scientific study of international relations. However, there are features of Morgenthau's account that seem to undermine this aspiration. In the first place, it is clear that states and statespersons do not have to obey the laws of politics – otherwise, what would be the point of trying to persuade them that they should? Second, and perhaps more important, the ways in which Morgenthau generates and establishes his laws seem highly unscientific. A key text here is in the Preface to the second edition of *Politics Among Nations,* where Morgenthau quotes with approval a comment by Montesquieu to the effect that the reader should not judge the product of a lifetime's reflection on the basis of a few hours' reading. This seems to run against the scientific ethos, which holds that seniority and breadth of experience must always take second place to the logic and quality of an argument. If a smart undergraduate spots a genuine flaw in the lifetime's work of a distinguished scholar this is (or, at least, is supposed to be) a matter for congratulation, not rebuke.

In short, the scientific claims of realism are seemingly belied by its apparently unscientific methods – a point that was seized on in the 1950s and 1960s by the comparatively large number of former natural scientists who were attracted to the field, especially in the United States. These people were either former physicists with a guilty conscience over nuclear weapons, or systems analysts employed by bodies such as the RAND Corporation to improve the quality of United States policy-making, especially in the area of defence. These figures were joined by imports from the behavioural sciences, who were attuned to a version of the social sciences that involved an attempt to study the actual behaviour of actors rather than the meanings they assigned to this behaviour.

The aim of the behaviouralists was to replace the 'wisdom literature' and 'anecdotal' use of history represented by Morgenthau and the traditional realists with rigorous, systematic and scientific concepts and reasoning. There were various dimensions to this. It might involve casting old theories in new, rigorous forms – as with Morton Kaplan's 'balance of power' models in *System and Process in International Politics* (Kaplan 1957). It might involve generating new historical databases and time-series to replace the anecdotalism of traditional diplomatic history – as in J. D. Singer and associates' 'Correlates of War' Project at Ann Arbor, Michigan (Singer *et al.* 1979). It might involve the use of mathematical models for the study of decisions – as in game theoretic work and early rational choice theory in the hands of people such as Thomas Schelling at Harvard University (Schelling 1960). Less conventionally, it might involve the creation of new concepts that undermined state-centric International Relations altogether – as in the work of social theorists such as John Burton (1972), Kenneth Boulding (1962) and Johan Galtung (1971).

In the mid-1960s, this work generated a fierce counter-attack on behalf of traditional, or, as they called it, classical International Relations, led by British scholars, in particular Hedley Bull (Bull, in Knorr and Rosenau 1969); however , unlike the contest between utopianism and realism, this debate only engaged the interests of a minority of scholars, except, perhaps, in the United Kingdom, where an educational system still divided into two cultures meant that the majority of International Relations scholars were more amenable to attacks on 'scientism' than their North American cousins. In practice, by the 1960s, the majority of US graduate students in International Relations (which means the majority of the future members of the profession) were receiving training in the methods of the behavioural sciences, and a methodology that essentially reflected this training took hold and has not yet weakened its grip. Moreover, the traditionalists/classicists had little to offer by way of an alternative to the behavioural revolution, largely because their own ideas of science and reliable knowledge were, in practice, very close to those of the scientists. The aspirations to science of Morgenthau and Carr have been noted, and any doctrine that claims to be based on how things really are is obviously open to those who claim to have a better grasp of this reality. Positivism — which, in this context, means the belief that the facts are out there to be discovered and there is only one way to do this, only one form of reliable knowledge – namely, that generated by methods based on the natural sciences – reigned in both camps, and the differences were largely of style rather than substance. Indeed, the most effective critiques of behaviouralism – until, that is, the post-positivist revolution of the late 1980s – came from the so-called 'post-behaviouralists': scholars who accepted the goal of science, but who were critical of the behaviouralists for their unwillingness to engage with the pressing political issues of the day.

The so-called 'behavioural revolution' did, however, generate a number of new ideas, and these, combined with changes in the real world, brought about quite striking changes to International Relations theory in the 1970s.

Challenges to the realist synthesis

For the most part, the behaviouralists were realists – their aim was to fulfil the realist claim to scientific status rather than to undermine it. However, in the 1960s and the early 1970s, major challenges to realism did emerge, driven not by developments in the academy, but by events in the real world. Two sets of events were of particular significance, one set focusing on changes in the world of great-power diplomacy ('high' politics), the other pointing to the significance of less dramatic socio-economic changes ('low' politics). Taken together, these changes produced the dominant theories of the 1980s and 1990s – 'neorealism' and 'neoliberal institutionalism' (institutionalism or neoliberalism for short) – as well as fuelling challenges to this new orthodoxy such as 'structuralism', 'constructivism' and 'globalization' theory, and assisting in the revival of the English School theory of international society. The final section of this chapter will set the scene for these contemporary notions.

The first set of changes reflect the shift in the nature of 'high' politics in this period. Realism as a doctrine originated in the troubled years of the 1930s and was established as an orthodoxy at the height of the Cold War, which is to say, in times when the reality of great-power competition could not be denied, or the dangers underestimated. By the beginning of the 1960s, and in particular after the Cuban Missile Crisis of 1962, the Cold War took a new turn, and relations between the superpowers became markedly less fraught – having looked over the brink in 1962, both sides decided that nothing was worth the risk of fighting a nuclear war. This new mood – which led eventually to the process of 'détente' – was accompanied by a new focus of attention in the United States, namely the developing disaster of the Vietnam War. The most striking feature of this, from the point of view of realist theory, was the inability of the USA to turn its obvious advantages in terms of power into results on the ground or at the conference table. Perceptions and psychology are important here. In point of fact, it is not too difficult to explain either the lessening of tension in great-power relations or the failure of US policy in Vietnam using sophisticated realist categories, but, in superficial terms, it did look as if power politics were becoming less important in this period. This dovetailed with the second, more significant set of changes that led to a reassessment of the post-war synthesis, the changes in the area of 'low' politics.

The post-war realist synthesis was based on the assumption that the state is the key actor in international relations (and a unitary actor at that), and that the diplomatic–strategic relations of states are the core of actual international relations. Gradually, through the 1960s and 1970s, both of these assumptions seemed less plausible. Studies of foreign policy decision-making revealed that the unitary nature of (at least, Western, pluralist) states was illusory. Whereas bodies such as the United Nations could plausibly be seen as no more than arenas wherein states acted, new international organizations such as the European Economic Community (the then title of the European Union) or the functional agencies of the United Nations seemed less obviously tools of the states who brought them into being. Business enterprises had always traded across state boundaries, but a new kind of firm (rather confusingly termed the 'multinational corporation', or MNC) emerged, engaging in production on a world scale, and, allegedly, qualitatively different from the old firms in its behaviour. International diplomatic–strategic relations are of central importance when the stakes really are matters of life and death, but as the possibility of the Cold War turning into a 'Hot War' declined, so the significance of international social and, in particular, economic relations increased. All told, the feel of international relations seemed to be changing quite rapidly.

The changes were caught nicely in the title of a book, *Transnational Relations and World Politics* (1971), edited by figures who would be almost as significant for the next generation of IR theory as Morgenthau had been for the previous generation: Robert Keohane and Joseph Nye. This collection did not develop a theory as such, but its description of the world posed an interesting theoretical challenge. Conventional, realist, state-centric International Relations assumes that the significant relations between different societies are those that take place via the institutions of the state. It is universally acknowledged that there are a myriad of ways in which the peoples of one country might relate to the peoples of another – via a great number of cross-border transactions, movements of money, people, goods and information – but the conventional assumption is, first, that the relations that really matter are interstate relations; and, second, that the state regulates, or could regulate if it wished, all the other relations. The model suggested by Keohane and Nye relaxes both parts of this assumption. First, it can no longer be assumed that interstate relations are always the most important; in the modern world, the decisions and actions of non-state actors can affect our lives as much as, if not more than, the decisions and actions of states (the decision taken by Al-Qaeda in 2001 to attack the USA on 9/11 being just the most obvious recent example). Second, it can no longer be assumed that states have the power to regulate these actors effectively; in principle, some states may have this capacity but, in practice, they are loath to exercise it given the potential costs of so doing in economic, social and political terms. Much of the time states are obliged to negotiate with non-state actors – Chapter 9 will examine the effects on the state system of the emergence of global civil society and MNCs in this context. Conventional International Relations endure, but they are now accompanied by many other 'Transnational Relations' – relationships that involve transactions across state boundaries in which at least one party is not a state. To reiterate an important point, realists have never denied the existence of such relationships but they had downplayed their significance. The transnational relations model questioned this judgement.

Pluralism and complex interdependence

Keohane and Nye's transnational relations collection espoused no theory of the new IR; their *Power and Interdependence* (1977/2000) went some way towards meeting this need. In this classic work they proposed *complex interdependence* as a new account of international relations to run alongside realism, and set out three key differences between the two approaches. First, complex interdependence assumes that there are *multiple channels of access* between societies, including different branches of the state apparatus as well as non-state actors, as opposed to the unitary state assumption characteristic of realism. Second, complex interdependence assumes that, for most international relationships, *force will be of low salience,* as opposed to the central role that force is given in realist accounts of the world. Finally, under complex interdependence there is no *hierarchy of issues*; any 'issue-area' might be at the top of the international agenda at any particular time, whereas realism assumes that security is every-where and always the most important issue. as between states (Keohane and Nye 1977/2000). These latter two points are, of course, related; it is largely because of the low salience of force in these relationships that there is no hier-archy of issues. The complex interdependence model does not assume that these three features exist everywhere; there may be – indeed are – relations where realism still holds. The point is to challenge realism's claim to be the only theory of international relations, holding for all relationships.

States have always been interdependent; what is new about *pluralism* is that, rather than seeing relationships as a whole, they are seen as disaggre-gated. Different *issue-areas* – such as security, trade or finance – display differ-ent modes of mutual dependence. The politics of complex interdependence stems from these differences. The *sensitivity* of actors varies according to circumstances, as does their *vulnerability*. By sensitivity is meant the degree to which actors are sensitive to changes in a given issue-area, and by vulnerabil-ity is meant the extent to which they are able to control their responses to this sensitivity – thus, for example, all advanced industrial nations in the early 1970s were very sensitive to the price of oil, but they varied considerably in their vulnerability to price changes; some had options to deal with the situa-tion (such as developing their own resources, or increasing industrial exports), which others did not. This opens up the possibility of actors employing strengths in one area to compensate for weaknesses in another. A favourite case study for this process was the 'Smithsonian Crisis' of 1971, which revolved around the decision of the US government to attempt to force a change in the rate at which dollars were changed into gold. Under the rules of the Bretton Woods system, finance was supposed to remain separate from trade, and both were to be isolated from military–security concerns – but in 1971 the USA employed trade sanctions as a means of forcing parity changes, and US diplomatic heavyweights such as Henry Kissinger were wheeled on to back up the American stance by making veiled threats about a re-evaluation of US security guarantees to Germany and Japan if these countries failed to respond positively. Since the USA was not reliant on foreign trade, and was a clear provider of security, it was able to use its comparative invulnerability and insensitivity in these areas in order to compensate for its greater sensitiv-ity and vulnerability in the realm of international finance (Gowa 1983).

Another feature of the world as seen by pluralists is that '*agenda-setting*' is a matter of some significance. In the realist world of power politics, the agenda sets itself: what is or is not significant is easy to determine in advance, because only the big issues of war and peace are truly significant. Not so for pluralism, where, in principle, any issue could be at the top of the international agenda – here, the ways in which actors are able to promote issues in international organizations and elsewhere becomes a significant subject for study. In some issue areas there may be a quite clear-cut route for promoting items to the top of the agenda. Such issue-areas may be characterized by quite a high degree of international order; they may constitute *regimes*. A regime is to be found where there are clearly understood principles, norms, rules and decision-making procedures around which decision-makers' expectations converge in a given area of international relations (Krasner 1983: 2). The politics of regimes is an interesting feature of pluralist analysis, and will be explored in greater detail in Chapter 7 below.

In the mid-1970s, pluralism seemed to be in the process of establishing itself as the dominant approach to the theory of International Relations, and traditional realism looked decidedly passé. Pluralism had preserved some of the more convincing insights of realism – for example, about the importance of power – while offering a far more complex and nuanced account of how these insights might be operationalized in international political analysis. Indeed, some of the most convincing critiques of pluralism came from the so-called 'structuralists' who stressed the extent to which the pluralists were modelling a rich man's world – their account, examined in more detail in Chapter 8, stressed the dependence of one group of countries on another rather than their interdependence, and argued that the poverty of the poor was directly caused by the wealth of the rich. The alleged chain of exploitation that linked rich and poor, the development of underdevelopment that had over the centuries created present-day inequalities, was the focus of these writers. However, pluralists were able to respond that, on their account of the world, 'mutual dependence' did not amount to equal dependence and the structuralists were simply describing a special case that could be subsumed under the complex interdependence model. All told, in the mid-to-late 1970s, pluralism looked like a research programme that was in pretty good shape.

Further reading

The history of theories of international relations from the Greeks to the present day is well surveyed in David Boucher, *Political Theories of International Relations* (1998); Brian Schmidt's *The Political Discourse of Anarchy: A Disciplinary History of International Relations* (1998) is a pioneering work of disciplinary historiography. Hidemi Suganami, *The Domestic Analogy and World Order Proposals* (1989), offers a useful history of how the 'domestic analogy' (seeing relations between states as being directly comparable to relations within states) has been used to conceptualize international relations since 1814.

To understand fully the evolution of theory in the first half of the twentieth century it is necessary to form a view about the causes of the two world wars and the crises of the 1930s. William Keylor, *The Twentieth Century World and Beyond: An International History Since 1900*, 5th edn (2005), is the best available overview. James Joll and Gordon Martel, *The Origins of the First World War* (2007), synthesizes the debate on the origin of the war. and H. Koch (ed.) The *Origins of the First World War* (1972) provides extracts from the key controversialists. A. J. P. Taylor's famous work, *The Origins of the Second World War* (1961), the thesis of which is that Hitler's diplomacy was not significantly different from that of previous German leaders, is now widely regarded as unsatisfactory; current thinking is summarized in E. M. Robertson (ed.), *The Origins of the Second World War: Historical Interpretations* (1971); and G. Martel (ed.), *The Origins of the Second World War Reconsidered: The A. J. P. Taylor Debate after Twenty-Five Years*, 2nd edn (1999). D. C. Watt's *How War Came* (1989) offers a measured account of the diplomacy of the last year of peace and is equally valuable on appeasement, as is Paul Kennedy, *The Realities Behind Diplomacy* (1981). Christopher Hill, '1939: The Origins of Liberal Realism' (1989), is a fine combination of history and theory. Gerhard L. Weinberg, *A World at Arms: A Global History of World War II* (1994), is the best single-volume account of the history and diplomacy of the Second World War.

A collection of essays on the liberal internationalists of the inter-war period, David Long and Peter Wilson (eds), *Thinkers of the Twenty Years' Crisis: Interwar Idealism Reassessed* (1995), provides for the first time a convenient, sympathetic and scholarly account of these writers. Wilson's *The International Theory of Leonard Woolf* (2003) is a valuable re-examination of the work of one of the most prolific yet overlooked liberal thinkers of the early twentieth century. Additional critiques of the framing of the 'First Debate' and the interwar period in IR can be found in Joel Quirk and Vigneswaran Darshan, 'The Construction of an Edifice: The Story of a First Great Debate' (2005), and Lucian Ashworth's 'Where are the Idealists in Interwar International Relations?' (2006). David Long and Brian Schmidt (eds), *Imperialism and Internationalism in the Discipline of IR* (2005), rewrites the first debate in terms of imperialism versus internationalism. Apart from the works of classical realism by Niebuhr, Spykman, Kennan and Carr cited in the text, attention should be drawn to Herbert Butterfield, *Christianity, Diplomacy and War* (1953), and Martin Wight, *Power Politics* (1946/1978). Morgenthau's *Politics Among Nations* (2006) has been through a number of editions; it is still worth reading, but the heavily-cut 1988 version is to be avoided. Of recent works by classical realists, by far the most distinguished is Henry Kissinger's monumental *Diplomacy* (1994).

These works are discussed in a number of valuable studies: book-length works include Michael J. Smith, *Realist Thought from Weber to Kissinger* (1986); Joel Rosenthal, *Righteous Realists* (1991); A. J. Murray, *Reconstructing Realism* (1996b); and Jonathan Haslam, *No Virtue like Necessity: Realist Thought in International Relations since Machiavelli* (2002). Less sympathetic but equally valuable is Justin Rosenberg, *The Empire of Civil Society* (1994). Martin Griffiths, *Realism, Idealism and International Politics: A*

Reinterpretation (1992), argues that the so-called 'realists' are in fact, in a philosophical sense, idealists. Chapters by Steven Forde and Jack Donnelly on classical and twentieth-century realism, respectively, are to be found in Terry Nardin and David Mapel (eds), *Traditions of International Ethics* (1992); Donnelly has followed this up with *Realism and International Relations* (2000). Campbell Craig's *Glimmer of a New Leviathan: Total War in the Realism of Niebuhr, Morgenthau, and Waltz* (2003) examines the import of realism to the US academy and subsequent evolution. Michael Williams' *The Realist Tradition and the Limits of International Relations* (2005) is a recent reappraisal of the key figures of classical realism.

On Morgenthau, Peter Gellman, 'Hans Morgenthau and the Legacy of Political Realism' (1988), and A. J. Murray, 'The Moral Politics of Hans Morgenthau' (1996a), are very valuable. More recently, Michael Williams (ed.), *Realism Reconsidered: The Legacy of Hans Morgenthau in International Relations* (2007) is key reference in the growing literature re-examining Morgenthau. Other recent references not found in the Williams collection include: William Scheuerman, 'Realism and the Left: The Case of Hans J. Morgenthau' (2008); Robbie Shilliam, 'Morgenthau in Context: German Backwardness, German Intellectuals and the Rise and Fall of a Liberal Project' (2007); and Veronique Pin-Fat, 'The Metaphysics of the National Interest and the Mysticism of the Nation-State: Reading Hans J. Morgenthau' (2005).

On Carr, the new edition of *Twenty Years Crisis* (2001) edited with an extended introduction by Michael Cox makes this core text much more accessible; essays by Booth and Fox cited in the text are crucial; see also Graham Evans, 'E. H. Carr and International Relations' (1975); and Peter Wilson, 'Radicalism for a Conservative Purpose: The Peculiar Realism of E. H. Carr' (2001). John Mearsheimer returns to Carr's realism in 'E. H. Carr vs. Idealism: The Battle Rages On' (2005). For the response of British IR scholars to Mearsheimer's charge that British IR has abandoned Carr's insights, see International Relations, 'Roundtable: The Battle Rages On' (2005).

On the debate over methods, Klaus Knorr and James Rosenau (eds), *Contending Approaches to International Politics* (1969), collects the major papers, including Hedley Bull's 'International Theory: The Case for a Classical Approach'; and Morton Kaplan's equally intemperate reply 'The New Great Debate: Traditionalism vs. Science in International Relations'. The best account of what was at stake in this debate is to be found in Martin Hollis and Steve Smith, *Explaining and Understanding International Relations* (1991). Bull's critique is probably best seen as part of a wider British reaction to American dominance of the social sciences in the 1950s and 1960s, but it has some affinities with more sophisticated critiques of positivism, such as Charles Taylor, 'Interpretation and the Sciences of Man' (1971), or William E. Connolly, The Terms of Political Discourse (1983).

Many of the leading 'pluralist' writers of the 1970s became the 'neoliberal institutionalists' of the 1980s, and their work is discussed in the next chapter; the third edition of Keohane and Nye's Power and Interdependence (2000) clarifies their relationship with realism.

At something of a tangent to the preceding readings, but very much worth looking into because of their significance for future IR theorizing, are contemporary works on human nature. Richard Dawkins' The Selfish Gene (1989) is the classic here, but *The Blank Slate: The Modern Denial of Human Nature* (2003) by Steven Pinker is more clearly relevant to our subject – see especially ch.16 on Politics, and ch. 17 on War. Bradley Thayer has made one of the first attempts to apply post-Dawkins evolutionary theory to realism – see 'Bringing in Darwin: Evolutionary Theory, Realism and International Politics' (2000) and *Darwin and International Relations* (2004). Also valuable are Stephen Peter Rosen, *War and Human Nature* (2005), and Raphael D. Sagarin and Terence Taylor (eds), *Natural Security: A Darwinian Approach to a Dangerous World* (2008). Ken Binmore's *Natural Justice* (2005) and Jason Alexander's *The Structural Evolution of Morality* (2007) are philosophical studies purporting to trace scientifically the development of morality as a social institution through evolutionary and game theory.

Chapter 3

International Relations Theory Today

Introduction: rational choice theory and its critics

Just as the post-war synthesis was dominated by Morgenthau's 1948 text, so contemporary IR is fixated on Kenneth Waltz's 1979 volume, *Theory of International Politics*. Not only was realism revitalized by this book, but anti-realists have also felt obliged to respond to its arguments. In the 1960s, it was said (by Kenneth Thompson) that IR theory constituted a debate between Morgenthau and his critics; in the 1980s, 1990s and 2000s the name of Waltz should be substituted for that of Morgenthau (although, in both cases, it is what the author is believed to have written rather than what was actually on the page that is crucial).

The merits of *Theory of International Politics* will be discussed below, but the success of the book does not simply rest on its own qualities, impressive though these are. The wider context is provided by the rise to dominance of *rational choice theory* in the political science community in the United States. The presupposition of rational choice thinking is that politics can be understood in terms of the goal-directed behaviour of individuals, who act rationally in the minimal sense that they make ends–means calculations designed to maximize the benefits they expect to accrue from particular situations (or, of course, minimize the losses). This overall perspective – sometimes termed 'neo-utilitarian' – draws much of its strength from the discipline of economics, where rational choice assumptions are fundamental, and was widely applied in the study of domestic politics in the USA from the 1960s onwards, with electoral, interest group and congressional politics at the forefront. It encourages the application of tools such as game theory to the study of politics, and opens up the possibility of quantitative studies employing regression analysis (and other statistical techniques largely developed by econometricians). Arguably, both the individualism of rational choice theory and its scientific aspirations are particularly congenial to the American psyche, which accounts for the dominance of this approach in the USA, as opposed to its comparative unimportance in Britain and, until recently, on much of the European continent.

While Waltz's realism is sometimes described as *structural realism,* and structuralism is generally seen as the polar opposite of rational choice theory, it is the possibilities opened up by assimilating his approach to rational choice theory that account for the long-term significance of his work – and, perversely, the bitterest and most sustained critiques of Waltz have come from opponents of rational choice theory. In effect, Waltz made possible the integration of IR theory into the dominant mode of theorizing politics in the US – what remains to be seen is whether this constitutes a giant leap forward in our abilities to comprehend IR, or a major detour down a dead-end. The rest of this chapter sets out these alternatives.

From realism to neorealism

The very term *neorealism* is somewhat contentious, because many realists regard the ideas it conveys as containing nothing that would merit the prefix 'neo'; nevertheless, most observers disagree, and feel that something *did* change with realism in response to the pluralist challenge, and neorealism is one way of noting this change. In any event, there is general agreement that the most significant realist/neorealist work is Kenneth Waltz's *Theory of International Politics* (1979). Waltz is a scholar with a classical realist background. His first major work, *Man, the State and War* (1959), is still a starting-point for modern thinking about the causes of war and, for the most part, is a work of international political theory in the traditional mould; in the 1950s, Waltz had been the secretary of the American Rockefeller Committee for the Study of the Theory of International Relations, founded in 1954, and was conventionally realist in orientation and traditionalist in method. *Theory of International Politics,* on the other hand, is anything but traditionalist in style and presentation, or conventional in its arguments.

Waltz's basic strategy for preserving realism in the face of the pluralist challenge is to restrict its scope. First, whereas for Morgenthau 'theory' is quite a loose term – despite his frequent references to laws of politics and so on – for Waltz, theory is defined quite precisely in his first chapter, and in terms drawn from the thinking on scientific method of Karl Popper as refracted through the lens of modern economic theory. Waltz is concerned to produce interrelated, linked, law-like propositions from which testable hypotheses can be drawn – though he does acknowledge that 'testing' is likely to be a more impressionistic process in International Relations than it is in the exact sciences. Waltz vehemently denies being a 'positivist' in any wider sense of the term, but his apparent belief that there are real-world regularities that it is the role of theory to explain would seem to put him in that camp, at least given the usual implications of the term positivism within IR theory (Waltz 1997, 1998).

However, Waltz does not just restrict the kind of theory he is producing; crucially, he also restricts its scope. His aim is to produce a theory of the *international system* and not a general account of all aspects of international relations. This enables him to gaze benignly on many of the changes described by the pluralists, because they do not address the nature of the international system as such, only aspects of its component units. One of the positions he advocates most forcefully is that it is only possible to understand the international system via *systemic* theories; to attempt to understand the system through theories that concentrate on attributes of the units that make up the system is to commit the ultimate sin of *reductionism*. We know reductionism is wrong, because we know that there are patterns of the international systems that recur over time even when the units that make up the system change; these patterns must be the product of the system itself, and cannot be the product either of mutable features of its sub-systems, or of human universals, such as an alleged tendency towards aggression, which, by definition, appear throughout history and not simply in international systems. Thus, to take one of his examples, Lenin must be wrong to explain imperialism in terms of the dynamics of monopoly capitalism, because imperialism has been around for ever, while monopoly capitalism is of recent origin (Waltz 1979: 19ff.). In fact, this is not a compelling critique of Lenin, because the latter recognizes this point and stresses that modern imperialism is different from its predecessors – nevertheless, Waltz's general point is clear.

Once we focus on the system, we can see, he suggests, that there are only two kinds of system possible – *hierarchical* or *anarchical*. In a hierarchical system, different kinds of units are organized under a clear line of authority. In an anarchical system, units that are similar in nature, even though they differ dramatically in capabilities, conduct relations with one another. The distinction between hierarchy and anarchy is crucial to Waltz; the present system, he argues, is clearly anarchical, and has been since its late medieval origins. None of the changes identified by the pluralists amounts to a change of system – this would only come if hierarchical institutions were established; that is, some kind of world government. Much of *Theory of International Politics* is devoted to demonstrating that this is not taking place, and that the sorts of developments identified by pluralists only scratch the surface of things; the underlying reality of the system remains the same.

The international system is a 'self-help' system; states (which for theoretical purposes are assumed to be unitary actors) are obliged to look after themselves, because there is no one else to look after them. Waltz does *not* assume that states are self-aggrandizing, necessarily aggressive bodies, but he does assume that they wish to preserve themselves. This means that they are obliged to be concerned with their security, and at the same time obliged to regard other states as potential threats. They must continually adjust their stance in the world in accordance with their reading of the power of others and of their own power. The result of these movements is the emergence of a *balance of power*. The balance of power is *the* theory of the international system. Balances of power can be defined in terms of the number of 'poles' in the balance – the metaphor gets a bit confused here – and the number of poles is defined by the number of states that are a serious threat to each other's basic survival; Waltz argues that this means that the system (in 1979) is *bipolar*. Only the United States and the USSR have the ability to threaten each other's survival. As we shall see, most writers on the balance of power see bipolar balances as inherently unstable, because changes in the capacity of one actor can only be met by similar changes in the other – and this process is always likely to get out of sync. Waltz disagrees; according to him, bipolar systems are easier to manage because there are fewer interested parties involved.

This is a theory of the structure of the international system, and a good question would be how structure relates to 'agency' – what does it mean to say that states *must* behave in certain kinds of ways? We shall examine the agent–structure debate in the next chapter, in the context of the study of foreign policy, but this is clearly also an issue for structural theories. Again, how can it be assumed that a balance of power will always emerge, or that states will be able to manage a bipolar system, given that they do not consciously wish to create balances – indeed, most states would prefer to eliminate potentially threatening states (that is, all states other than themselves)? Waltz's answer to these questions is that there is no guarantee that balances will appear or that power management will be successful; however, states that do not respond to the signals sent to them by the international system – that is to say, states that ignore the distribution of power in the world will find that they suffer harm as a result; indeed, under some circumstances, they could face loss of independence. Since states do not want this to happen, the likelihood is that they will take the necessary steps (Waltz 1979: 118). But they may not; some states, but not very many across the past century, have actually lost their independence, while others, because of a favourable geographical position, or some other natural advantage, have the luxury of being able to make quite a few misreadings of the demands of the international system without suffering serious harm. None the less, the tendency is for states to respond to their cues.

Here, and at other points throughout the work, Waltz employs analogies drawn from neoclassical economics; in particular, the theory of markets and the theory of the firm. The pure competitive market is a classical example of a structure that comes into existence independent of the wishes of the buyers and sellers, who nevertheless create it by their actions. Each individual actor must respond to the signals sent by the market – but 'must' in this sense simply means that, say, farmers who attempt to sell at a price higher than the market will bear will be unable to unload their crops, while farmers who sell for less than they could get are passing up opportunities for gain, which will be taken up by others who will drive them out of business. Similarly, buyers will not want to pay more than is necessary and will not be able to pay less than the going rate. The market structure emerges out of these decisions, yet the decisions are shaped by the market structure. The analogy can be taken further. In an uncompetitive market, an oligopoly, a small number of firms are able to manage prices and output in such a way that, by avoiding direct competition, each is better off than they would otherwise be. These firms have no interest in each other's survival – Ford would like to see General Motors disappear, and vice versa – but as profit-maximizers they realize that positive attempts to get rid of the competition would be far too dangerous to contemplate; a price war might bring down both firms. In the same way, the United States and the Soviet Union had a common interest in regulating their competition, even though each would have preferred the other to disappear had this been achievable in a riskless, costless way.

It is this economic analogy that might be said to justify the 'neo' in 'neorealism'. In effect, and crucially in terms of the influence of his work, Waltz is offering a 'rational choice' version of the balance of power, in which states are assumed to be self-interested egoists who determine their strategies by choosing what maximizes their welfare. This is a long way in spirit from the agonized reliance on the mainspring of the sinfulness of man characteristic of Morgenthau and the 'righteous realists' (Rosenthal 1991). In this respect, he is closer to Carr, whose quasi-Marxist emphasis on scarcity and the human condition seems to parallel Waltz's account of anarchy and the desire for self-preservation. Carr did not adopt a rational choice mode of theorizing, but even this style of reasoning is not unknown in the classical tradition. Rousseau's fable of the stag and the hare is similar in import to Waltz's account of the egoism of states: a band of hunters can collectively meet their needs by bringing down a stag, but if at the crucial moment one leaves the hunt in order to catch a hare, thus satisfying his individual needs, this action causes the stag to be lost – an excellent illustration of the problems involved in collective action. None the less, in spite of these predecessors, there is something new here in the way in which Waltz puts together the argument.

The extraordinary influence of Waltz's work can also be seen in the impetus it has given to other scholars to develop structural realist thought, which has resulted in a conceptual split within the paradigm between 'defensive' and 'offensive' realists. The two strands of thought agree on the basic assumption that states' desire for security is compelled by the anarchic structure of the international system. However, defensive realists, who include Stephen Van Evera (1999), Stephen Walt (1987, 2002) and Jack Snyder (1991) as well as Waltz himself, hold that states attain security by maintaining their position within the system, so their tendency is towards achieving an appropriate amount of power, in balance with other states. Offensive realists, the most influential of whom is John Mearsheimer (1990, 1994/5, 2001), assert instead that security is so elusive in a self-help system that states are driven to attain as much power (defined as material, particularly military, capability) as possible: to become the global, or at least regional, hegemon. This leads them to pursue aggressive, expansionist policies, argued by offensive realists to be much less costly and more rewarding than they are considered to be by defensive realists, who see such policies as irrational. Defensive realists argue that more power can lead to less security, therefore that the rational state has little incentive to seek additional power once it feels secure relative to other powers within the system. Contrary to offensive realist assumptions, the international system does not reward states who seek to dominate, but rather those that maintain the status quo. Because of this, perhaps the main contribution of offensive realism has been to explain the behaviour of 'revisionist' states, an account of whose actions is absent from Waltzian neorealism.

A further break with Waltzian thought can be seen in the impulse in the recent work of scholars such as Wohlforth (1993), Schweller (1998) and Zakaria (1998) to supplement structural neorealism with unit-level analysis. This work, labelled 'neoclassical' or 'postclassical' realism, contends that state behaviour cannot be explained using the structural level alone, and uses the insights of classical realists such as Machiavelli, Morgenthau and Kissinger in order to reintroduce individual and domestic governmental level variables (rejected by Waltz in *Man, the State and War,* 1959) into explanations of state behaviour in the international system.

In summary, Waltz's neorealism is obviously controversial – but it remains not only the most convincing restatement of the realist position in recent times, but also a restatement that links IR theory to the mainstream of (American) political science. *Theory of International Politics* deserves its status as the most influential book on International Relations theory of its generation.

From neorealism to liberal institutionalism

From the perspective of the late 1970s, it might have been anticipated that the way International Theory would develop in later decades would be along the lines of a contrast between (neo)realism and pluralism, with, perhaps, a left-wing critique of both theories hovering in the background. To some extent this has happened, and a number of accounts of contemporary International Relations theory are presented in terms of three perspectives or 'paradigms' (Little and Smith 1991; Viotti and Kauppi 1999). However, in the United States, which is the effective home of the discipline, theory developed in a rather different way. The pluralists of the 1970s largely became the 'neoliberal institutionalists' of the 1980s and 1990s, and in the process came rather closer to neorealism than might have been expected.

Scholars such as Robert Axelrod and Robert Keohane developed models that shared much with neorealism (Axelrod 1984; Keohane 1984, 1989; Axelrod and Keohane 1985): they accepted the two basic assumptions of international anarchy and the rational egoism of states; and the aim of their analyses was to show that it was possible for rational egoists to co-operate, even in an anarchical system. Drawing material from the same kinds of sources as the neorealists – in particular, game theory, public choice and rational choice theory – they recognized that co-operation under anarchy was always liable to be fragile. 'Free rider' states – which took the gains of co-operation without contributing to the costs – would always be a problem, and the 'prisoner's dilemma' game modelled very clearly the difficulty of relying on promises of co-operation made in circumstances where enforcement was impossible. However, if international regimes could be established within which information could be exchanged and commitments formalized, the possibilities for co-operation would be enhanced. Establishing regimes is a difficult process, and most of the existing regimes in, especially, the international political economy were established by a 'hegemonic' power, the United States, in the immediate post-war era – a 'hegemon' in this context being defined as a state that has the ability to establish rules of action and enforce them, and the willingness to act on this ability. One of the key propositions of most of these writers is that US hegemony has declined dramatically in recent years, thus posing a problem – is it possible for co-operation to continue 'after hegemony'? The answer usually given is 'yes' – but at sub-optimal levels, because what is happening is that the regime is living on the capital built up under hegemony; the details of this argument will be examined in Chapter 7 below.

The neoliberal institutionalists are clearly saying something rather different about international co-operation from the neorealists, but a common commitment to rational choice theory makes them part of the same broad movement. The neorealist Joseph Grieco helpfully sets out the points of disagreement between the two camps (Grieco 1988).

Grieco suggests that a key issue concerns *absolute* as opposed to *relative* gains from co-operation. Neoliberals assume that states are essentially concerned with the absolute gains made from co-operation; as long as they are happy with their own situation, they will not be too worried about how well other states are doing. There is a clear parallel here with liberal trade theory, where the fact that parties will gain unequally from trade that reflects comparative advantage is deemed to be less important than the fact that they will all gain something. Neorealists, on the other hand, assume that each state will be concerned with relative gains from co-operation; that is, with how well other states are doing as well as how well *it* is doing. This follows from the neorealist focus on the balance of power, which rests precisely on the assumption that states will scan each other continually for signs that their relative power position is changing. This difference in orientation, Grieco suggests, means that neorealists and neoliberals focus on quite different problems when it comes to the limits of co-operation. For neoliberals, it is not at all difficult to see why states co-operate – it is in their (absolute) interest to do so. The problem, rather, as we have seen, is that states have a tendency to cheat, to become 'free riders', and what is needed is some mechanism that prevents cheating. This would allow states to realize their true long-term interest in co-operation as opposed to falling prey to the temptation to settle for short-term gains – it is easy to see why this branch of theory is termed neoliberal. For neorealists, on the other hand, 'cheating' is something of a non-problem. From their point of view, the difficulty is getting co-operation going in the first place, because states will only co-operate when they expect that the gains they will receive will be greater than, or at least equal to, the gains of all other relevant parties – is quite a tough criterion to meet.

Grieco argues that the neorealist assumption that states concentrate on relative gains is backed up by observations of how states actually behave in the international system, as well as by public opinion data which, as he shows, suggests that the US public at least is more concerned with relative rather than absolute gains. On the other hand, neoliberals can point to the extensive network of international institutions that exists and, indeed, is added to continually, which rather undermines the proposition that states are chronically unwilling to co-operate. From the neorealist perspective, the neoliberals are engaging in a doomed enterprise. While accepting an essentially Hobbesian definition of the situation – that is, the two criteria of anarchy and rational egoism – neoliberals argue that co-operation can take place without the presence of a Hobbesian 'sovereign'; this cannot be so. Neoliberals argue that, while co-operation will be sub-optimal it will still be possible.

However this debate is resolved, what is clear is that neoliberals and neorealists are much closer together than their non-neo forebears. Whereas the latter understood the world in fundamentally incompatible terms, stressing either harmony or disharmony of interests, and the importance or unimportance of domestic structures, the 'neos' both rest their position on what are taken to be the facts of anarchy and of the rational egoism of states. It may be going too far to write of a unified 'neo–neo' position (Waever 1996), but certainly the two positions are close enough to be seen as offering different understandings of what is essentially the same (rational choice) research programme. Moreover, this is a research programme within which the work of the majority of IR scholars can be located. As will become apparent in subsequent chapters, within this research programme there is room for a great deal of variation, and even basic notions such as the balance of power can be challenged – perhaps states 'bandwagon' rather than 'balance', or engage in soft rather than hard balancing? None the less, implicitly or explicitly, the 'anarchy problematic' established by Waltz sets the agenda for most contem-

porary IR research. But, especially in the last few years, opposition movements have been growing, and the rest of this chapter provides an overview of
these movements, though perhaps the most fundamental challenge over
matters of substance, that of theorists of globalization, is covered in its own
terms in Chapter 9.

Constructivism and the 'English School'

As we shall see, theorists of globalization reject the 'state-centrism' involved
in neorealist/neoliberal rational choice theory in favour of an approach that
stresses global social, economic, cultural and political forces. Other critics of
rational-choice IR are less concerned by its focus on the state, and more critical of the implicit assumptions that underlie that focus, in particular the
assumption that the nature of the state is, in some sense, given, and that the
rules that govern state behaviour are simply part of the way things are, rather
than the product of human invention. By definition, rational choice IR theories assume that states engage in goal-directed behaviour, but within a context
that is stated in advance; they study how states play the game of being rational
egoists in an anarchic world, but they take for granted that states *are* rational
egoists and that the identification of the world as anarchic is unproblematic;
in other words, that the game is preordained. Critics challenge this set of
assumptions.

These critics share a hostility to rational choice approaches, but relatively
little else, and finding even a rudimentary classification schema here is difficult; for the purposes of exposition they are divided here into two groups.
First, the work of *constructivists* and their *English School* cousins will be
examined; then, moving progressively further away from the mainstream of
IR theory, *critical theorists, poststructuralists* and others misleadingly termed
postmodern writers will come under scrutiny.

Constructivism is the fastest-growing oppositional movement within IR
theory, but a good part of this growth is a by-product of the lack of any clear
definition of what this approach might involve. Unfortunately, constructivism
has become a bumper-sticker term, a label appropriated by those who wish to
assert a degree of independence from mainstream American IR theory while
maintaining a certain level of respectability – it has come to be seen as a kind
of acceptable 'middle way' (Adler 1997). In the late 1980s and early 1990s,
this was not the case. At that time, the writings of Alexander Wendt (1987,
1992), Friedrich Kratochwil (1989) and Nicholas Onuf (1989) established
constructivist ideas as a genuinely radical alternative to conventional IR.

The central insight of constructivist thought can perhaps best be conveyed
by the notion that there is a fundamental distinction to be made between
'brute facts' about the world, which remain true independent of human

action, and 'social facts', which depend for their existence on socially established conventions (Searle 1995). There is snow on the top of Mount Everest whether anyone is there to observe it or not, but the white and purple piece of paper in my pocket with a picture of Adam Smith on it is only a £20 note because it is recognized by people in Britain to be so. Mistaking a social fact for a brute fact is a cardinal error – and one constructivists believe is made with some frequency – because it leads to the ascription of a *natural* status to conditions that have been produced and may be, in principle, open to change. Thus, if we treat 'anarchy' as a given, something that conditions state action without itself being conditioned by state action, we shall miss the point that 'anarchy is what states make of it' and does not, as such, dictate any particular course of action (Wendt 1992). We live in 'a world of our making', not a world whose contours are predetermined in advance by non-human forces (Onuf 1989).

So far so good, but how are these approaches to be developed? A variety of different possibilities emerge. First, unfortunately, there may be no development at all, and in the 1990s a number of essentially empirical IR scholars proclaimed themselves to be 'constructivist' in so far as they accepted the above points, but did not change their working methods in any significant way, at least not in any way that outsiders could discern. This is constructivism as a label. More to the point, and second, it might be noted that because a structure is the product of human agency it by no means follows that it will be easy for human agents to change its nature once it has been established – *agent–structure* questions tease out the relationships between these two notions (Wendt 1987). Such questions are of particular importance in the study of foreign policy and will be discussed in Chapter 4 below. Third, once we recognize that the nature of the game of international politics is not simply to be taken for granted, the road is opened up for a Wittgensteinian analysis of the *rules of the game,* an account of the ways in which the grammar of world politics is constituted. Kratochwil and Onuf have been particularly important in developing this side of the constructivist project; for a paradigm of this kind of analysis the reader is referred to Kratochwil's account of the place of the rule of non-intervention within the Westphalian game of 'sovereignty-as-*dominium*' (Kratochwil 1995). Alternatively, some German constructivists have adopted an essentially Habermasian approach, focusing on communicative action in world politics (Risse 2000).

However, perhaps the most popular line of development has been in another direction, towards using constructivist ideas to throw light on normative issues, in particular those that revolve around matters of identity, and, by extension, on issues of co-operation between states (Ruggie 1998; Wendt 1999). As noted above, 'neo-neo' IR theory assumes that co-operation takes place between egoists under conditions of anarchy, if, that is, it takes place at all. The identities of the actors in question is a matter of no significance, and norms promoting co-operation will have no purchase on what is essentially a process of ends–means calculation, in which the end ('security') is given in advance and is the same for all actors, and the context is provided by a notion of anarchy that is essentially incontestable and unchanging. Of course, specific actors will pursue particular goals in order to achieve security, but these goals are effectively given in advance – state interests are conceptualized as exogenous to their calculation of the right thing to do in any given circumstances. Constructivists challenge each item in the formulation of these ideas. Identity *does* matter: US relations with, for example, Canada and France are different from the country's relations with Egypt and the People's Republic of China, not simply for reasons of security, but because the first two countries share with the USA a common (broad) identity that the latter two do not – more dramatically, as Ruggie points out, it mattered enormously that the USA became (briefly) hegemonic post-1945 rather than the USSR, in ways that cannot be captured by those who simply portray 'hegemony' as an abstract requirement for a particular kind of co-operative regime. Interests are not simply exogenous variables, but are subject to continual change as a result of interactions with others. Equally, the idea that there is only one 'anarchy problematic' will not do; anarchy means 'no rules', but need not (though it may) mean chaos. The possibility exists that within an anarchical framework norms can emerge.

This latter thought is developed extensively in the second half of Alexander Wendt's ambitious *Social Theory of International Politics* (1999). As the title suggests, this book is a deliberate attempt to set up an opposition to Waltz's *Theory of International Politics* (1979), though, as the title also suggests, it also pays a kind of homage to the earlier volume. The first part of *Social Theory* presents a clear, albeit at times somewhat anodyne, version of constructivist epistemology, while the second half develops notions of the importance of identity and norms, and the politics of different kinds of anarchy – including the possibility of the emergence of an 'anarchical society'. This latter possibility highlights the connections between this version of constructivism and the work of a group of theorists generally known as the 'English School'.

The 'English School' is so named because its major figures, though often not English, worked in England (in particular at the London School of Economics, and at Oxford and Cambridge Universities) during its formative years. It is best defined as a group of scholars – most notably Martin Wight, Hedley Bull, Adam Watson, R. J. Vincent, James Mayall, Robert Jackson, and more recently Tim Dunne and N. J. Wheeler – whose work focuses on the notion of a 'society of states' or 'international society': the history of the English School is well told in Dunne (1998). The term 'international society' conveys two points, both of which are examined at length in the masterwork of the School, Hedley Bull's *The Anarchical Society* (1977/1995/2002); first, the focus of study should be primarily on the world of states and not on sub-state entities or universal categories such as 'humanity'; however, second, states when they interact do not simply form an international *system,* a non-normative pattern of regularities; rather, they form a *society,* a norm-governed relationship whose members accept that they have at least limited responsibilities towards one another and to the society as a whole. These responsibilities are summarized in the traditional practices of international law and diplomacy. States are assumed to pursue their interests in the international arena, but not at all costs – or, rather, if they do pursue them at all costs, international society will be in danger. The link between this kind of thinking and Wendt's constructivist thought is clear. International relations take place under conditions of anarchy, but in an 'anarchical society'; states act within a system of norms which, most of the time, they regard as constraining. Moreover, these norms are created by the states themselves; Dunne makes this explicit connection in an article entitled 'The Social Construction of International Society' (1995).

This is not the only direction in which English School thought can be taken; Barry Buzan, the inspiration for a recent attempt to revitalize the School as a research programme, draws connections with neoliberal institutionalist thought on regimes (Buzan 1993, 1999, 2004). Perhaps more to the point, the notion of international society is connected quite closely to an older, pre-rational choice kind of realism. One way of looking at the concept is to see it as an occasionally idealized conceptualization of the norms of the old, pre-1914 European states system. This is the real version of European statecraft, as opposed to the 'crib' that Hans Morgenthau and others prepared for the American domestic political elite in the 1940s. If this is right, a good question would be whether 'international society' provides a satisfactory starting-point for understanding the contemporary world order, where the majority of states are non-European. It is at least arguable that the old order worked as well as it did because there was quite a high level of cultural homogeneity in the system; Europeans shared a common history, albeit one of frequently violent relationships, and common Graeco-Roman cultural origins. Even so, the divide between (Greek) Orthodox and (Roman) Catholic Europe was a source of some tension, as had been, in the sixteenth and seventeenth centuries, the divide in the West between Protestant and Catholic Europe. How much more problematic would be the normative basis for an international society composed, as today it must be, of states based in many cultures – Islamic, Hindu, Confucian and African as well as 'Western'?

There are two possible answers here. One is that while the modern world is incontestably multicultural in social terms, the Western invention of the nation-state has proved remarkably attractive to a great many different cultures. Whether because they genuinely meet a need, or because, given the existing order, territorial political units are more or less unavoidable, nation-states seem to be desired everywhere. The only part of the world where the institution is under serious threat from an alternative form of political organization is at its place of origin in Western Europe in the form of the European Union. A second answer is less contingent and more complex. It is that the very rationale of 'international society' is its ability to cope with cultural diversity, with the practices of the society supporting the freedom of its members to pursue their own conceptions of the Good (Nardin 1983). This view is explored further in Chapter 10.

To summarize, some versions of constructivism, especially that associated with Wendt's recent writings and the English School, offer not-dissimilar critiques of the current intellectual dominance of rational-choice IR theory, and cognate accounts of how the world might be studied other than through the assumption that rational egoists maximize their security under the anarchy problematic. In opposition to positivism, they share the view that theory in part constitutes the world. However, on some accounts, the critical impulse of early constructivist writings has been lost by Wendt; it is noticeable that, in the *Review of International Studies* Forum on Wendt's *Social Theory of International Politics*, mainstream IR theorists were disposed rather more favourably towards his arguments than were more radical critics, and Friedrich Kratochwil has argued that Wendt is in the process of constructing a new orthodoxy (*Review of International Studies* 2000; Kratochwil 2000). Certainly, Wendt has cast himself as a 'loyal opposition', challenging the mainstream, but eager for dialogue with it; the title of Wendt's 1999 book conveys this very nicely, being at once a challenge and a tribute to Waltz. In any event, in the final section of this chapter, the work of oppositionists who can by no stretch of the imagination be thought of as loyal, will be examined.

Critical, poststructuralist and 'postmodern' international thought

All constructivists are, in some sense post-positivist, indeed anti-positivist in so far as they reject the rational choice, neo-utilitarian reasoning of mainstream IR theory, but the currently dominant trend of constructivist thought, represented by Wendt and Ruggie, remains closely in touch with the research agenda of the mainstream – that is, the relations of states, and specifically problems of co-operation and conflict. The writers to be considered in this final section on contemporary IR theory are much less wedded to this conventional agenda; they take their inspiration from elsewhere; in fact from a variety of elsewhere, since there is no single source of inspiration for this 'new learning'. We find here Frankfurt School Critical Theorists, feminist writers, writers inspired by the French masters of thought of the last half century – Foucault and Derrida in particular – and even, although the word is much misused, the occasional genuine 'postmodernists'. These thinkers do not have a great deal in common, save for two important intellectual commitments: all desire to understand International Relations not as a free-standing discourse with its own terms of reference, but rather as one manifestation of a much broader movement in social thought; and all hold that theory must unsettle established categories and disconcert the reader. On both counts, IR must be seen in the context of Enlightenment and post-Enlightenment thought. Just *how it is* to be seen in this context is what is contested, and to understand this context a step back has to be taken, in the direction of the Enlightenment itself.

To answer the question 'What is Enlightenment?' in a study of this scope is not possible, but a rough-and-ready account of what it has become customary to call the 'Enlightenment Project' can be given, building on Kant's famous answer to this question – Enlightenment is 'humanity's emergence from self-imposed immaturity' (Reiss 1970: 54). In other words, the Enlightenment mandated the application of human reason to the project of human emancipation. Human beings were challenged by the great thinkers of the Enlightenment to know themselves and their world, and to apply that knowledge to free themselves both from superstition and the forces of ignorance, and, more directly, from political tyranny, and, perhaps, the tyranny of material necessity. Originally, the main carrier of the project of emancipation was 'liberalism' in one form or another, but one belief held by all the writers examined here, and by most constructivists, is that contemporary forms of liberalism, such as the neo-utilitarianism represented by rational choice theory and mainstream IR theory, no longer perform this function. To use the influential formulation of Robert Cox, contemporary liberal theory is 'problem-solving' theory – it accepts the prevailing definition of a particular situation and attempts to solve the problems this definition generates – while emancipatory theory must be 'critical', challenging conventional understandings (Cox 1981). Thus, whereas neorealist/neoliberal thinking accepts the 'anarchy problematic' as given, and seeks devices to lessen the worst side-effects of anarchy, the new approaches wish either to explore and elucidate the ways in which this problematic serves particular kinds of interests (and closes down particular sorts of arguments) or to shift the argument on to an altogether different subject.

If it is generally agreed by these authors that contemporary liberalism can no longer be seen as an emancipatory discourse, there is no agreement as to whether the project of emancipation itself is recoverable. Here, a quite sharp divide emerges between those who believe it is, though not on modern liberal lines, and those who believe that the failure of liberalism in this respect is symptomatic of a problem with the goal of emancipation itself. The former look back to, variously, Kant, Hegel and Marx to reinstate the Enlightenment Project; and the latter, variously, to Nietzsche, Heidegger and Foucault to critique the underlying assumptions of emancipatory theory.

The former group – call them 'critical theorists' for the sake of convenience – are clearly related to left-orientated, progressivist, international thought since the French Revolution, including radical liberalism before it became part of the official world-view of the dominant international powers. The single most influential critical theorist was, and remains, Karl Marx; it was Marx who set out most clearly the propositions that 'emancipation' could not be simply a political process, leaving economic inequalities untouched (which has been the failing of liberalism); that capitalism, while its subversion of traditional forms of rule was to be welcomed, itself created oppression; and, most important in this context, that capitalism was, at least potentially in his day, a world-system, a force that had to be understood in global rather than local terms – which means that 'emancipation' must be a global project. Unfortunately, these core insights, which most critical theorists would endorse, were embedded by Marx within a framework that contained much that contemporary history has shown to be decidedly un-emancipatory. The direct descendants of Marx – the Bolsheviks in the Soviet Union, Mao and the Chinese Communist Party, and various national communist regimes in Cambodia, Cuba, North Korea and Vietnam – were, between them, responsible for more human misery in the twentieth century than the adherents of any other world-view, Nazism included. Moreover, the various directly-inspired Marxist theories of IR – Lenin's theory of imperialism, and numerous variants of centre–periphery and world-systems analysis – have proved to be equally unsatisfactory, despite being highly influential in the non-Western world (as will be seen in Chapter 8 below). As a result of this record, contemporary critical theorists tend to work with Marx via intermediaries, the most important of whom have been, for international political economists, the Italian/Sardinian Marxist and victim of fascism, Antonio Gramsci, and for international political theorists, the Frankfurt School – and, in particular, its leading modern theorist, Jürgen Habermas.

Setting aside the Gramscian heritage for later consideration, the contribution of Habermas to critical theory has been to move Marx-influenced thought away from economic determinism and the class struggle, and towards an engagement with Kantian ethics and Hegelian notions of political community. Habermas shares Kant's universalist account of ethical obligation, which he recasts for our age in terms of 'discourse ethics'; moral issues are to be understood as resolvable via dialogue under ideal conditions (the influence of this notion on German constructivists was noted above); that is, with no voice excluded and without privileging any particular point of view or taking for granted that inequalities of wealth and power are legitimate. Politics is an ethical activity that takes place within communities – but communities must be understood to be as inclusive as possible; some level of exclusion may be inevitable if citizenship is to be meaningful, but the basis for inclusion and exclusion is subject to moral scrutiny.

Habermas has written on the theory and practice of international relations in books and articles on such diverse subjects as Kant's international theory, the Gulf War of 1990–1 and the Kosovo Campaign of 1999, but his standard-bearers in English-language International Relations have been scholars such as David Held and Andrew Linklater, with a rather more Marx-orientated, wider Frankfurt School perspective represented by Mark Neufeld and Richard Wyn Jones (Habermas 1994, 1997, 1999, 2002; Held 1995; Neufeld 1995; Linklater 1998; Jones 1999, 2001). Linklater and Held have developed different aspects of the notion of cosmopolitan democracy. Held's work is orientated towards an explicitly normative account of the need to democratize contemporary international relations; the central thesis is that, in an age of globalization (of which Held has been a major theorist) the desire for democratic self-government can no longer be met at a national level and so the project of democratizing the international order must be prioritized, however difficult a task this may be. Linklater is less concerned with institutional change; more with the transformation of notions of political community, and the evolution of an ever-more inclusive dialogue. These are themes that clearly relate to Habermas's thought, but many writers in critical international studies – particularly in sub-fields such as 'Critical Security Studies' – take a broader view of the critical theory project. Both Neufeld and Jones remain closer to the Marxian roots of critical theory than do Linklater and Held, and are rather more critical generally of the 'powers that be' in contemporary world politics.

These few comments can only give a flavour of the work of critical theorists – readers are urged to follow up the suggested reading listed below – but enough has been said to make it clear that the account of International Relations they offer is radically different from that of mainstream IR. A valuable illustration of the chasm in question can be found in the *Review of International Studies* (1999b) Forum on Linklater's *The Transformation of Political Community* (1998); the blank incomprehension of Randall Schweller, representing the mainstream, results in an almost-comically hostile response. However, in the same Forum, the equally critical comments of R. B. J. Walker point in another direction. Linklater's brand of critical theory is ultimately devoted to the rescue of the emancipatory project of the Enlightenment – but can this project be rescued? And ought it to be? Perhaps it is not so much a case of work such as rational choice IR betraying the Enlightenment Project, but rather of representing it all too faithfully.

This is the approach taken by writers characteristically referred to as post-structuralist – or sometimes, usually inaccurately, postmodern – and if the above account of Habermas and critical theory is dangerously thin, any attempt to provide an equivalent background for these scholars within a study of this scope presents even more difficulties; once again, readers are urged to follow up some of the references given below. A few themes only can be identified; first, following up the reference to Walker above is 'inside/outside'; then, closely related, a new approach to ethics and to pluralism; next, speed, simulation and virtual reality; and finally, the contribution of feminist writing.

For the critical theorist, Linklater, the community is necessarily to some degree exclusionary, but the aim is to be as inclusive as possible and to make the costs of exclusion as low as possible – this is, of course, an explicitly normative project, though Linklater insists that trends supportive of this end are immanent in our current world order. Walker may share some of these normative goals, but is concerned more directly with the way in which the very system of sovereign states is constituted by and rests on a sharp inside/outside distinction (Walker 1993). It was the emergence of this sharp distinction in the early modern era that created the Westphalia System, and, more recently, has created the discourse of International Relations itself; moreover, the emancipatory discourses of the Enlightenment rest on a structurally similar distinction: the privileging of a particular voice by the Enlightenment – European, rationalist, male – is not something that is incidental and can be eliminated by a better dialogue, any more than the bounded community can be redesigned to avoid the privileging of the interests of its inhabitants.

It is not always clear where Walker wishes to take these points, but writers such as William Connolly and David Campbell offer some suggestions. Both focus on issues of 'difference' and 'otherness', and both propose strategies for dealing with otherness that reject the universalism of conventional emancipatory politics. Campbell, in studies of the Gulf War and the Bosnia conflict, attempts to show the emptiness of rule-orientated approaches to ethics, symbolized by such constructions as Just War theory, in which the actions of parties to a conflict are tested against an allegedly impartial and objective ethical yardstick (Campbell 1993, 1998). Instead, he proposes an ethics of encounter, a more personal, less general approach to the identities and interests of groups and individuals, in which those identities and interests are not taken as given but are seen to be constructed in the course of conflicts – a classic illustration being the way in which the various parties to the Bosnian conflict are created by that conflict rather than representing pre-existent monolithic identities such as 'Muslims' or 'Serbs'. Connolly's interests are less obviously international, his contribution more closely related to the 'Culture Wars' of the modern USA, but his critique of American pluralism as a unifying and categorizing force as opposed to the kind of 'pluralization' that he would favour, in which no attempt is made to privilege particular kinds of interest and where the self-definition of actors is respected, draws on similar resources (Connolly 1995, 2002).

Campbell and Connolly are self-described 'late-modern' writers, who have by no means lost contact with the notion of emancipation – their worry, most explicit in Connolly, is that conventional notions of emancipation are likely to combine with contemporary technology to create a world in which 'difference' is abolished, in which human variety is 'normalized' and, as Nietzsche put it over a century ago, everyone thinks alike, and those who do not voluntarily commit themselves to the madhouse (Connolly 1991). The theme that the speed of modern life, the capacity for simulation and the creation of 'virtual reality' will fundamentally shift the ways in which we are able to think of ourselves as free and emancipated has been taken up in the discourses of IR, most prominently by James Der Derian. His early and pioneering work on the genealogy of diplomacy pursued Foucauldian themes, but his later work on spies, speed and 'anti-diplomacy' has rested in particular on the work of Paul Virilio – one of the only writers referred to in this section who could accurately be described as postmodernist, in so far as his oeuvre suggests that the pace of contemporary existence (in every sense of the term) is actually taking us beyond the modern into a new era (Der Derian 1987, 1992, 1998, 2001). Der Derian's work on 'virtual war' has interesting connections with other attempts to trace the changing nature of warfare, and will be discussed briefly below, in Chapter 6.

There is no particular reason why feminist writings should be associated with poststructuralism as opposed to the other positions outlined in this chapter – and, indeed, one of the most influential of feminist writers on IR, Jean Bethke Elshtain, certainly could not be described in these terms (Elshtain 1987, 1998). None the less, the majority of feminist writers in the field do fall naturally into this section rather than, say, the constructivist or critical theoretical section. The central point here is that the voice of the European Enlightenment is seen as masculine, and feminist writers such as J. Ann Tickner (1992, 2001), Cynthia Enloe (1993, 2000, 2004), Christine Sylvester (1994, 2001) and Cynthia Weber (1999) are not prepared to see the association of 'European, rationalist and male' as being contingent (in the way that, for example, a liberal feminist simply concerned with 'women's equality' might). These writers share with the authors discussed above the view that the project of emancipation of the Enlightenment is not recoverable by, in this case, simply adding women to the equation. Instead, they attempt, in various ways, to develop accounts of the social world that trace the influence of gender in all our categories, most particularly, of course, in this context, in our notions of the 'international'.

As with the other writers in this section, the goal is to dislocate our sense of what is 'normal', to cause us to re-think assumptions that we did not even know *were* assumptions. Tickner and Enloe engage in this project in ways that ultimately connect back to the wider goals of critical theory and an expanded, revised notion of human emancipation. Other writers have no such ambitions. Perhaps the most striking and controversial piece of writing in the latter camp is Cynthia Weber's account of US policy towards the Caribbean and Central America over the last generation in terms of the projection of fears of castration created by the survival of Castro's regime in Cuba (1999). This particular example of feminist IR writing is by no means typical, but the forging of links with another substantial body of contemporary social theory – in this case, gender studies and so-called 'queer theory' – certainly illustrates the general ambition of post-positivist IR to break away from the statist assumptions characteristic of mainstream theory.

One final category of writers deserve attention. Most of the schools of thought described in this and the previous section can be characterized as both self-consciously radical, and anti-'positivist', positivism being seen here as the belief that a reality exists that can be discerned by the methods of the natural sciences suitably adapted to cope with the particular circumstances of the social sciences – the belief that reality is socially constructed is common to nearly all these writers. In recent years, another approach to the issue of 'science' has emerged, or, better, re-emerged. This is 'scientific realism' – the belief that the goal of science is to describe how things really are; that the objects of science exist in the real world; that unobservable phenomena can be described with reference to their effects; and that notions such as causation are real, and not simply the product of human thought. The way in which scientific realism has had the most impact in the international field has been via the work of Roy Bhaskar and his notion of 'critical realism'; here are to be found writers who are indisputably of the radical, often Marxist, left but who reject the anti-scientism of the poststructuralists and postmodernists. This is an interesting development, but time will tell whether the relatively few writers currently working in this field will have a major impact on the discipline; in the meantime, the work of scholars such as Colin Wight, Jonathan Joseph and Milja Kurki certainly deserves attention.

Conclusion

The aim of this chapter has been to provide an overview of contemporary International Relations theory. As with any other sketch-map, it may not be possible to find a particular location by employing it – the further reading suggestions below provide the information needed for that task – but the reader ought now to have some sense of how the often bewildering variety of IR theories relate to each other. As the above discussion suggests, one answer is 'not very closely'. As suggested in the introduction to this chapter, IR theory since 1980 has involved a dialogue with the work of Kenneth Waltz – at times 'running battle' would be more appropriate – and the authors discussed in the second half of the chapter agree in their rejection of neorealism, despite agreeing on little else. Perhaps the only features post-positivist writers have in common is their post-positivism – that is, their rejection of the epistemological stance of rational choice theory, and, more generally, their rejection of a 'foundationalist' account of the world, in which knowledge can be grounded by the correspondence of theory to a knowable reality – the scientific realists described above are an obvious exception to this point. Contrary to the occasional slur of their opponents, post-positivists do not deny the existence of a 'real world' but they do deny our ability to grasp that world without the aid of theoretical categories that cannot themselves be validated by an untheorized reality. Beyond these epistemological commonalities, it is difficult to characterize the opponents of the 'neo-neo' consensus.

However, the hope is that when, in future chapters, a particular theoretical position is mentioned it will to be possible for the reader to have a sense of what conceptual baggage is associated with that position, and where he or she needs to go to find a fuller account. With this in mind, it is now possible to turn away, for the time being at least, from an emphasis on theory and look to the actual picture of the world that these theories have created. In the following three chapters, the issues with which realism is concerned will be examined, then the next three chapters will open up the debate to include the agendas of the theories that challenge the realist orthodoxy: looking at global forces and at the theoretical issues specifically orientated towards globalization.

Further reading

While the books referred to in the main body of this chapter have obviously been significant for the debate between pluralists, neorealists and neoliberals, the most interesting contributions to this debate have been in the form of journal articles, generally in *International Organization, World Politics* and *International Security*. These articles are also available in a number of convenient collections, with some overlap in terms of contents.

Robert O. Keohane (ed.), *Neorealism and its Critics* (1986), contains extensive extracts from Waltz, *Theory of International Politics* (1979), in addition to critiques by J. G. Ruggie, 'Continuity and Transformation in the World Polity: Towards a NeoRealist Synthesis' (1983); Robert Cox, 'Social Forces, States and World Orders: Beyond International Relations Theory' (1981); and an edited version of Richard K. Ashley, 'The Poverty of Neorealism' (1984). It also contains papers by Keohane himself; Robert Gilpin's response to Ashley, 'The Richness of the Tradition of Political Realism' (1984); and a response to his critics by Kenneth Waltz. This is certainly the best collection on the early stages of the debate.

David A. Baldwin (ed.) *Neorealism and Neoliberalism: The Contemporary Debate* (1993) is the best collection; it is largely shaped around Joseph M. Grieco, 'Anarchy and the Limits of Cooperation: A Realist Critique of the Newest Liberal Institutionalism' (1988). It also contains, among other important papers, Robert Axelrod and Robert O. Keohane, 'Achieving Cooperation under Anarchy: Strategies and Institutions' (1985); Robert Powell, 'Absolute and Relative Gains in International Relations Theory' (1991); and Arthur Stein, 'Coordination and Collaboration: Regimes in an Anarchic World' (1982); as well as a valuable summary of the debate by Baldwin, and reflections on the reaction to his original article by Grieco.

Friedrich Kratochwil and Edward D. Mansfield (eds), *International Organization and Global Governance: A Reader* (2005), has a wider remit and contains a number of articles that are very valuable for the study of regimes (see Chapter 7 below). The general theory sections contain a number of classic articles that are critical of the neoliberal–neorealist way of setting things up. Cox (1981) is again reprinted, along with edited versions of Kratochwil and J. G. Ruggie, 'International Organization: The State of the Art or the Art of the State' (1986), and, especially important, Alexander Wendt, 'Anarchy Is What States Make of It: The Social Construction of Power Politics' (1992). Also reprinted is Robert O. Keohane's classic, 'International Institutions: Two Approaches' (1988).

Charles W. Kegley, Jr. (ed.), *Controversies in International Relations Theory: Realism and the Neoliberal Challenge* (1995), is somewhat less focused on the immediate debates than its competitors, and contains a number of original pieces: it reprints Grieco (1988) and Kenneth Waltz, 'Realist Thought and Neorealist Theory' (1990), as well as valuable, state-of-the-art summaries by Kegley and James Lee Ray.

Michael E. Brown, Sean M. Lynn-Jones and Steven Miller (eds), *The Perils of Anarchy: Contemporary Realism and International Security* (1995), is an *International Security* Reader, especially valuable on realist thought on the end of the Cold War. Of general theoretical interest are Kenneth Waltz, 'The Emerging Structure of International Politics' (1993), and Paul Schroeder's critique of neorealist accounts of the development of the international system, 'Historical Reality vs. Neo-Realist Theory' (1994). On offensive, defensive and neoclassical realism, the following are useful review pieces that capture the main issues: *Review of International Studies* 29 Forum on American Realism (2003); Stephen G. Brooks, 'Duelling Realisms' (1997); Colin Elman, 'Horses for Courses: Why Not Neorealist Theories of Foreign Policy?' (1997); Gideon Rose, 'Neoclassical Realism and Theories of Foreign Policy' (1998); and Jeffrey Taliaferro, 'Security Seeking under Anarchy: Defensive Realism Revisited' (2000/01).

Important articles and essays not collected above include Robert Powell, 'Anarchy in International Relations: The Neoliberal–Neorealist Debate' (1994); Joseph Nye, 'Neorealism and Neoliberalism' (1988); Ole Waever, 'The Rise and Fall of the Inter-paradigm Debate' (1996); and, particularly important, Robert Jervis, 'Realism, Neoliberalism and Co-operation: Understanding the Debate' (1999). Book-length studies in addition to those referred to in the text include Robert Gilpin, *War and Change in World Politics* (1981), and Barry Buzan, Charles Jones and Richard Little, *The Logic of Anarchy: Neorealism to Structural Realism* (1993).

A Special Issue of *International Organization*, 'International Organization at Fifty' (1998), edited by Peter Katzenstein, Robert O. Keohane and Stephen Krasner provides an overview of current mainstream theory, including constructivist voices such as that of J. G. Ruggie. New looks at both liberalism and realism, but still within a rational choice framework, can be found in Andrew Moravcsik, 'Taking Preferences Seriously: The Liberal Theory of International Politics' (1997), and Jeffrey W. Legro and Andrew Moravcsik, 'Is Anybody Still a Realist?' (1999). A forum in *American Political Science Review,* December 1997, on Waltzian neorealism contains a number of valuable contributions, including a reply to his critics from Kenneth Waltz himself.

More recently, the focus of both neoliberalism and neorealism has been on making sense of the war on terror and US power. Particular attention has been paid to issue of hegemony, hierarchy and unipolarity. The *World Politics* special issue 'International Relations Theory and the Consequences of Unipolarity' (2009) features articles by important scholars. Stephan Waltz addresses the issue in *Taming American Power: The Global Response to U.S. Primacy* (2005). Other useful articles include Jack Donnelly, 'Sovereign Inequalities and Hierarchy in Anarchy: American Power and International Society' (2006), and David Lake 'Escape from the State of Nature: Authority and Hierarchy in World Politics' (2007).

The main constructivist writings by Kratochwil, Onuf, Ruggie and Wendt are referenced in the text. The *European Journal of International Relations* is a major source for the journal literature in this area – see, for example, Emmanuel Adler, 'Seizing the Middle Ground' (1997); Richard Price and Christian Reus-Smit, 'Dangerous Liaisons: Critical International Theory and Constructivism' (1998); and Stefano Guzzini, 'A Reconstruction of Constructivism in International Relations' (2000). Vendulka Kubalkova *et al.*, *International Relations in a Constructed World* (1998), is a useful overview. Rodney Bruce Hall's *National Collective Identity: Social Constructs and International System* (1999) is a model of serious constructivist scholarship, as is the collection by Yosef Lapid and Friedrich Kratochwil (eds) *The Return of Culture and Identity in International Relations Theory* (1996). Kratochwil's critique of Wendt's *Social Theory of International Politics*, 'Constructing a New Orthodoxy? Wendt's *Social Theory of International Politics* and the Constructivist Challenge' (2000), is itself a major statement and now collected in Stefano Guzzini and Anna Leander *Constructivism and International Relations: Alexander Wendt and his Critics* (2006) along with a number of important essays. Wendt remains a central figure for constructivists, as evidenced in exchanges with Vaughn Shannon, 'Wendt's Violation of the Constructivist Project: Agency and Why a World State Is Not Inevitable' (2005), in *European Journal of International Relations*.

For the 'English School', Hedley Bull, *The Anarchical Society* (1977/1995/2002), remains crucial, and an earlier collection, Herbert Butterfield and Martin Wight (eds), *Diplomatic Investigations* (1966), is still the best general introduction to the approach. Tim Dunne, *Inventing International Society* (1998), is establishing itself rapidly as the standard history of the School. The most interesting development in this mode is the attempt of two younger scholars to develop a 'critical' international society theory: N. J. Wheeler, 'Pluralist and Solidarist Conceptions of International Society: Bull and Vincent on Humanitarian Intervention' (1992); Tim Dunne, 'The Social Construction of

International Society' (1995); and Dunne and Wheeler, 'Hedley Bull's Pluralism of the Intellect and Solidarism of the Will' (1996). A useful general collection of articles can be found in the Forum on the English School in the *Review of International Studies* (2001). Barry Buzan's *From International to World Society? English School Theory and the Social Structure of Globalization* (2004) is a major statement, as are the recent works on legitimacy by Ian Clark, *Legitimacy in International Society* (2005) and *Legitimacy in World Society* (2007). Recent reflection on the English School includes Alex Bellamy (ed.), *International Society and its Critics* (2004); Andrew Linklater and Hidemi Suganami, *The English School of International Relations: A Contemporary Reassessment* (2006); and Andrew Hurrell, *On Global Order* (2007). The exchange between Tim Dunne (2005) and Barry Buzan (2005) in *Millennium* highlights the diversity in the work of those carrying on the English School tradition. Following an initiative by Barry Buzan, with Richard Little and Ole Waever, there is now a very useful website promoting the English School as a research programme: http://www.leeds.ac.uk/polis/englishschool/.

Hazel Smith, 'Marxism and International Relations' (1994) is a valuable bibliographical survey. Anthony Brewer, *Marxist Theories of Imperialism: A Critical Survey* (1990), is the best survey of both older and newer theories of imperialism. Fred Halliday, *Rethinking International Relations* (1994), offers the most accessible and best overview of the field from a (somewhat) Marxist perspective. Works on dependency theory and centre–periphery analysis will be discussed in Chapter 8 below. Gramscian international political economy is also discussed in Chapter 8; Stephen Gill (ed.), *Gramsci, Historical Materialism and International Relations* (1993) is a useful collection, and a good survey is Randall D. Germain and Michael Kenny, 'Engaging Gramsci: International Relations Theory and the New Gramscians' (1998).

Habermasian critical theory is well represented by Linklater's *The Transformation of Political Community* (1998); see also his *Beyond Realism and Marxism* (1990) and the programmatic 'The Question of the Next Stage in International Relations Theory: A Critical-Theoretic Approach' (1992). The collection by James Bohman and Matthias Lutz-Bachmann (eds), *Perpetual Peace: Essays on Kant's Cosmopolitan Ideal* (1997), contains essays by a number of important critical theorists, including Jürgen Habermas himself. The latter's *The Past as Future* (1994) contains some of his explicitly 'international' writings on the Gulf War and German politics, and in *The Inclusion of the Other* (2002), he reflects on the future of the nation-state and the prospects of a global politics of human rights. Habermas's *Die Zeit* essay (1999) on the Kosovo Campaign of that year (translated in the journal *Constellations)*, is a very fine example of critical thinking in practice. *Review of International Studies* has a recent Forum and a Special Issue that provide a quick and accessible entry to the state of critical theory in IR; see Forum: 'Useful Dialogue? Habermas and International Relations' (2005a) and Special Issue: 'Critical International Relations Theory after 25 Years' (2007).

Major poststructuralist collections include James Der Derian and Michael Shapiro (eds), *International/Intertextual: Postmodern Readings in World Politics*

(1989); Richard Ashley and R. B. J. Walker (eds), 'Speaking the Language of Exile: Dissidence in International Studies', Special Issue, *International Studies Quarterly* (1990); Michael Shapiro and Hayward R. Alker (eds), *Challenging Boundaries: Global Flows, Territorial Identities* (1996); and Jenny Edkins, Nalini Persram and Veronique Pin-Fat (eds), *Sovereignty and Subjectivity* (1999). Jenny Edkins, *Poststructuralism and International Relations: Bringing the Political Back In* (1999) is an excellent, albeit quite difficult guide to this literature; easier-going guides include Richard Devetak, 'Critical Theory' and 'Postmodernism' in Burchill et al., *Theories of International Relations* (2009); and Chris Brown, 'Critical Theory and Postmodernism in International Relations' (1994a) and '"Turtles All the Way Down": Antifoundationalism, Critical Theory, and International Relations' (1994c). Also very valuable are Yosef Lapid, 'The Third Debate: On the Prospects of International Theory in a Post-Positivist Era' (1989), and Emmanuel Navon, 'The "Third Debate" Revisited' (2001). On the issue of memory and trauma in war, Jenny Edkins, *Trauma and the Memory of Politics* (2003) and Maja Zehfuss, *Wounds of Memory: The Politics of War in Germany* (2007) provide intriguing case studies. Recent focus has been on the application of Foucault's notions of Governmentality and Biopolitics to IR; Michael Dillon and Luis Lobo-Guerrero 'Biopolitics of Security in the 21st Century: An Introduction' (2008); and Iver Neumann and Ole Jacob Sending, '"The International" as Governmentality' (2007) are recent developments of these ideas. Kimberly Hutchings' *Time and World Politics: Thinking the Present* (2008) is a comprehensive statement on the current world politics from a postmodern and feminist perspective.

Apart from the feminist writers mentioned in the text, readers are referred to V. Spike Peterson (ed.), *Gendered States: Feminist (Re)Visions of International Relations Theory* (1992); Marysia Zalewski and Jane Papart (eds), *The 'Man' Question in International Relations* (1997); and, best of recent textbooks on the area, Jill Steans, *Gender and International Relations: An Introduction* (1998). The debate between Adam Jones and his critics in the *Review of International Studies* provides an interesting insight into the issue of feminism and emancipation: see Jones, 'Gendering International Relations' (1996); Jones, 'Engendering Debate' (1998); and Terrell Carver, Molly Cochran and Judith Squires, 'Gendering Jones' (1998). Key collections on feminism and gender in IR are Rebecca Grant and Kathleen Newland (eds.), *Gender and International Relations* (1991), drawn from the *Millennium* special issue, 'Women and International Relations' (1988); and Louiza Odysseos and Hakan Seckinelgin *Gendering the International* (2002), from the *Millenium* special issue 'Gender and International Relations' (1998). A twentieth-anniversary forum, 'Reflections on the Past, Prospects for the Future in Gender and International Relations' (2008) is featured in *Millennium*. The recent *British Journal of Politics and International Relations*' special issue, 'Beyond Being Marginal: Gender and International Relations in Britain' (2007) is also good. Brooke Ackerly et al. (eds), *Feminist Methodologies for International Relations* (2006) is an important contribution to the field. Contemporary issues are covered from a feminist perspective in Shirin Rai and Georgina Waylen (eds), *Global Governance: Feminist Perspectives* (2008), and in

Krista Hunt and Kim Rygiel (eds), *(En)Gendering the War on Terror: War Stories and Camouflaged Politics* (2006). Finally, important journals for feminist work include *International Feminist Journal of Politics, Hypatia* and *Women's Philosophy Review.*

For critical and scientific realism, the best introduction is probably the *Millennium* forum 'Scientific and Critical Realism in International Relations' (2007), which features contributions from Colin Wight, Miljia Kurki and Jonathan Joseph. See also Chapter 4 for further references on scientific and critical realism in relation to the agent–structure problem in IR.

Chapter 4

Agency, Structure and the State

Introduction

In the previous chapter we noted the shift in focus in mainstream IR theory, from studying states as actors to examining the environment or structure in which states act – an 'international system', or perhaps an 'international society'. In this chapter, the relationship between actors and their environment, and the nature of the key actors in IR will be examined. To do so, we need to recap one of the oldest and most intractable debates in social science: the agent–structure problem. The debate centres not on the detail of who or what it is that acts in international politics – states, individuals, firms, international institutions and so on – but on whether 'agency' (the actions of actors, or their capacity to act) or 'structure' (the broad constraints within which actors act, such as international anarchy or society, global capitalism, or international law) is the key determinant of our social world. The argument here can sometimes seem rather abstract, but there are important real-world issues at stake and it is worth persevering – in any event, much recent work in this area does focus on the study of particular cases rather than rehashing old epistemological or ontological controversies. After setting out the agent–structure problem in slightly more detail, we shall focus in this chapter on agency and the most important agent in IR – the state – exploring the making of foreign policy and the relationship between this particular agent and the international system. Further discussion of the structure of the international system is to be found in Chapters 5 and 6.

The agent–structure problem and levels of analysis

The agent–structure problem is a critical and unresolved debate in the social sciences. Alexander Wendt identifies two truisms about social life which between them set out what is at stake: '1) human beings and their organizations are purposeful actors whose actions help reproduce or transform the society in which they live; and 2) society is made up of social relationships which structure the interactions of these purposeful actors' (Wendt 1987: 337–8). Marx made the same point in slightly different language in the nineteenth century – 'Men make their own history, but they do not make it just as they please; they do not make it under circumstances chosen by themselves, but under circumstances directly encountered, given and transmitted from the past' (Marx 1973: 96). Agents act, but they do so within the constraints of structures. How do agents and structures, separately or together, create the principal features of international relations? This is the agent–structure problem.

After Marx, the most influential classical theorist to address this problem was Emile Durkheim (see, especially, Durkheim, 1982), who, early in the twentieth century, argued that long-term structural factors, or 'social facts', such as law, religious beliefs or the norms associated with acting out particular social roles, were the most important determinants of individual behaviour. This was in opposition to the prevalent view in Anglo-American thought which was, and to a large extent still is, that social phenomena can be explained entirely by reference to the actions and motives of individuals – a position sometimes termed 'methodological individualism'. This controversy has implications for all the social sciences, including International Relations. Classical realist IR theory tended to be agent-centred, with states as the agents in question, but Kenneth Waltz, in his book *Man, the State and War* (1959), brought about something of a revolution in the discipline by suggesting that the nature of the international system (a structural variable) was the best, though not the only, explanation for war, and, as noted below, generalized the point by focusing on the imperatives imposed by international anarchy in his later *Theory of International Politics* (1979). Waltz's work is in fact somewhat ambiguous and can be interpreted as supporting the apparently agent-centred work on the behaviour of rational egoists that came to dominate US IR in the 1980s and 1990s, but other recent theories have been more unambiguously structuralist; dependency theory, core–periphery analysis and world-systems theory (on all of which, see Chapter 8).

Redefining the problem slightly, J. David Singer (1961) identified the problem of explanation in IR as a 'levels of analysis' problem. He argued that IR theorists relied on two distinct sources of explanation for international politics: the state and the international system (agent and structure), and suggested that these two sources of explanation could not be reconciled. Since then, the number of levels has been expanded. Buzan, Waever and de Wilde (1997) identify five levels at which international politics are frequently studied: international systems; international sub-systems or groups within international systems such as ASEAN or the OECD; units such as states or transnational firms; sub-units such as bureaucracies or lobby groups; and individuals. They, like many others, argue that 'levels of analysis' is a useful way to approach IR, and may even be the most useful concept that IR theorists have contributed to social science, but they also note two dangers of the approach. First, the debate over levels tends to confuse *ontological* questions about what exists, and therefore what our objects of study should be in IR (the state; individual action; the system as a whole) with *epistemological* questions about how we should study what we study – the appropriate sources of explanation for the characteristics or behaviour of states, individuals or systems. The second danger is that, as recent IR theory has been dominated by neorealism, we may be tempted to define the levels solely in terms of states – states as units, sub-units and individuals simply as components of states, and international systems as constituted by states. To do this would be to lose sight of the many other actors that influence international relations. Nevertheless, the idea that we can analyse international politics at different levels, and generate different theories and findings depending on from which level we decide to approach the subject matter is very valuable, and helps to explain why so many theories in IR – as discussed in previous chapters – seem to talk *past* rather than *to* each other.

Waltz's *Theory of International Politics* is a key contribution to modern debates on this subject. As described in Chapter 3, Waltz narrows the scope of IR theory to concentrate on the international system level (that is, the international system – a structural variable – is his principal object of analysis). He argues that the characteristics of the international system – an anarchy in which sovereign states, differing only in terms of their relative capabilities, must act and interact – are the best explanations for international politics (that is, structural factors are his source of explanation). Yet, the most interesting questions we face in IR arise when states seem to act counter to Waltz's structural imperatives. Why did the Soviet Union surrender its empire without a fight in 1989? Why have Germany and Japan not sought to balance US power post-1991, or to arm themselves with nuclear weapons? Waltz's answer to these questions is that the agents in the international system – states – are not forced to comply with structural imperatives, but over the long run the system is likely to discipline them into doing so, though large and powerful states can sometimes persist in error for a long time. In short, agents have *some* freedom from structure, but only at significant cost to their ongoing security.

This account of the relationship between agents and structures is unsatisfactory for a number of reasons. It is difficult to see how Germany and Japan are actually suffering for ignoring alleged systemic imperatives, and, at a more philosophical level, Waltz can be attacked for his ontological claim that the system should be our object of analysis (which seems to imply that structure is ontologically prior to agency at the international level, and thus that states were in some sense created by the international system – an implication that Waltz would dispute but which does seem to follow). Many theorists, especially of a constructivist persuasion (see Chapter 3), have questioned Waltz's approach, and have looked to build more subtle models of how structures and agents interact in IR. They start by questioning Waltz's assumptions that agents (states) are rational, self-contained, self-interested and autonomous, and that the international system is, for the most part, a material structure consisting of military and economic resources rather than ideas and norms. Wendt (1992, 1999, 2004) has been very influential in moving the debate forward. He argues that we cannot identify either agents or structures as the main causes of events in IR, but rather we need to understand how the two interact, and, specifically, how they constitute each other. Causal explanations, according to Wendt – that is, those that use rules of cause and effect to explain phenomena – can explain how features of the international system such as rules or institutions change or are reproduced by the actions of agents. Constitutive explanations use interpretation to understand the perspectives of the actors involved and the contexts in which they believe themselves to be. Both types of explanation are necessary in order to understand how actors in IR behave, and how the structures they act within come into being and change over time.

Wendt imports from sociology the concept of 'social structures', or patterned relationships between elements of society that are repeated across time and space (see Giddens 1986). These structures are not observable entities, but abstract formulations whose effects can be perceived. Wendt (along with other constructivists such as Dessler 1989) argues that systems of norms, beliefs and ideas are social structures that function as enablers and constraints in largely the same way that material structures do in international relations, and should be taken into account when trying to explain action. Normative structures, such as international law and the human rights regime, affect action by shaping the interests and identities of actors, which in turn limit the range of actions the agent considers as legitimate. However, constructivism also recognizes that these structures are the result of the knowledgeable (although not necessarily intentional) behaviour of agents. Thus, agents and structures are mutually caused.

Constructivists do not limit their analysis to causal explanation. They argue that the relations between agents and structures cannot be properly understood without also using constitutive theory, which brings the concept of social rules to the fore. According to Wendt (1991: 390), constitutive theory explicates the rules governing social situations, showing how actors can engage in certain practices in certain contexts, and how these practices instantiate the rules (or fail to do so). To use some Wittgensteinian language, constitutive rules are the rules of the game – they do not simply regulate how the game is played; in a sense they *are* the game. To use a well-worn example drawn from chess, a rule such as 'touch a piece, you must move it' is a regulative rule and can be relaxed when playing with a novice, but the rule that bishops move diagonally is constitutive of the game; relax this rule and you are no longer playing chess. Constitutive theory invites us to attempt to understand the perspectives of the actors involved in social situations and the contexts within which they believe themselves to be acting. It shows that agents and structures (that is, the rules and the game) are co-constituted (in contrast to causal theory, which shows that they are co-determined or mutually caused).

But how, exactly, are agent and structure co-determined and mutually constituting? Dessler conceptualizes structure as a means to action, following the Aristotelian argument that structure is a *material* rather than an *efficient* cause of behaviour. Aristotle's notion of causation is too complex to go into in detail here, but interested readers might start with Milja Kurki's recent work on causation (Kurki 2006, 2008). In brief, structure creates the possibility of agency, but does not dictate it, in the same way that language creates the possibility of speech, but cannot cause any particular conversation. For Roy Bhaskar, a major source for Dessler's position, agents and structures are ontologically distinct, with social agents being like 'a sculptor at work, fashioning a product out of the material and with the tools available to him' (Bhaskar 1979: 43; see also Bhaskar 2008). Bhaskar's work has been used in some of the latest thinking on the agent–structure problem: work by 'critical realist' scholars, exemplified by Colin Wight ('realism' in this context is very different from the IR use of the term). Critical realism is critical of both positivist and postpositivist approaches to the study of IR, and puts forward instead a method of analysis that is 'ontologically realist' – arguing that there is one reality and that this reality exists independently of what we think about it; 'epistemologically relativist' – contending that all beliefs are socially produced and hence potentially fallible; and 'judgementally rationalist' – holding that, despite epistemological relativism, it is still possible in principle to provide justifiable grounds for preferring one theory or social explanation/interpretation over another (Patomäki and Wight 2000: 224–5).

Wight (1999, 2004, 2006) argues that, while agency is 'embedded within, and dependent upon, structural contexts' (Wight 1999: 109), agency is not reducible to structure. Wight goes on further to argue that the real question we should be asking is not whether international politics is essentially shaped or caused by structural forces or by agency, but rather what we mean by the terms structure and agency – an ontological question about what actually exists in the international world. For Wight, this question of what agents and structures actually are needs to be answered before we can investigate the effects they have on each other, and he believes (rightly) that IR scholars have failed to do this so far. The agent–structure problem cannot be resolved definitively, according to Wight, as agents and structures are never totally independent of one another. We cannot therefore know which of the four levels of analysis Wight identifies – material, intersubjective, social role and personal subjectivity – is most appropriate to the study of IR in general: the most appropriate level will depend on the questions we are looking to answer. But what we can do is to use empirical analysis to establish the causal significance of particular agents and particular structures in particular situations. This is anathema to theorists such as Waltz, who want to simplify the study of IR, but does seem to be the most reasonable way to think about agents and structures, and, very importantly, it pushes us back towards real-world problems, and away from those more abstract questions that are best dealt with by philosophers of science rather than scholars of International Relations.

Turning now to the more substantive questions, in the rest of this chapter we shall examine the actor that remains dominant in IR: the state. In so doing we remain, for the time being, with an essentially realist or at least state-centric agenda; there is no doubt that other actors are increasingly important. Keohane and Nye identified as far back as 1971 the critical role that non-state actors play in IR, and developments since then have borne out their work: the approximately 54,000 non-governmental organizations, 60,000 multinational corporations and 7,500 intergovernmental organizations that now exist have profound effects on world politics. But these effects will be explored in detail in Chapter 8 when looking at the global economy and the increasing interconnectedness of states through trade and commerce; in Chapter 9 in discussion of the putative growth of a 'global civil society'; and indeed throughout the book, because references to the actions of NGOs, MNCs and IGOs can be found almost anywhere. However, since it is still impossible to understand IR without reference to states, and, despite a perceived loss of state power since the halcyon days of sovereignty after the Peace of Westphalia (of which more below), the state is still the most dominant agent in international politics and thus it will be the focus here.

The state and international relations

To recap, realism offers a *state-centric* account of the world, and, because realism takes the state to be central to international relations, topics such as the study of foreign policy decision-making or the analysis of the components of national power loom large; for the same reason, interstate 'war' is taken to be *sui generis,* unlike any other form of social conflict. This state-centricity suggests that realism ought to have a clear theory of the state, and that this should be the natural jumping-off point for the rest of its thinking. As it happens, this is not the case; the lack of such a theory is an important problem at the heart of realism, and indeed of International Relations as an academic discourse. It is striking that there are so few good studies of 'the state and IR' – John M. Hobson's book is the first introduction to the subject to be published for many years (Hobson 2000).

However, while *theory* is missing, realism offers quite an elaborate *description* of the state and of its emergence. The state is a *territorially-based political unit* characterized by a central decision-making and enforcement machinery (a government and an administration); the state is legally 'sovereign' in the sense that it recognizes neither an external superior, nor an internal equal; and the state exists in a world composed of other, similarly characterized, territorial, sovereign political units. These criteria can each best be established by reference to alternative modes of political organization, some of which were the points of origin of the modern state. Thus we can see what the state is, by contrasting it with what it is *not*.

The state is a territorial political unit, and there is clearly no necessity that politics should be arranged on a territorial basis. In classical Greece, the political referent was the inhabitants of a place rather than the place itself – hence in the writings of the day it is never 'Athens' that is referred to, always 'the Athenians'. Obviously, the Athenians lived in a territory, but they were the focal point, not the territory as such, and while the walls of the city were well defined, the boundaries of the wider territory occupied by the Athenians were not. In the medieval European world out of which the modern state emerged, political authority was personal or group-based rather than necessarily territorial. While a ruler might, in principle, claim some kind of authority over a territory, there would always be other sources of authority (and indeed power) to contest such a claim. The universal Church under the authority of the Pope operated everywhere, and its members, both lay and clergy, were obliged to deny the secular ruler's writ in a number of critical areas of policy. Guilds and corporations claimed 'liberties' against kings and princes, often successfully. Many individuals owed allegiance to powerful local magnates, who might in turn owe allegiance to 'foreign' rulers rather than to the nominal king of a particular territory. All of these factors fed into issues such as 'political identity'; any particular individual was likely to have a number of different identities, of which territorial identity might well be the least politically significant (see Chapter 10 for a discussion of the re-emergence of non-territorial identities in the twenty-first century). For the average villager, being the bondsman or woman of a particular lord would be of far greater significance than being 'English' or 'French', as would one's identity as a Christian. Moreover this latter, wider identity was a reminder that once upon a time in Europe the political order as well as the religious order had been universal; the Roman Empire cast a long shadow – understandably, since, at its peak, it had offered a more effective rule than any of its medieval successors.

The emergence of a system of states is the product of the downfall of this world, usually dated to the fifteenth and sixteenth centuries; the Peace of Westphalia, which ended the Thirty Years' War in 1648, is often seen as a convenient starting-point for the new order, though this should not be taken too literally – in fact, Westphalia changed very little. The new system emerged for a number of reasons. New military techniques and technologies – especially the professionalization of the infantry and improvements in siege-craft – favoured larger political units and undermined the defensive viability of towns and castles. Economic growth, connected to, but also promoting, the conquest of the Americas and voyages of exploration to the East, also allowed for the development of larger political units. On the other hand, administrative techniques and the technology of communication did not favour continent-wide political organization, and the break-up of the universal Church undermined the ideological basis of European unity. The result was the emergence of relatively strong territorially-based political units, capable of exerting control domestically, but obliged to accept the existence of similarly formed political units externally. This is the *Westphalia System,* and over the centuries it has reproduced itself successfully throughout the world to create the modern global system.

This is the story of the origins of the system that state-centric International Relations tells, and a good story it is too, with plenty of opportunities for variation in the re-telling. Thus Marxists (and political economists more generally) can tell the story from a materialist perspective, stressing changes in the world economy and the processes of production. Technological determinists and military historians can point to the impact of new weapons technology and improvements in ship design. Others look to the importance of ideas, in particular to the revival of classical learning (the Renaissance), including classical ideas on politics, and the emergence of the Protestant religion and the concomitant break-up of the universal Church. Most probably, some combination of these factors led to the emergence of the Westphalia System.

In any event, whichever version is adopted, even if we can tell where states *come from,* it still remains for us to say what states actually *do.* The standard account of the origins of the system does not offer a theory of the state – and this is a crucial omission since, if, for example, we wish to understand 'foreign policy' and 'statecraft', we shall be seriously handicapped in this ambition if we do not have a clear sense of what it is that states are motivated by, what is their function, and how they work. In practice, of course, state-centric International Relations does have something approaching a theory of the state – the problem is that because this theory is largely implicit and not clearly articulated, it pulls together a number of contradictory elements that need to be sorted out if progress is to be made. What, then, is the state?

One answer to this question is that the state is purely and simply a *concentration of power,* of brute strength, of basic (military) force. This is the *Machtpolitik* conception of the German thinker Treitschke in the nineteenth century, and it does, indeed, correspond quite well to the realities of state-formation in sixteenth-century Europe – or, for that matter, in parts of the Third World today (Treitschke 1916/1963). As described by, for example, Charles Tilly, what states did in the sixteenth century was to raise taxes and make war, activities that complemented each other (Tilly 1975, 1990). States that made war successfully expanded their territory, and hence their tax base; with the expanded tax base they could raise more money to expand their armies and thus conquer more territory, and so on. The idea that the state is essentially a military entity has a certain plausibility, and has recently been reinforced by the work of historical sociologists such as Michael Mann and social theorists such as Anthony Giddens. Mann suggests that 'societies' are artificial constructs held together by force, and the story of the Westphalia System is the story of militarism and successful conquest, while for Giddens the role of the nation-state and violence has been an undertheorized topic, an omission he wishes to rectify (Giddens 1985; Mann 1986/1993).

Some realist writers have signed up to this militarist account of the state, with approval (more or less) in the case of Treitschke; but resignedly in other cases. The pacifism practised by some Christian realists such as Reinhold Niebuhr and Martin Wight stemmed partly from their sense that, once one understood the working of the state and the states-system, the only moral attitude that could be adopted towards international relations was one of detachment from the struggle. However, in both cases, things are not clear cut. Niebuhr did believe in the possibility that the state could be based on something other than force, while Wight's ambiguity on the matter allows us to see him as an intellectual leader of the English School as well as the leading British post-war realist (Bull 1976). More characteristic of realism than a simple military account of the state has been a Weberian notion of power coupled with responsibility. Weber stresses that, ideally, the state should possess a monopoly of violence, but what it actually possesses is a monopoly of *legitimate* violence. This opens up a second front with respect to the theory of the state – the idea that the state is an institution legitimated by its people, because it represents them, acting on their behalf at home and abroad.

Whereas the idea that the state is a pure expression of power fits comfortably with absolutism and the pretensions of the princes and kings of early modern Europe, the idea that the state has this *representative* function is resonant of contract theory and the ideas of the Enlightenment, but perhaps especially of the post-Enlightenment emphasis on 'community' and the 'nation'. German thought is crucial here; it is to Herder that we owe the idea that the proper basis for political authority is the nation, the pre-given identity of a 'people' expressed in their folkways and, especially, their language (Barnard 1969). In Hegel we find the idea that the constitutional *Rechtstaat* is the forum within which the tensions and contradictions of social life are resolved (Hegel 1821/1991). Combined with the revival of Roman-style republican patriotism promoted by French revolutionaries after 1789, these German ideas feed into the nationalist movements of the nineteenth century, and out of this mix emerges the 'nation-state' – the idea that the only legitimate form of state is the state that embodies and represents the nation.

Clearly, this is an account of the state that can be filled out in at least two directions. On the one hand, the nation-state could become simply a new manifestation of the *Machtstaat*. Instead of collecting and employing power in the name of the prince, the power of the state is wielded on behalf of the nation. National glory and national honour replace the personal glory and honour of the ruler. *Raison d'état,* the logic of *Realpolitik,* power politics, is replaced by the *national interest* as the driving motivation of state conduct – but little else changes. Though not given to ruminations on national glory, Carl Schmitt, with his notion that the concept of the political is about a division between friends and enemies, and that the modern state is an entity which rests on the externalizing of this dichotomy, can also be seen in this light (Schmitt 1932/1996). On the other hand, once the idea that the state represents the nation is current, the possibility exists that the state will come to see the welfare of its people, rather than its power as such, as being central. The warfare state comes to be superseded by the welfare state. National well-being rather than national honour or glory defines the national interest. Nor is this simply a theoretical possibility; it is striking that some of the contemporary European states that have the strongest reputation for being peaceful, non-threatening, co-operative, good neighbours are also states that have a very strong sense of identity as *nation-states* – the Scandinavian countries are obvious examples here of countries that seemed to have been able to harness the sentiments of nationalism away from the drive for power, and towards a concern for the welfare of the people.

   In whatever way the influence of the nation/community makes itself felt, it is clear that this conception of the state is different from that of the state simply as a concentration of power. There is, however, a third conception of the state that stands somewhere between both the idea that the state is simply an accumulation of power, and the idea that the state has a positive role in promoting the interests of the people. This is the notion that the state *does* play a positive role in social life, but a role that is *facilitatory* rather than constructive, enabling rather than creative. This is a conception of the state that could be termed 'liberal' – so long as one was prepared to accept Thomas Hobbes as a proto-liberal – and which is certainly characteristic of English social contract theory and the thinking of the Scottish (as opposed to the French or German) Enlightenment. The thinking here is that individuals have interests and desires that drive them to co-operate with others, but that this co-operation is either impossible (Hobbes) or likely to be achieved only at sub-optimal levels (Locke) in the absence of some mechanism for ensuring that agreements are adhered to; that is, without the coercive power of the state.

   This is a theory of the state that makes it of very great importance in social life, but denies it a creative role in forming the national interest – indeed, it denies that the 'national interest' has much meaning beyond being a kind of catch-all description of the sum of the individual interests of citizens. It is a theory of the state that has been the dominant line of thought for several centuries in English-speaking countries – a fact of some significance, given that International Relations is an academic discipline that has always been predominantly British and American in inspiration – and has obviously influenced liberal internationalist theory. Indeed, it could be argued that one of the weaknesses of liberal internationalism was its inability to grasp that, within some political traditions, the state is given a far more exalted role than it is in liberalism, while from other perspectives the state is simply a concentration of power. The Anglo-American liberal account of the state is in fact closer to a theory of 'administration' than it is to a theory of the state in the continental European sense. Some of the Anglo-American realists, in particular continentally-trained Anglo-Americans such as Morgenthau, were conscious of this difference, but it is noticeable that the neorealists and neoliberals, possibly because of the debt they owe to the economics profession, largely operate within a liberal theory of the state. Robert Gilpin's remark that the role of the state is to solve the problem of 'free riders' is a perfect expression of this point (Gilpin 1981: 16).

Finally, one the most compelling modern alternatives to this liberal theory of the state is the Marxist conception of the state as the executive arm of the dominant class – under capitalism, the ruling committee of the bourgeoisie. Marxism shares with liberalism the notion that the state is a secondary formation, but rather than seeing it perform a valuable function for society as a whole, Marxists argue that the state cannot be a neutral problem-solver, but will always represent some particular interests – radical liberals such as the earlier John Hobson would agree, as would the very influential modern anarchist, Noam Chomsky, whose critiques of US/Western foreign policy rest on the notion that state power is exercised on behalf of an unrepresentative elite (Hobson 1902/1938; Chomsky 1994). While Marxism is no longer the official ideology of one of the two superpowers, Marxist ideas remain influential, especially when filtered through figures such as Chomsky; in fact, since many Marxist theorists now stress the 'relative autonomy' of the state, Chomsky and his followers are the main contemporary group of theorists who adhere to a crude Marxist account of the role of the state. Finally, in this connection, it should be noted that the practical result of this crude position is usually to align Marxist/Chomskyan ideas with the 'hard' realist notion of the state as simply a concentration of power – Chomsky shares with realism a total rejection of the idea that the state could represent the 'people' or a community, much less be some kind of ethical actor; Chomskyans, Marxists and realists all agree that such talk represents liberal obfuscation. More than anything else, it is perhaps the opportunity he offers to be a 'left-wing' realist that accounts for the extraordinary popularity of Chomsky's conspiracy theories. In Chomsky, the saloon-bar, cynical realist can find justification without having to abandon progressivist sympathies.

Is the state properly characterized as an actor at all in international relations? The nation-state would appear to be an actor according to the theories discussed above, as would the warfare state. But if the state simply facilitates social life, or is the point around which power accumulates in society, are we mistaken to see the state as an agent? Alexander Wendt (1999, 2004) argues that the state should not only be seen as an actor, but as a person. For Wendt, 'states are people too' in the sense that states are unitary actors that are capable of experiencing desires, intentions and beliefs via emergent mental properties, including collective intentionality and collective identity (Wendt 1999: 194ff., and 2004). It is through the process of collective identity formation that Wendt sees the development of a world state as being inevitable (Wendt 2003). Colin Wight takes issue with Wendt's conception of the state as a person, arguing instead that the state (more specifically, the capacities that go to make up the power of the state) is an institutional ensemble of structures rather than an individual agent. He emphasizes that the way that state power is actualized depends on the actions of agents – individuals and groups – located within the ensemble of the state (Wight 2004: 279). So, for Wight, the state is not an agent in itself, and certainly not a person, but rather a body that facilitates the exercise of power by the agents within it, a position with which foreign policy analysis (FPA), examined below, should have much sympathy.

Foreign and domestic policy: agency within the state

These theories of the state are obviously very different, and it might be expected that they would generate different theories of foreign policy and statecraft. Yet, on the whole, this has not happened; as we shall see, most accounts of foreign policy do not relate back to an explicit theory of the state, somewhat to their disadvantage. Rather, a vaguely liberal account of the state as a problem-solver exists in the background of a great deal of foreign policy analysis but is rarely articulated.

The working assumption of most FPA is that the state as a social institution exists in two environments: on the one hand, there is the (internal) environment that is composed of all the other institutions located in the territory demarcated by the state and their interactions with it and each other; and on the other, there is the (external) environment composed of all other states and their interactions with it and each other. Conventional International Relations theory assumes that the state is involved constantly in attempts at intervening in both environments;, that is, it engages in both 'domestic' and 'foreign' policy. Realist theory, as distinct from, for example, pluralism, assumes that these two forms of policy are different; in the case of domestic policy, the state is, in principle, capable of getting its way once having decided on a course of action; that is, it possesses both the authority to act, and the means to do so. In foreign policy this is not so; outcomes are the product of interdependent decision-making. The state cannot expect that other states will respect its authority, because in an anarchical system no state possesses authority, and whether the state has the means to get its way or not is a contingent matter – whereas domestically the state, in principle, possesses a monopoly of the means of coercion, internationally no state is in this position. What this means is that we can distinguish two aspects of the study of foreign policy; the way in which foreign policy is formulated – which might be rather similar to the way in which domestic policy is formulated; and the way in which foreign policy is implemented – which is likely to be very different. The latter is largely dealt with in the next chapter; policy formulation in this.

On the traditional account of foreign policy formulation, what is involved is recognizing and articulating the 'national interest' in so far as it affects a particular issue. Thus, for example, in the years prior to 1914, the British foreign policy establishment had to formulate a policy with respect to the changing pattern of forces in Europe, and in particular the perceived growth of German power and the attempt by Germany to project this power on to the world stage. British diplomacy already had a long-standing view with respect to the pattern of forces in continental Europe – namely, that it was against any concentration that might control the Channel ports and the North Sea, and thus undermine the Royal Navy and oblige Britain to develop a large enough army to defend itself from invasion. The policy-making process of the decade prior to 1914 can be seen as a matter of adapting this view to new circumstances by shifting the focus of concern away from the traditional enemy, France, towards the new challenger, Germany. How and why did this adaptation come about? Rather more dramatically, in a few years in the 1940s the United States abandoned its long-held policy of 'isolationism', and, for the first time, became committed to an extensive range of peace-time alliances. How and why did this reversal occur?

One way of answering these and similar questions is by employing the methods of the diplomatic historian. Assuming that the relevant documents are available, this may give us a satisfactory account of particular changes, but it is not really what we want. As students of international relations, we wish to possess a general account of how foreign policy is made and the national interest identified. We are looking to identify patterns of behaviour rather than to analyse individual instances. We may sometimes employ the methods of the historian in our 'case studies', but our aim is to generalize, whereas the historian particularizes. How do we achieve generalizations about foreign-policy formulation? Foreign-policy analysis for most of the period since the 1950s tells us that the best way to do this is to break down the processes of foreign-policy-making into a series of 'decisions', each of which can in turn be analysed in order to ascertain which factors were influential and in what circumstances. Thus a general theory of foreign-policy-making may slowly emerge.

The originators of the foreign-policy decision-making approaches were American behavioural scientists working in the 1950s, who saw themselves as effectively 'operationalizing' the idea of the national interest, developing large-scale classificatory schemas in which a place was made for all the factors that might have gone into making any particular decision, from the influence of the mass media, to the personality of decision-makers, from institutional features of the policy-making body, to socio-psychological factors about threat perception. These schemata were impressive, but a classification is not the same as an explanation; a list of all factors that *might* be relevant is much less useful than a theory that predicts which factors *will* be relevant. Moreover, putting a schema into operation, filling all the boxes, was a horrendously complex task. What was required was not so much a classification scheme as a model that would simplify the myriad factors involved; this was provided in 1971 by *Essence of Decision,* Graham Allison's outstanding case study of the Cuban Missile Crisis of 1962, one of the few genuine classics of modern International Relations (Allison 1971; see also the fully updated second edition, co-authored by Allison and Philip Zelikow 1999).

In fact, Allison provides three models of decision-making, each of which is used to provide a different account of the decisions that characterized the crisis – which are simplified to, first, the Soviet decision to deploy Intermediate Range Ballistic Missiles (IRBMs) on Cuba; second, the American decision to respond to this deployment with a blockade; and third, the Soviet decision to withdraw the IRBMs. His point is that, contrary to his title, there is no 'essence of decision', only different ways of seeing the same events.

His first model is the *Rational Actor Model* (RAM). This corresponds to the kind of analysis favoured by traditional accounts of the national interest and those who see the state as an agent in itself. Foreign-policy decisions are assumed to be rational responses to a particular situation, formulated by a single unitary state actor. Rationality is seen in ends/means terms; that is to say, it is assumed that states choose the course of action that maximizes their gains/minimizes their losses in the context of a given set of values. Decisions can be studied by a process of rational reconstruction, armchair analysis in which the analyst puts him/herself into the position of the decision-maker, and attempts to simulate the processes of reasoning that might have led the decision-maker to act as he or she did. Thus, in order to explain why the Soviet Union deployed missiles when and where it did, one must specify the goals the Soviets wished to attain and the chain of reasoning that led them to think that such a deployment would meet these goals – always bearing in mind that the goals might not be those that are explicitly stated; indeed, the best way of approaching the real goals may be to work back from the actions taken. Rational reconstruction is a difficult business; a full 'simulation' would require the analyst to have all the information available to the decision-maker, and *only* this information – which is a tall order. None the less, we engage in this kind of reconstructive thinking all the time, and can usually come up with a fairly plausible account of how decisions are taken.

Allison suggests there are two kinds of problems with this model. First, the notion that action is fully 'rational' poses problems. The requirements for rational action are never in fact met. They involve a fully specified set of values to be maximized, an account of all the possible courses of action available to the decision-maker, and a set of algorithms that allow us to predict the consequences of each action. Perfect information such as this is simply not available – not to the original decision-maker, nor to later analysts. Such information would be the equivalent of, say, a fully specified decision-tree for a game of chess; still a practical impossibility even for the fastest computer. In fact, we make decisions in much the same way that we play chess – we have some rules of conduct that help us, particularly in the early stages of a game when we face known situations, and later, when faced with unknown situations, we explore what we take to be the most promising moves, and act when we are satisfied that we have found the best move we can given the time constraints. This is a 'rational' way to play the game or to make decisions – though the possibility always exists that the next option we might have examined will be better than our actual choice – but reconstructing a game played like this is extremely difficult. Intuition may be of more use than purely rational processes of thought, and one of the things that will need to be simulated is time pressure. We cannot assume that a move is always the best move even if made by a grandmaster; even they are known to make terrible mistakes when the clock is ticking. The RAM assumes that states always intend the consequences of their actions, but the real circumstances under which decisions are made may falsify this assumption.

A second problem with the RAM is more practical. Even when we come to a conclusion using rational reconstruction, there are almost always anomalies left unexplained. Thus Allison suggests that the most plausible RAM explanation of the Soviet IRBM deployment is that it was designed to close what they perceived to be a widening gap in capabilities between themselves and the USA, but this leaves unexplained some of the features of the actual deployment, which seem to have been almost calculated to encourage early discovery by the USA. The alternative view that they were indeed *designed* to be discovered covers the anomalies but explains less overall than the proposition that the deployment was designed to close the capability gap.

Possibly a better RAM explanation could be found, but Allison suggests instead that we shift to another model of decision. The rational actor model assumes that decisions are the product of calculation by a single actor; the *Organizational Process Model* (called the *Organizational Behaviour Model* in the second, revised, edition of the book) assumes that decisions are made by multiple organizations within the state, each of which have characteristic ways of doing things – organizational *routines* and *standard operating procedures* – and are resistant to being organized by any kind of central intelligence. Not by accident, this fits in with earlier comments about coping with the lack of perfect information. When faced with a problem, organizations such as the KGB, Soviet Rocket Forces, or the American Navy and Air Force do not attempt to solve it by starting from scratch; rather, they delve into their institutional memories and try to remember how they dealt with similar problems before. Thus, when tasked with building a missile base in Cuba, Soviet Rocket Forces (SRF) use the same basic layout they use in the Soviet Union, because experience suggests that this is the best way of building a missile base; the fact that it is identifiable to US air reconnaissance as such is apparently not something that occurs to them. Conversely, the KGB transported the missiles in secret and the dead of night, because that is how the KGB does things. This looks anomalous in the light of the almost publicity-seeking methods of the SRF – but it is only an anomaly if one assumes that someone is directing both organizations to behave in this way. On the contrary, it is possible that if the overall directors of the Soviet effort had known what was going on, they would have been horrified.

It might be thought that this exaggerates the autonomy of organizations, but a US example reinforces the point. The US Air Force under General Curtis Le May wanted to bomb the missile sites, but the report of probable casualties they produced was horrific and they could not guarantee 100 per cent success; as a result, the attack was put on hold by President Kennedy. A later investigation revealed that the Air Force had simply taken an existing plan to attack Cuban installations and added the missile sites – hence the predicted high casualties. Moreover, they had assumed that the missiles were mobile, and that some would be missed; in fact, the missiles were only 'mobile' in the context of a time-scale running into weeks, and an attack would have been very likely to have produced a 100 per cent success rate. This is an interesting example precisely because the US Air Force was actually in favour of the operation; usually when the military provide high casualty estimates it is because, for one reason or another, they wish to dissuade the politicians from using force, a point that leads to the next of Allison's models.

The organizational process model plays down the idea of rational central control of decisions. In his final *Bureaucratic Politics* model, Allison deconstructs rational decision-making from another direction, stressing the extent to which political factors external to the overt international issue might affect decision-making. One aspect of this is the way in which bureaucracies see the world from the perspective of their own organization. As the slogan has it, 'where you sit determines where you stand' (revised in the second edition, 1999, to the significantly less punchy, but much more accurate 'where one stands is influenced, most often influenced strongly, by where one sits'). In the United States, the State Department usually favours negotiation; the UN Representative favours action by the UN; the US Navy action by the US Navy and so on. It is not to be expected that organizations will promote courses of action that do not involve enhancements to their own budgets. More important is the fact that leaders have their own political positions to protect and defend. During the Cuban Missile Crisis, President Kennedy knew that his actions could have posed severe political problems to his chances of re-election, and, more immediately, the Democratic Party's prospects in the mid-term Congressional elections in November 1962 – though, interestingly, research now suggests that this was not a determining factor in his actions (Lebow and Stein 1994: 95). The assumption of the Rational Actor Model (and of realism in general) is that foreign-policy decisions will be taken on foreign-policy grounds. The bureaucratic politics model suggests that this often will not be the case.

The conceptual models Allison established in *Essence of Decision* have survived remarkably well, despite criticism of the political implications of his work – he was accused of playing down the roles that the president, Congress and the public played in foreign-policy decision-making and suggesting that policy-making in democracies was anti-democratic because of the power held by bureaucracies (see the snappily titled 1972 piece by Stephen Krasner: 'Are Bureaucracies Important? (Or Allison Wonderland)'). Allison's work has also remained influential even though his case study has been superseded by later work drawing on Soviet and American sources available since the end of the Cold War. It is, however, clear that the models need to be supplemented. The biggest lack in Allison is a sufficient account of the *socio-psychological, cognitive* dimension of decision-making. Decision-makers interact with their *perceived* environment, and it may well be that their perceptions are incorrect (Jervis 1976; Cottam 1986). It might be thought that one way to correct misperceptions would be to listen to as many voices as possible when making a decision, but Irving Janis, in *Victims of Groupthink*, demonstrates that collective bodies of decision-makers are just as likely to be vulnerable to misperceptions as are individuals (Janis 1972). It is the lack of a good account of these issues that has caused Allison's case study to become outdated – later research emphasizes the extent to which the Soviet decision to act was based on fears created by US policy; ironically, in particular, by policies designed specifically to deter the Soviets. US warnings of the consequences of deploying missiles on Cuba were interpreted as threats and signals of an intent to undermine Soviet positions (Lebow and Stein 1994). An emphasis on cognitive processes is also present in recent work on the role of ideas and ideologies in foreign-policy decision-making (Goldstein and Keohane 1993); again, the ending of the Cold War has provided much stimulus to this work (Lebow and Risse-Kappen 1995).

There are other general problems with Allison's models. The distinctions between his Organizational Process Model and Bureaucratic Politics model are at times very unclear, and he later conceded that he had placed too much emphasis on the role that organizations and bureaucracies play versus political leaders and the media in democratic states. Allison's elaborate models may only work in countries that have highly differentiated institutional structures; certainly, it is difficult to apply the organizational process model in those countries that do not have extensive bureaucracies. He also studies decision-making in a time of crisis, and crises – situations in which high-value stakes are played for under pressure of time – may produce patterns of behaviour that are very different from those in operation during 'normal' decision-making. However, it would be surprising if an almost 40-year-old case study were not to be superseded in some respects, and Allison's models themselves are still in use. There are two ways in which one could read this. It may be that this demonstrates how well-designed the models were; on this account, foreign-policy decision-making is one of the best-established areas in International Relations, and the lack of recent innovation in this field is a point in its favour. On the other hand, this longevity could be seen as a sign of weakness, an indicator that this is an area of International Relations theory where not much is happening – where a few basic points have been made and there is little else to say. Similar points could be made with respect to a number of other areas of foreign-policy analysis. For example, the study of public opinion and foreign policy, or pressure groups and foreign policy, also seem to be areas where there have been relatively few recent innovations. Most of the work being done takes the form of empirical case studies which shuffle and reshuffle a small number of ideas rather than create new theories – though Brian White offers a number of reasons why this judgement might be contested (White 1999).

Why is this? Here the agent–structure problem comes back into play; both the neorealist and liberal institutionalist approaches that dominate contemporary IR theory emphasize analysis of the international *system* at the expense of foreign-policy analysis. Despite Waltzian neorealism paying lip service to the importance of the study of foreign policy, as we have seen, it essentially offers a top-down, structure-first account of international relations, the implication of which is that the supreme skill of the foreign-policy decision-maker lies in recognizing the signals sent by the system rather than in exercising responsible agency. The decision-maker is a skilled craftsman rather than a creative artist. As we have seen, neoliberalism also offers an account of international relations that works from the top down, albeit one that emphasizes the possibilities of co-operation. In each case, the assumption that states are unitary, rational egoists operating under conditions of anarchy limits the space available for foreign policy as an autonomous area of enquiry. Effectively, the rational actor model is being reinstated, albeit under new conditions. One of the ironies of the dominance of rational *choice* in contemporary mainstream International Relations theorizing is that it appears to be antithetical to foreign-policy analysis. One might have thought that 'choice' and 'policy' would go together, but in practice the way in which rational choice thinking is expressed undermines this potential partnership. The system is the focus, and the behaviour of the units that make up the system is assumed to be determined by the system, rather than an expression of agency; as Waltz puts it, any theory to the contrary is 'reductionist' and patently false, because the persistence of patterns over time in the system is unconnected with changes in the units (Waltz 1979). On this account, traditional components of foreign policy analysis, such as 'public opinion', the influence of the media, pressure groups, organizational structure and so on, can do little more than confuse the policy-maker, deflecting his or her attention from the real issue, which is the relationship between the state and the system.

Few foreign-policy analysts have taken the fight to neorealists – a significant exception being Walter Carlsnaes (1992) who works through the agent–structure problem in FPA and argues that Wendtian constructivism as well as traditional approaches to the problem may be able to document the effects that structures have on agents, but they fail to take into account the effects that agents have on structures, because they do not look at foreign-policy-making over a long enough time-frame. He distinguishes between three explanatory levels in FPA: (i) the *intentions* of foreign policy actors – what the policies were designed to achieve; (ii) explanations of why the actors had these intentions or purposes, which involves examining the *dispositions* of actors; and (iii) the domestic and international structural *environment* of actors and how it affects (i) and (ii) in specific instances. Carlsnaes supports an institutional or structural approach to FPA, but insists that within such an approach we can and must try to understand the values and perceptions of the sub-state-level actors involved, as actor-specific intentions and dispositions feed back to the level of the domestic and international institutions that constrain and enable particular foreign policy actions, and can change structural environments over time.

A key battlefield for the contest between FPA as conventionally understood and neorealist understandings of international structure – and indeed for the significance of the agent–structure debate more generally in International Relations – concerns the relevance or irrelevance of 'regime-type' to foreign-policy behaviour. From a neorealist perspective, the nature of a domestic regime, whether liberal-democratic, authoritarian or totalitarian, is of relatively little significance. A state is simply an egoistic actor attempting to survive under the anarchy problematic. All else pales into insignificance in the face of this imperative. Consider, for example, a highly influential essay by the leading realist John Mearsheimer; in 'Back to the Future: Instability in Europe after the Cold War' (1990), Mearsheimer envisages a reappearance of the old pre-1914 patterns in Europe, and suggests that one way of controlling and stabilizing this process would be to assist Germany to become a nuclear-weapons state. This is an interestingly counter-intuitive suggestion, but what is striking in the present context is that virtually all sections of German public opinion, bar a neo-Nazi fringe, would be wholeheartedly opposed to this policy troubles Mearsheimer not at all. If this is the 'right' policy, then the assumption is that it will be adopted – 'right' in this context means appropriate to international conditions (that is, the requirements of the balance of power) rather than domestic pressures. This is a structural argument and there is clearly a problem of agency here – a problem of finding a German government that could introduce this policy without being hounded from office – but to Mearsheimer this is a secondary matter. Foreign policy on this count becomes analogous to completing a crossword puzzle – we have the grid and the clues, the task is to get to the right answer; the policy-maker/solver cannot influence or determine this answer, only discover it, and implement it as effectively as possible.

From virtually every other perspective (with the possible exception of that of Chomsky) the idea that regime-type is of no significance is seen as plain silly. It seems intuitively implausible that the leaders thrown up by liberal-democratic political systems will react to external stimuli in the same way as the makers of military coups or the leaders of totalitarian mass parties. There may be pressures pointing them in the same direction, but, surely, their own values will have some impact on the decisions they eventually take – as the example of modern Germany and nuclear weapons illustrates. Moreover, it seems inherently implausible that domestic social and economic structure is irrelevant to foreign policy – that the shape of a nation's society has no influence on its international behaviour. One, very controversial but interesting, investigation of these intuitions comes from the so-called 'democratic peace' hypothesis – the proposition that constitutionally stable liberal-democratic states do not go to war with each other (though they are, in general, as war-prone as other states when it come to relations with non-democracies). The reason this is particularly interesting is because, unlike some other challenges to the neorealist mode of thinking, it is an argument that uses the same kind of positivist methodology that the rational choice realists employ. While the idea was first popularized as a somewhat unconventional extrapolation by Michael Doyle of the work of the political philosopher Kant to contemporary conditions, its main developers in the 1990s were empirical researchers using the latest statistical techniques to refine the initial hypothesis and identify a robust version of it (Doyle 1983; Russett 1993; Gleditsch and Risse-Kappen 1995; Brown *et al.* 1996). Possible explanations for the democratic peace are discussed in Chapter 10.

If democratic-peace thinking were to become established it would – and to some extent already has – reinstate and relegitimize a quite traditional research programme with respect to foreign-policy analysis. Institutions, public opinion, norms, decision-making – these were the staple diet of foreign-policy studies before the dominance of structural accounts of international relations shifted them from centre-stage. The 'Democratic Peace' has brought this older agenda back as a potential central focus for contemporary

International Relations, and it is interesting that its main, and vociferous, opponents have been neorealists and Chomskyans, both of whom recognize how important it is for their position that the proposition be refuted or defeated (Layne 1994, Barkawi and Laffey 1999). Moreover, it should be noted that here, more than with any other topic in foreign-policy analysis, we have a theory of foreign-policy that grows out of an explicit theory of the state.

While attempts to widen the scope of democratic-peace thinking have been largely unsuccessful, the core proposition that constitutionally stable liberal democracies do not go to war with each other remains unrefuted – the worst that can be said about this proposition is that it may be that this highly specific kind of peacefulness is the product of some factor other than regime-type, or a statistical artefact produced by generalizing from too few cases. If this core proposition remains unrefuted, then we are left with a large anomaly in contemporary International Relations theory – because, while the practical implications of neorealist thinking on these matters seem to be challenged by a successful argument that is clearly agent-centred or 'reductionist', the structural logic of neorealism remains untouched. The two bodies of thought seem to point in opposite directions. We have here, in effect, something quite similar to the discontinuity that exists in economics between 'microeconomics', whose dominant theory of the firm does not seem to gel very well with the 'macroeconomic' theories concerning the economy as a whole. Whether we should regard this as a problem or not is a moot point; economists seem not to be too worried by their particular problem, and perhaps their strategy of advancing on all fronts and hoping that eventually some unifying notions will emerge is the sensible one to adopt.

Conclusion: from foreign policy to power

The next stage in this investigation is to move from the making of foreign policy to its implementation – the realm of diplomacy or, to employ an old term that has made something of a comeback recently, 'statecraft'. In a larger-scale study, such an examination would involve a full-length exploration of the arts and crafts of diplomacy, the art of negotiation and so on. In later chapters, on, for example, the establishment of international economic regimes, such matters will be mentioned, but in this part of the book, which is overtly concerned with state-centric International Relations, and shaped by the realist tradition, it makes more sense to shift to another aspect of implementation – the ways in which power is employed by states to get their way in the world. A focus on 'power', however, inevitably introduces considerations that go beyond foreign policy as such – hence the next chapter will examine power as a whole, and the problems it generates.

Further reading

On the agent–structure problem, Alexander Wendt, 'The Agent/Structure Problem in International Relations Theory' (1987) and Colin Wight, *Agents, Structures and International Relations* (2006) are the key texts. See also Martin Hollis and Steve Smith, *Explaining and Understanding International Relations* (1991) – a debate between Wendt, and Hollis and Smith has been under way in the *Review of International Studies* since 1992. Beyond the works cited in the text, Hidemi Suganami, 'Agents, Structures, Narratives' (1999) and Roxanne Lynn Doty, 'Aporia: A Critical Exploration of the Agent–Structure Problematique in IR Theory' (1997) are important contributions to the debate. On the older issue of the 'levels-of-analysis' problem, see Nicholas Onuf, 'Levels' (1995), and H. Patomäki, *After International Relations: Critical Realism and the (Re)Construction of World Politics* (2002). Milja Kurki, *Causation in International Relations: Reclaiming Causal Analysis* (2008), is an outstanding primer on critical realism and controversy over the nature of causation in social science. For article-length work by critical realists, see M. Kurki, 'Causes of a Divided Discipline: Rethinking the Concept of Cause in International Relations Theory' (2006), and Jonathan Joseph, 'Hegemony and the Structure–Agency Problem in International Relations: A Scientific Realist Contribution' (2008), both in *Review of International Studies*. James Rosenau, in *Turbulence in World Politics: A Theory of Change and Continuity* (1992) and *Along the Domestic–Foreign Frontier: Exploring Governance in a Turbulent World* (1997) argues that the relationship between agents and structures in international politics is currently undergoing a radical shift, with turbulence at the intermediate and systemic levels creating more room for agents to bring about significant change. A recent forum in *International Studies Review*, 'Moving Beyond the Agent–Structure Debate' (2006b), is constructivist discussion of the epistemological and methodological problems that plague the debate.

On pre-Westphalian 'international' systems, A. B. Bozeman, *Politics and Culture in International History* (1960) and Martin Wight, *Systems of States* (1977) offer contrasting views; close to Wight but more in the nature of a textbook is Adam Watson, *The Evolution of International Society: A Comparative Historical Analysis* (1992), which is the best short guide to the origins of the Westphalia System.

The work of historical sociologists on the origins of the system and the nature of the state has become important in recent years: for overviews, see Richard Little, 'International Relations and Large Scale Historical Change' (1994); and Anthony Jarvis, 'Societies, States and Geopolitics' (1989); apart from books by Giddens, Mann and Tilly cited in the main text above, important substantive works include Ernest Gellner, *Plough, Sword and Book: The Structure of Human History* (1988); George Modelski, *Long Cycles in World Politics* (1987); Paul Kennedy, *The Rise and Fall of the Great Powers* (1988); Charles Tilly (ed.), *The Formation of National States in Western Europe* (1975); and Michael Mann, *States, War and Capitalism* (1988). *Empires, Systems and States: Great Transformations in International Politics* (2002), edited by Michael Cox, Tim Dunne and Ken Booth, is a collection of essays that cover not just the history of the state system, but also the experiences of non-European cultures and communities, and theories of why the state triumphed over other forms of political organization. Adam Morton, in 'Waiting for Gramsci: State Formation, Passive Revolution and the International' (2007), looks at state formation from a critical perspective.

On the state, P. Evans, D. Rueschemeyer and T. Skocpol (eds), *Bringing the State Back In* (1985), is, as the title suggests, a reaction to the absence of theorizing about the state. Friedrich Meinecke, *Machiavellism: The Doctrine of Raison d'Etat and its Place in Modern History* (1957) is a monumental, irreplaceable study. John M. Hobson, *The State and International Relations* (2000) is an excellent text on the subject. 'The "Second State Debate" in International Relations: Theory Turned Upside-down' (2001) by John M. Hobson examines conceptualizations of the state within a range of theoretical positions. Colin Hay *et al.* (eds), *The State: Theories and Issues* (2006) is a survey of contemporary theorizing on the state; Bob Jessop's *The Future of the Capitalist State* (2002) documents the crisis of the state under advanced capitalism and examines state forms in a globalized world, and Jessop, *State Power* (2007) sets out his strategic-relational state theory. Essays in the *Review of International Studies*' 'Forum on the State as a Person' (2004) consider the implications of Wendt's theory of the state, and are continued in the exchange between Peter Lomas, 'Anthropomorphism, Personification and Ethics: A Reply to Alexander Wendt' (2005), and Wendt 'How Not to Aruge against State Personhood: A Reply to Lomas' (2005b) in *Review of International Studies*. Cornelia Navari, 'States and State Systems: Democractic, Westphalian or Both?' (2007) examines rival accounts of the state and its formation.

From a broadly Marxist perspective, Ralph Miliband, *The State and Capitalist Society* (1973), and Nicos Poulantzas, *State, Power, Socialism* (1978/2001), are influential works. More recent writing on the relationship between international relations and capitalism can be found in Alex Callinicos, 'Does Capitalism Need the State System?' (2007) and Ray Kiely 'US Hegemony and Globalization: What Role for Theories of Imperialism?' (2006).

Deborah J. Gerner, 'Foreign Policy Analysis: Exhilarating Eclecticism, Intriguing Enigmas' (1991) and Steve Smith, 'Theories of Foreign Policy: An Historical Overview' (1986) are good surveys of the field, though somewhat dated. Important general collections include Richard C. Snyder, H. W. Bruck, Burton Sapin and Valerie Hudson, Derek Chollet and James Goldgeier (eds), *Foreign Policy Decision Making Revisited* (2003), an update on Snyder, Bruck and Sapin's classic 1962 text; Charles F. Hermann, Charles W. Kegley and James N. Rosenau (eds), *New Directions in the Study of Foreign Policy* (1987); Michael Clarke and Brian White (eds), *Understanding Foreign Policy: The Foreign Policy Systems Approach* (1989); and, on actual foreign policies, the classic Roy C. Macridis (ed.), *Foreign Policy in World Politics* (1992). Brian White, 'The European Challenge to Foreign Policy Analysis' (1999) is an interesting riposte to some disparaging remarks on FPA in the first edition of this volume. Christopher Hill, *The Changing Politics of Foreign Policy* (2002) is now the standard work in this area. See also his article 'What Is to Be Done? Foreign Policy as a Site for

Political Action' (2003) for a powerful argument in favour of looking beyond the systemic answers offered by neorealists and globalization theorists in order to understand politics in the modern world. Recent critical works on Allison's classic study include Jonathan Bender and Thomas H. Hammond, 'Rethinking Allison's Models' (1992), and David A. Welch, 'The Organizational Process and Bureaucratic Politics Paradigm' (1992). The second, revised, edition of Allison's classic (with Philip Zelikow, 1999) is reviewed at length in Barton J. Bernstein, 'Understanding Decisionmaking, US Foreign Policy and the Cuban Missile Crisis' (2000). On the features of crisis diplomacy, see Michael Brecher, *Crises in World Politics: Theory and Reality* (1993); James L. Richardson, *Crisis Diplomacy* (1994); and Richard Ned Lebow, *Between Peace and War: The Nature of International Crisis* (1981). On cognitive processes and foreign policy, see works by Jervis, Janis and Cottam cited in the main text. For a positivist reply to post-positivist work in foreign policy, see Fred Chernoff, *The Power of International Theory: Reforging the Link to Foreign Policy-Making through Scientific Inquiry* (2005), which also touches on broader theoretical issues. An *International Studies Perspectives* symposium 'Policy and the Poliheuristic Theory of Foreign Policy Decision Making' (2005) looks at advances in decision theory. David Houghton's 'Reinvigorating the Study of Foreign Policy Decision Making: Toward a Constructivist Approach' (2007) appraises the state of the field and suggests that Constructivism has an important contribution to make.

Micro–macro problems in International Relations theory are discussed in Fareed Zakaria, 'Realism and Domestic Politics: A Review Essay' (1992), and the domestic–international interface in Peter B. Evans, Harold K. Jacobson and Robert D. Putnam (eds), *Double-Edged Diplomacy: International Diplomacy and Domestic Politics* (1993). Much older but still valuable is James N. Rosenau (ed.), *Domestic Sources of Foreign Policy* (1967). Daniel Byman and Kenneth Pollack, in 'Let Us Now Praise Great Men: Bringing the Statesman Back In' (2001), use case studies to demonstrate the role individual agents can play in international affairs.

On the 'Democratic Peace' thesis, Bruce Russett, *Grasping the Democratic Peace: Principles for a Post-Cold War World* (1993), is crucial. For a Kantian perspective, see Michael Doyle, 'Liberalism and World Politics' (1986) and the articles cited in the text. Tarak Barkawi and Mark Laffey, 'The Imperial Peace: Democracy, Force and Globalization' (1999) challenge the thesis from a 'left' position, while realist opponents are well represented in the *International Security Reader, Debating the Democratic Peace*: Brown *et al.* (1996). Joanne Gowa, *Ballots and Bullets: The Elusive Democratic Peace* (1999) is an important study. A selection of additional articles might include: Chris Brown, '"Really-Existing Liberalism" and International Order' (1992b); Raymond Cohen, 'Pacific Unions: A Reappraisal of the Theory that "Democracies Do Not Go To War with Each Other"' (1994); Bruce Russett, J. L. Ray and Raymond Cohen, 'Raymond Cohen on Pacific Unions: A Response and a Reply' (1995); and John MacMillan, 'Democracies Don't Fight: A Case of the Wrong Research Agenda' (1996). Edward Mansfield and Jack Snyder, *Electing to Fight: Why Emerging Democracies Go to War* (2005) reconsiders aspects of the democratic peace thesis, as does Karen Rasler and William Thompson (eds) in *Puzzles of the Democratic Peace* (2005). Recent work is summarized in an *American Political Science Review forum* (2005). Azar Gat critiques the democratic peace by emphasizing the impact of technological change in 'The Democratic Peace Theory Reframed: The Impact of Modernity' (2005).

Chapter 5

Power and Security

Introduction: statecraft, influence and power

From a foreign-policy perspective, states attempt to change their environment in accordance with aims and objectives they have set for themselves. From a structural perspective, states attempt to adapt to their environment, making the best of the cards the system has dealt them. Either way, states are agents; they act in the world. How? What is the nature of diplomacy or 'statecraft' – a slightly old-world term that has recently been given a new lease of life? The best discussion of this topic is that of David Baldwin, who produces a four-way taxonomy of the techniques of statecraft that provides a useful starting-point for this discussion. He defines *propaganda* as 'influence attempts relying primarily on the deliberate manipulation of verbal symbols'; *diplomacy* refers to 'influence attempts relying primarily on negotiation'; *economic statecraft* covers 'influence attempts relying on resources which have a reasonable semblance of a market price in terms of money'; and *military statecraft* refers to 'influence attempts relying primarily on violence, weapons, or force' (Baldwin 1985: 13). The rest of this chapter examines the questions raised (or in some cases, avoided) by his classification.

A common feature of these techniques is that they are techniques of '*influence*'. The best way to think of influence is in terms of its two antonyms – authority and control – and then to ask whether influence is synonymous with power. States attempt to exert influence rather than *authority*, because authority is something that can only emerge in legitimate relationships, which *ex hypothesis* do not exist between states. That is, it is an essential feature of the nature of authority that those over whom it is exercised acknowledge that those exercising it have a right to do so – they are *authorized* to act. In international relations there is no authority in this sense of the term, or at least not with respect to issues of any real political significance. The contrast between influence and *control* works rather differently. When control is exercised, those who are controlled have lost all autonomy; they have no decision-making capacity; they are no longer agents. From a realist perspective, states would like to exercise control over their environment, but if any one state ever was in a position to control another, the latter would cease to be a 'state' in any meaningful sense of the term; and if any state were able to control all other states, then the current international system would be replaced by something else, namely an empire. Some contend that this process is already under way, with the establishment of an American empire, though in recent years this judgment has been put in question by US policy failures in Iraq and elsewhere.

Recasting these points, the exercise of influence is the characteristic way in which states relate to one another, because we have neither a world government (a world-wide source of legitimate authority) nor a world empire (a world-wide source of effective control). In the absence of these two polar positions, only relationships of influence remain. Of course, in practice, there may be some relationships that approach the two poles. In an elaborate military alliance such as NATO, the governing council, the Supreme Allied Military Commander in Europe (SACEUR), and, in some circumstances, the president of the United States, could be said to exercise a degree of legitimate authority, having been authorized by the members of NATO to act on their behalf. However, this authority is tenuous and could be withdrawn at any time, albeit at some cost. Conversely, the degree of influence exercised by the former Soviet Union over some of its 'allies' in Eastern Europe came at times close to actual control, although even at the height of Stalinism the freedom of action of the weakest of the People's Republics was greater than that of the Baltic States that were incorporated into the Soviet Union in 1940. Sometimes freedom of action may only mean the freedom to submit to the inevitable, but even this can be meaningful; in the pre-war crises of 1938 and 1939, neither Czechoslovakia nor Poland had any real freedom, apart from that of determining the circumstances under which they would fall into Nazi control, but the way in which they exercised this final freedom had a real influence on the lives of their populations.

The relationship between influence and *power* is more complicated. Power is one of those terms in political discourse that are so widely used as to have become almost devoid of meaning; the suggestion that its use should be banned is impracticable, but understandable. Common-sense usage of the term 'power' suggests that it is quite closely related to influence – a 'powerful person' is an influential person – but there are forms of influence that do not seem to rely on power as the term is usually understood, and there are forms of power that are connected only indirectly to influence. This is a particularly important relationship for a state-centric (especially a realist) view of the world, and, unlike the distinctions between influence and authority or control, this matter is too sensitive to be determined by definition. It is only by generating quite a sophisticated understanding of power that the realist view of the world can be comprehended – but, equally, such an understanding is required if realism is to be transcended.

Dimensions of power

Power is a multi-faceted and complex notion, and it makes sense to think of the term under three headings, always bearing in mind that the three categories this will generate are closely interrelated. Power is an *attribute* – it is something that people or groups or states possess, or have access to, have at hand to deploy in the world. Power is a *relationship* – it is the ability that people or groups or states have to exercise influence over others, to get their way in the world. These two dimensions of power are clearly not separable, and most realist accounts of international relations have a story to tell about them. A third dimension of power, in which it is seen as a property of a *structure*, is less easily incorporated into realist accounts of the world, at least in so far as these accounts rely on the notion that power can only be exercised by an actor or agent.

The idea that power is an *attribute* of states is a very familiar notion in traditional accounts of international relations. Most old textbooks, and many new ones, offer a list of the components of national power – the features of a country that entitle it to be regarded as a 'great' power, or a 'middle' power, or, more recently, a 'superpower'. These lists generally identify a number of different kinds of attributes that a state might possess in order to entitle it to claim its position in the world power rankings. These might include: the size and quality of its armed forces; its resource base, measured in terms of raw materials; its geographical position and extent; its productive base and infrastructure; the size and skills of its population; the efficiency of its governmental institutions; and the quality of its leadership. Some of these factors are immutable – geographical position and extent would be the obvious examples (though the significance of geographical features can change quite sharply over time). Others change only slowly (size of the population, rates of economic growth) while yet others can change quite rapidly (size of the armed forces). These points allow us to make a distinction between *actual* power and *potential* or *latent* power – the power that a state actually possesses at any one point in time as opposed to the power it could generate in a given time period.

The significance of any one of these factors as against the others will change over time. Population size and geographical extent can only add to the power of a state to the extent that the administrative, communication and transport infrastructure allows it to do so. For example, until the construction of the Trans-Siberian Railway in the 1890s, the quickest way to get from St Petersburg or Moscow to Vladivostok was by sea via the Baltic and North Seas and the Atlantic, Indian and Pacific Oceans, which meant that Russian land power in the East was at the mercy of British sea power, and in those circumstances the great size of Russia could rarely be translated into a genuine political asset. A relatively small country with a highly productive economy may be more powerful than a much larger country with a less productive economy – but there are limits. For example, no matter how economically successful Singapore is, or how skilful its army, it will never be major military power, nor have the capacity to project military power at a distance in the absence of a sufficiently large population base. A culture that gives great respect to those who bear arms may be an important factor in developing effective armed forces, but the nature of modern mechanized warfare may mean that technically skilled civilians can be more effective than old-style warriors, always presuming, that is, that such civilians are prepared to risk their own lives and take those of others. Nuclear weapons may act as the great equalizers of military power, and yet it may be that only those states which possess a very large land mass and dispersed population are actually able to threaten to use them.

These sorts of propositions amount to the folk wisdom of power politics. As with most examples of folk wisdom, there are alternative and contradictory versions of each proposition, and it is very difficult to think of ways of validating them short of the exchange of anecdotes. In any event, most of the time in international relations we are not just interested in power as an attribute of states, but in power as a *relational* concept. Indeed, all the attributes listed above only have meaning when placed in a relational context – thus, for an obvious example, whether a country has a 'large' or a 'small' population is a judgement that only makes sense in relation to some other country. Relational power also, of course, takes us back to the notion of influence.

The American political scientist, Robert Dahl, offered a classic formulation of relational power when he suggested that power is the ability to get another actor to do what it would not otherwise have done, or not to do what it would otherwise have done (Dahl 1970); the first of these relationships we could call 'compellance', and the second 'deterrence'. Either way, on this count, power is not something that can be measured in terms of the attributes of a state but only in action, in the effect one state has on another. There is a real distinction being made here, even if the contrast between power-as-attribute and power-as-influence-in-a-relationship is somewhat obscured by the ambiguity of ordinary language, at least of the English language, where 'power' can be synonymous with both 'strength' and 'influence' – unlike the French language, where *puissance* (power, might) and *pouvoir* (capability) are more clearly delineated.

Of course, it might be the case that what we have here are simply two different ways of looking at the same phenomenon. Such an argument lies behind the *basic force* model of power, which suggests that it is a reasonable assumption that the power an actor is able to exercise in a relationship is a direct reflection of the amount of power in the attribute sense possessed by that actor. In other words, we can, in effect, pass over the relational aspect of power fairly quickly, because it is the resources that are brought to the relationship that really count. The suggestion is that, if we wish to know whether in any particular situation one actor will be able to exert power over another, the obvious method of answering this question is to compare the resources that the two actors bring to the relationship. As folk wisdom has it, God is on the side of the big battalions.

The problem with this account of power is that it is self-evidently false – or rather can only be made true by the addition of so many qualifications that the clarity of the original idea is lost, and the proposition simply becomes the tautology that the more powerful state is the state that gets its way in any relationship. To employ an often-cited example, it is clear that, by any attribute measure of power, the United States was a stronger country than North Vietnam, and that even in terms of the resources devoted to the Vietnam War, the United States had more men, tanks, planes and ships committed than had the North Vietnamese. If we want to explain why, none the less, the United States was effectively defeated by North Vietnam, we have to develop our analysis in various ways. In the first place, we have to introduce into our calculations factors such as the quality of the leadership of the two countries, and the effects of their domestic political and social structures on the conduct of the war – the role, for example, of the American media in undermining support for the war in the United States, the skill of the Vietnamese army at irregular jungle warfare, and the inability of the United States to find local allies with sufficient support in the countryside of Vietnam. Each of these factors could be assimilated to a basic force model – after all, the skill of its army and political elite has always been identified as an element of the power of a state – but only at the cost of introducing highly subjective elements into the calculation. The merit of the basic force model is that it allows us to make more-or-less precise calculations – this is lost if we have to start assessing the relative skills of national leaderships.

However, there are two more fundamental objections to the basic force model; first, the context within which power is exercised is important; as is, second, the asymmetrical nature of many power relationships. As to *context*, very few relationships in reality involve only two actors. Generally, there are many other parties involved indirectly. In the Vietnam War, numerous third parties influenced the outcome. We simply cannot say what would have happened had the United States been able to act without bearing in mind the reactions of, on the one hand, North Vietnam's potential allies, China and the Soviet Union, or, on the other, America's own allies in the Pacific and Europe. A pure two-actor power relationship is very unusual, and certainly was not present here.

If anything, *asymmetry* is even more important than context. The difference between compellance and deterrence, referred to above, is part of this. What exactly it was that the United States wanted in Vietnam was never clear (that was one of their problems), but it certainly involved a number of positive changes to the political architecture of Vietnam, such as the emergence of a government in the South capable of winning the allegiance of the people. The North Vietnamese, on the other hand, simply wanted the Americans to go away; they were confident that if the Americans did go away they would be able to deal with any local opposition – as indeed proved to be the case. The North Vietnamese could wait; their aim was to win by surviving, rather than to bring about any positive change in their relationship with the United States.

This opens up a dimension of relational power that goes well beyond the basic force model of power. One definition of power is that power is the ability to resist change, to throw the costs of adaptation on to others, and, characteristically, the ability to resist change requires fewer resources to be placed on the line than the ability to bring change about. In international politics, as in war, the assumption must be that there are tactical advantages to a defensive posture as opposed to an offensive one.

What all this suggests is that it is not possible to assimilate attribute and relational power into one algorithm, or at least that such an algorithm would have to be so complicated, and hedged around with so many provisos, that it would not be able to perform the role of simplifying the analysis of power. This is unfortunate, because there are a number of circumstances where we might actually want a *measure* of power, and measuring the influence of a state is, in every respect, more difficult than measuring its attributes. When, for example, we move on to consider the notion of the 'balance of power' we shall want to ask ourselves what it is that is being balanced, and how we could tell whether a balance exists. In each case it would be helpful if we were able simply to assume that power is measurable in terms of attributes. Once we are obliged to accept that power-as-influence is not directly related to power-as-attribute we are bound to encounter problems.

The measurement of influence is bound to be difficult, because what we are looking for are changes in the behaviour of an actor that are *caused* by the attempt of another to exert power, and, of course, in any practical situation there are always going to be a range of other possible reasons why an actor's behaviour might have changed, which either could have been determined even in the absence of the actions of another, or, at the very least, that reinforced the effects of the latter. There may be some cases where it is possible to identify a moment in the course of negotiations, or in the process of making a particular decision, where it can be said that such-and-such a consideration was decisive, but the standard literature on decision-making suggests that this kind of 'essence of decision' is rare. Moreover, even when a particular decision can be pinned down in this way, the circumstances leading up to the decisive moment are always going to have been complex and involve a number of different factors. In effect, the attempt to isolate one factor, a particular influence-attempt, involves the construction of a counter-factual history – what would the world have been like had someone acted differently? None the less, these difficulties should not be exaggerated; historians cope with this dilemma all the time – any historical narrative is obliged to confront the problem of assigning influence to particular factors, and this seems to be achieved without too much hardship.

In any event, while power-as-influence is not based directly on the resources a state has at its disposal, indirectly these resources remain crucial. Influence rests on the ability to make threats in the event of non-compliance, and/or offer rewards for compliance – that is, on *positive and negative sanctions*, or 'sticks and carrots' as the vernacular has it – and this ability is clearly related to the attributes of power possessed by a state. States that attempt to exert influence in the world, to alter the international environment in their favour, solely on the basis of reasoned argument or by relying on the skills of their representatives, are likely to be disappointed. This does not mean that all attempts at influence rest on explicit threats or promises; the ability of a state to make effective threats/promises will generally be known and taken into account by interested parties without having to be made explicit. In fact, explicit threats – and even more so, action to back up threats – tend to be made when it is unclear that the message is getting across, or when credibility is at stake. It should also be noted that threats and rewards need not relate directly to tangible factors – some states may have a degree of prestige so that other states wish to be associated with them.

These propositions can be illustrated by reference to a number of recent episodes in international relations. The negotiations in 1993 and 1994 that brought about real progress in relations between the Israeli government and the Palestine Liberation Organization, and the creation of limited self-rule in some areas of the Gaza Strip and the West Bank, were brokered by the good offices of a number of parties, ranging from the government of Egypt to private individuals in Norway. However, when an initial deal was struck, the signing ceremony took place on the White House lawn, because it was deemed necessary by all parties that the power of the United States be associated with the outcome. Only the United States possesses the ability to reward progress and punish the lack of it – underwriting by Norway or Egypt would not be sufficient. As the peace process has unfolded, this fact has become if anything even more salient, as has the fact that the exercise of this influence is crucially related to domestic politics in the USA; there is a limit to what any American politician seeking election or re-election can demand in the way of concessions from Israel. This become a live issue in the American Academy with the publication of John Mearsheimer and Stephen Walt's work on the Israel Lobby (2006, 2007). Arguably, they overstate the influence of the lobby, partly because they use a very flexible definition of what the lobby actually stands for, but no one doubts that there are genuine domestic constraints on US policy in the region.

In any event, the efficacy of threats and rewards offered by the US or anyone else will vary according to the issues at stake; as time has passed and a Palestinian Authority has been established, core values have come closer to the surface for both parties, and the ability of outsiders to persuade them to compromise has diminished. The failure of the Camp David talks in 2000, and the unwillingness of either side to adhere to the various 'road maps' with which they have been presented by third parties (such as the USA, the UK and the EU) illustrates the point, and the success of Hamas in the elections of 2005 in the Palestinian territories drove the message home. Gaza and the West Bank are now governed by Palestinian factions opposed to each other, and the capacity of any external actor to influence events has plummeted.

In the peace process in Bosnia which led in 1995 to the Dayton Accords, the movement can be observed from implicit to explicit threats, and finally to overt action. In this case the United States had stayed in the background of the process during 1993–5, but with the implicit threat that it would become involved if the Bosnian Serbs refused to compromise. This had no effect; eventually the USA became involved and the threat became explicit. This also had no effect, and it was not until a short bombing campaign by US and NATO forces in response to the fall of the town of Srebrenica and the accompanying atrocities that the Bosnian Serb leadership finally, grudgingly, moved towards a degree of compliance. Action was necessary here perhaps because intentions had been misread – although it may also have been the case that the Bosnian Serb leadership found it easier to justify to their own people giving way to actual coercion than they would have yielding even to an explicit threat. Such at least was believed by some NATO analysts in 1999 when the campaign to end Serbian oppression of ethnic Albanians in Kosovo began, though in the event it transpired that a far more substantial military effort would be necessary before Serbian policy was reversed. In both instances, a continuing American presence is required – without the power of the United States at its disposal it seems unlikely that the international force in Bosnia charged with implementing the Dayton Accords could perform its mandate, even given the involvement of the major European NATO members, and, similarly, KFOR in Kosovo can only act effectively because it is known that ultimately US military power backs up the local commanders (Chapter 11 considers these interventions in terms of their professed humanitarian goals and outcomes).

Finally, it is worth noting the impact of a very different kind of power – that associated with the great prestige of a particular figure, such as Nelson Mandela of South Africa. Thus, the South African delegation played an important role in bringing about the relatively successful outcome of the Nuclear Non-Proliferation Treaty Review Conference of 1995, partly through skilful diplomacy, but also because they were able to exploit the unwillingness of other delegations to find themselves in opposition to South Africa. And, as another example, the willingness of the Libyan government to hand over for trial its nationals who were suspects in the Lockerbie bombing owed something to the good offices of (by then) ex-President Mandela. On both occasions, the more conventional lobbying of the US government was rather less successful – partly, no doubt, because the US did not have enough to offer on these particular issues. On the other hand, the limits of this sort of power are also apparent; for example, in the unwillingness of the then military rulers of Nigeria to respond favourably to South African pressure to grant a reprieve to condemned dissidents. The execution of Ken Saro-Wiwa while the 1995 Commonwealth Heads of Government Conference was under way suggests that the disapproval of Nelson Mandela took second place in the minds of these rulers to the need to preserve their power at home.

Staying within the African continent, and taking a less dramatic example, it is clear that the relative effectiveness of the African nations in the still-continuing Doha Round of trade talks under the WTO owes a great deal to the work of President Paul Kagame of Rwanda. Here it is neither the power of Rwanda, nor the past history of Kagame as the man who ended the genocide in that country that is significant. Rather, his 'power' rests on the sheer competence of his government, and his command of the issues involved. Sometimes, knowing what to do and how to do it can be the source of a kind of power. Of course, this sort of influence can be directed towards the malevolent ends of individuals and can also have deleterious effects – see the power of Osama Bin Laden to win converts to his cause, which is comparable to, or greater than Mandela's in terms of impact, but is being used exclusively to bring harm.

Before moving on to consider structural power, there is one further feature of relational power that needs to be addressed. Dahl's definition of power, cited above, was formulated in the context of American debates on 'community power', and one of the strongest criticisms of his approach stressed the way in which his definition only allows us to see power in operation when a decision is to be made; there may be, it was argued, cases of *'non-decision-making'* where power is exercised more effectively than in the making of decisions (Bachrach and Baratz 1970). The ability to control what gets on to the agenda is more important than the ability to determine what happens when items are actually raised in discussion. This is widely regarded as a valid criticism of Dahl's definition of power in the context of a governmental system – does it apply to international relations? Whereas much of the earlier discussion of power could apply to many versions of pluralism as well as to realist notions, we now reach a point at which paths diverge. Clearly, the power of non-decision-making is crucial to the analysis of agenda-setting within regimes, and thus of great significance to all versions of pluralism, including modern neoliberal institutionalism; however, for realists, neo- or otherwise, non-decision is a 'non-concept'. This is because, from a realist perspective, it is not possible for a state to be prevented from placing an item on the agenda, there being no agenda in any formal sense of the term. The key issues in international relations at any particular time are the issues that states with sufficient power to gain the attention of other states wish to be the key issues. No powerful state can be prevented from raising an issue; by definition, if an issue is not raised it is because the state that wished to raise it had insufficient power to do so. From a realist point of view, there is no second meaning of power.

It might be that a similar point will emerge with respect to structural power – but this requires a more extensive examination. So far in this chapter, power has been treated as though it were something that is exercised by actors whom realists presume to be states, but who might, in some circumstances, be other entities, such as individuals or groups. This agent–actor-orientated approach is a necessary feature of the way in which the consideration of power grew out of a consideration of foreign policy. We began with agent–structure problems, shifted attention to the state, moved on to consider how states formulate policy, took a short detour to examine the proposition that state action is determined by the international system, concluded that we had reason to doubt that this was entirely so, and then moved to the issue of foreign-policy implementation. Consideration of implementation raised the issue of techniques of statecraft, and this led to a discussion of power, in which power has been seen as something that states possess either as an attribute or exercise in a relationship. This is a natural enough way to think of power if one's starting-point is the state – but there is another way of thinking of power that is not actor-orientated, which returns us to the agent–structure problem discussed in the last chapter.

If we think of power as something in social life that brings about states of affairs, that instigates or prevents change – if, in other words, we take as our starting-point *outcomes* – it rapidly becomes clear that not all states of affairs come about because of the actions of individuals or groups or states (including as 'actions' in this case the legitimate exercise of authority as well as the exercise of influence). Some things happen without any apparent human agency. A society or a system may be structured in such a way as to bring about certain kinds of outcomes independently of the will of any of its component parts. It makes sense to talk about power existing in these circumstances – powerful forces are at work, as it were – but it is *structural* power that is involved.

A good way of making sense of the idea of structural power can be found in the work of the Italian Marxian revolutionary, Antonio Gramsci. Gramsci's concern was to start a revolution and overthrow capitalism, but he came to realize in the 1920s that overthrowing capitalism in Italy, a relatively-developed bourgeois state, was a different, and certainly a more difficult, task than the one that had faced Lenin in 1917. In Russia, which had been a very underdeveloped capitalist state, the power of capital was embodied in particular institutions that could be identified and engaged with in struggle – once defeated, capitalism was overthrown. In Italy, on the other hand, capitalism was so well established that it permeated all aspects of society; it controlled the 'common sense' of society, the ways in which ordinary people thought about politics, economics and social life in general. The effect of this capitalist 'hegemony' is that bringing about change becomes very difficult – checking and overthrowing capitalist/bourgeois institutions such as the firm or the liberal-democratic state is only the first step; the structural power of capitalism would remain as a more formidable obstacle to revolution than the resources of the overtly capitalist institutions.

How does this notion of structural power work in international relations? The direct application of notions of hegemony to international political economy will be discussed in Chapter 9; here, the focus will remain on power understood more generally, and it will be noted that apparently similar ideas have been encountered above, in the neorealist account of the international system; we now need to re-examine this account in the light of this new focus. To recapitulate in a slightly different way points made in the previous chapter, what we find is that, somewhat contrary to first impressions, Waltz's version of systemic power is only partly structural in the sense outlined above. As we have seen, the international system allegedly sends messages to its members, which, if correctly interpreted, will tell them what courses of action they should engage in – and Waltz assumes that, since states wish to survive, they will become quite skilled interpreters of the state of the system. There is obviously an element of structural power in this. The rules of the game – the 'common-sense' understanding of how one should conduct international relations – stem from the imperatives of the system. It is clearly not the case that these rules, in general, reflect the power of any particular state; they are not understood as the product of the will of any state or group of states, even though they clearly do operate to the benefit of some states as opposed to others, by, for example, giving some more options than others possess.

However, Waltz's conception does not quite capture the full idea of structural power, because the states that make up the system have an existence that seems to be independent of it, and they possess the ability not only to exploit structural power in the manner that, say, capitalist enterprises exploit the structural logic of capitalism, but also to interact with, and even to change the nature of, the rules of the game. Thus, in a bipolar system, according to Waltz, the two states concerned have the ability to regulate their competition and override the systemic imperative of 'self-help' which, unless regulated, might otherwise be expected to lock them into a highly destructive arms race. Even in a multi-polar system where such regulation is more difficult, states have the ability to misread the signals sent by the system – whereas structural power that is really part of the common sense of a society does not need to be read at all. It just *is*. Waltz's system is a strange hybrid in which states are sometimes agents, sometimes automatons – too much of the latter for the foreign-policy analyst who looks for greater autonomy, too much of the former for a truly structural account of the system. Here we see, yet again, the impact of rational choice thinking on International Relations; states are rational egoists operating under conditions of anarchy and, however much Waltz wishes to deny it, his model cannot avoid being actor-orientated.

Better versions of structural power can be found elsewhere in the International Relations literature. From the realm of international political economy, Susan Strange makes a compelling case for the existence of four primary structures in world politics – the knowledge structure, the financial structure, the production structure and the political structure (Strange 1988). Each of these structures has a logic of its own, independent of its members, and structural power can be found in operation in each. The historical sociologist Michael Mann also identifies four key structures – in his case, ideological, economic, military and political (Mann 1986/1993). His is a work of large-scale historical sociology and he is concerned not simply with the ways in which each of these structures determines outcomes, but also with changes in the relative importance of each structure over time.

What is interesting about these writers is that although both are, in some sense, providing realist accounts of the operation of international relations, neither accepts a state-centric view of the world, or a clear distinction between the domestic and the international – both of which are generally seen as key criteria for identifying realists. Neither of these two criteria is compatible with a truly structural account of the operation of power, and their determination to provide such an account takes them away from realism in the sense that the term has been used so far in this chapter and the previous one. In effect, as with the matter of non-decisional power, structural power in the full meaning of the term is not a category that works from a realist state-centric perspective – which provides yet one more reason for going beyond this perspective. However, before taking this step, there are still quite a few elements of the state-centric view of the world that need to be established and investigated.

Power, fear and insecurity

One of the defining features of realist accounts of international relations – of state-centric accounts in general – is an emphasis on the inherently *dangerous* nature of international relations. A level of watchfulness, if not fearfulness, which would be regarded as paranoid in other circumstances, seems a necessary feature of international relations. A brief review of the story so far will clarify why this is so.

First, it is a premise of state-centric accounts of international relations that states determine their own aims and objectives in the international system, and that primary among these aims and objectives will be a concern for survival, both in the physical sense of a concern to preserve the territorial integrity of the state, and, more intangibly, in terms of a concern to preserve the capacity of the state to determine its own destiny, its way of life. This premise emerges from the notion that the state is *sovereign* and wishes to remain so, and the assumption holds independently of the nature of the state – thus, *Machtstaat* or *Rechtstaat,* absolutist monarchy or liberal democracy, it makes no difference; states wish to preserve their sovereignty, come what may. Second, it is a premise of state-centric views of international relations that, given the absence of world government – that is, of a mechanism whereby interests can be pursued in the hope of achieving authoritative decision – the pursuit of interests is conducted by attempting to exercise power in the world; and power, in this sense, means the ability to make threats and offer rewards. Moreover, coercive means are part of the repertoire of positive and negative sanctions at the disposal of states in their conduct of foreign affairs, and the decision to use coercion is one that sovereign states reserve to themselves, with any commitment not to employ coercive means being contingent on circumstances.

Taken together, these two premises – each of which is no more than an elaboration of the implications of a system of *sovereign* states – ensure that insecurity and fear are permanent features of international relations. The very bare bones of the basic situation point to this conclusion, and the different ways in which flesh can be added to these bare bones may make the situation more or less dangerous, but they do not and cannot produce the qualitative change that would be necessary to remove danger completely.

The traditional realist account of state-centric international relations clearly makes life even more dangerous than the basic situation would suggest, because it adds to the pot the assumption that human beings have naturally aggressive tendencies that can only be constrained by the coercive force of government. The aims and objectives of states will include a desire to dominate, not simply because this is a systemic imperative, but because human beings are like that. Domination is what they do. It may be that, as Carl Schmitt suggests, as between states the visceral hatreds of a 'friend–foe' relationship can be transformed into the political hostility of a friend–enemy relationship, and the impersonal quality of this relationship may mitigate some of the worst features of our primordial aggressiveness (Schmitt 1932/1996). As against this, the very impersonality of modern means of violence may undermine whatever natural restraints we have inherited as part of our animal nature. In any event, for a classical realist, aggression and violence are part of who we are, whether these features are perceived in theological terms or as having socio-psychological or socio-biological origins.

The neorealist emphasis on systemic imperatives as a source of conduct removes this notion of aggressiveness from the equation. It is the basic situation that is dangerous, not the nature of the human beings who are obliged to work within the international anarchy. Moreover, states are assumed to be rational in their decision-making, and not liable to be overcome by instinctual fears or hatreds. The neorealist state is a cold, impersonal entity, with no friends, but also no enemies. On the other hand, the neorealist account of the international system puts great stress on the dangers of the basic situation in which states find themselves. States are enjoined to pay constant attention to the relations of power that exist in the world; watchfulness is needed, because, in a Hobbesian sense, international relations is a state of war. For Hobbes, life in the state of nature – a clear analogy to the neorealist international system – is a state of war, not in the sense that fighting is continual, but in the sense that it is an ever-present possibility (Hobbes 1946).

The state-centric view of the English School theorists of *international society*, and of constructivists such as Alexander Wendt, looks at first sight to be offering a rather less fear-dominated account of the world. The assumption here is that while states are sovereign and the basic situation outlined above still holds, nevertheless they are in a social relationship with one another, and there are some rules and practices that work to reduce the fear and tension that otherwise might exist. The rules of international law mandate non-aggression and non-intervention, and are taken seriously by states. There are certain kinds of 'settled norms' in international relations which regulate conduct. Such norms are settled not in the sense that every state always obeys them, but in the sense that, even when breaking them, states will pay allegiance to them; that is, they will attempt to show that they are not really breaking them, or that they are doing so for wholly exceptional reasons (Frost 1996: 105). These rules are backed by diplomacy – an institution with a culture of its own orientated towards problem-solving and negotiation rather than violence and coercion. States are sovereign, but this does not stop them, most of the time, from obeying the rules; a degree of watchfulness is justified, but not the extent of fearfulness that full-blown realist accounts suggest should be normal.

There are two problems with this: one fairly obvious, and one that may need more elaboration. In the first place, no theorist of international society has ever suggested that all states will play by the rules all the time – the possibility that there will be dissatisfied customers in the international arena who will be prepared to use their power to damage others cannot be discounted. But there is a more serious problem here, which is that even with the best will in the world, even assuming that all states are abiding by the rules – and do not wish to employ violence and coercion in their relations with one another – there is still the possibility that this fact will not be recognized, and that insecurity will increase even if there is no 'objective' reason why it should.

This notion – the 'security dilemma' – is based on the complex relationship between 'intentions' and 'capabilities', and the ways in which the system of sovereign states encourages emphasis on the latter rather than the former, with the result that a spiral of insecurity may emerge on the basis of misperception. Thus, because there is a background level of possible insecurity even in an international order where the majority of states are unaggressive and broadly satisfied with life, states feel obliged to preserve the means of self-defence and to do so in a cost-efficient but also effective way, which sometimes involves enhancing this capacity. However, the capacity to defend oneself is also, most of the time, a capacity to act offensively. Following the same chain of reasoning that leads the first, peaceful, state to preserve and occasionally enhance the effectiveness of its armed forces, a second state may see this as a potentially hostile act. The defensive intentions – which cannot easily be demonstrated, much less proven – will be less important than the offensive capabilities. If the second state reacts to these capabilities by expanding its own coercive capacity this is likely to be perceived as potentially hostile, and so the spiral sets in. The US debate over National Missile Defense offers an interesting illustration of the reasoning here; a partial missile defence for the USA would be purely defensive in intent, designed to deter attacks from 'rogue' states, but, if effective, such a system would render Russian and Chinese deterrent forces less credible and probably stimulate them to upgrade their systems, in turn increasing US anxiety, and so on. There are things the USA can do to try to prevent this vicious circle from emerging, such as offering to share the technology with rivals, but the history of recent years suggest that such strategies do not, in fact, allay fears, but may actually increase them by demonstrating an effortless superiority that is, in itself, threatening.

This is a security *dilemma* rather than, for example, a simple mistake, because no one is behaving unreasonably or making unreasonable assumptions. It might, in fact, be a mistake to perceive hostility where there is none, but it is a reasonable mistake; better safe than sorry. There are too many historical examples of states not reacting in time, taking overt intentions as a reason for ignoring capability enhancements, and suffering as a result, for this possibility to be ignored. We do not have access to the intentions of states – we can only see their capabilities and work back from these. It is in the nature of the 'self-help' system in which states exist that they are likely to take a pessimistic view of the world, even in an international society. National leaders consider themselves to have a responsibility to their populations to be cautious and prudent, and not to turn a blind eye to potential threats.

The idea of the security dilemma can be taken too far to imply that *all* international insecurity stems from some such process of reaction and overreaction. There seems no reason to hold to such a view. Sometimes states *do* have hostile intentions towards each other, in which case reacting to a build-up of capabilities is a sensible move. But the point is that even in a world largely composed of states that do not have any hostile intent, and that make rational, calculated decisions about their place in the world, insecurity is still endemic. Anarchy is anarchy even in an anarchical *society* – the existential situation of sovereign states coexisting in a world without government is inherently insecure and dangerous.

Conclusion: managing insecurity

And yet the international system is not as anarchic in the usual, pejorative sense of the term, as these ruminations would imply. Much of the time there is a degree of order in the world, and insecurity, while ever present, is kept at manageable levels. How? There are two institutions of international relations which, according to the state-centric tradition, preserve a degree of order and security in the international system. The first, predictably, is the *balance of power* – the idea that while force is the defining characteristic of the international system, some patterns of force may induce a degree of stability. The second institution for managing insecurity is, counter-intuitively, the institution of *interstate war*. Whereas from a common-sense point of view war is a disaster and represents the breakdown of order, in the traditional state-centric view of the world, war, while still disastrous, nevertheless plays an important role in the preservation of the system. Quite plausibly, nowadays, neither of these institutions can work in the way the tradition wants them to, and this may be one more reason for abandoning the state-centric view of the world. However; before we can legitimately reach this conclusion, we must carry the argument through to the end, which is the task of the next chapter.

Further reading

For this chapter the readings in Part 1 of Richard Little and Michael Smith, *Perspectives on World Politics: A Reader* (2006) are particularly valuable.

On diplomacy in general, see G. R. Berridge, Diplomacy: Theory and Practice (2002), and Adam Watson, *Diplomacy: The Dialogue of States* (1982); also Keith Hamilton and R. T. B. Langhorne, *The Practice of Diplomacy* (1995). For a wider notion of how states act, see Steve Smith and Michael Clarke (eds), *Foreign Policy Implementation* (1985); and, for postmodern accounts of diplomacy, see James Der Derian, *On Diplomacy: A Genealogy of Western Estrangement* (1987); Costas Constantinou, 'Diplomatic Representation, or, Who Framed the Ambassadors?' (1994); and Constantinou, *On the Way to Diplomacy* (1996).

David Baldwin, *Economic Statecraft* (1985) is a seminal study on the exercise of power/influence. On 'coercive diplomacy', see A. L. George, *The Limits of Coercive Diplomacy* (1971); Gordon C. Craig and A. L. George (eds), *Force and Statecraft* (1983); and Robert Art and Kenneth Waltz (eds), *The Use of Force: Military Power and International Politics* (1993). The journal *International Security* is a major source of high-quality material on the exercise of power – see, for example, the debate between Robert A. Pape, 'Why Economic Sanctions Do Not Work' (1997) and 'Why Economic Sanctions *Still* Do Not Work' (1998); and David A. Baldwin, 'Correspondence Evaluating Economic Sanctions' (1998) and 'The Sanctions Debate and the Logic of Choice' (1999/2000). Joseph Nye's *Soft Power: The Means to Success in World Politics* (2005) is a major contribution.

The best recent collection on the conceptualization of power is Felix Berenskoetter and Michael Williams, *Power in World Politics* (2007), which features contributions from Joseph Nye, Steve Lukes and Joseph Grieco among many important contributions. The collection originally saw publication as a *Millennium S*pecial Iissue on 'Facets of Power in International Relations' (2005). Michael Barnett and Duvall Raymond provide a useful taxonomy of power in 'Power in International Politics' (2005a), and their edited volume, *Power in Global Governance* (2005b), is also a good resource.

Most textbooks have extended discussions on power: particularly interesting are Hans J. Morgenthau, *Politics Among Nations: The Struggle for Power and Peace* (1948), and Raymond Aron, *Peace and War: A Theory of International Relations* (1967). George Liska, *The Ways of Power: Patterns and Meanings in World Politics* (1990); Robert Cox, *Production, Power and World Order: Social Forces in the Making of History* (1987); and David A. Baldwin, *Paradoxes of Power* (1989) are diverse but stimulating discussions of different kinds of power. Geopolitics is currently becoming fashionable again – a good survey is Daniel Deudney, 'Geopolitics as Theory: Historical Security Materialism' (2000). For Gramscian notions of hegemonic power, see Chapter 9. Alexandre Bohas, 'The Paradox of Anti-Americanism: Reflections on the Shallow Concept of Soft Power' (2006) examines soft power in the light of recent developments in world politics. Fahreed Zakaria reflects on the challenges to, and continued predominance of, US power, in 'The Future of American Power' (2008).

Moving away from the international context, the standard work on community power is Robert Dahl, *Who Governs?* (1961). Classic critiques are in Paul Bachrach and Morton S. Baratz, *Power and Poverty* (1970), and Steven Lukes, *Power: A Radical View* (1974/2004). For a brief, but powerful, critique of Lukes, see Brian Barry, 'The Obscurities of Power' (1989).

Robert Jervis, *Perception and Misperception in World Politics* (1976) is the classic account of the 'security dilemma' and the 'spiral of insecurity', although Ken Booth and Nicholas Wheeler *The Security Dilemma: Fear, Cooperation and Trust in World Politics* (2007) sets a new standard on these topics. Ken Booth (ed.), *New Thinking about Strategy and International Security* (1991a) contains a number of articles critical of the notion. Michael E. Brown *et al., New Global Dangers: Changing Dimensions of International Security* (2004a), looks at critical security dilemmas facing states in the twenty-first century, including non-military threats. Further readings on new approaches to security are listed after Chapter 9; David Baldwin, 'The Concept of Security' (1997), is a useful survey that bridges old and new. Daniel Deudney's *Bounding Power* (2007) looks at republican security theory from antiquity to the present. Other recent work on security include: Holger Stritzel, 'Towards a Theory of Securitization: Copenhagen and Beyond' (2007); Thierry Balzacq 'The Three Faces of Securitization: Political Agency, Audience and Context' (2005); and Tarak Barkawi and Mark Laffey, 'The Postcolonial Moment in Security Studies' (2006).

Chapter 6

The Balance of Power and War

Introduction

The state-centric view of the world, especially in its realist variant, paints a picture of great insecurity and fear. Concerned for their own security, possibly desiring to dominate others, states are obliged to keep a watchful eye open for ways of enhancing their own power, and reducing that of others. Unrestrained and unprotected by any international government, states must look after their own security, even though they cannot but be aware that their attempts to do so may induce insecurity in others. Thus, the scene seems set for a wretched world, in which the idea of an international 'order' would be preposterous. Yet there is a degree of order in the world; international relations may be anarchic in the formal sense of lacking government, but they are not anarchic in the sense of being lawless and disorderly – or at least not entirely so. How can this be?

According to realist International Relations theory, order of a kind and to a degree is preserved by two key institutions – the *balance of power* and *war*. The idea that the balance of power generates order is plausible enough, but to suggest that war is a source of order seems counter-intuitive, implausible and, indeed, somewhat distasteful. None the less, this thought, however distasteful, must be borne with, because war, seen as a political instrument, does indeed play this role (or, at least, it has done in the past). It does so in two senses: first, as part of the balance of power, because, contrary to some accounts which suggest that the balance of power is designed to prevent war, war is an essential mechanism for preserving a balance; and, second, as a conflict-resolving mechanism that does something that the balance of power cannot do – namely, to bring about (rather than frustrate) change. In other words, war both complements and completes the balance of power. Without war, the balance of power could not operate as a functioning institution of an international system or society. War and the balance of power stand together – or, perhaps, fall together, because it may well be that there are features of international relations in the early twenty-first century which mean that an account of the world in which war plays this central role is indefensible for one reason or another; not simply on moral grounds, but as a practical proposition. If this is so, yet more doubt will be cast on state-centric International

Relations, to be added to the reservations already expressed in Chapters 4 and 5.

The first section of this chapter will examine the balance of power. After a cursory examination of the long tradition of balance-of-power thinking in the European states system, two modern versions will be examined (or, in one case, re-examined) – those of Kenneth Waltz and Hedley Bull. The next section will outline the political, Clausewitzian theory of war – in contrast to other accounts of war that stress its irrational, cataclysmic nature – and the role of war as a conflict-resolving mechanism in classical international relations. The final section will offer a number of reasons why this account of war, and the account of international relations upon which it rests, is, under current conditions, no longer plausible.

The balance of power

The balance of power is one notion that is virtually inescapable in the discourse of International Relations as it has developed over the last three or four centuries. The term goes back to at least the sixteenth century – though not to pre-modern times; according to Hume (1987), the Greeks knew nothing of it – and was theorized in the eighteenth century and after. It appears in treaties (for example, that of Utrecht 1713), in the memoirs of statesmen and diplomats, and in the writings of historians and lawyers. To the diplomats of the *ancien régime,* it was the underlying principle that created stability. By contrast, to radical liberals such as Richard Cobden it was a mere chimera, a simple collection of sounds with no meaning (Cobden in Brown *et al.* 2002). In the twentieth century, it has been invoked at one time or another by all the major international actors.

Unfortunately, no one can agree on what it means. Scholars such as Martin Wight and Herbert Butterfield have between them collected examples of at least eleven different meanings revealed in the writings or speeches of its adherents. Neither is there internal consistency in the way particular writers use the term – Inis Claude, for example, notes that Hans Morgenthau shifts back and forth between several different meanings in his chapter on the subject in *Politics Among Nations,* a chapter explicitly designed to clear up confusions (Claude 1962: 25). No doubt almost every other writer could be exposed in the same way.

What is to be done about this confusion? Claude more or less gives up, and tries to restrict the term to a description of the system of states as a whole – thus, a balance of power system is simply the term we give to a system that is based on sovereignty and the absence of world government. However, this is a little too defeatist. There is a root idea of some importance here, and it would be a shame to lose this as a result of past confusions. This root idea is the notion that only force can counteract the effect of force, and that in an anarchical world, stability, predictability and regularity can only occur when the forces that states are able to exert to get their way in the world are in some kind of equilibrium. The notion of a 'balance' is rather a bad metaphor here, if it suggests the image of a pair of scales, because this implies only two forces are in equilibrium. Better, though less conventional, is the image of a chandelier. The chandelier remains level (stable) if the weights that are attached to it are distributed in such a way that the forces they exert (in this case the downward pull of gravity) are in equilibrium. There are two advantages to this metaphor; in the first place it makes more difficult some of the more perplexing usages associated with the idea – it would become clear, for example, that 'holding the balance' is rather difficult, while a balance 'moving in one's favour' is positively dangerous if one is standing under a chandelier.

More seriously, it conveys the idea that there are two ways in which equilibrium can be disturbed, and two ways in which it can be re-established. The chandelier moves away from the level if one of its weights becomes heavier, without this being compensated for – if, let us say, one state becomes more powerful than others for endogenous reasons; for example, as a result of faster economic growth than other states. It also becomes unstable if two weights are moved closer together without compensatory movement elsewhere – if, for example, two states form a closer relationship than previously. Restoring stability can also take two forms – another weight increasing, or two other weights moving closer together. Put differently, disruptions are both created and potentially rectified by *arms racing*, or by *alliance* policy, or by some combination of the two.

To illustrate these points in more concrete terms, consider a highly simplified account of the international system in Europe after 1871. In 1871, the system was more or less in equilibrium, following Prussia's victories over Austria-Hungary (1866) and France (1870–1), and, crucially, following Bismarck's decision not to use these victories to create a Greater Germany by incorporating parts of the Dual Monarchy in the new German Empire. There were tensions in the system, and loose, temporary alliances between states, but, on the whole, the system was in equilibrium. However, on one reading, in the late nineteenth century, German power increased as a result of German industrialism and population growth, to the point that a German superpower began to emerge, contrary to Bismarck's intentions. This industrial strength transmitted itself into an active German foreign policy via such measures as a larger army, and the growth of a navy virtually from scratch. The response of the other European powers was, first, to attempt to enhance their own power (by, for example, in France, extending periods of military training, and in Britain, engaging in naval enhancement); and, second, to re-align, creating new military alliances. France and Russia ignored ideological differences and signed a formal alliance in 1892; and Britain disregarded imperial rivalries and set aside a long policy of peacetime non-entanglement to become associated effectively with these two countries, in 1904 and 1907, respectively. In short, both the methods identified above to deal with incipient disequilibrium were attempted.

There are three interesting points about this story, two of which can be made here, and the third being held over to the end of this section. The first is that the flexibility of the system decreases as alliances become firmly established, because then the system begins to look bipolar, and in a bipolar system, by definition, disturbances to stability can only be met by internal changes, and not by the construction of alliances. This is one of the reasons why classical balance-of-power theorists say that the ideal number of states in a balance is five – this allows for three-versus-two formations, which can be adapted as appropriate, compared to bipolar systems, which are inherently inflexible. However, Kenneth Waltz argues that, in a bipolar system, power management is easier, as two parties can negotiate their way to stability more easily than is the case with any larger number.

This first observation is somewhat arcane; more significant is the second point, the difficulty of thinking about the balance of power while using theoretically sophisticated notions of 'power'. Balance-of-power theorists tend to see power as an attribute of states – Claude, for example, defines power in military terms throughout his work – and thus tend to be committed to a 'basic force' model of influence. However, as was shown in Chapter 5, basic-force models are either wrong or tautological. If, on the other hand, we try to work with power-as-influence as our starting point, then simple stories that advocates of balance of power relate become very complex narratives. For example, returning to the post-1871 narrative offered above, the idea that German power was the major disruptive influence rests on a basic force model of power; once we look at influence as revealed in outcomes, things look very difficult. We find that, in most of the diplomatic crises of the period, the German government was on the losing side, quite unable to convert its undoubted physical strength into favourable results at the conference table. This was why the German political elite in the years up to 1914 had such a strong sense that the rest of the world was against them; they were conscious of their own *lack of influence*, while others were conscious of their *superabundance of power*.

How do balances of power become established? Morgenthau argues that, when states pursue their national interests and seek power in the world, a balance will emerge, 'of necessity' – but this is a very dubious argument, since he is well aware that sometimes balances of power do not emerge (Morgenthau 1948: 161). If he were not so aware, his advocacy of balance-of-power policies would be hard to explain; one does not need to proselytize on behalf of something that is really going to happen 'of necessity'. Moreover, the historical record gives little support to the idea that balances of power are in some way 'natural' phenomena – as Martin Wight remarks, the historical record shows a tendency towards the concentration of power rather than towards its balanced distribution (Wight in Butterfield and Wight 1966: 167). More generally, anyone who wishes to argue that balances of power will always emerge is obliged to provide some account of agency; some explanation of how this automatic process becomes translated into state policy.

Two accounts of the balance of power that do meet, or successfully avoid, this criterion are given by Bull and Waltz. Waltz's theory, as outlined in *Theory of International Politics*, was discussed briefly in Chapter 3. On his account, the 'balance of power' is what will happen if states take notice of their surroundings, adjust their policies to changes in the configuration of power worldwide, and, a critical proviso, if the actual distribution of power is such that a balance *can* emerge. Waltz does *not* argue that balances of power will always emerge – for example, when discussing the bipolar nature of the then current (1979) world, he remarks that the most likely shift away from bipolarity would be towards unipolarity (that is, an end to the anarchical system) – if the Soviet Union were unable to remain in competition with the United States (Waltz 1979: 179). His point is, rather, that other states would not want this to happen, and would do everything they could in terms of realignment and enhancing their own capabilities to stop it from happening – a point neorealists have repeated since the end of the Cold War.

On Waltz's account, the system influences agents via the imperatives of rationality. To act in such a way that balances of power emerge is to act as a rational egoist in the face of a particular set of circumstances; namely, in response to changes in the distribution of power that might have an adverse effect on a state's capacity for self-preservation. It should be stressed that states do not wish to create balances of power, at least not as a first preference. This is even true (perhaps especially true) of bipolar balances. Each party would in reality like the other to disappear, and would be prepared to take steps to bring this about if it could do so without risk. But, of course, this is not possible, and the 'second best' solution is to manage jointly a bipolar balance. Again, generalizing the point, no state really wants to see a balance of power emerge; balances of power are accepted because there is no better game in town; no alternative source of security anywhere near as effective.

Waltz is clear that the balance of power *is* the theory of international politics, but it should be stressed that other writers employing the same general line of argument have come to different conclusions. One alternative to balancing is 'bandwagoning' – that is; lining up behind a state that is rising in power – and it has been argued quite cogently both that this is sometimes a rational strategy to follow and that the historical record suggests that states are every bit as likely to bandwagon as to balance (Walt 1987). Arguably, in the post-1989 world, the dominant tendency has been for states to bandwagon behind the USA, though this may now be changing (on which, see

Chapter 12). However one judges the argument here, the central point is that it is not quite as obvious that states will engage in balancing behaviour in the way that Waltz assumes; there are other rational responses they might have to the security dilemmas they face.

Hedley Bull, in his *The Anarchical Society,* briefly considers the idea that a balance of power might emerge, as he puts it, 'fortuitously', simply as an unintended consequence of the actions of states (Bull 1977/1995/2002: 100). However, having considered this possibility, he rejects it on the grounds that such fortuitous circumstances could not be expected to provide the basis for any kind of medium- to long-term stability. States motivated only by rational egoism would take the first chance to upset the balance. Instead, the burden of Bull's argument is that the balance of power is a necessary adjunct to any kind of international order; that only when power is balanced have states any real freedom in the world; and that balances of power will only emerge and be sustained when states are aware that this is so and are willing to act accordingly. In other words, the balance of power is a kind of artefact, something that states, or a significant proportion of states, are willing to see as a desirable end. If a balance of power is to work, states must *want* it to work, and must be committed to the idea that the preservation of the system of states is desirable. As always with theorists of international society, it is the normative basis of the relationship that is crucial. To return to the European example outlined above, the balance of power was established initially in 1871 because Bismarck was committed to at least a version of these norms; he wanted Germany to be the most powerful state in Europe, but he did not want the system to be replaced with a German empire – thus he was willing to assist in the birth of a new balance of power, in contrast to at least one of his successors, Hitler, and possibly also to the Emperor Wilhelm II.

On this account, the balance of power is an *artefact,* something made by human beings; is it a *cultural* artefact? It might be thought that the motivation Bull seems to think is necessary could only come from a society that is, to some degree, culturally homogeneous, and it might be doubted whether the normative basis for the balance of power could work in the modern, post-European world. Bull was clearly concerned about this, as evidenced by his last pieces of work, *Justice in International Relations,* and on the expansion of the international system (Bull 1984; Bull and Watson 1984). On the other hand, Frost has argued that the 'settled norms' of the modern system, norms that have been tacitly accepted by almost all states, include a commitment to the continuation of the system, and that this entails the need to preserve a balance of power – there is no need to assume that this is a specifically European attitude (Frost 1996).

On Bull's account, we aim to preserve a balance of power in order to preserve international 'order'. Does this mean 'peace'? Not necessarily. Here, the third point raised by discussion of the post-1871 system and deferred can be made. Post-1871 was also pre-1914; what does the outbreak of war in 1914 tell us about the balance of power system that preceded it? It might be thought that it tells us that this system failed in 1914 – but it could equally well be argued that in terms of the preservation of international order, the 1914–18 war and subsequent events amount to a *vindication* of the balance of power. At a human level, this is a terrible conclusion, but one that is difficult to avoid if one accepts that preventing the dominance of the system by any one power is good, and if one acknowledges that, in some circumstances, this can only be achieved by violence and war. It may well be that, generally, international order equates to peace, but this cannot be guaranteed; sometimes the price of peace will be too high. This is a view sanctioned by history across the past four centuries, which can easily be described in terms of a series of bids for hegemony that were resisted successfully by a balance-of-power politics that relied on war as a possible tactic.

War plays an important role in maintaining a balance-of-power system, as a concomitant to alliance politics and arms races – that is, these are ways of maintaining a balance without war, but if they fail, then war may be necessary. However, there is a further role for war in this kind of international system. The balance of power is about stability, equilibrium, the prevention of change, but, sometimes, the resolution of conflict requires change, change that can only come via war. In this sense, war does not indicate the failure of conflict resolution – rather, war is *a means* of conflict resolution. This is a point that needs to be explored in some depth.

The political conception of war

In the twentieth century, the common-sense view of war came to be that it is a pathological phenomenon; that war represents a breakdown, a malfunctioning, of the international system, or perhaps a sign of the immaturity of a people or a civilization – the latter was the view of, for example, Freud (1985) and remains the view of the so-called Anti-War Movement today, at least in so far as anti-war is a genuine sentiment and is not synonymous with anti-wars-waged-by-Western-powers-especially-the-USA. However, to understand the role of war in a balance-of-power system, it is necessary to realize that this is mistaken. War is a *normal* feature of international relations, a normal part of the functioning of the international system, and in no sense pathological, though it may be regrettable. To see how this could be so, we need to examine briefly some alternative accounts of the causes of war, before outlining the view of war that makes sense of this position – the Clausewitzian or political conception of war.

The causes of war is a subject dominated by one study, and it is extraordinary that Kenneth Waltz, the author of *Theory of International Politics*, the book that raised the level of theoretical discourse in the discipline so dramatically in 1979, should also have authored, in 1959, *Man, the State and War,* the standard work in question – though, from some perspectives, the later book could be regarded as an elaboration and re-working of the third section of the earlier study. In the 1959 volume, Waltz identifies three 'images' of the causes of war, the third of which formed the basis for his later study.

The first image stresses *human nature*. Wars occur because of some aspect of human nature, an argument that can be cast in theological, psychological, psychoanalytic or, popular nowadays, socio-biological terms. We are fallen creatures, cast out of the Garden of Eden, preternaturally prone to violence. We are possessed by *thanatos,* a death-wish. We are the only animal that kills intra-specifically, that does not possess an inhibitor to prevent us killing our own kind (it should be noted that this is not in fact the case, although it is widely believed to be true). These are elaborate arguments, and they may contain some element of truth, but they do not explain war. War is not similar to murder, grievous bodily harm, or individual acts of violence – war is a *social* institution, and as such requires a social explanation. To explain social phenomena by reference to the nature of individuals is 'reductionist' – a term Waltz would also employ to some effect in his later study.

The second image focuses on the nature of societies rather than of human beings. War is caused by a particular kind of *society* – the choice here is very wide, ranging from autocracies and monarchies (the liberal view) to democracies (the autocratic view), from capitalist societies (the Leninist view) to communist societies (the capitalist view). Once again, one can tell a good story in support of the war-proneness of each of these kinds of society, but each explanation misses a crucial point. As far as we can tell, all societies that have had any kind of regular contact with other societies seem to have experienced some kinds of war – even those democracies that do not fight other democracies fight non-democratic systems with some regularity. The only exceptions to the ubiquity of war are a few rare cases where extreme climatic conditions – as with the Inuit in the Arctic – make war effectively impossible. This suggests that the second image is no more capable of providing general explanations of war than the first.

This leaves the third image, which, as will have been anticipated, points to the international *system* as being the essential cause of war. The argument here has been rehearsed above enough times to make any lengthy restatement redundant. States have interests, which at times may clash; in an anarchical system there is no way of resolving such a clash of interests that is binding on the parties; most of the time, the parties will not wish to resolve their difficulties by violence, but sometimes they will – war is the ultimate resort of states who can see no other way to have their interests met. It should be noted here that the third image explains why war is *possible* – in order to explain why any *actual* war takes place we shall need to bring into play societal and individual factors.

One final way of making the same point is to stress the difference between *civil* and *international war.* A civil war is a pathological condition, since it represents the breakdown of normality. In principle, states have methods of conflict resolution that forbid the use of force; sometimes, a problem emerges that cannot be contained by these mechanisms, and violence – civil war, if on a large enough scale – ensues. International war is *not* like this; as between states, war *is* the (ultimate) mechanism for the resolution of conflict.

This is a political account of war, and an account of war as the product of a rational choice, a weighing of the costs and benefits of the instrumental use of force. This sounds quite modern, but the writer who first set out this position and identified the key points in the argument did so nearly two centuries ago. This was the Prussian general and prototypical military intellectual, Karl von Clausewitz, whose master work, *On War,* was published posthumously in 1831. Clausewitz was a moderately successful senior staff officer, with campaign experience in the service of the Tsar and the King of Prussia in wars against Napoleon, and later an instructor at the Prussian Staff College, the most advanced centre for military thought of its day. In this latter capacity he produced the drafts for *On War,* and its origins are reflected in the fact that most of its contents examine the minutiae of tactics and strategy, and, given the changes in technology and society generally, are of little relevance today. However, Clausewitz was an intellectual soldier, a product of post-Enlightenment German thought, someone who was steeped in current thinking on the state and society. As a result, in addition to the technicalities, his book also includes some (quite short) reflections on the nature of war and its role in the international relations of the day – reflections that have been required reading ever since.

The gist of these reflections is that war is (or should be) a controlled, rational, political act. War is an act of violence to compel our opponent to submit to our will; in Clausewitz's famous words, it is not a mere act of policy but 'a true political instrument, a continuation of political activity by other means' (Clausewitz 1976: 87). Here we see the continuity between war and peace. War is not the end of political activity; it is conducted for political purposes. Clausewitz was a soldier, but a soldier who stressed the importance of political control of the armed forces. On his account, war rests on a triad of factors – animosity directed against the enemy, which is provided by 'the people'; the management of contingency; which is the role of the army; and the aims and objectives of the war, which are determined by the political leadership. It is crucial that these three moments are not confused; the army are entitled to ask of the government that they be given resources appropriate to the tasks in hand, but they are not to set these tasks. The government sets objectives but should not interfere with the means chosen for their achievement. The people should support the army and government, but not restrict their freedom of action.

In a few pages of Clausewitz we see, in condensed form, the essential features of the realist view of the world – and perhaps of any state-centric view of the world (though theorists of international society and Wendtian constructivists would resist this conclusion). The extent to which Clausewitzian ideas chime with neorealist thought is striking. While the former does not use the terms 'costs' and 'benefits', it is clear that this is what he understands by the instrumentality of war. An interesting question is whether Clausewitz was an 'offensive' or a 'defensive' realist, to use current terminology. Defensive realists assume that states are essentially reactive, prepared to defend their position but not likely to pre-empt potential opponents, while offensive realists assume that states will attempt to solve their security dilemmas by striking first if they can get away with it (see Chapter 3 for more detail on the two positions). One suspects that he would have sympathized with the latter position, but, at the very least, the prudent, calculating manner he advocates involves the rejection of crusades and vendettas. Moreover, for Clausewitz and his philosophical contemporaries, war is fought on behalf of the nation, and underwritten by national support, but it is not fought by the nation. As in the writings of his great contemporary, Hegel, war is for armies, and a clear distinction is to be drawn between combatants and non-combatants. Civilian, or, at least, political, control, is central – Clausewitz would have subscribed to Lloyd George's maxim that war was too important to be left to the generals, and would have had no sympathy for the bombast of some twentieth-century commanders, or the view (held, for example, by Eisenhower against Churchill in the Second World War) that war is a technical business and that politicians have no business interfering in strategic concerns. A Clausewitzian approach would have spared the twentieth century many disasters. The downside is also readily apparent – a willingness to use force that seems not to grasp the moral seriousness of the decision to employ violence for political ends, an acceptance of the notion that states must always be the judges in their own cases, an inability to see beyond the confines of the nation to a wider humanity. We might accept that a Clausewitzian view of war in the nineteenth century is an accurate description of how things were, and, on the whole, a more satisfactory view than any alternatives, but in the twentieth century there were many reasons to doubt this.

War in the twentieth century

In the nineteenth century, the view that war was a legitimate act of state was broadly accepted by international lawyers as a concomitant to the doctrine of sovereignty. So long as the war-making body had the authority to act, and followed the correct legal procedures (a proper declaration of war, for example), war could be waged lawfully, and without any legal interest in the reasons for this act of state. This is no longer the case. The Covenant of the League of Nations of 1919, the Pact of Paris of 1928, the United Nations Charter of 1945 and the London Charter of the same year – which established the War Crimes Tribunal that sat at Nuremberg – taken together have established a new legal regime in which war is only legitimate in two circumstances: as an act of self-defence; or as an act of law enforcement to assist others in defending themselves. Not only is this the current legal position; it also seems to correspond to the ways in which most people thought about war in the twentieth century, namely as a disaster that should be avoided at almost all costs – indeed, the current law on war is more likely to be criticized for being too permissive than for restricting the activity too closely. Both morally and legally, a Clausewitzian view of war seems today to be unacceptable.

Of course, from a realist point of view, all this is by the by. If states still make war on Clausewitzian lines, then the fact that law and public opinion goes against them is neither here nor there. At best, it explains some of the peculiarities of modern war, in particular the unwillingness to call a spade a spade – hence the British government always refers to the South Atlantic Conflict of 1982 rather than the Falklands War, the problems involved in fighting a declared war being too complicated to contemplate. But do states still make war as a rational act of policy? Some try to, sometimes – but on the whole, twentieth-century conditions worked against war being fought in terms of Clausewitzian calculations. There are two points here, one about the *actual* calculations, the other about the *role* of calculations in decisions for war.

The first point is simple; in the twentieth century, the costs of war rose dramatically, while the benefits either remained the same or, more often, fell. As mentioned in Chapter 1 above, Norman Angell saw this in the years before 1914 and it has become even more true post-1945. The rise in the destructiveness of war has been exponential – from the mayhem of machine guns, breechloading artillery and barbed wire in the First World War, to the strategic bombing of the Second, to the threat of nuclear annihilation of a potential Third World War. The economic structures of society are destroyed by war, financial resources dissipated, political stability undermined. The benefits of success have not risen in the same way; in material terms, the rewards for a successful war are now less significant than they once were. National wealth does not, on the whole, come from the conquest of territory or the cornering of raw materials – although, as the invasion of Kuwait in 1990 suggests, there may still be, in some circumstances, possibilities here. A successful war may remove an enemy or competitor, and there may be circumstances in which this is a very worthwhile result – but on the whole one would expect far fewer wars to emerge from rational calculation in the twentieth century than in the nineteenth. Yet the former was a century of warfare; by most statistical indices more war-prone than the latter, which suggests that war is no longer fought as a rational act, but for some other reason.

A clue to this other reason comes when we examine the fate of Clausewitz's triad under modern conditions. The people, the army and the government are supposed to have one function each, which fits in with the other two – the raw feelings of the people are harnessed to political ends by the government, and are then translated into action by the military. This can still work, but only rarely. Returning to an earlier example, the North Vietnamese were remark-ably Clausewitzian in their approach to the Vietnam War, not altogether surprisingly since their ideological influences – Marx, Engels, Lenin and Mao – were all avid readers of Clausewitz. The North Vietnamese people were mobilized behind the war, but not allowed a say in its execution. The politi-cal leadership maintained tight control over the objectives of the war, and the army was given freedom of action only in its proper sphere of operation. By contrast, the US army was given no clear objectives in Vietnam. The US pres-ident interfered with military operations, to the point of choosing bombing targets from the White House briefing rooms. The US public was never mobi-lized behind the war effort, and, via the media and Congress, set political constraints on the war that were detailed, inconsistent and deeply harmful to the development of a coherent strategy.

The key point here is that this latter state of affairs is far more common than the Clausewitzian purity of the North Vietnamese. North Vietnam, the Prussia of South East Asia, recreated a Clausewitzian environment by having nationalism without democracy, and a state strong enough to control the army and not to be constrained by informal expressions of popular opinion. This is a very unusual combination. In the advanced industrial countries, public opinion and democratic institutions mean that 'the people' are hard to mobi-lize, and, once mobilized, will refuse to play their designated role as cheer-leaders of the government and army – they insist on playing a major role in determining goals and approving (or more likely disapproving) strategies and tactics. Congressional and parliamentary investigations in the USA and UK into the reasons for and intelligence concerning the 2003 Iraq War, as well as in-depth and often critical media coverage of the conflict, have infuriated the governments concerned, but such questioning is, nowadays, more or less inevitable. In the less-developed countries, nationalism without democracy is quite common, but the state rarely has the capacity both to control its own armed forces and to ignore the disaffection of its people. Riots and civil unrest can be every bit as effective in influencing war aims as a democratic media and free elections.

In short, Clausewitzians face two problems when dealing with public opinion. In the first place, it may be very difficult to get the public 'on side', as the phrase goes. In the 1930s it took a long time for opinion in Britain and the United States to realize that war was probably necessary – but in the 1960s the USA was never able to persuade a large enough majority of Americans that Vietnam justified the effort they put into it. However, once public opinion is 'on side' it is very difficult to restrain it. Whatever the merits of the 'unconditional surrender' doctrine of the Allies in the Second World War, it is clear that any alternative approach – and in particular any suggestion that in future the Soviet Union might prove more of a problem than post-war Germany – would have been ruled out by public opinion. Perhaps public opinion would have been right, and was right, over Vietnam – but the point is that it is not a very Clausewitzian way of doing business.

There is, however, an even more fundamental problem with the Clausewitzian account of war, which is that it may be *culturally specific*. Nineteenth-century European war was a very formal business, with uniformed armies occupying clearly delineated territory, a code of conduct that was usually (although not always) observed, a formal declaration and a formal end – the peace treaty. The 'decisive battle' was a feature of Napoleonic, Clausewitzian and Victorian accounts of war – Creasy's *Fifteen Decisive Battles* is a key text here, showing a clear progression from Marathon to Waterloo (Creasy 1902). States fight in a formal way and make peace in a formal way. Hanson calls this *The Western Way of War* (1989) and traces it back to the wars of the Classical Greek cities, in which citizen heavy-infantry would fight one, highly stylized, battle per campaigning season, with a clear-cut way of determining winners and losers based on possession of the battlefield. This, he suggests, gives modern Europe its governing idea of what a war is like. However, he argues that it is highly untypical of the warfare of most civilizations, which is much more informal, is not dominated by set-piece battles, and rarely leads to any kind of decisive moment, much less a peace treaty.

The West is, of course, aware of this kind of warfare, but regards it as the exception rather than the rule and gives it special labels – guerrilla war, low-intensity conflict, police action, dirty war – Kipling's 'savage wars of peace'. The point to make here is that the exception may be becoming the rule. As we have seen, constitutionally secure liberal democracies do not fight each other – but then *no one* fights each other in the old way any more, except on very rare occasions such as the Falklands/Malvinas War of 1982 or the Gulf War of 1990–1. Even in these two cases, the parties that were clearly defeated have refused to behave like nineteenth-century gentlemen and make treaties that acknowledge this fact. Instead, they hang on, hoping something will turn up. Again, the Israelis have repeatedly 'defeated' their enemies in set-piece battles but they have been unable to turn these victories into political results – indeed, every 'successful' military action seems to have weakened their bargaining power by undermining the sympathy previously shown to the underdog by Europeans, and by many Americans. More characteristic of modern warfare was the imbroglio in former Yugoslavia in the 1990s, where quasi-regular armies vied with armed bands of 'volunteers', and local warlords owed only tenuous loyalty to their nominal superiors, where alliances shifted on a day-by-day basis and the 'frontline' was difficult to define, where territory changed hands without set-piece battles, and where formal armistices and peace treaties were signed and broken, signed again and broken again. This was the non-Western way of warfare encroaching on the West in a most painful way. The sensational victories in war-making, but equally spectacular failings in peace-building following both the 2002 Afghanistan war and the 2003 Iraq war of the US and its allies, also demonstrate the point. In both cases, the overwhelming military force of the Coalition has experienced serious problems in controlling the haphazardly organized and poorly armed insurgents in each state, and has been unable, so far, to build and protect new political systems.

There is at least some evidence that can be read as suggesting that some Western military thinkers have understood this shift in the nature of warfare rather better than Western governments or public opinion. The US armed forces have been developing doctrines for the employment of coercive measures of a non-conventional kind for some time. The new American soldier ('land warrior') will be expected to display his or her prowess by employing the latest technologies, not in set-piece battles against regular opponents, but in more informal situations where the political interests of the United States need to be supported by a show of violence. This capacity for 'virtual war' which, given the publicity surrounding it, may be intended to be 'virtual deterrence', has been mapped by postmodern enthusiasts such as the Tofflers (1993) and Der Derian (1992).

One of the reasons why the Western way of war is being rejected in the West itself is, perhaps, traceable to wider changes in late modern society, and in particular to the apparent ending of the 'warrior culture' in the West. Although Western public opinion has not abandoned the idea that it may sometimes be necessary to use force in international relations, the demand nowadays is to minimize casualties among one's own troops, and among 'enemy' civilians. The US reliance on air-power and its refusal to commit its troops in battle until the ground has been thoroughly prepared by 'precision' bombardment has been noted by many writers, and is in part a reflection of this changing ethos (Coker 1994, 1998; Ignatieff 2000). The Kosovo Campaign of 1999 represents the apotheosis of this approach – a 'zero casualty' war, for NATO at least, and to most people's surprise, apparently actually won (in the short term at least) by air-power.

The apparent political acceptability of the level of casualties in Afghanistan at the time of writing, and in Iraq, at least initially, may suggest that, for some Americans at least, 9/11 and the War on Terror have changed the nature of this particular game; Afghanistan is not seen as a 'war of choice' in the way that Somalia and Kosovo were. But the very nature of the 'War on Terror', or the 'Long War' as it has now been rebranded, reinforces the general point that the nature of war has changed. Some writers, who remain fixated on the 'Western Way of War' and expect wars to have beginnings, middles and ends, resist naming the Long War a war at all – they argue that what is needed is police action to apprehend wrongdoers (with an implicit acceptance that wrongdoing as such will not be ended thereby). But this is to discount the changing nature of modern warfare; just as the current Afghan campaign bears many resemblances to previous Afghan wars (some of which, it should be recalled, were in fact won by the British) so the Long War resembles other counter-insurgency campaigns. Interestingly it was only once the US military realized that they were engaged in such a campaign in Iraq that things have improved there – under General Petraeus, who has consistently argued the point against the Pentagon and the neo-conservatives since the war began.

In any event, a central feature of this kind of warfare is that, unlike Clausewitzian war, it *cannot* so easily be seen as a viable means of conflict resolution. In the 1860s there were conflicting views of the future shape of German politics. Prussia under Bismarck settled the matter by allowing von Moltke to win him three Western, Clausewitzian wars in succession – decisive battles at Sadowa in 1866 and Sedan in 1870 determined the outcome. Defeat was reluctantly accepted, peace treaties were signed, and the German Empire was formed under the aegis of Prussian military might. A problem was solved, though a new problem emerged, as is usually the way. It seems inconceivable that a sequence of events such as this could happen today. Wars are not formally declared, they do not formally end; they peter out or they fester on. Sometimes a stalemate emerges, sometimes imposed from outside – the 'non-war' in Cyprus in 1973 has been stifled by a UN peacekeeping force but the conflict remains unsolved; indeed, the very stalemate removes the impetus for solution. In other circumstances, such as Somalia and Rwanda, the impact of informal war may be the collapse of a society and a descent into anarchy, a descent that outsiders are effectively powerless to halt because, in the absence of clear enemies, clear battle lines and regular armies, external intervention becomes almost impossible. Even in Kosovo, where the military outcome was decisive, it is by no means the case that the losers have accepted the verdict of the (air) battlefield – instead, NATO is faced with the prospect of maintaining Kosovo as a protectorate for the foreseeable future. All this suggests that any account of war that tries to give the modern phenomenon its older, European function will miss the point in a very big way.

Conclusion: the end of state-centric International Relations?

Over the last three chapters we have seen a number of cracks appear in the edifice of state-centric International Relations theory. We have seen that theorists of decision-making have undermined the idea that foreign policy is radically different from domestic politics; the notion that states follow the national interest is difficult to support from these studies. Structural theories of international relations shift the emphasis away from foreign policy, but in turn are unable to resolve the problem of agency – and their emphasis on the irrelevance of domestic factors is undermined somewhat by the phenomenon of the 'democratic peace'. Power is a notion that seems clear and easy to understand, but once the distinction between power-as-attribute and power-as-influence is introduced, many of the usual certainties about the operation of power disappear. The balance of power, again, is an idea that has a degree of intuitive plausibility, but, again, it crumbles once the logic of the notion is exposed.

At one level, the weakness of the political conception of war is simply one additional reason for suspicion about state-centricity, yet one more example of a feature of international relations not behaving in quite the way it is expected. In reality, the malaise here goes much deeper. A Clausewitzian view of war is an essential requirement for the balance of power to operate; the two institutions stand together, and if, as suggested here, they fall together, the whole state-centric edifice is in ruins – certainly, this is so for any variant of realism. The point is that war and the balance of power are not simply additional extras that can be set aside if things do not work out. On the contrary, they are at the heart of both Waltz's anarchical system and Bull's anarchical society. They are the devices that permit the system or society to operate, and if they are in difficulties, *it* too is in trouble.

And yet the logic of state-centricity remains compelling. If the initial premises hold – that is, we live in an anarchical world, in which states are the major actors – and if states are motivated by rational egoism, then a neorealist world seems inevitable. But if states are able to temper this egoism with a concern for norms, then some kind of international society might emerge. If, none the less, we live in a world that in many respects is not characterized by this kind of international relations, which seems to be the case, then it seems likely that there is something wrong with these assumptions. We have already seen that one of these assumptions, that of rational egoism, can only be sustained by some quite heroic surgery. In the chapters to come, the other assumptions will equally be put to the test. The most basic of these assumptions is that of anarchy, and there are two ways in which the notion of anarchy can be challenged.

In the first place, we need to take seriously some of the propositions about the role of theory outlined in Chapter 1. In particular, we need to pay serious attention to the implications of the view that knowledge is constructed, not found; that it rests on social foundations and not upon some bedrock of certainty. If we acknowledge the sense in which 'international anarchy' is a construction by states – 'Anarchy Is What States Make of It' – we shall be less surprised by its illogicalities, and more willing to ask whose interests it serves (Wendt 1992, 1999). Partly, this is a question of historicizing international anarchy, of grasping the insubstantial nature of the timeless generalities of (neo)realism and placing them in some kind of historical context. This task is undertaken very ably by Rosenberg, though, unfortunately, the historical narrative he wishes to employ to replace realism's a-historicism is based on a Marxism that seems equally problematic, given the political and intellectual failings of that nineteenth-century doctrine (Rosenberg 1994). However, there are also questions here about power and knowledge that need to be raised.

The *anarchy problematic,* to anglicize Richard Ashley's phrase, does not simply serve the interests of rich and powerful states by legitimizing certain ways of exercising power; it also sets in place a particular conception of politics that privileges *all* states (Ashley 1989c). The notion that states exist in order to protect their populations from external dangers is legitimized in this way – even though it is quite clear that most people most of the time are in far more danger from their 'own' governments than they are from foreigners. The private–public distinction that pervades Western conceptions of politics and has characteristically supported the exclusion of women from public life in the West rests on the same foundations as the Western way of warfare – the original public figures were the soldiers who fought the set-piece battles of the Greek cities (Elshtain 1987). In short, a state-centric conception of *international* politics carries with it a quite extensive amount of political baggage from other areas of social life – the notion that international relations is different from all other spheres of social life, and thus that International Relations is a different kind of discipline from the other social sciences is one of the least compelling propositions of conventional realist international thought.

These are thoughts that will be pursued in the rest of this book, which begins with an attempt to cross-examine 'anarchy' in an essentially empirical way. Is it actually the case that we live in an ungoverned system? Clearly, there is no 'government' in the conventional, Western sense of the term – a limited set of institutions that makes and enforces authoritative decisions – but is this the only available model of what a government is? Realists, neorealists, neoliberals and international society theorists all stress that, in international relations, 'in the last instance' there is no 'ultimate' decision-making power. Thus sovereignty is a defining feature of the system, and nothing has really changed, or ever will, short of the emergence of a world empire. But how important is 'the last instance'? It might well be argued that we only very rarely and *in extremis* come close to reaching 'the last instance'. Can the network of quasi-governmental institutions within which the states system is today embedded really be dismissed quite so readily? We may not have world government, but perhaps we do have 'global governance', and it is to this phenomenon that we now turn.

Further reading

Classical texts on the balance of power by Brougham, Von Gentz and Cobden are collected in M. G. Forsyth, H. M. A. Keens-Soper and P. Savigear (eds), *The Theory of International Relations* (1970); a similar collection with a wider remit is Chris Brown, Terry Nardin and N. J. Rengger (eds), *International Relations in Political Thought* (2002). Hume's excellent essay, 'The Balance of Power', is very much worth reading 250 years on, and is most conveniently found in David Hume, *Essays: Moral, Political and Literary* (1987).

Modern 'classics' on the balance of power include E. V. Gulick, *Europe's Classical Balance of Power* (1955); Chapters 2 and 3 of Inis L. Claude, *Power and International Relations* (1962); Ludwig Dehio, *The Precarious Balance* (1965); and essays by the editors, both entitled 'The Balance of Power', in Herbert Butterfield and Martin Wight (eds), *Diplomatic Investigations* (1966), as well as discussions in Morgenthau and other standard texts. Morton Kaplan, *System and Process in International Politics* (1957), is a classic of a different kind from the behavioural movement of the 1950s, containing an attempt to pin down the rules of a balance system. J. N. Rosenau (ed.), *International Politics and Foreign Policy: A Reader* (1969), contains extracts from Kaplan, Waltz, Singer and others, still valuable over thirty years on. Contemporary debate on the balance of power is dominated by Kenneth Waltz, *Theory of International Politics* (1979) – see the articles from *International Security* in Michael E. Brown, Sean M. Lynn-Jones and Steven E. Miller (eds), *The Perils of Anarchy* (1995), especially Stephen M. Walt, 'Alliance Formation and the Balance of World Power' (1985) and Paul Schroeder, 'Historical Reality vs. Neo-Realist Theory' (1994) for critiques and alternatives largely from within the neorealist camp. A non-neorealist alternative to Waltz is provided by Hedley Bull, *The Anarchical Society* (1977/1995/2002). A good, fairly conventional collection on the balance of power is a Special Issue of *Review of International Studies*, Moorhead Wright (ed.), 'The Balance of Power' (1989).

Recent mainstream focus on the balance of power has been on 'soft balancing', which is accessibly presented and critiqued in the *International Security* forum on 'Balancing Acts' (2005). Richard Little's *The Balance of Power in International Relations: Metaphors, Myths and Models* (2007) rethinks the analytical framework of the balance of power and is something of companion piece to Stuart Kaufman *et al.*, *Balance of Power in World History* (2007). William Wohlforth *et al.*, 'Testing Balance-of-Power Theory in World History' (2007) presents a series of historical case studies. From a slightly different perspective, Ken Booth and Nicholas Wheeler's *The Security Dilemma* (2007) is an important recent study. Ruminations on the future nature of US–China relations has become a cottage industry, but still reflects on important issues; see Aaron Friedberg, 'The Future of US–China Relations: Is Conflict Inevitable?' (2005); G. John Ikenberry, 'The Rise of China and the Future of the West' (2008); and David Kerr, 'The Sino-Russian Partnership and U.S. Policy Toward North Korea: From Hegemony to Concert in Northeast Asia' (2005).

Lawrence Freedman (ed.) *War* (1994) is a very useful reader which contains short extracts from a wide range of sources. The acknowledged classic on the subject is Karl von Clausewitz, *On War* (1976): this edition/translation by Michael Howard and Peter Paret contains extensive commentary and fine introductory essays, and is to be preferred to the many alternatives available. Michael Howard, *Clausewitz* (1983) is the best short introduction. Beatrice Heuser, *Reading Clausewitz* (2002) synthesizes the main arguments in *On War*, but more interestingly looks at how others have read (or misread) him. Paret (ed.), *Makers of Modern Strategy from Machiavelli to the Nuclear Age* (1986) is a reissue of a classic collection on the great strategists. Colin Gray, 'Clausewitz Rules, OK! The Future is the Past with GPS' (1999), is, in principle, a defence of Clausewitzian ideas; in practice, it is a somewhat intemperate attack on those authors unwise enough to think that one or two things might have changed since the beginning of the nineteenth century (including the present writer in the first edition of this book).

On the causes of war, two major studies stand out: Kenneth Waltz, *Man, the State and War* (1959); and its only equal, Hidemi Suganami, *On the Causes of War* (1996), an earlier, brief version of which is 'Bringing Order to the Causes of War Debate' (1990); Stephen Van Evera's *Causes of War: Power and the Roots of Conflict* (1999) is rightly highly regarded, but too much focused on the offensive/defensive realist debate for non-rational choice orientated readers – a short version is 'Offense, Defense and the Causes of War' (1998). The *International Security* reader, M. E. Brown *et al.*, *Offense, Defense and War* (2004b), is totally focused on the debate, but brings together most major scholarship (including Van Evera's shorter piece) to evaluate the positions. Other useful works include Geoffrey Blainey, *The Causes of War* (1988), and John G. Stoessinger, *Why Nations Go to War* (2005). Attempts to think about war in new terms can be found in Vincent Pouliot 'The Logic of Practicality: A Theory of Practice of Security Communities' (2008), and William Thompson, 'Systemic Leadership, Evolutionary Processes, and International Relations Theory: The Unipolarity Question' (2006). Taj Dingott Alkopher's 'The Social (and Religious) Meanings that Constitute War: The Crusade as Realpolitik vs. Socialpolitik' (2005) is a recent contribution to the debate over the social construction of the idea of war.

For more recent thinking on Just War and legal restraints on violence, see Adam Roberts and Richard Guelff (eds) *Documents on the Laws of War* (2000); Geoffrey Best, *War and Law since 1945* (1994); Michael Walzer, *Just and Unjust Wars* (2000) and *Arguing about War* (2004); Terry Nardin (ed.), *The Ethics of War and Peace* (1996); looking specifically at justice in the War on Terror, Jean Bethke Elshtain, *Just War Against Terror: The Burden of American Power in a Violent World* (2004); and Mark Evans (ed.), *Just War Theory: A Reappraisal* (2005). Further reflections on the legality and legitimization of war can be found in the *Review of International Studies* forum on 'Force and Legitimacy in World Politics' (2006); Shirley Scott and Olivia Ambler's 'Does Legality Really Matter? Accounting for the Decline in US Foreign Policy Legitimacy Following the 2003 Invasion of Iraq' (2007); and Marieke De Goede's 'The Politics of Preemption and the War on Terror in Europe' (2008), which highlights a continued European trend towards the legalization of war and intervention. Related debates about intervention and preventative war, especially in light of the 'War on Terror' are also relevant to the issues discussed here, see Wolf-Dieter Eberwein and Bertrand Badie 'Prevention and Sovereignty: A Vision and Strategy for a New World Order?' (2006); Michael Doyle, *Striking First: Preemption and Prevention in International Conflict* (2008); and Robert Lieber's *The American Era: Power and Strategy for the 21st Century* (2007).

Wider reflections on the changing nature of warfare are to be found from a number of sources, some 'academic', some not: a selection of recent books that raise serious questions about the nature of war and its shape in the future would include John Keegan, *The Face of Battle* (1978); Jean Bethke Elshtain, *Women and War* (1987); Victor Davis Hanson, *The Western Way of War: Infantry Battle in Classical Greece* (1989); James Der Derian, *Antidiplomacy: Spies, Terror, Speed and War* (1992) and *Virtuous War: Mapping the Military–Industrial–Media–Entertainment Network* (2001); Alvin and Heidi Toffler, *War and Anti-War* (1993); Christopher Coker, *War in the Twentieth Century* (1994), *War and the Illiberal Conscience* (1998) and *Humane Warfare: The New Ethics of Post-Modern War* (2001); and Michael Ignatieff, *Virtual War* (2000). Ignatieff focuses on the Kosovo campaign of 1999 – interesting military strategic analyses of that conflict are Daniel A. Byman and Matthew C. Waxman, 'Kosovo and the Great Air Power Debate' (2000), and Barry Posen, 'The War for Kosovo: Serbia's Political Military Strategy' (2000), both from *International Security*. Michael E. O'Hanlon, 'A Flawed Masterpiece' (2002), is interesting on the Afghanistan campaign; while John Keegan, *The Iraq War* (2004) conveys the military side of the 2003 Iraq war very well; and Rick Fawn and Raymond Hinnebusch (eds.) *The Iraq War: Causes and Consequences* (2006) is a more recent study. Further consideration on the changing nature of war include Andrew Hurrell's *On Global Order: Power, Values and the Constitution of International Society* (2007), and Tarak Barkawi's *Globalization and War* (2005); the latter's edited volume with Mark Laffrey, *Democracy, Liberalism and War* (2001) is an important critique of the Democratic Peace. Norrin Ripsman and T.V. Paul 'Globalization and the National Security State: A Framework for Analysis' (2005) and Sven Chojnacki 'Anything New or More of the Same? Wars and Military Interventions in the International System, 1946–2003' (2006) both examine the idea that the nature of war is changing radically. Philip Bobbitt's magisterial *Terror And Consent* (2008) builds on his equally authoritative *The Shield of Achilles* (2002) to present a compelling picture of the clash between states of terror and states of consent in a world where 'market states' are coming to dominate.

Chapter 7

Global Governance

Introduction: sovereignty, anarchy and global governance

Anarchy is basic to state-centric International Relations because *sovereignty* is basic to state-centric International Relations. As Hinsley and others have demonstrated, 'sovereignty' emerged in the sixteenth and seventeenth centuries as a double-headed notion (Hinsley 1966). On the one hand, rulers were sovereign in so far as they accepted no internal, 'domestic' equals; while on the other, they were sovereign in so far as they accepted no external, 'international' superiors. This notion gained normative acceptance in the second half of the seventeenth century – conventionally, following the Westphalia Peace Treaties that ended the Thirty Years' War – and remains the base upon which the structures of anarchy are constructed. The extent to which the norms of Westphalia have governed international practice is debatable; the Westphalia notion of sovereignty may indeed, as Krasner suggests, be a matter of 'organized hypocrisy', given the extent to which rulers have actually always intervened in each others affairs, but, at least in principle, the claim to be a sovereign entails acknowledgement of the sovereignty of others (Krasner 1999; Kratochwil 1995).

In any event, the absence of an external superior implies the absence of 'government', which is the definition of anarchy. This is clear enough, but it does involve glossing over the distinction between sovereignty as a *juridical status* and a *political concept*. On the one hand, to say of a state that it is sovereign is to make a judgement about its legal position in the world, namely that it recognizes no legal superior; that it is not, for example, a colony or part of a suzerain system. On the other hand, to say that a state is sovereign generally implies that it possesses certain sorts of capacities; the ability to act in certain ways, to perform certain tasks. One essential difference between these two meanings of sovereignty is that the first is unqualified – states either are, or are not, legally sovereign – while the second clearly involves matters of degree; that is, both the tasks themselves can be added to and subtracted from without losing the basic idea, and the manner in which they are performed can be more or less effective. On the one hand we have sovereignty as a *status*, which states either possess or do not possess; and on the other, we have sovereignty as a *bundle of powers and capacities* that can become larger or smaller.

This distinction was of no great significance in the early years of the 'Westphalia System', because the powers that states exercised were limited in scope and range. Tax collection and 'pacification' – the establishment of law and order – were the main domestic activities of states, and warfare and imperialism the main external activities; here, differential capabilities were most striking, but this in no sense undermined the idea of anarchy – indeed, as Kenneth Waltz insists, a key feature of anarchy is that the units in an anarchical system try to perform the same functions with different capabilities (Waltz 1979). However, once it became accepted that among the functions of a sovereign state are the achievement of certain kinds of social goals, and the successful regulation, if not actual management, of the economy, the situation does change quite dramatically, because it is clear that exercising these powers effectively might well, in some circumstances, be impossible without external co-operation and a degree of *pooling* of sovereignty. Thus, to take a very simple example, one of the 'powers' a state has is the power to set up a postal service – but such a service will be of limited value unless it is possible to send and receive letters across state boundaries, and to arrange this effectively states have had to give up certain powers to an international body, originally the Universal Postal Union of 1874. The bundle of powers that a state possesses as a 'sovereign' body is thereby simultaneously diminished *and* enhanced – the state now has the capacity to set up an effective postal system, but it buys this capacity by giving up part of its capacity to regulate this system. Paradoxically, to be truly sovereign it may be necessary to surrender part of one's sovereignty.

Another way of putting the same point is that the 'fit' between state and society/economy has altered since the beginning of the Westphalia System. Initially, social policy was minimal, and economic activity was, for the most part, agricultural, local and small-scale. However, with the coming of manufacturing and the factory system, and recognition that efficiency gains – economies of scale – could be achieved via production for a wider market, the range and scope of economic activity expanded, and with it the possibilities for social policy. The first consequence here was a step up in the optimum size of states; Britain and France created 'single markets' by removing local obstacles to trade, while Germany moved from being a customs union to a single state. However, the needs of the new societies went beyond these steps, and gradually, from the 1860s onwards, regulatory international bodies were established: the International Telegraphic Union of 1865; the establishment of an International Bureau of Weights and Measures in 1875; and the International Labour Office in 1901 (Murphy 1994). In the twentieth century, the League and UN systems accelerated the institutionalization of functional co-operation, and institutions such as the IMF, the World Bank and the WTO attempted to regulate ever-wider areas of state activity. Each of these new institutions grew out of the exercise of sovereign powers, but each constituted a diminution of sovereignty, in the sense that here we have powers that can only be exercised effectively by a degree of pooling of sovereignty.

Moreover, this process of institutionalized regulation does not simply involve the new social and economic forces of the last two centuries. It is also the case that the most basic external capacity of the state – the capacity to make war – is now regulated, albeit somewhat ineffectively, in a way that would have been difficult to believe 150 years ago. The various Hague and Geneva Conventions, the legal restraints of the UN Charter, and the emergence of customary restraints on the employment of force do place some inhibitions on the use of military power. In short, what these reflections suggest is that, although the world lacks government (because states have been unwilling to surrender their *juridical* status as sovereign) their attempts to rule effectively and exercise their *political* sovereignty have created extensive networks of global 'governance' – a somewhat archaic word that was originally synonymous with government, but which has been pressed into service as a convenient term for the collective impact of the various disparate quasi-governmental institutions that have proliferated (internally and externally) over the last century or more (Rosenau and Czempial 1992). In this chapter, the basic institutional framework of global governance will be examined, along with some theories of international co-operation – functionalism, neo-functionalism, federalism, regime theory and collective security.

One final caveat; the relevance of 'global governance' varies quite dramatically from issue to issue, and from one part of the world to another. It would be a mistake to see the growth of global governance as a steady process encroaching on all areas of international life and all regions of the world. There are many parts of the world where a savage Hobbesian realism is the most accurate way of theorizing politics, both domestic and international, and there are some aspects of international politics where no states have proved willing to give up their sovereign prerogatives. In short, and to reiterate an earlier point, global *governance* is not the same thing as global *government* – and much less, responsible and representative government; the extent to which the world as a whole is orderly and norm-governed should never be exaggerated.

Functionalism

Federalist ideas can be dated back at least to the peace projects of the eighteenth century, and thus, strictly speaking, are the earliest attempts to reach an understanding of the growth of international institutions; however, there are good reasons for beginning this survey with an examination of *function-*

alism. Functionalism is the most elaborate, intellectually sophisticated and ambitious attempt yet made not only to understand the growth of international institutions, but also to plot the trajectory of this growth into the future, and to come to terms with its normative implications. It is an original set of ideas, parallel in scope to realism, but, unlike realism, it has little contact with past diplomatic tradition. While one figure, David Mitrany, could reasonably claim to be the originator of functionalism, his account of the world has been taken up and employed in case studies and theoretical work by scholars such as Joseph Nye, Ernst Haas, J. P. Sewell, Paul Taylor, A. J. R. Groom and, in a rather idiosyncratic way, by John Burton and theorists of *world society*, such as Christopher Mitchell and Michael Banks. Functionalism is certainly the most important approach to international institutions to have emerged in the twentieth century – which is not to say that all its ideas, or even most of them, stand up to critical scrutiny.

The key to an understanding of functionalism is that while it offers an explanation for the past growth and future prospects of international institutions this is not its primary intention. Rather, it is an account of the conditions of peace. It emerged in the 1940s as a reaction to state-centric approaches to peace, such as federalism and collective security. Mitrany's insight was that these approaches failed not because the demands they made on states were too radical – the common criticism – but because they were not radical enough. Collective security leaves untouched the sovereign power of states to determine whether or not to respond to its imperatives; legally, states may be bound to act in certain ways but they retain the power to disregard legality when it suits them. Federalism on a world scale might create the conditions in which states are no longer capable of acting in this way, but, for precisely this reason, states are unwilling to federate. Both approaches fail because they attempt to work with the grain of sovereignty while producing results that go against the grain of sovereignty – a *frontal assault on juridical sovereignty that leaves political sovereignty intact is bound to fail.* Instead, Mitrany argued that a 'working peace system' could only be constructed from the bottom up, by encouraging forms of co-operation that bypassed the issue of formal sovereignty but instead gradually reduced the capacity of states to actually act as sovereigns (Mitrany 1966). Two formulas summarize the argument: 'form follows function' and 'peace in parts' (Nye 1971).

'Form follows function' collapses a number of propositions. First, co-operation will only work if it is focused on particular and specific activities ('functions') that are currently performed by states but would be performed more effectively in some wider context. Second, the form that such co-operation takes should be determined by the nature of the function in question – thus, for some functions, a global institution will be appropriate while for others regional, or even local, institutions are all that is necessary. Sometimes the exchange of information is all that is required; while in other cases power of decision may need to be vested with functional institutions. Workers' organizations and employers' groups should be concerned with labour standards; and doctors and health administrators with the eradication of disease. Each functional organization should be set up in such a way that it is appropriately designed to cope with its particular function.

'Peace in parts' describes the hoped-for collective outcome of these individual cases of functional co-operation. The functionalist model of sovereignty stresses the primacy of the political dimension of sovereignty described above. Sovereignty is a bundle of powers. As these powers are gradually shifted from the state to functional organizations, so, gradually, the capacity of the state to act as a sovereign will diminish. There is an element of political psychology involved here; the assumption is that the loyalty individuals give to states is a product of the things states do for them and, as other institutions take over the performance of particular activities, so loyalty will drain away. Moreover, the result of functional co-operation is not to create a new, larger and more effective state – instead, the territorial basis of the system will, itself, be undermined by the precept that form follows function. Gradually the territorial state will come to exercise fewer and fewer functions – states will become anomalous institutions attempting to be multi-functional and territorial in a world in which most of the business of governing and administration will be carried out by bodies that are functionally specific and non-territorial.

Mitrany's basic ideas have inspired a number of later theoretical works, and some very famous case studies, in particular, *Beyond the Nation State,* Ernst B. Haas's account of the International Labour Organization (ILO), and *Functionalism and World Politics,* J. P. Sewell's account of UNESCO (Haas 1964; Sewell 1966). Clearly, the 'functional agencies' of the United Nations system provide a range of possible case studies – though, for the most part, they breach the injunction that 'form follows function', being global bodies, largely dominated by states rather than the performers of functions. Functionalism has also influenced thinking on regional organizations, though, as the next section will suggest, only in a 'neo' form. The connection between functionalist ideas and Burton's notion of the 'cobweb' model of world society (Burton 1972) is clear, and acknowledged by writers such as Mitchell and Groom, if not by Burton himself. Accounts of the world economy that stress *globalization* owe much to functionalist thinking; similarly recent work on the *de-bordering* of states. In short, we have here a model of global governance that has quite widespread influence even if the full version of Mitrany's vision is subscribed to by very few. What are the problems with functionalism – why has it not been even more influential?

In a comment on Haas's famous study, the English realist F. S. Northedge remarked that the ILO is 'beyond the nation-state' in the same way that Trafalgar Square is beyond Charing Cross station. The meaning of this somewhat enigmatic remark is that, while the ILO with its tripartite structure of state, trade unions and employers' representatives is undoubtedly in a different place from (cf. spatially beyond) the nation-state, it can in no sense be said to have *transcended* that institution. An extremely elaborate network of institutions has emerged in the world but, contrary to the expectations of functionalists, the Westphalia System remains in place and sovereignty is undiminished as a guiding principle. It seems that the sovereign state has been able to ring fence functional co-operation, and isolate itself from the supposedly corrosive effects of functionalism. From a realist point of view, it is clear what has gone wrong; the political psychology of functionalism is misconceived. Loyalty to the state rests on two pillars. First, it is an affective phenomenon rather than purely instrumental; for many, the state represents the nation, and the nation is Edmund Burke's contract between generations past, present and future, a contract that rests on ties of birth, language, attachment to a territory, and a culture – and none of these are factors that can be diminished by functional co-operation across state boundaries. But second, in so far as loyalty is instrumental, it is the ability of the state to provide basic physical security that is the key, the ability to protect the people from outsiders – and the performance of this function is, literally under Mitrany's model, the last thing that governments will surrender.

It could be argued that this realist position rests on as implausible a view of political psychology as does functionalism: very few states are actually nations; most people are more in danger from their own governments than from foreigners; much of the time, 'loyalty' is coerced rather than freely given. However, behind the realist position lies a rather better general criticism of functionalism that rests on a less romantic view of the state. Mitrany – along with some at least of his successors – offered an essentially a-political account of functional co-operation. He approached problems with the soul of a technician. The underlying assumption is that the problems that functional co-operation is supposed to solve are essentially technical problems that admit to a technical solution. Administration can be divorced from politics – a very nineteenth-century, positivist view of the world, and one shared, for example, by John Burton, whose notion of 'systemic' problem-solving, as opposed to the non-systemic approach of states, rests on a similar distrust and marginalization of the political (Burton 1968).

The difficulty, of course, is that even the most technical of solutions to the most technical of problems will always have political implications, and will always have the potential to benefit one group and disadvantage another. The basic rule of the Universal Postal Union. which is that each state has an obligation to deliver international mail on its own territory, seems as purely technical a solution to the problem of an effective mail system as can be imagined, yet it has enormous political implications when it comes to issues such as the dissemination of political, religious or pornographic material through the mail. The gathering of information for effective weather forecasting seems innocuous, but will be resisted by closed societies. At the other extreme, no one needs to be reminded of the political implications of such matters as labour standards or the regulation of trade or international capital markets. All these examples of functional co-operation involve the distribution of gains and losses, a determination of who gets what, where and when. There are no technical problems, there are no technical solutions, and because of this, states are often very unwilling to allow problems to be dealt with 'functionally'. Thus it is that the state-centric nature of the functional agencies of the United Nations is not an accident. No major state has been willing to allow issues it regards as political to be dealt with in an allegedly non-political way, and even if any state were so willing it is moot whether their populations would be equally tolerant when the consequences became clear.

For this reason, the full-blown functionalist model of international co-operation has to be regarded as a failure. Still, no theory of similar range or scope has yet been produced, and some at least of the language of functionalism persists in other, less ambitious, but perhaps more successful, theories. Moreover, the functionalist opposition to the principle of territoriality strikes a chord in the context of an era of globalization in which new notions of political space are emerging.

Integration theory, federalism and neofunctionalism

Functionalism looks to the creation of a new world order, in which the sovereign state takes a back seat. By way of contrast, integration theory looks to the creation of new states by the integration of existing states, generally on a regional basis and possibly, in the long run, to the creation of a single world state. Since 1945, the most important testing ground for ideas on integration has been Europe, thus the following discussion of *federalism* and *neofunctionalism* takes a European focus – however, it should be remembered that most of the godfathers of the European process saw this as a stepping stone towards, in perhaps the very long run, the integration of the world.

In the immediate post-war world, many of the leaders of Western Europe, concerned to avoid a third European war, looked to the creation of a United States of Europe – a federal, or perhaps confederal, arrangement in which the sovereignty of its members would be suppressed. Some early institutions – in particular the Council of Europe – represented this aspiration in embryonic form, but it became clear in the course of the 1940s that a direct assault on the sovereignty of European states would not succeed; a fact that was finally confirmed by the failure of plans for a European Defence Union (EDU), scuppered by the French National Assembly in 1954. Instead, the founding fathers of European integration – Monnet, de Gasperi and Schuman – drew on some functionalist ideas, and on the experience of American aid under the Marshall

Plan, to chart a different route to European unity. Functionalists look to undermine state sovereignty from below, by stripping away the powers of the state piecemeal, salami-style: in the Committee for European Economic Co-operation – later to become the Organisation for Economic Co-operation and Development (OECD) – which was set up to distribute Marshall Aid, the European recipients were obliged to produce common plans for this distribution. The result of combining this strategy with that experience was a route to European *political* unity that went via European *economic* unity – hence the formation of the European Coal and Steel Community (ECSC) in 1952, and of Euratom and the European Economic Community (EEC) in 1956. These three institutions were later solidified as the European Community (EC), now rebranded as the European Union (EU).

These were, and are, unique organizations. While in formal terms much of the decision-making power in the EU rests with state representatives in the Council of Ministers, the European Commission, a body of appointed bureaucrats has the capacity to initiate policy, the European Court is empowered to decide many intra-Community disputes, and, more recently, a directly-elected European Parliament has some significant powers that it can employ independent of state control. These institutions taken together mean that the (current) twenty-seven member states and 400 million citizens of the Union are taking part in a unique process of international institutional co-operation.

How is this process to be understood? It clearly differs from the functionalist notions of Mitrany and his collaborators in two key respects. In the first place, the intention was – and is – to create a new *state* via international institution-building; the end result has always been intended to be the (con)federal Europe that could not be created by direct action. While politicians in some parts of the community, especially Britain and Scandinavia, may find it convenient to deny this aspiration, it remains central – though what federalism means in this context is contentious. In any event, the European institutions were not, and are not, designed on a 'form follows function' basis, hence the opposition of many integrationists to the quasi-functionalist principle of a 'two- (or n-) speed Europe' in which different parts of the Union integrate at different rates.

Perhaps even more important is the second difference from functionalism. As with functionalism, the aim was that institutional co-operation would expand as states discovered that co-operation in one area led naturally to co-operation in another; the difference is that, in the European system, this expansion (or 'spillover') is, and was intended to be, an overtly *political* process. The abolition of internal tariffs between member countries creates a political demand to equalize as far as possible production and transport costs. The idea is that political parties and pressure groups will gradually come to put pressure on central institutions rather than 'local' governments. Whereas politics is the enemy of functionalism, it was meant to be the driving force of European integration.

These two departures from the functionalist model lead some writers to distil from the European experience an approach to integration they called *neofunctionalism,* which could provide a theoretical basis for other examples of integration in, for example, Africa or Latin America. It is important to put the matter this way round because sometimes the impression is given that Europe has been some kind of test for the neofunctionalist model. Not so – the idea that integration between states could come as a result of a politically driven process of spillover, the heart of neofunctionalism, was *drawn from* European experience rather than *applied to* it. In any event, regarded as a model, how does neofunctionalism fare? Not very well has to be the basic answer. The European experience has not proved to be exportable; other examples of integration have generally not followed the European (neofunctional) model. Moreover, even within Europe, the model clearly has not worked in any consistent way. Sometimes spillover has taken place, sometimes not. Some pressure groups have operated at the European level, others have not – it is striking, for example, that despite the obvious importance of the Common Agricultural Policy (CAP) and the extent to which CAP rulings are made in Brussels, farmers' organizations throughout the Union remain largely orientated towards putting pressure on their home governments rather than the central institutions. 'Functional autonomy' is the watchword here. It is also the case that direct elections to the European Parliament have not led to the emergence of genuinely European political divides; instead, electorates use these elections to pass judgement on their national governments. In short, European integration has proceeded by stops and starts rather than as a smooth process of spillover – and the factors that have, at different times, restarted the process have not followed any obvious pattern. Integration has taken place in ways and at speeds determined by the course of events, and not in accordance with any theoretical model. Later writers have stressed 'inter-governmentalism' – on this account, the process of integration is driven by interstate bargaining; particular problems emerge and are solved politically by state governments and not in accordance with any functional logic. However, intergovernmental bargaining could lead in some circumstances to a degree of 'pooling of sovereignty', and the emergence of 'policy networks' on a European scale may be responsible for some kinds of change. In particular, a number of writers have noted that the EU is often employed by national governments to promote policies that are deemed to be necessary by the political elite but are unpopular at home, which implies a kind of Europeanization of politics, if not the kind envisaged by the founders. In any event, it seems clear that the European experience really is *sui generis* and it may not be sensible to look here to find any general lessons about the processes of co-operation and international institution building.

However, before turning to the institutions of the global economy and the United Nations system, it may be worth returning briefly to the starting-point of the post-war European experience – the aspiration to create a 'Federal Europe', which has returned to a kind of prominence in recent years. A great deal of debate in Britain since the 1980s, and in particular since the creation of a single European currency in 1999 (the 'euro'), has centred on whether a federal Europe is desirable – an important issue, since the Maastricht Treaty of 1992 refers specifically to this ambition, and the abortive constitution for the Union of 2004 has a number of obviously federal features. Resistance to this step in the UK (and possibly elsewhere in Europe) is considerable. Part of the problem here rests in the fact that 'federalism' has different connotations in Britain from much of the rest of Europe, especially Germany. In Britain, federalism is seen as a process of *centralization* that takes power away from the regions (that is, the nation-states of Europe); in Germany, on the other hand, federalism is seen in the light of the movement from the Second and Third Reich to the Federal Republic of Germany – that is, as a process of *decentralization*. When continental politicians talk of a European Federation they do not have in mind the 'European Superstate' deplored by British Eurosceptics. What makes this issue very complex is that, on some accounts, the European Union is already a federal system. Murray Forsyth points out that the defining characteristic of a federal system is that the federal authority has some powers it can exercise effectively without reference to the lower levels and vice versa, and this is certainly the case within the European Union (Forsyth, in Brown 1994c: 56). The EU is a 'weak' federal system, but a federal system none the less. There may be a wider point here. There are in the world today quite a number of organizations that have some powers of this kind, including, on some interpretations, the United Nations itself, and it may be that the general unwillingness of analysts to use older categories such as 'federalism' to describe this situation is a mistake.

In any event, returning briefly to the EU, the proposed Constitution of 2004 did not survive the process of national ratifications. Referenda in France and the Netherlands rejected the Constitution, not because of its putative federalism, but, ironically in view of the above discussion, because of fears that the allegedly neo-liberal features of the document, allegedly inserted by the British with their East–Central European allies, would undermine the social model upon which these states are built. The rejection by these two leading European countries also reflected fears about EU expansion, and in particular Dutch resistance to the proposed membership of Turkey. The Constitution was then withdrawn, but a very similar document without the pretensions of its predecessor was promulgated, only to be holed beneath the waterline by a referendum in Ireland in 2008; a similar result could certainly have been anticipated in the UK and perhaps elsewhere, had not the low-key nature of the new document allowed governments to argue, rather implausibly, that it differed substantially from a 'Treaty' and therefore did not need popular as opposed to parliamentary approval. It is incontestable that some institutional changes are needed to cope with the expansion of the EU – the current 27-person Commission is too large to be effective, and the voting arrangements in the Council and size of representation in the Parliament need to be addressed – but it seems clear that the European public is unwilling to sign up to a new grand statement of the European ideal. Most probably, these problems will have to be addressed piecemeal; in a way, this reflects the success of the EU – EU politics are no longer dominated by grand gestures; instead, they have become routinized.

Global economic institutions: Bretton Woods and after

In terms of global governance and the undermining of sovereignty, the EU is the most ambitious of contemporary international institutions, but on the world scene, an almost equally impressive set of institutions exists. Some historical background is necessary here. Before 1914, the world economy was nominally 'self-regulating'; in practice, British economic power provided a degree of actual regulation but most countries were on the gold standard, which meant no elaborate international monetary institutions were necessary and trade was relatively free, in accordance with the dictates of economic liberalism (to be discussed further in the next chapter). This economy collapsed under the strain of war – with most of the participants imposing physical controls on exports and imports, and going off the gold standard, ending the direct link between their currencies and the price of gold – but the intention was that this would be temporary and that the old liberal international economy would be re-established after the war was over. This proved impossible, and after a brief interlude of prosperity in the 1920s, the Wall Street Crash of 1929 and bank failures in Europe in 1930 and 1931, virtually all countries introduced high levels of protection for their trade, and extensive monetary controls.

The leader of the old system, Britain, left the gold standard for good in 1931, and in 1932 established a system of Imperial Preferences, at last abandoning free trade and following the lead of the highly protectionist Hawley–Smoot Tariff, which the United States Congress had passed in 1929. Between 1929 and 1933, trade crashed world-wide, declining by the latter year to less than a quarter by value of its 1929 figure. The Great Depression of the 1930s was trade-led – unlike, for example, the recessions of the 1980s, when trade actually increased year on year, even when overall output fell. When recovery began in the 1930s it was on the basis of trade blocs – the Dollar Area, the Sterling Area, the Gold Franc Area and so on – and with much resort to bartering, usually on a basis that reflected political power rather than economic advantage, as with some of the barters arranged by the Nazis in the late 1930s whereby, say, Romania would be obliged to exchange its oil for cuckoo clocks and other inessentials. In the collective memory of the world capitalist system, this whole period was a disaster, and it remains the case that the distant memory of the Great Depression is one of the factors that promotes co-operation in the world economy today.

On some accounts, it was a lack of leadership that produced the depression – Britain no longer had the ability to lead, and the United States did not have the will. In any event, by the mid-1930s the United States was already taking the initiative at international trade conferences, and with the coming of the war and the establishment of the United States as the arsenal of democracy and the world's leading financial power, America was in a position to determine the future shape of the world economy, along with its now junior partner, Britain. The US view was that it was the failure of the old liberal order that led to war, and thus it was absolutely essential to re-establish that order after the war ended – this involved a commitment to free trade (or at least the replacement of physical controls and trade blocs by tariffs) and the restoration of convertible currencies by the abolition of currency blocs and exchange controls. The British disagreed; led by John Maynard Keynes, the radical economist of the 1930s and a convinced protectionist, who was now Lord Keynes and a Treasury insider with great influence on policy, they were no longer free-trade-orientated, and were committed to the Sterling Area. But US economic power was, in the last resort, too great to be resisted – ironically, since the US wished, in principle, to remove power considerations from institutional arrangements. As noted above with respect to functionalism, this is rarely possible, and never when it comes to core economic matters.

Along with a number of minor players, the British and Americans met at Bretton Woods, New Hampshire, in 1944 to negotiate the shape of the post-war economic order, which thus became known as the *Bretton Woods System* (BWS). The BWS met American notions in several ways. In the first place, attempts were made to 'de-politicize' the international economy by dividing up the various international issues among separate institutions. Thus an International Trade Organization (ITO) would handle trade matters, a World Bank would handle capital movements, and an International Monetary Fund (IMF) would deal with international money and balance-of-payments crises. These separate institutions would be functional agencies of the UN but isolated as far as possible from the Security Council and other UN bodies dealing with 'political' affairs; indeed, in practice, the UN has had no effective control over these organs. Moreover, the new institutions were to be run by boards of directors and managing directors who, while appointed by states (in proportion to their relative economic strength – no question of 'one state, one vote' here), would have fixed terms of office and would be expected to act as functionaries rather than as political representatives. The emphasis would be on technical solutions to technical problems.

In the second place, these organs were to be regulatory rather than managerial. Thus the World Bank would not have funds of its own beyond a small amount of working capital, but would raise money commercially that it would then lend on to states at commercial rates to supplement private loans and intergovernmental dealings. The IMF would not be a world-wide central bank with the capacity to create international money (as Keynes had proposed) but a regulatory body designed to police a set of rules that required convertibility and national action to defend exchange rates. The IMF would help states to deal with balance-of-payments crises, but it would also lay down conditions for its help, thereby policing the policies of its members. The ITO would monitor the trade policies of its members, ensuring that the rules limiting quotas and promoting tariff reductions were enforced, though in the event it would be nearly fifty years before the World Trade Organization (WTO) was finally established in 1995, and in the meantime a more limited General Agreement on Tariffs and Trade (GATT) performed this function.

In the immediate post-war period it was impossible to bring these institutions on line. No country in the 1940s was able to compete with the United States, the home of over half of the capitalist world's industrial production. In practice, what led to the reconstruction of the capitalist world economy and a generation of prosperity was the Cold War. Marshall Aid, the European Recovery Programme, transferred some US$15 billion in grants to Europeans and the Japanese – far more capital and on easier terms than Keynes had envisaged in his schemes – but it operated explicitly as a response to the threat of communism. Without such a spur there was no possibility that Congress would have passed such a generous programme. The attempt to de-politicize international economic relations stood revealed as a pious hope rather than a reality. In any event, for two decades after the early 1950s the world economy experienced unprecedented growth and prosperity. This growth was concentrated heavily in Europe and Japan, but even Britain and the United States grew steadily, and growth rates in what was coming to be called the Third World were high, although often undermined by rising populations. By the end of the 1950s, most of the leading economies had re-established currency convertibility, and the GATT 'rounds' of tariff negotiations were well under way. Going into the 1960s, the system seemed to be working pretty well, albeit not quite as originally intended.

However, in the 1960s, crisis followed crisis for the BWS, and by 1973 – when the attempt to work with fixed currency rates was abandoned – it is widely regarded as having, to all intents and purposes, ceased to exist. Partly this was because of continual currency crises; the system worked via 'reserve currencies' (the dollar and, to a much lesser extent the pound sterling) which had somehow to be made widely available for use by third parties without this undermining the issuing countries. Squaring this particular circle remains impossible, hence the current system of floating exchange rates. The decline of Bretton Woods was also a function of the rise of new economic actors, to be discussed in Chapters 8 and 9. Still, despite the Bretton Woods *System* going into abeyance, the Bretton Woods *institutions* remain in existence, finding new roles.

The new roles of the IMF and World Bank are largely orientated towards the developing world; instead of handling the short-term currency and capital needs of the developed world, these two institutions have gradually become responsible for promoting growth in the so-called 'South'. Their role in this respect has been deeply controversial. IMF 'conditionality' – the terms under which assistance is given to borrowers – is widely regarded as incorporating advice that is inappropriate and burdensome for developing economies, and similar kinds of criticisms have been levelled at the World Bank and the WTO. Whereas genuine free trade might be to the advantage of the developing world, the unwillingness of the advanced industrial countries to liberalize trade in agriculture in particular is a source of deep resentment. In any event, the South has created its own global economic institutions. A key date here is 1964, which saw the formation of both the United Nations Conference on Trade and Development (UNCTAD) and the Group of 77. UNCTAD was a body set up by the UN to hold regular conferences on trade issues as they affected the South. Unlike the IMF or World Bank, UNCTAD works on a one-state, one-vote basis, thereby maximizing the key advantage held by the South in international forums – their sheer weight of numbers. The same is true, incidentally, of the WTO, where, with good leadership, such as that provided by Rwanda for African states in the Doha Round negotiations since July 2004, the South can exercise a great deal of power, and where major Third-World countries such as Brazil and India have real clout. The Group of 77 was the group of 'less-developed countries' that pressed for UNCTAD in the UN – which, given the pace of decolonization, more-or-less immediately had more than 77 members, but still retained the name. These groupings still have a certain amount of symbolic significance, but it is worth noting that in actual negotiations, such as the current Doha Round at the WTO, things are more complex than the simple division into North and South would suggest. India, China and Brazil, for example, have interests that differ from those of the rest of the South and from each other, and the actual processes of coalition building cross the boundaries of all these informal groups.

As well as all these formal institutions, economic decision-making also takes place in other forums such as the G8 – annual meetings of the heads of government of the leading industrial powers – via UN Conferences on particular big issues, smaller-scale local trade agreements, policy networks, and informal meeting-places of the rich and influential such as Davos and Bilderberg. For this reason it makes sense to think of the governance of international economic relations – and perhaps other, social areas – in terms that go beyond the merely institutional; in terms, that is, of *regimes*.

International regimes and regime theory

The notion of an international regime emerged out of the complex interdependence model of international relations of the 1970s, and became a prime focus of debate between neoliberals and neorealists in the 1980s. For once, there is a generally-accepted (albeit slightly contentious) definition of a *regime*, stating that it is a set of 'implicit or explicit principles, norms, rules and decision-making procedures around which actors' expectations converge in a given area of international relations' (Krasner 1983: 2). To illustrate, consider the current trade regime using Krasner's expansions of the key terms.

The *principles* ('beliefs of fact, causation and rectitude') upon which the trade regime is built are that trade is good, free trade is better than controlled trade, and free trade promotes peace. These principles constitute the 'embedded liberalism' of the trade regime, and they exist in the background even when contrary practices are sanctioned. The *norms* ('standards of behaviour defined in terms of rights and obligations') of the regime give these principles some practical content. Thus, for example, it is a norm that if it is not possible for trade to be free, tariffs are a better mechanism for restraint of trade than physical quotas because they cause less interference in the market and are less discriminatory in impact. The *rules* ('specific prescriptions or proscriptions for action') of the trade regime set out in detail what these norms imply, and set out the sanctioned exceptions to these norms; they are to be found in the WTO Charter, in the Multi-Fibre Arrangement (MFA) and in various other legal and quasi-legal documents. The *decision-making procedures* ('prevailing practices for making and implementing collective choice') in this case focus on meetings of the WTO, the conference diplomacy of bodies such as UNCTAD, and, at a different level, on the trade dispute procedures set out in the WTO Charter.

Principles, norms, rules and decision-making procedures may be *explicit* or *implicit*. Explicit rules are written down somewhere, while implicit rules are understood without being written down. Thus, for example, 'customs unions' and 'free trade areas' such as the European Union and the North American Free Trade Area are explicitly licensed even though clearly discriminatory, while 'voluntary export restraints' (VERs) are implicitly accepted. VERs are agreements whereby one party promises to limit exports to the other; such restraints are discriminatory and breach the norms and principles of the trade regime, but are acceptable because of the fiction that they are voluntary, a fiction that everyone goes along with, for their own reasons. This is a case of an 'implicit' rule of the trade regime and it is every bit as important as the explicit rules set out in the various treaties that establish the regime.

'Around which actors' expectations converge' – here we come to the heart of the matter. The 'actors' in world trade – firms, states and individual consumers – have expectations about the principles, norms, rules and decision-making procedures that will apply in this area, and if these expectations converge, there is a regime, but if not, not. 'Converge' is a word deliberately chosen to avoid the idea that expectations have to be exactly the same (which, much of the time, they clearly are not) or that rules will always be obeyed (which, equally clearly, will not always be the case). Instead, 'expectations converge' suggests that most of the time the actors will have similar expectations and most of the time they will be fulfilled – thus, for example, there is a degree of predictability and regularity about trade matters that is appreciably greater than would be expected in the absence of a regime.

Regimes are clearly seen as part of global governance, but it should be noted that, despite the importance of the WTO in the trade case, they represent a clear break from the emphasis on institutions characteristic of the BWS. The WTO is important, but so are other institutions such as UNCTAD and the MFA, and informal 'institutions' based on implicit rules may be as important as, or more important than, the official bodies. Regime theory emerges out of the neoliberal theory of International Relations; that is, its root assumption is that states – and, for that matter, firms – are rational egoists operating in an anarchical system. How are regimes possible? That is, how is co-operation possible among rational egoists under anarchy? From a neoliberal perspective, it is not too difficult to see why states (and firms) would want to co-operate: there are absolute gains to be had from co-operation – that is, from mutual adjustments; and on neoliberal assumptions, states are concerned to make absolute gains. The problem is that the temptation to cheat may be overwhelming. States will continually be placed in a situation where it is in their interests that co-operation takes place, but even more in their interests that the cost of co-operation be carried by others. This is a classic collective action problem. In domestic societies, one of the roles of government is to solve problems of collective action by enforcing compliance with a system of rules that are, in principle, in the common interest. By definition, no such solution is available internationally – so how do states set up regimes in the first place; and why do these regimes persist to the extent they do? The most influential explanation for this phenomenon is the theory of *hegemonic stability*.

An important early statement of the theory of hegemonic stability is that of Charles Kindleberger in the final chapter of his economic history of the 1930s, *The World in Depression 1929–1939* (1973). In examining explanations for the Great Depression, he tells the basic story as follows: the international economic system before 1914 was not, as it was usually taken to be, self-regulating. Instead, the hegemonic financial power of Great Britain, exercised by the quasi-autonomous Bank of England, had been employed to smooth over problems of co-operation generated by the operation of the gold standard. Britain had had the *capacity* to do this, given its enormous holdings of overseas capital. It had also had the *will* to do this, because, as the largest financial power, it had the biggest stake in the preservation of the system. Its role as the hegemon was widely, albeit tacitly, accepted as *legitimate* by other members of the system. Capacity, will and legitimacy need to be found in one country if the system is to work. In the 1930s they were not, and the system collapsed. But, after 1945 a new hegemonic economic power emerged: the United States.

The USA had the capacity to provide hegemonic leadership, the will to do so and, because of the poverty of the rest of the capitalist world, and their fear of the Soviet Union, American leadership was widely accepted. Thus it was that the post-war institutional structure was underwritten by the power of the USA, which largely obeyed the rules itself, but was able, because of its basic strength, to turn a blind eye to infractions of the rules by other states, if by so doing it was able to preserve the system. Thus the hegemonic power of the United States was able to act as a kind of substitute for international government, but without violating the basic assumption of rational egoism; the US performs this role because it is in its interests to do so. As the country with the largest stake in the preservation of the system, it is willing to act in accordance with the rules and to bear most of the transaction costs of running the system, not as an act of altruism but on the basis of enlightened, medium-term self-interest (Ikenberry 2001).

However, hegemonic leadership is a wasting asset that creates the conditions for its own downfall. The hegemon is required to play fair, but its rivals are not so hampered. They will use the regime set up by the hegemon to the full, taking advantage of access to the hegemon's market, but relying on the hegemon not to overreact to their own measures to prevent its access to *their* markets. Gradually, the material basis on which hegemony rests will be eroded and the hegemon will cease to have the capacity to act as such – instead, it will itself start to play fast and loose with the formal rules, and, as a result, will lose legitimacy. In the end, it will be perceived by other members of the system as acting solely in its own interests; this, it is suggested, is more or less what has happened to US economic hegemony since the 1950s – gradually its trade rivals out-produced it, partly because it was hampered in its actions by its responsibilities, and the USA then became liable to succumb to the temptation to act on the short-term basis of self-interest – financing the Vietnam War by inflation rather than taxation, for example.

The good news is that regimes may well survive 'after hegemony' (Keohane 1984). The hard work of setting up regimes has been done, and the remaining task is the easier one of keeping them ticking over. The very fact that rules are written down and thus institutionalized makes it more likely that states will abide by them, while the institutions can provide a great deal of useful information that will prevent states acting against their own interests. The hypothesis is that most of the time when states act as free riders it is either because they do not believe they will be found out, or because they do not appreciate the longer-term consequences of their actions. The existence of institutions makes it unlikely that either position will hold, which creates an incentive to co-operate. Thus it is that co-operation can continue – but at 'sub-optimal' levels by comparison with the co-operation that can be generated by a hegemon. Before leaving behind the notion of a regime, it is worth noting that the issue of hegemonic stability arises as it does partly because the 'Krasner' definition of a regime given above is so closely connected to main-stream American rational choice IR. Other notions of a 'regime', associated particularly with European scholars and the constructivist turn in IR theory, place more emphasis on the ideational component of regimes, rather than the rational egoism of social choice theory – thus co-operation may be sustained because states come to believe that it constitutes a good in itself rather than simply because it is in their immediate or even medium-term interest to co-operate, and the need for some kind of mechanism to enforce co-operation may be less compelling (Rittberger 1993; Hasenclever *et al.* 1997, 2000).

Global governance and (collective) security

As suggested at some length in previous chapters, issues of security and inse-curity have always been at the heart of the anarchy problematic, and it might have been expected that a chapter on global governance would begin by addressing these issues directly and substantively, rather than by examining regional co-operation and economic governance. The 'Peace Project' designers of the eighteenth century would have expected this, as would most theorists of international organization in the 1920s and 1930s, who regarded the design and re-design of the League of Nations as their primary task. Even after 1945, the 'world peace through world law' movement continued to think in terms of reform of the central security institution rather than the indirect approach to peace via functionalism and integration theory (Clark and Sohn 1966). In fact, it is clear that frontal assaults on sovereignty in bodies such as the League of Nations or the UN have been among the least successful inno-vations of the last hundred years – why is this? And has the record been quite as bad as this might suggest?

The most important twentieth-century attempt to change directly the way the world handles security issues was the doctrine of 'collective security' – the attempt to replace the 'self-help' balance-of-power system that prevailed before 1914 with a system that involved a commitment by each state to the security of every other state. We have already seen, in Chapter 2, the fate of this doctrine in the 1930s in the context of the theoretical debate between liberal internationalism and realism; a second 'take' on this failure, concentrating more on the institutional side, and carrying the story through to the post-1945 era, is now called for.

The formation of the League of Nations in 1919 emerged out of the contingencies of the First World War, and the United Nations was formed from the wreckage of the League at the end of the Second World War, but the roots of these institutions go much further back in the history of the European states system. 'Roots' in the plural is important here, because a central problem of these bodies has always been that they have attempted to institutionalize and fuse two quite separate traditions, with quite different normative approaches to the problem of international order and global governance – the tradition of the 'Peace Project' and the tradition of the 'Concert of Europe'.

The most famous 'Peace Project' was Kant's 'Perpetual Peace' of 1795, but while the phrase 'perpetual peace' was a commonplace among the creators of 'Peace Projects' in the seventeenth and eighteenth centuries, Kant's work was untypical of most others (Reiss 1970). The basic idea of these projects was clear, even though they differed markedly as to detail (Hinsley 1963). In order to overcome the scourge of war, the states of Europe would form a kind of parliament or federal assembly wherein disputes would be solved. Projectors differed as to such matters as voting mechanisms and enforcement procedures, but collective decision was central – states would no longer have the power to act as judges in their own cases. Impartial rules would be impartially applied to all. International relations would become a realm of law and not a realm of power – though the 'projectors' were suspicious of the international lawyers of the day, regarding them as, in Kant's phrase, 'sorry comforters'; that is, apologists for power politics and the rights of states.

The Concert of Europe was very different in approach. This notion emerged in the nineteenth century, initially via the medium of the formal congresses that dealt with the aftermath of the Napoleonic Wars, and later on a more informal basis. The idea of the Concert was that the Great Powers would consult and, as far as possible, co-ordinate policy on issues of common concern. The root idea was that great power brought with it great responsibility; managing the system in the common interest was something that the powers should do if they could – but, crucially, it should be noted that the 'common interest' was weighted towards the interests of the Great Powers themselves. Sometimes 'managing the system' might involve preserving a balance of power among the great at the expense of lesser players – as with the wholesale reorganizations of boundaries that took place after 1815. Sometimes, if the great powers were in conflict, it could not work at all, and Bismarck for one was wont to regard the notion of a European interest with disfavour. In any event, the Concert of Europe was, in no sense, an impartial body, dispensing impartial laws. If it worked at all, it worked partially, in the interests of order perhaps, of the Great Powers certainly.

Both of these traditions still exist at the beginning of the twenty-first century. Movements for institutional reform of the UN and global 'democratization' clearly draw on the tradition of peace projects, but, on the other hand, for example, the informal 'contact group' of the United States, Russia, Germany, France and Britain, which oversaw policy on the former Yugoslavia during the Bosnian war of the early 1990s, was clearly a (wider) reincarnation of the Concert of Europe, with a similar attitude to the rights of smaller countries, as the Bosnian government discovered to its cost. However, the actual institutions set up in the League of Nations and UN represent an uneasy and unsuccessful hybrid of both traditions.

Thus the doctrine of Collective Security draws on the universalism of the Peace Projects – one for all and all for one – but is meant to be operated by states which retain the power of deciding when the obligations of collective security are binding, unlike the institutions envisaged by most of the projectors. Moreover, collective security defends the status quo, with only a passing nod in the direction of mechanisms for peaceful change, while the peace projectors envisaged that their deliberative bodies would be able to bring about such change in a lawful manner. The Council of the League and the Security Council of the UN clearly reflect the idea of a Concert of Great Powers, but they also attempt to be representative of the rest of the system, and the norms the Security Council is supposed to enforce are norms that stress the equality of states, not their differentiation. As with the Concert, it has been tacitly recognized that the Councils would operate effectively only when there was consensus among the Great Powers. In the League, unanimity in the Council was required, with the exception of the interested parties, who, if they were unable to find any friends, generally responded to a negative vote by walking out, while in the UN the famous 'veto' for the five permanent members of the Security Council made such a walkout unnecessary. However, the universalism of the organizations has made it difficult for this prerequisite to be explicitly defended, and hence the persisting sense that the veto was some kind of mistake made in 1945, rather than an essential feature of the system. The (Security) Council has been expected to enforce the norms of collective security and universalism, while, in its very nature, it represents the alternative, Concert, tradition.

A great deal of the rather poor record of these global institutions since 1919 can be explained in terms of the contradictory impulses of these two traditions. In effect, the system works properly only when they both point in the same direction, which does happen sometimes, but obviously cannot be relied upon. The only clear-cut example of a collective security enforcement action occurred in Korea in 1950 as a result of the temporary absence of the Soviet Union (one of the veto powers) from the Security Council. Even in 1990, when universal principles and the interests of most of the Great Powers pointed in the same direction with respect to Iraq's invasion of Kuwait, the Coalition that enforced the law acted outside UN control, albeit with the sanction of a Security Council resolution. For a while after 1989 it seemed as if the UN Security Council could act as the Charter intended it to, but the revival of Russian power, and a more self-assertive China have removed what chance there was that consensus could frequently be generated, and the attempts by the Council to reach a common position on issues of potential breaches of the peace have usually failed.

Nevertheless, it is possible to exaggerate the extent to which the UN system as a whole has failed to address problems of security. As in the case of European integration, the failure of grand theory has been accompanied by quite a high degree of institutional and conceptual innovation. When, in the 1950s, the UN was stymied by the Cold War, the then Secretary General of the UN, Dag Hammarskjöld, invented the notion of 'preventive diplomacy' – proactive attempts to keep the Cold War out of particular areas – and, with others, pioneered the notion of 'peacekeeping' (the employment of troops in UN uniforms with a mandate to assist all sides in a conflict if they wished to be kept apart). The UN has also offered mediation services, truce observers, and a number of other 'good offices' that parties to a conflict could use. There can be little doubt that these innovations have been genuinely helpful in a number of cases – there have been sixty-three Peacekeeping Operations since 1948, with some twenty still current; very few have been totally successful, but almost all have made some positive contribution to world peace.

What is striking about these innovations is the way in which they combine the pragmatism of the Concert tradition with a 'politics from below' element that is universalist in origin. As with Concert politics, peacekeeping is, in the jargon of social work, 'non-judgemental'; the UN is able to act to help preserve order because it does not take sides, and does not concern itself with the rights and wrongs of the case. This refusal to judge is, of course, totally against the ethic of collective security, which rests crucially upon a willingness to identify the wrongdoer – and it is noticeable that the UN's attitude is often criticized by those who feel they can tell right from wrong: witness, for example, the resentment of the Bosnian government at the apparent willingness of the UN to treat Bosnian Serbs on a par with the 'legitimate' authority. However, the non-judgemental quality of the UN is much appreciated by many smaller member states, who fear that if judgement is to be the norm they are more likely to be in the dock than on the bench.

Preventive diplomacy and peacekeeping are not substitutes for collective security; they do not answer the basic question, which is whether it is possible for international institutions to take us beyond a realist, self-help system in matters of security. Functionalism tries to do this by undermining sovereignty directly, but has been no more successful than were the Peace Projects of the eighteenth century. The attraction of collective security was that it did not try to undermine state sovereignty as such; rather, it attempted to get sovereign powers to support a wider interest than merely national concerns. In the formal sense it failed: there have been very few cases that have been overtly collective security operations – however, in an informal sense, some elements of a collective security system do seem to have taken hold. The closest analogy to an informal collective security system may be the old English common law idea of a *posse comitatus* – men called out by the sheriff to assist in the enforcing of the law, a notion which encompasses both medieval England and the 'posse' of Western movie fame. Something like this seems to be the best way of looking at the Gulf War of 1990–1. A group of states acted together to expel Iraq from Kuwait – the Coalition as posse – and the lawfulness of this action was attested to not by the presence of a sheriff, but by a positive vote of the UN Security Council. In 1995, the posse – this time in the guise of NATO – intervened in Bosnia to create a 'level killing-field' (again with the approval, but not under the command, of the UN), while in 1999 the NATO posse operated in Kosovo without the approval of the UN Security Council (albeit without its opposition either). In 2003, a much attenuated posse invaded Iraq, this time very much against majority opinion in the UN.

In the realm of security, the most important task that global institutions can perform today is not to solve problems, but to give – or withhold – their blessing to those who can and do act. The UN's role comes close to that of the medieval papacy, rewarding an enterprise with its blessing – not really something those in power actually need, but something that they feel better for none the less. When they do not receive the blessings of UN approval, powerful states may act in any case , if they believe this to be the right thing to do, or if their interests are crucially involved – but, as the examples of Kosovo and a fortiori Iraq 2003 illustrate, action without UN approval can generate deep unease. Legitimacy is important to all international actors, and when it comes to the use of force, the UN is a, if not *the*, major source of legitimacy. These issues will be investigated further in Chapter 11, when the notion of humanitarian intervention in defence of human rights will be examined.

Further reading

Anne-Marie Slaughter, *A New World Order* (2004), is a comprehensive account of the global networks that constitute the global governance of today's world. and Michael Barnett and Martha Finnemore, *Rules for the World* (2004) argues against the rationalist mainstream. J. N. Rosenau and E. O. Czempial (eds), *Governance without Government: Order and Change in World Politics* (1992) is a useful collection providing an overview of the subject. An earlier collected volume by the same editors, Czempial and Rosenau, *Global Changes and*

Theoretical Challenges (1989), contains a number of articles prefiguring the approach, including a valuable critique by Richard Ashley, 'Imposing International Purpose: Notes on a Problematic of Government' (1989a). Craig Murphy, *International Organization and Industrial Change: Global Governance since 1850* (1994), gives an historical perspective. An official view from the UN is *Our Global Neighborhood: Report of the Commission on Global Governance* (1995). Readings on international political economy (Chapter 8) and globalization (Chapter 9) are generally relevant. The *International Relations* forum 'Rethinking the Rules' (2006) is a good introduction to the role of rules in global governance. Klaus Dingwerth and Philipp Pattberg, 'Global Governance as a Perspective on World Politics' (2006) offers an overview of global governance as a concept and looks into its broader application.

On 'functionalism', David Mitrany's writings are central: see *A Working Peace System* (1966) and *The Functional Theory of Politics* (1975). A. J. R. Groom and Paul Taylor (eds), *Functionalism: Theory and Practice in World Politics* (1975), is an excellent collection, and other collections by the same editors are highly relevant: Taylor and Groom (eds), *International Organization: A Conceptual Approach* (1978); Groom and Taylor (eds), *The Commonwealth in the 1980s* (1984); Groom and Taylor (eds), *Frameworks for International Cooperation* (1994). Peter Willetts (ed.) *Pressure Groups in the International System* (1983), is a pioneering collection.

On the functional agencies of the UN, works by Haas and Sewell referred to in the chapter are crucial: see also Robert W. Cox and Harold K. Jacobson (eds), *The Anatomy of Influence* (1973). More recent work on these bodies casts its theoretical net a little wider into the area of 'regime' analysis: for example, Mark W. Zacher with Brent A. Sutton, *Governing Global Networks: International Regimes for Transport and Communication* (1996). For Burtonian adaptations of functionalism see, for example, J. W. Burton, *World Society* (1972). Paul Taylor, *International Organization in the Modern World* (1993), is a good overview of theory in the area of international organization in general, including recent thinking about the UN.

On theories of integration, Michael Hodges (ed.), *European Integration* (1972), provides useful extracts from the early theorists. William Wallace, *Regional Integration: The West European Experience* (1994), and Robert O. Keohane and Stanley Hoffmann (eds), *The New European Community* (1991) are good overviews, though both are a little dated. Andrew Moravcsik, *The Choice for Europe: Social Purpose and State Power from Messina to Maastricht* (1998), has become an instant classic. Thoughtful reflections on sovereignty and contemporary European developments are William Wallace, 'The Sharing of Sovereignty: The European Paradox' (1999b), and 'Europe after the Cold-War: Interstate Order or Post-Sovereign Regional System' (1999a). Recent collections on the EU include Jeffrey Checkel (ed.), *International Institutions and Socialization in Europe* (2007); Antje Wiener and Thomas Diez (eds), *European Integration Theory* (2004); Mette Eilstrup-Sangiovanni (ed.), *Debates on European Integration*; and Charlotte Bretherton and John Vogler, *The European Union as a Global Actor* (2005). The *International Studies Review* forum 'The Changing

Face of Europe: European Institutions in the Twenty-First Century' (2006a) and the *International Affairs* special issue on 'Europe at 50' (2007) provide quick general introductions to the current work on the EU.

The Bretton Woods institutions are well covered in the standard textbooks: Robert Gilpin, *The Political Economy of International Relations* (1992) and *Global Political Economy* (2001), offer an orthodox, (neo)realist account; Stephen Gill and David Law, *The Global Economy: Prospects, Problems and Policies* (1988), is neo-Marxist, Gramscian, in inspiration; Susan Strange, *States and Markets* (1988), is *sui generis* and highly entertaining. Less characterful than these three offerings, but reliable, are Joan Spero and J. Hart, *The Politics of International Economic Relations* (2003); David Balaam and Michael Veseth, *Introduction to International Political Economy* (2004); and Robert O'Brien and Marc Williams, *Global Political Economy* 2nd (2007). There are also a number of very valuable edited collections. G. T. Crane and A. M. Amawi (eds), *The Theoretical Evolution of International Political Economy: A Reader* (1999) has good historical coverage; Jeffrey A. Frieden and David A. Lake (eds), *International Political Economy: Perspectives on Global Power and Wealth* (1999) –reprinted articles; and Richard Stubbs and Geoffrey Underhill (eds), *Political Economy and the Changing Global Order* (1999) – original essays – are best on recent approaches; with Craig Murphy and Roger Tooze (eds), *The New International Political Economy* (1991) reflecting an interest in critical theory and epistemological sophistication. Most of the above books appear in various editions – the most recent should always be sought out. Specifically on the rise and fall of Bretton Woods, Richard N. Gardner, *Sterling–Dollar Diplomacy in Current Perspective: The Origins and Prospects of our International Economic Order* (1980), is the expanded version of the author's classic *Sterling–Dollar Diplomacy* (1969), the standard account of the origins of the Bretton Woods System. Andrew Shonfield (ed.), *International Economic Relations of the Western World 1959–1971, Vol. I, Politics and Trade* (Shonfield *et al.*), Vol. II, *International Monetary Relations* (Susan Strange) (1976) is the standard history of the system. Strange, *Sterling and British Policy* (1971) is an account of the crises of the 1960s from a London perspective. Fred Block, *The Origins of International Economic Disorder* (1977), and E. A. Brett, *The World Economy since the War* (1985), look at things from a Marxian perspective. The standard texts cover the crisis of 1971; also useful is Joanna Gowa, *Closing the Gold Window: Domestic Politics and the End of Bretton Woods* (1983).

Recent work on the legacy of the Bretton Woods institutions includes Elizabeth Smythe and Peter J. Smith, 'Legitimacy, Transparency, and Information Technology: The World Trade Organization in an Era of Contentious Trade Politics' (2006) looks at debates over the legitimacy of the WTO; *Global Governance* (2006/2007) is a good source; recent special issues on the IMF and the World Bank provide convenient starting points.

On regimes, two collections are very important: Stephen D. Krasner (ed.), *International Regimes* (1983); and Volker Rittberger (ed.), *Regime Theory and International Relations* (1993). Apart from being more recent, the Rittberger collection involves European as well as American scholars – but Krasner has many classic papers and is still relevant. Also very valuable is the survey article by Marc A. Levy, Oran R. Young and Michael Zürn, 'The Study of International Regimes' (1995). The 'European' approach to regimes is well represented by Andreas Hasenclever, Peter Mayer and Volker Rittberger, *Theories of International Regimes* (1997), and the same authors' 'Integrating Theories of International Regimes' (2000). On post-war regimes and 'hegemonic stability' theory, J. G. Ruggie, 'International Regimes, Transactions and Change: Embedded Liberalism in the Postwar Economic Order' (1982); Robert O. Keohane, *After Hegemony* (1984) and 'The Theory of Hegemonic Stability and Changes in International Economic Regimes, 1967–1977' (1980), are crucial. On hegemonic stability, see also two valuable overviews of the debate: David Lake, 'Leadership, Hegemony and the International Economy: Naked Emperor or Tattered Monarch with Potential' (1993); and Jarrod Wiener, 'Hegemonic Leadership: Naked Emperor or the Worship of False Gods' (1995). Paul Kennedy, *The Rise and Fall of the Great Powers* (1988), is a classic of 'declinism', while a robust rebuttal of the thesis is offered by Joseph S. Nye, *Bound to Lead: The Changing Nature of American Power* (1990), and, predictably, Susan Strange, 'The Persistent Myth of Lost Hegemony' (1987); see also Strange's final book, *Mad Money* (1998b). Thomas Pederson carries arguments over hegemony into regional politics in 'Co-operative Hegemony: Power, Ideas and Institutions in Regional Integration' (2002). Michael Cox continues the discussion of the fall of the US hegemony and the transatlantic rift in 'Beyond the West: Terrors in Transatlantia' (2005), and for those who cannot get enough of cheering the downfall of the US empire, *European Journal of International Relations* contains a response by Vincent Pouliot (2006) and a rejoinder by Cox (2006).

G. John Ikenberry, 'Constitutional Politics in International Relations' (1998), 'Institutions, Strategic Restraint and the Persistence of American Post-War Order' (1998/99), and *After Victory* (2001) makes many of the same points as conventional US regime theorists, but without buying into some of intellectual baggage carried by the latter. More recent takes on global governance include Richard Haass, 'The Age of Nonpolarity' (2008) which looks towards global governance without unipolarity; Helen Thompson, in 'The Case for External Sovereignty' returns to non-intervention and the pragmatic case for sovereignty; Alex Warleigh, 'Learning from Europe? EU Studies and the Re-thinking of 'International Relations'' (2006) argues that post-national or transnational relations would benefit from engagement with EU studies; and Ole Jacob Sending and Iver Neumann, 'Governance to Governmentality: Analyzing NGOs, States, and Power' (2006) present current research on the application of Foucault to issue in global governance.

On antecedents to the UN: for the Peace Projects, see F. H. Hinsley, *Power and the Pursuit of Peace* (1963); for the Concert of Europe, Carsten Holbraad, *Concert of Europe* (1970); for the UN today, Taylor and Groom (eds), *The United Nations at the Millennium* (2000); and the slightly dated Adam Roberts and Benedict Kingsbury (eds), *United Nations, Divided World: The UN's Role in International Relations* (1993). On the history of the United Nations, classics such as I. L. Claude, *Swords into Plowshares* (1971), and H. G. Nicholas, *The*

United Nations as a Political System (1985) are still useful. For the recent politics of the UN, Mats Berdal, 'The UN Security Council: Ineffective but Indispensable' (2003), is a useful short study; the Brahimi Report (2000) is an internal view on peacekeeping operations. For recent UN interventions, James Mayall (ed.), *The New Interventionism: 1991–1994* (1996) is invaluable; for a good, albeit journalistic, account, see William Shawcross, *Deliver Us from Evil* (2000). David Rieff, *A Bed for the Night: Humanitarianism in Crisis* (2002), is more sceptical. Michael Doyle and Nicholas Sambanis, *Making War and Building Peace: United Nations Peace Operations* (2006), is a good recent study, and Kurt Mills, 'Neo-Humanitarianism: The Role of International Humanitarian Norms and Organizations in Contemporary Conflict' (2005) examines the changing perspective of IOs and NGOs as regards humanitarian relief and intervention.

On the first Gulf War, see Paul Taylor and A. J. R. Groom, *The UN and the Gulf War, 1990–1991: Back to the Future* (1992). On Rwanda and the UN, see Michael Barnett, *Eyewitness to Genocide* (2003), and Romeo Dallaire, *Shake Hands with the Devil* (2003). On Kosovo, see Lawrence Freedman, 'Victims and Victors: Reflections on the Kosovo War' (2000), and Ivo Daalder and Michael Hanlon, *Winning Ugly* (2001). Chapter 11 has further reading on humanitarian interventions, and Chapter 12 on the war in Iraq 2003.

A final word on global governance (for the time being): Alexander Wendt, 'Why a World State Is Inevitable' (2003) is a fascinating and challenging attempt to resuscitate the notion of a world state, by one of today's leading theorists of constructivism. Other such arguments are listed in the further reading for Chapter 3.

Chapter 8

The Global Economy

Introduction

One of the defining characteristics of state-centric international relations has been to draw a clear distinction between 'domestic' and 'international' politics. When the volume of transactions that crossed state boundaries grew ever larger in the 1960s and 1970s, a subsidiary distinction became common, that between 'high politics' – the traditional interstate agenda of war and peace – and 'low politics' – the projection of essentially domestic concerns on to the international agenda. The assumption of realist, especially neorealist, thinking was that whatever 'global governance' might emerge it would be in this latter sphere rather than the former, and the essentially anarchic nature of 'high' politics would remain unchanged. In one sense, this assumption has turned out to be accurate. As established in Chapter 7, attempts to introduce collective management of security problems have not been markedly successful, and the great increase in the number of international institutions has come about because of other kinds of needs, other kinds of problems. Where, however, the realist position falls is at the outset, in the distinction between 'high' and 'low' politics – a distinction that collapses in the face of the 'high political' importance of what was once seen as the characteristically 'low political' activity of international economic relations. The world economy and attempts to manage and regulate it are now at the heart of international relations in a way that would have been difficult to believe a century ago and very surprising even as recently as the 1970s.

The changing salience of the world economy is obviously tied up with a number of factors, but for the moment a fairly basic account of the importance of the world economy will suffice. Nowadays, most governments in the world that do not rely on direct physical coercion to stay in power (as well as some that do) understand that their well-being and survival in office is determined more or less directly by their success at economic management, and this is a task that cannot be understood in isolation from the international economy. This, it is worth remembering, is a relatively new state of affairs. A century ago, most governments would have rejected the idea that they were responsible for the state of the economy, and their electorates, such as they were, tended to agree – though issues such as free trade and protectionism could on occasion be crucial. Even when economic management did become critical it was not automatically the case that politics drove governments towards attempts to collectively manage the world economy; sometimes isolation was the aim, at other times the world economy was seen as a self-regulating mechanism that did not need, or was positively averse to, political management.

In Chapter 7 the basic structure of the state-based institutions of the global economy – the IMF, the WTO, the World Bank, UNCTAD and so on – was briefly described. These institutions are interesting in their own right, but the nature of the global economy is far too complex, and there are far too many non-state actors involved, to be summarized via a purely institutional account. It is also far too anarchic; the study of international or global political economy may lead one to believe that realist accounts of the world err by placing too much emphasis on the importance of the sovereign state, but their account of the importance of power is by no means undermined by an accurate rendering of the workings of the world economy. That corporations as well as states seek power, and the impact on power relations of the workings of commodity and capital markets are consistent themes in the study of international political economy. The use of the term *political economy* here is deliberate; one of the weaknesses of contemporary *economics* is the difficulty it experiences in modelling the political process and the importance of power. Just as contemporary political scientists characteristically underestimate the importance of markets, so contemporary economists usually set to one side political phenomena; in reaction, a major sub-field of International Relations, International Political Economy (IPE), has developed since the 1970s, based on the proposition that to understand the modern world economy it is necessary to understand both states and markets (Strange 1988). The founders of modern economics – figures such as Adam Smith, David Ricardo and John Stuart Mill – would have no difficulty in agreeing with this position.

This chapter and the next will focus on IPE very broadly defined. Chapter 8 begins with a brief backward look at the development of the world economy over the last half-millennium, and will then focus on the theories and perspectives that have been generated to understand this development, starting with classical liberalism, mercantilism, Marxism and structuralism; the final section of the chapter will outline recent dramatic changes in the nature of the world economy. Chapter 9 will generalize from these changes to the notion of globalization. Initially the focus will be on the global economy, discussing contemporary neoliberalism and neo-Gramscian thought – but inevitably the scope of the discussion will widen to examine global social and political issues.

The growth of the world economy

Along with war, trade has been a feature of 'international' relations for millennia – indeed, among the classical and pre-classical Greeks the distinction between war and trade was only loosely drawn. Flotillas of ships would cruise the coast, trading if they met strength, engaging in piracy if they found weakness – the Vikings seem to have adopted a similar practice. However, the mere existence of the exchange of goods does not create an economy, much less a world economy. Here, it may be helpful to introduce some distinctions made by Immanuel Wallerstein in his monumental study of the origins of the modern world system (Wallerstein 1974/1980/1989). Wallerstein begins by defining a 'world' in social rather than geographical terms. A world consists of those who are in regular contact with each other and in some extended sense form a social system – the maximum size of a world being determined by the effectiveness of the technology of transportation currently available; it is only in the twentieth century that the social and the geographical worlds are effectively the same. He then identifies 'microsystems' as self-contained societies, small 'worlds' that are either entirely self-contained or exist with only limited exchanges with other worlds, exchanges limited to luxuries, and conducted, characteristically, by trade caravans. Such microsystems still exist in places such as New Guinea and the Amazon basin and are fascinating for social anthropologists, but they are of little interest in this context.

Our interest is in worlds where there is significant exchange; that is, where the long-distance movement of essential, bulk, goods takes place: Wallerstein suggests that there are two kinds of worlds in which this happens. On the one hand there are *empires*, and on the other, *world-systems* (his term – for our purposes the term *world economy* is more appropriate). In empires, exchanges take place within the same political structure, characteristically in the form of *tribute*. Thus Rome conquered Sicily and then Egypt in order to extract from those territories the grain it needed to feed the enormous population of the imperial city. The grain so transferred was tribute paid by the conquered to their conquerors. Within a world economy, on the other hand, exchanges takes place between territories under different political control, and thus tribute cannot be extracted; instead, exchanges take place on an economic basis as *trade*. Wallerstein suggests that such world economies occur quite often but are usually short-lived, filling spaces between empires; Volume I of *The Modern World System* traces the formation of such an economy in Europe in the 'long sixteenth century' (1492–1648), while subsequent volumes demonstrate that, rather than disappear, this system has spread and now dominates the world as a geographical and not just a social whole.

Wallerstein presents an account of the structure of this world economy as necessarily divided into cores, peripheries and semi-peripheries; this is over-mechanical and contentious – though quite influential in the 'South', as we shall see below – but his account of the early formation of the system makes good sense and can be divorced from other aspects of his model. Initially, two sets of transactions were under way; the large-scale movement of sugar and spices, mainly in the form of tribute, within the Spanish Empire, and the trading of craft products and early manufactures from the 'advanced' areas of Europe (the Low Countries, England and Northern France) for grain from Eastern Europe, and sugar from the Spanish Empire. This basic set of exchanges was initially based on very small differences of productivity between north-west Europe and the rest, but gradually it worked to widen this differential. The 'core' in north-west Europe was able to develop comparatively effective and powerful states and to dominate politically and economically both the 'feudal' systems of Eastern Europe and the overextended Habsburg/Spanish power to the South. The strength of this description is that it makes the point that, from the beginning, the world economy and the world political system were closely intertwined. It also reflects the importance of communication and transport technologies in determining the power of states relative to their size. Contemporaries in the sixteenth century were deeply impressed by the scale and scope of Spanish/Habsburg power, but in fact, given existing technologies, smaller, more compact states such as England and the United Provinces had major advantages over such an unmanageably unwieldy conglomerate.

Over the next two centuries this economy expanded. The 'agricultural revolution' in England, in particular, increased productivity markedly, and the spread of empire generated important new commodities, in particular tea and slaves. Ever greater areas of the world were integrated into a single economy, still with the states of north-west Europe occupying the core positions, but with England – now the United Kingdom – increasingly becoming the 'core of the core'. In the Atlantic, the 'Golden Triangle' brought together basic manufactures from Britain, slaves from West Africa and sugar from the Caribbean. Somewhat later, in the early nineteenth century, in the East the demand for tea from China, the lack of a product desired by the Chinese and the inability (at that time) to directly coerce the Chinese Empire led to the development of another triangle, this time involving British cotton goods, Indian opium and Chinese tea. However, for all the importance of this activity, it remained the case that, as late as the end of the eighteenth century, virtually all states were still, in large measure, self-sufficient, and while foreign trade was important to some, in particular the Netherlands and Britain, this importance was still largely marginal. Even Britain, the most important trading country, largely fed itself – the Corn Laws would not have been effective in excluding foreign competition had not the highly productive local agriculture been able both to feed the country and release labour for the new manufacturing concerns.

All this changed with the emergence of industrial society in the nineteenth century; by the second half of the century, for the first time ever, a genuinely world-wide, large-scale division of labour existed. To a great extent, Britain was at the centre of this change – with the highest level of urbanization the world had ever seen, and the lowest numbers on the land. this was a society that could only exist as part of a complicated web of exchanges, in which textiles, machine tools and machinery were exchanged for cotton, and later grain, from the United States, beef from Argentina, and mutton and wool from the Antipodes. This was possible because of changes in the technology of communication and transport. Railroads, steamships and refrigeration made possible the transport of perishable goods over long distances, and the telegraph made the creation of a genuine market possible. Many of these innovations depended also on the export of capital – American and Argentinian railways were largely financed by British capital, and the British shipbuilding industry and British shipping fleets met the demand for sea transportation directly. As the twentieth century arrived, so did competitors to Britain in the form of the new industrial powers of Germany and the United States. Although these newcomers dominated some industries, chemicals for example, until 1914 Britain remained at the centre of the system – but it was clear to far-sighted observers, including the British political class, that this dominance was unlikely to survive much longer. The two world wars of the twentieth century brought it to an end, and the geographical core of the system moved to the United States, with the tacit approval of British capital, the old core state defining its interests in terms of retaining close relations with the new core – a common pattern, demonstrated earlier by Anglo-Dutch relations which, after a shaky start, eventually became very close.

What is particularly striking about the emergence of this complicated structure of exchanges of money, goods, services and people across national boundaries is the extent to which it emerged unplanned and unprepared for. Questions such as how can a large-scale division of labour work in a world based on territorial states; what difference does crossing a political border make to economic activity; and how has this world economy changed international relations were not answered because they were not posed. The system seemed to regulate itself; indeed, it was widely believed to have grown as fast as it did not in spite of, but because of the absence of planning. However, after 1914 and the outbreak of the First World War and subsequent failures to re-establish the old system, it becomes clear that these questions are in fact unavoidable. The institutional solutions to these questions were sketched in Chapter 7 – but now some extended consideration needs to be given to a more theoretical response, because how we actually think about international economic relations has been, and remains, as important as the institutional structures we create.

Problems and perspectives

What difference *does* crossing a political border make to economic activity? Consider a very basic situation – so basic in fact that, as we shall see later, it has now been superseded – wherein a firm in one country (A) produces goods bought by consumers in another (B). How is this different from production and consumption taking place in the same country?

The first issue concerns *money*. The producer wishes to be paid in the currency of A, while the consumer wishes to pay in currency B. Until 1914, there were relatively few technical problems here, because virtually all currencies were convertible into precious metals, mainly gold, but sometimes silver. The Victorian Londoner travelling to Paris could be confident that his gold sovereigns would be readily convertible into gold francs – literally convertible, since each coin was effectively a weight of a certain quality of gold. And since paper money issued by the Bank of England was equally convertible into gold ('I promise to pay the bearer the sum of ...' is still, meaninglessly, reprinted on British paper money) it also met few obstacles abroad, although paper issued by lesser banks might be unacceptable. As far as large-scale trading was concerned, bills of exchange issued by the great merchant banking houses were widely accepted throughout Europe and in the rest of the world.

A gold-based system was readily comprehensible, and required no special mechanism to operate, but there was one feature of the system that potentially posed political problems. If one country had firms that were more successful at selling abroad than another, or consumers keener to buy foreign goods, this might lead to a flow of gold in or out of the country. Ought this to be a source of concern? In the seventeenth century, when for the first time it became possible to measure gold flows, if not accurately then at least to degrees of magnitude, the new proponents of 'political arithmetic', the 'mercantilists', argued that a positive, inward, flow of gold was good, and a negative, outward flow bad. In the eighteenth century, David Hume, in a splendidly concise essay, demonstrated that, in principle, negative and positive flows would be self-correcting – inward flows would raise price levels and make exports more expensive, and imports cheaper, and thus reverse the flow, and vice versa with outward flows of gold – though his argument begs the question of whether governments would allow this mechanism to work (Hume 1987).

In any event, since 1914 a different problem has emerged. Since that date, most currencies most of the time have not been directly convertible into gold, and thus domestic price levels are not directly affected by the flow of precious metals, but this simply allows *balance of payments* crises to emerge and persist more readily. Under the Bretton Woods system international payments were still linked indirectly to the price of gold, but since 1973 this has not been the case, and, in any event, an indirect link requires management in a way that the old, self-regulating system did not. Once gold is no longer the key, *exchange rate policy* is something that all states have to have, and the essentially political problem of establishing a reliable medium of exchange for international transactions becomes unavoidable.

Assuming this problem can be solved, an international economy based on a large-scale division of labour can emerge. In a system of uncontrolled exchange, patterns of specialization will develop, with some countries producing one range of goods, others another. Some countries may become specialists in agricultural products, others in industrial goods. Does this matter? Ought states to have positive policies to promote the production of certain kinds of goods, or is this something where market forces can be allowed to decide? *Trade policy* joins *balance of payments policy* and *exchange rate policy* as areas where, like it or not, states must have a position – and in this context not to have a position is itself a position, and one with very considerable implications.

Two quite distinct orientations may be adopted towards these problems, which can be termed *liberal* and *nationalist* – although, as we shall see, nationalist political economy can take widely different political and social forms. Historically, the *nationalist* approach to international economic relations came first. As suggested above, following Hume, the mercantilist idea that states should aim for a positive inflow of gold has been seen to be a self-defeating policy, because the effect on the trade balance of the consequent changes in price level will reverse the trade flow, but the general idea that the way one judges economic matters is in terms of the effect they have on the nation's position in the world and not from some other, less partial, perspective has never lost its appeal. Economic nationalism is still part of the common rhetoric of the political life of most countries, as witnessed by the universal desire of states to have a balance of payments surplus – impossible for all to achieve, of course, since every surplus is someone else's deficit. Equally, no government minister ever returns from a trade negotiation to announce with pride that a particular deal will increase the general welfare even though, regrettably, it will have harmful effects at home; that the universal expectation is that states will promote their own interests in such negotiations illustrates the continuing salience of economic nationalism.

Still, if economic nationalism came first in history and is still in certain respects politically dominant, economic *liberalism* has been the intellectually dominant position for most of the last two centuries. The basic liberal proposition is that while in some areas a degree of regulation may be a necessary evil, in general free market solutions to economic problems maximize welfare in the system taken as a whole, and should be adopted. There were three essential steps along the way to this conclusion, spread over a nearly century from the mid-eighteenth to the early nineteenth centuries. The first was Hume's demolition of the mercantilist love affair with gold, noted above. The second was Adam Smith's demonstration of the gains to be had from an extended division of labour in *The Wealth of Nations,* gains that are a function of the size of the market and therefore can, in principle, be increased by foreign trade. The third and crucial step was David Ricardo's 'theory of comparative advantage' which, although published in 1817, remains in an amended form the basis of liberal trade theory and the liberal international economic order (Ricardo 1971).

Ricardo's achievement was to provide a logically sound, albeit counter-intuitive, answer to one of the fundamental problems posed by international trade. It is intuitively easy to see why trade takes place when two countries have different kinds of resources, and thus produce different kinds of products. Europe could produce bananas under glass, and the Windward Islands could set up small-scale craft audio-visual and 'white goods' workshops, but it is not too difficult to see why, in fact, this does not happen, and the Windward Islands grow bananas and import televisions and refrigerators from the industrial world. More generally, it is easy to see why two similar countries that are efficient in the production of different products would trade (though how they became efficient in different areas if they are really similar is another issue). But what is very difficult to see is how trade could be desirable and profitable in the quite common situation where two countries produce similar products and one of them is more efficient at producing *everything* than the other. Ricardo provides the answer, which is that while one country may be more efficient at producing everything, it will almost always be the case that the *comparative* costs of producing different products will be different, and thus even the least efficient country will have a comparative advantage in some product.

Ricardo's demonstration of this proposition assumed a two-country, two-commodity economy in which the costs of production are measured in labour-time. Nowadays, this is, of course, much too simple, and the modern demonstration of Ricardo's principle takes a chapter or more in the average economics textbook – but the basic idea is of enormous significance and underlies liberal economic thought to this day. What Ricardo demonstrated was that under virtually all circumstances trade would be beneficial to both parties. This is very much in contrast to the eighteenth-century belief, present, for example, in Rousseau and even in Kant – as well as, of course, in the work of the mercantilists, that trade was necessarily an activity that generated winners and losers. After Ricardo, economic liberals were able to argue that the removal of restrictions on trade would be to the benefit of all, because the general welfare would be maximized by the lowering of barriers between regions and countries. Each country, by specializing in the products in which it has a comparative advantage and engaging in trade, is contributing to the general good *as well as to its own welfare.* This belief is still at the heart of the 'embedded liberalism' of the modern trade system.

Ricardo provided liberals with a powerful argument, but he did not silence all opponents. The key issue for opponents was (and, in a different form, still is) the pattern of specialization established by free trade. If one country has a comparative advantage in the production of industrial foods. and another in the production of agricultural goods, then the welfare of the system as a whole is maximized if specialization takes place – but might there not be other considerations involved here? One issue that features largely in structuralist accounts of international relations, to be discussed shortly, is the terms of trade at which products are exchanged, and whether or not there is a trend moving against primary products. More important for the moment is the power-political objection to the view that any pattern of specialization is, in principle, as good as any other.

This argument was articulated by the American statesman Alexander Hamilton in the 1790s in his 'Report on Manufactures' to the US Congress, but the central figure here is the German political economist and liberal nationalist, Friedrich List, whose 1841 work *The National System of Political Economy* (republished in 1966) is the most impressive attack on liberal international political economy to be mounted in the nineteenth century. List's basic position was that, in the conditions of the 1840s, free trade was a policy that would set in concrete Britain's industrial pre-eminence as the workshop of the world, leaving the German states – and others – in a subordinate position as the hewers of wood and drawers of water for the more sophisticated producers across the Channel. Because Britain was first in the field it would have a comparative advantage in heavy industry. It would therefore be cheaper for a country such as Germany to buy machine tools and other advanced technology from the British – but the dependence that this would create would turn the German states into second-rate powers. Moreover, the British had not achieved their predominance by following the precepts of free trade. On the contrary, British economic strength was fostered behind many protective devices: the Navigation Acts, which obliged British trade to be carried in British ships; the Corn Laws, which protected the profitability of British agriculture; and so on. The British, remarked List in an illuminating metaphor, were kicking away the ladder up which they had climbed to their present position, denying others the advantages they had exploited.

His solution was to develop German industry behind a protective wall of tariffs: the so-called 'infant industry' argument that the early stages of industrial development can only take place if local industries are protected from international competition. Perhaps when these industries grow up they will no longer need protection – though List, along with many later neomercantilists, envisaged a continuation of protection even after maturity, because the industries in question would remain central to German power and could not be exposed to the risks of competition. List's wider point here is that free trade and economic liberalism are generally promoted as being in the common interest by those who are satisfied with the existing pattern of specialization. Those who, for one reason or another, are not so satisfied will be sceptical.

List's argument assumes that patterns of specialization will not shift rapidly. However, another objection to economic liberalism is based on the opposite assumption, namely that open markets will lead to very rapid change. This seemed plausible in the late twentieth century, where competition from the 'newly industrializing countries' very quickly undermined many sectors of the old industrialized world. Liberal economic relations rely on a willingness to adapt to change whatever the cost – but sometimes the cost in terms of social dislocation can be very high. Consider, for example, the run-down of the coal industry in Britain from the 1980s, with over 200,000 jobs lost to foreign competition in less than twenty years – similar patterns could be observed throughout the developed industrial world; for example, consider the collapse of heavy industry in the American 'rust-belt' which has caused widespread social disruption, and opposition to agreements such as the North American Free Trade Area (NAFTA) which, allegedly, export American jobs. The social dislocation these shifts have caused has been very high, and it is by no means clear that measures to slow down the rate of change ought not to have been taken. Allowing the market to determine results on the basis of an abstract calculation of the general welfare presents major political and social difficulties. Modern 'protectionists' are not necessarily motivated by a desire to preserve the nation's power; they may, instead, desire to protect social and community values – though it should be said that any kind of protectionism, including this social democratic variant, throws the costs of adaptation on others and therefore cannot be innocent of nationalist implications. This is one of the reasons why, until comparatively recently, Marxist writers have been very suspicious of positions that were not based on free trade.

Karl Marx himself appears not to have contested the basic logic of Ricardo's argument. His point was to stress the extent to which liberal economic relations were a recent construction and not part of the 'natural' way of doing things. He is bitterly critical of the 'Robinson Crusoe' style of argument, in which liberal economic relations are assumed to emerge naturally on the basis of simple common sense – they are, instead, the product of a particular way of life, a mode of production, which emerged out of class struggle and the victory of the bourgeoisie over feudalism. However, once this is acknowledged, Marx seems to be quite willing to recognize the achievements of the political economists, holding Ricardo in particularly high esteem. That there were gains from trade was not contested by him, though these gains were seen as accruing to the dominant class and not to the general welfare of all. Moreover, Marxist political economists of the early twentieth century observed that trade was very clearly no longer conducted on liberal terms. 'Finance capital' dominated the state, and had a clear foreign policy based on the use of tariffs to extend the national economic territory and thereby allow national conglomerates to make monopoly profits. One of the reasons why socialists should oppose this policy was because it went against the requirements of internationalism, which included free trade.

In the second half of the twentieth century, the commitment to free trade remained firm among most of the small Trotskyite groups that survived in the West, but most other Marxists (and social democrats more generally) made their peace with nationalism. In the Northern industrial world, 'labour' and 'social democratic' parties (including, much of the time, the Democratic party in the USA) found that a precondition for survival was to advocate the adoption of political measures to put some limits on freedom of trade. The basic political point here is that the gains from protectionism are always concentrated, while the gains from free trade are dispersed; conversely, the costs of protectionism are dispersed among the general population, whereas the costs of free trade bear heavily on vulnerable groups rather than the population at large. Other things being equal – which, of course, much of the time they are not – protectionism will be more politically popular than free trade. In the Third World, in particular, neo-Marxist theories of dependency or 'structuralism' were explicitly and unapologetically anti-liberal in trade matters. These ideas are of sufficient political importance that they need to be discussed at greater length.

Structuralism

The notion that there is a 'South' or 'Third World' is, today, contested quite hotly by those who point out that the states making up the putative South are many and various, with very little in common – thus, say, Brazil and India are both large industrializing countries, but differ in every other respect; the Maldives and Brunei are both small, but one is oil-rich and Muslim while the other is not, and the other 130 or so states which might be thought of as Southern are equally ill-matched. All these states have in common is *not* being members of the OECD, the rich-states club – but even there, some OECD members (Singapore and South Korea) were once thought of as Southern. And where China fits into 'the South' is anyone's guess. However, around the 1960s, it was possible to identify a fairly coherent group of states – mostly poor, mostly non-European in population, mostly recently de-colonized, mostly non-aligned – who did identify themselves as the 'Third World' (the other two 'worlds' being Western capitalism and the Soviet bloc) and did develop a distinctive approach to international economics. While the term itself has many meanings in social theory, in International Relations *structuralism* is a convenient term to refer to this distinctive approach, a cluster of theories that emerged in the 1950s, 1960s and 1970s whose aim was to give an account of the political and economic subordination of the South to the

North. These theories – dependency theory, centre–periphery/core–periphery analysis, world-systems analysis – share the idea that North and South are in *a structural relationship* one with another; that is, both areas are part of a structure determining the pattern of relationships that emerges. Structuralism is a general theory of international relations in the sense that it purports to explain how the world as a whole works, but it is also a 'Southern' theory in two senses; uniquely among modern theories of International Relations it actually originated in the South, and it is orientated explicitly towards the problems and interests of the South, designed to solve those problems and serve those interests. It is because of this 'Southern-ness' that structuralism maintained its appeal for so long, in spite of serious intellectual shortcomings.

A key figure in the development of structuralist ideas was the Argentinian economist Raúl Prebisch, a guiding light of the UN's Economic Commission for Latin America (ECLA) in the 1950s, even though his own position was rather less radical than that of later structuralists. Prebisch was influenced by Marxist-Leninist ideas on political economy, but rejected the assumption, common to Marx, Lenin and orthodox communist parties in Latin America, that the effects of imperialism would be to produce capitalist industrialization in the South; in this he was influenced by the revisionist Marxist political economist, Paul Baran, who argued, in *The Political Economy of Growth,* that monopoly capitalism in the mid-twentieth century was no longer performing a progressive role – instead, the industrialization of the rest of the world was being held back in the interests of maintaining monopoly profits in the centres of capitalism (Baran 1957). Prebisch's innovation was to identify the mechanism by which the capitalist centres held back the periphery. On his account, it was via the pattern of specialization that so-called 'free trade' became established in the world economy. This pattern involved the South in the production of primary products (food, raw materials), which are exchanged for the manufactured goods of the North. Why is this pattern undesirable? Because, Prebisch argues, there is a long-term, secular trend for the terms of trade to move against primary products – to put the point non-technically, over time, a given 'basket' of a typical primary product will buy fewer and fewer baskets of manufactured products. Where x bushels of grain bought a tractor in 1950, in 2009 it will take $x + y$ bushels to buy a tractor.

This is a fundamental challenge to liberal economic thinking, which, as we have seen, assumes that all economies have a comparative advantage in the production of some product(s), and that for purposes of trade and the general welfare it does not matter what the product in question is – hence, in the example given above concerning bananas and manufacturing goods, Prebisch's point is that, in order to continue to import the *same* value of manufactured goods, the Windward Islands will have to continually *increase* the value of banana exports, which will be difficult because of competition from other banana-producing countries, and because the demand for bananas is limited in a way that the demand for manufactured goods is not. In manufacturing, new products are being developed all the time, and new 'needs' are being produced via technological innovation and the power of marketing. In agriculture, productivity gains are likely to be less dramatic, while there is a limit to the market for even so desirable a product as a banana. Countries that specialize in agricultural and other primary products will be continually running on the spot in order to preserve existing living standards, let alone improve upon them. Does this argument stand up? The simple answer is that this is still hotly contested. Liberal economists on the whole deny that there is a trend of the sort that Prebisch identifies. Prices of commodities rise and fall in response to general and particular factors, and there is no clear trend; moreover, whereas a bushel of grain is much the same in 2009 as in 1950, a tractor may be a much better product at the later date, justifying a higher price. Keynesian and (some) Marxian economists tend to be more sympathetic to the general thesis. As we shall see below, to some extent the argument has been overtaken by events, as industrial production has moved South, and, in any event, much primary production has always been 'Northern' – the USA, Canada and Australia, along with Russian Siberia are, and always have been, the most significant producers of raw materials. However, none of this really matters, because in political terms Prebisch has been wholly triumphant. Until very recently, virtually all Southern governments and informed Southern opinion have been convinced of the basic truth of his position – that the liberal international economic order is biased towards the interests of the North, and that free trade is detrimental to Southern interests.

What are the policy implications of this position? In the 1950s, ECLA thinking was statist and nationalist, and summed up by the policy of *Import Substitution Industrialization* (ISI). The thrust of this policy was to protect and develop local industries in order to allow local suppliers to meet local demand, importing capital goods and technology but as few manufactured products as possible. By the mid-1960s there was no sign that this policy was working, and a rather more radical approach emerged – key names here include André Gunder Frank, Fernando Cardoso, Thestonio dos Santos, and, later, drawing on African experiences to support the Latin Americans, Arghiri Emmanuel, Immanuel Wallerstein and Samir Amin. The difference between these 'structuralist' writers and the proponents of ISI is the difference between reform and revolution. ISI was designed as a strategy to improve the standing of the South within the capitalist world economy; many supporters of ISI, including Prebisch, wanted to overthrow this system in the long run, but, as fairly orthodox Marxists, they believed this could not happen until the forces of production had been sufficiently developed; until, that is, 'the time was ripe'. Orthodox, Moscow-leaning communist parties in Latin America supported local capitalists – according to them, the bourgeois revolution had to take place before the socialist revolution could arrive. According to the structuralists, all parts of the world economy were already capitalist by virtue of producing for the world market, hence there was no need to wait for capitalism to develop before making the revolution. Consequently, they opposed official communism – except in Mao's China and Fidel Castro's Cuba – instead, giving their allegiance to rural guerrilla movements. The aim was to break the chain of exploitation that bound together the metropolitan centres and peripheral satellites of the world system; the world trading system works to transfer resources from the poor to the rich, from the South to the North, and there is no way this system can be reformed and made to work in the interests of the peoples of the South.

From a structuralist perspective, the statism and nationalism of import substitution strategies works to conceal the true nature of the world political economy – which is not, ultimately, about states, but about *classes and relations of production*. Capitalists everywhere exploit workers everywhere. Southern capitalists are junior partners to their counterparts in the great Northern centre; in principle, the workers everywhere also have a common interest – though here things are muddied by the propensity of the Northern proletariat to enter into (junior) partnership with capital. Developing Lenin's rather limited idea of a labour aristocracy in the imperialist countries bought off by the profits of imperialism, and adopting the fashionable 1960s notion, associated in particular with Herbert Marcuse, of the 'one-dimensionality' of the Northern proletariat, structuralists tended to write off the Northern working class. In any event, the structuralist model of the world was, in principle, resolutely non-statist. Capitalists everywhere were the enemy.

The intellectual strength of the structuralist view lay for the most part in its account of the history of the system. Frank's classic *Capitalism and Underdevelopment in Latin America* (1971) was largely a set of case studies defending in detail the view that close contact with the world economy resulted in the 'underdevelopment' of Latin America, while temporary breakdowns of the system (for example, in the two world wars) provided the only examples of successful development. Wallerstein's thought-provoking essays and lectures rest on the monumental achievement of his multi-volume *The Modern World System* (1974/1980/1989), which provides an account of the emergence and development of the system since the sixteenth century. The strength of these studies lies in the way that they outline in combination the 'political' and 'economic' dimension of the systems, unlike the more conventional historical accounts, upon which International Relations and liberal political economics usually rely.

However, the political strength of structuralism rests on shakier foundations. As Bill Warren has suggested, a mixture of 'romantic' anti-capitalism and nationalist mythology has been important here, though Warren was somewhat unfair in suggesting that the originators of the model shared these views (Warren 1980). The unorthodoxy of the Marxism of the structuralists is clear; structuralists place far too much emphasis on trade as opposed to production, and fail to grasp the achievement of capitalism in transforming the world by the development of the productive forces (hence the label 'romantic'). Moreover, while structuralism is in principle non-statist, it is easy to see how it could be turned into a defence of the interests of Southern states – after all, most of the dispossessed of the world live in the South, and, given the Northern workers' betrayal of the revolution, it is easy to see how an anti-capitalist struggle could turn into a North–South conflict. The anomalous figures here are the Southern capitalists and Southern elites more generally, and these groups have a clear interest in blaming outsiders for the failure of development in the South, skating over as quickly as possible the thought that they might be implicated in this failure. Such an attitude was very much in evidence in the Southern demand for a New International Economic Order (NIEO) articulated in the UN in the 1970s.

The NIEO had a number of components. In the area of *trade* it called for the establishment of a Generalized System of Preferences (GSP) for industrial goods from the South to increase the Southern share of manufacturing production to 25 per cent of the total by the year 2000, and an Integrated Programme for Commodities (IPC) to level out fluctuations in the prices of commodities. *Aid* targets should be increased to 1 per cent of the industrial world's GDP, two-thirds in the form of official aid. *Debt* should be cancelled and soft loans made available from the World Bank and its subsidiaries. In the area of *production* there should be extensive transfers of technology and research and development (R & D) to the South; investment should be increased, but multinational corporations should be subject to a strict code of conduct – indeed, the control of MNCs was a major plank in all Southern programmes at this time.

It should be noted that these are *reforms* of the liberal international economic order (LIEO), albeit very radical reforms. Structuralists criticized the NIEO, and later manifestations of NIEO policy, such as the two Brandt reports, as failing to grasp the nettle of world revolution. This is clearly true – NIEO is a statist programme which looks to the continuation of a capitalist world economy. However, the reforms it envisaged are very radical, and share some elements of the structuralist position. In particular, the underlying assumption is that the failure to develop on the part of the South is to be attributed to the operation of the system and not, for example, to failings in the South itself. The obstacles to development are structural and must be removed. Moreover, this cannot be done with a free-trade, non-discriminatory system; scepticism about trade runs through NIEO thinking. A key theme of the NIEO is management, the need to replace reactive regulation with proactive management. The best way to see this is as a response to vulnerability. Southern states are vulnerable states who find it difficult to cope with the swings and roundabouts of the market; hence the desire for regulation.

In the 1970s, the prospects for the NIEO looked moderately good. Despite the major industrial powers abstaining or voting against the programme, there was evidence that within the North many of its ideas were popular, and the Southern coalition at the UN seemed to be putting the North on the defensive generally, and combining quite effectively with the Soviet bloc who, though critical of the NIEO programme, were happy to join in the critique of the West. In the 1980s and 1990s, however, momentum behind the NIEO was lost, and even though the term is sometimes still employed at the UN it has little current purchase. This failure followed partly from political mistakes on the part of the South, which clearly overplayed its hand in the 1970s, mistaking votes in the UN General Assembly and UNCTAD for the reality of power, and which made the false assumption that powerful members of the bloc would use their power in the general interest of the South. In fact, and predictably, oil-rich countries such as Saudi Arabia developed a strong interest in the prosperity of the West, and behaved like their wealthy peers when they took up their seats on the IMF Board. Also in the 1980s, the emergence of the so-called 'debt crisis' derailed other North–South economic negotiations. Still, the real reason for the current irrelevance of the NIEO goes much deeper and relates to changes in the world economy that undermined many of the assumptions upon which both the NIEO and conventional theories of international political economy were based.

The new global economy

The theories of international political economy presented above – with the exception of some variants of Marxism – mostly share certain core assumptions: that the state encompasses a national economy; that international economic activity took place between such national economies; that international trade took place between national firms; and that the primary function of international financial transactions was to facilitate trade. Each of these assumptions is now under threat.

The most important of these changes is the rise in significance of the international business enterprise, or MNC ('multinational' is something of a misnomer, because many of the firms in question are mono-national in ownership and management, but the use of MNC as a generic term is so widespread that it would be pedantic to try to replace it). There are perhaps 60,000 or so MNCs which now account for around a third of the world's trade. The size and power of these firms in the contemporary world is unprecedented. To give a broad indication of their scale, in 2007, the stock market value of each of the ten largest companies in the world exceeded the gross domestic product of 156 of the UN's 192 member states, and each of the top two largest firms – Exxon Mobil and PetroChina, worth US$452.5

billion and US$424 billion respectively – were larger than all but nineteen UN member states. Such firms have enormous transnational influence and interests. Sixty-one per cent of Exxon Mobil's employees and almost half of General Electric's (the third-largest firm in the world) are employed outside the USA, where both firms are headquartered. Corporations are becoming increasingly transnational, with high percentages of assets, sales and employees being foreign. The size and value of these firms give them tremendous global influence via their decisions over where to invest, where to manufacture or employ service personnel, and where and at what price to sell their goods and services. States find it increasingly difficult to control and legislate over MNC activity, as they rely heavily on the employment and tax income that these firms generate, and states have even started to contract out their most central functions to private companies: the private military industry is now worth more than US$100 billion a year.

It is easy to see why MNCs are regarded by many as the root of all international evil, but it is important to keep a sense of proportion when examining their influence. The first step is to make it clear that there are many different kinds of business enterprises that are multinational; their common defining feature is that they all operate across national boundaries and are based on *direct* foreign investment – the ownership and control of assets located abroad – as opposed to *indirect* or *portfolio* investment in which assets are purchased for the financial return, rather than the control, they bring, and as opposed to simply trading across frontiers.

Some MNCs are engaged in the *extraction of raw materials*; this is an activity whose location is determined by accidents of geography and geology. Copper companies go where the copper is, oil companies where the oil is, and so on – which means that these corporations do not usually have relocation as an easy business strategy, and, in turn, means they have an incentive to try to preserve good relations with local political elites. Unsurprisingly, some of the most egregious acts of political interference by MNCs have involved such corporations. Other corporations engage in *manufacturing,* generally in the markets for which they are producing; that is, in the industrialized world. Here, direct political influence is comparatively unusual, though indirect influence is great. Some MNCs have world-wide integrated production strategies, although the extent of this phenomenon is contestable. A third important category of MNCs is made up of those corporations who engage in the *global manipulation of symbols* – the great multi-media and entertainment corporations, but also international banks – whose activities are highly deterritorialized, though, for the time being at least, their chief executives are still unable to avoid locating in one state or another, thus retaining a territorial link. Finally, for the sake of completion, mention should be made of international *holding companies,* where different firms producing different products in different countries are owned by the same corporation, but where there is no attempt to produce a common business strategy; such holding companies may have little political significance in comparison with the other types of MNC.

While there are sharply contrasting views of the significance of these corporations, there are a few points that are accepted by all. First, there are a great many more MNCs operating in the world today than there were in the 1960s and 1970s, and many of these new corporations are engaged in 'cutting edge' economic activities, in the production of high-technology manufactures, or in global finance or information and entertainment rather than in the extractive industries or old-style 'metal-bashing'. Second, and largely because of the nature of these activities, these newer corporations carry out most of their activities in the advanced industrial world and the 'newly industrializing countries' (NICs) rather than in the less developed countries generally, or the least developed countries in particular. Third, whereas up to the 1960s nearly all large MNCs were based on American capital held abroad, the situation today is rather different; the United States is still the country with the largest individual *stock* of overseas capital, but in recent years the net flow of capital has been to the United States from Europe and Japan, and the total stock of American capital held by foreigners is larger than that of foreign capital held by Americans.

To reiterate, the point about the emergence of the MNC is that many of the assumptions that have guided past thinking now have to be abandoned. Today, a high proportion of international trade is 'intra-firm' trade – that is, between different branches of the same corporation –though just how high a proportion is difficult to say because of the weakness of official statistics; it is probably between a quarter and a third by value of the trade of the advanced industrial countries. The possibilities for manipulating markets opened up by this phenomenon are tremendous; in principle, via 'transfer pricing', firms can move profits and losses from one area of operation to another at will, with a devastating effect on the effectiveness of national tariff and taxation policies, and on international attempts to regulate trade.

Transfer pricing is an activity open only to MNCs – and, in practice, more easily controlled by tax authorities than this summary would suggest – but in other respects too much emphasis on MNCs as such can be misleading. Effectively, all large corporations today are behaviourally 'multinational' – that is, to some extent they think and plan globally even if they do not possess foreign assets. The old distinction between multinationals and others relied on a national compartmentalization of economic activity to which MNCs were an exception, a situation that no longer applies. The new technologies on which production is now based work against any such compartmentalization.

The same point can be made with respect to a change in some ways more radical in its implications than the rise of MNCs – the emergence of *global financial markets*. One of the reasons for the collapse of the IMF's exchange-rate regime in the 1960s and 1970s was the existence of the 'Eurodollar' market. Once it was determined at Bretton Woods that private movements of capital would be allowed, and once the City of London was allowed to return to its traditional role with the ending of controls in 1951, the emergence of new capital markets was inevitable. 'Eurodollars' were foreign currencies held in banks beyond the regulatory reach of the country that issued them – the generic title derives from the fact that these were originally US dollars held in European (mainly British) banks. A market in Eurodollars existed alongside domestic capital markets – originally on quite a small scale and initially established for political reasons, it grew very quickly, largely because various features of US banking regulations encouraged US MNCs to keep working balances abroad. By the mid-1960s the 'Eurodollar slop' of currencies being moved from one market to another was a major destabilizing factor in the management of exchange rates.

The Eurodollar market still exists, but under different conditions. Whereas in the 1960s this was a market that was separate from, albeit linked to, domestic capital markets, at present all currency holdings are potentially 'euro' holdings; with the end of regulation in most countries, national capital markets and national stock exchanges are simply local manifestations of a world-wide market and the creation of credit is beyond the control of national authorities. Trading takes place on a 24-hour basis, following the sun from Tokyo to Hong Kong to Frankfurt and London to New York and back to Tokyo. Some transactions in this market are clearly 'international' – foreign currency loans, the purchase of Eurobonds, and so on – whereas others are 'local', but the compartmentalization that once kept such activities apart and made a limited specialization of the former no longer exists. Just as the distinction between multinational and national corporations is no longer of great interest, so the distinction between international and national capital markets is now somewhat unreal. In the aftermath of the rush to create new financial instruments in the 1980s, virtually any economic or financial activity can be 'securitized' and traded internationally. Thus it is possible to buy assets whose value is calculated on the basis of the cash flow generated by the repayments of loans for the purchase of automobiles in the USA, and foreign bankers can exchange dollar debts for shares in Brazilian soccer teams. All this assumes the system is working well, but, by the same token, when things go wrong the global financial system ensures that problems in any of the major markets are transmitted to all the others. The development of the 'credit crunch' in 2007/8 (discussed briefly in Chapter 12 below) illustrates this point all too clearly.

The end of the South?

The full implications of the changes will be discussed in the next chapter, but to end this chapter, the story of the South, structuralism and the NIEO will be brought to a kind of conclusion. A few basic points will make clear the impact of these changes. In classic Southern/structuralist thinking, from Prebisch onwards, the South is seen as a source of primary products for the world economy, and this is deemed to be a source of problems; however, since the 1980s, the South – or at least *parts of the South* – have become major centres for manufacturing production, easily reaching the NIEO targets in this respect without much assistance from the Northern states; indeed, the expansion in the South has been to an extent at the expense of jobs in the North. The significance of this can be underlined by examining classic writings of structuralists on industrialization in the South, where the possibility of such shifts is simply ruled out. Some have attempted to undermine the significance of these moves by, for example, describing Southern industrialization as *dependent* development – but without explaining adequately what *independent* development would look like.

Again, in the 1980s, the MNC was regarded as an enemy of Southern development, exploiting local raw materials or cheap labour and repatriating profits; thus, in order to avoid allowing the giant oil companies to share in the profits from exploiting its newly-viable oil-fields, Mexico borrowed from the banks to finance this development – forgetting that banks have to be paid whether the investments they finance are profitable or not, while MNCs actually share the risks associated with new ventures of this kind. In any event, while MNCs continue to exploit their strengths, advanced production techniques have limited the amounts of raw materials used in production processes, and cut the proportion of the value of products which represent labour costs to the bone. At present, manufacturing MNCs are concerned to find political stability, trained workers and access to global markets before they will invest or franchise, and profits that are not invested in R&D will be wasted. At the time of writing, in other words, Southern countries have to engage in the same kind of triangular diplomacy between national and international capital and the state that is characteristic of Northern countries – albeit with slightly, but not greatly, different bargaining power. *Some* Southern countries have done very well out of this; but others have been ignored completely by the giant corporations.

Clearly, one of the features of the past two decades has been stratification *within* the South. Some countries have done very well, such as the NICs of the Pacific Rim, and, to a lesser extent, of Latin America, while others have done very badly, particularly in sub-Saharan Africa. Still others have experienced some success, but from a very low base, and mixed with the continuation of extremes of poverty, as is the case in India and the Philippines. China is rapidly becoming one of the world's leading industrial powers, while Singapore is richer than many Northern industrial countries. Meanwhile, living standards are actually falling in Bangladesh and Pakistan. There is no longer a characteristic Southern economy – hence the rhetoric about the 'end of the Third World' alluded to in the heading of this section, which dates back to the 1980s (Harris 1986).

It should be apparent that what is being suggested here is not that all is well in the South, and that oppression and injustice are coming to an end. This is obviously not the case; poverty, malnutrition and hunger remain real problems, and are perhaps of increasing significance, certainly from the point of view of the 'bottom billion' (Paul Collier) and, even in those areas where industrialization is taking off, exploitation is rife. There is no difficulty finding examples of workers (often young women) living on starvation wages while assembling luxury goods for consumers in the advanced industrial world. High-pollution industries abound, and in many cases these industries have been deliberately exported from the North. The point is that this exploitation is rather different in kind from the exploitation described and anticipated by the structuralists in the 1970s. At that time, the assumption was that the South would be pushed down as a concomitant to the North continuing to rise – the world economy was described as a zero-sum game in which the 'winnings' of the North matched the 'losses' of the South. Now, things look rather different. Certainly the North has continued to grow (albeit unevenly) and develop new products and industries, but the South has also experienced (equally uneven) growth. Contrary to expectations, capital has moved to (some) Southern countries. Moreover, real living standards, measured by such indicators as life-expectancy at birth as well as by GDP growth have, in general, improved; average life expectancy in the South increased by 17 years between 1960 and the mid-1990s, though remaining 10 years or more below that of the North.

How is this stratification to be understood? Most plausibly, what is required is to reinstate some thinking about developing countries common to both liberal and orthodox Marxist writings in the 1950s and earlier. On this account, there is a natural tendency for the capitalist mode of production (or, if you prefer, 'free enterprise') to spread throughout the world, and the basic obstacle to this spread is to be found in local policies. Capitalists wish to 'exploit' the world via industrialization and development (though they do not express their intentions in such a manner) if they are allowed to, and they will do so unless prevented by local circumstances. Sometimes these local circumstances are outside the control of particular societies – for example, Paul Collier writes of the problems that land-locked states with poor neighbours experience; irrespective of their own policies, they simply cannot get their exports to market – but the most important point is that, in general, policy matters. If we look at the history of the South since the early 1980s, those countries that have adopted appropriate policies have reaped the reward of foreign investment, and those that have been unable to develop a coherent policy have suffered. Getting the policy right in this context does *not* mean simply adopting free market, liberal economic policies, as is sometimes suggested, and as the neoliberal proponents of the 'Washington Consensus' for some time in the 1980s and early 1990s made part of the conditions for assistance laid down by the IMF and the World Bank (on which more in the next chapter). Instead, it has usually involved quite extensive state intervention in free markets in order to shape development in the right direction, and has often involved overtly protectionist, and nationalist, policies. In short, the new global economy continues to be open to nationalist interpretations, but the particular variant of nationalism that was the 'structuralist' model is no longer as relevant – though, as stressed above, it remains politically very important.

Further reading

For texts on international political economy and the rise and fall of the Bretton Woods System, see the further reading for Chapter 7.

Karl Polanyi, *The Great Transformation* (1975), is a fine overview of the changes wrought by industrialization over the past 200 years, and a sustained account of the nature of the liberal society it has created. The volumes of the *Pelican History of the World Economy in the 20th Century* are generally valuable: Derek H. Aldcroft, *From Versailles to Wall Street 1919–1929* (1977); C. K. Kindleberger, *The World in Depression 1929–1939* (1973); and Herman Van der Wee, *Prosperity and Upheaval 1945–1980* (1986), are particularly useful. Kari Levit, 'Keynes and Polanyi: The 1920s and the 1990s' (2005) offers a quick historical introduction and useful appraisal of the contemporary significance of these earlier thinkers.

Classic texts by Ricardo, List and Rudolf Hilferding are collected, with extended commentaries, in Chris Brown, Terry Nardin and N. J. Rengger, *International Relations in Political Thought* (2002). On List, see also David Levi-Faur, 'Economic Nationalism: From Friedrich List to Robert Reich' (1997).

Paul Krugman and Maurice Obstfeld, *International Economics: Theory and Policy* (2002), is a standard text on international economics, but any introductory economics text will convey the basics of comparative advantage and the gains from trade. Paul Krugman is a vigorous, accessible and entertaining defender of liberal orthodoxy on trade; see his *Rethinking International Trade* (1994), *Pop Internationalism* (1996) and *The Accidental Theorist and Other Despatches from the Dismal Science* (1998). More recently, he has turned his fire on the Bush Administration: see *The Great Unravelling* (2004). Susan Strange, 'Protectionism and World Politics' (1985), makes a case for protectionism in some circumstances; Benjamin Cohen's review article, 'The Political Economy of International Trade' (1990), is also useful. Cohen's recent article in *Review of International Political Economy*, 'The Transatlantic Divide: Why Are American and British IPE so Different?' (2007), while ostensibly a bit of disciplinary navel-gazing, provides a good introduction to current broad issues in the subject and the global economy; responses by Richard Higgot, Matthew Watson and John Ravenhill expand the discussion.

Apart from the works by Frank and Wallerstein cited above, classic broadly 'structuralist' works would include Samir Amin, *Accumulation on a World Scale*, Vols I and II (1974), and *Imperialism and Unequal Development* (1977); Fernando Cardoso and Enzo Faletto, *Dependency and Development in Latin America* (1979); Arghiri Emmanuel, *Unequal Exchange* (1972); Johan Galtung, 'A Structural Theory of Imperialism' (1971); Raúl Prebisch, *The Economic Development of Latin America and Its Principal Problems* (1950); Walter Rodney, *How Europe Underdeveloped Africa* (1983); Immanuel Wallerstein, *Geopolitics and Geoculture: Essays on the Changing World System* (1991a); and most recently, André Gunder Frank and Barry Gills (eds), *The World System: Five Hundred Years or Five Thousand?* (1993). See also Special Issue on 'Dependence and Dependency in the Global System', *International Organization*, ed. James Caporaso (1978). Classic critiques of structuralism from the left include: Robert Brenner, 'The Origins of Capitalist Development' (1977); Ernesto Laclau, *Politics and Ideology in Marxist Theory* (1976); and Bill Warren, *Imperialism: Pioneer of Capitalism* (1980). Proving that no idea ever goes totally out of fashion, Erik Wibbels, 'Dependency Revisited: International Markets, Business Cycles, and Social Spending in the Developing World' (2006) returns to the idea that the structures of the global economy are hardly fair. Ray Kiely, 'Poverty Reduction through Liberalisation? Neoliberalism and the Myth of Global Convergence' (2007) is a critical rebuttal of self-satisfied neoliberal approaches to the global economy, which is expanded in Kiely's *The New Political Economy of Development* (2007). Phil Cerny, Susanne Soederberg and Georg Menz (eds), *Internalizing Globalization: The Rise of Neoliberalism and the Erosion of National Models of Capitalism* (2005) is similarly dissident from the mainstream. Brendan Donegan, 'Governmental Regionalism: Power/Knowledge and Neoliberal Regional Integration in Asia and Latin America' (2006) is one of the better applications of Foucault's ideas to IPE.

More orthodox approaches to development are still well represented by Ian M. D. Little, *Economic Development: Theory, Policy and International Relations* (1982). Powerful critics of structuralism from the position of neoclassical economics include Peter Bauer, *Equality, The Third World and Economic Delusion* (1981); and Deepak Lal, *The Poverty of 'Development Economics'* (1983). Stephen Krasner, *Structural Conflict: The Third World Against Global Liberalism* (1985) is an excellent work by a leading US International Relations theorist. On the 'debt crisis', see Miles Kaher (ed.), *The Political Economy of International Debt* (1986); and, for a different perspective, Susan George, *A Fate Worse than Debt* (1988). *International Organization* is a reliable source for mainstream work on the institutional aspects of global economics, the continued reconsideration of the neoliberal orthodoxy is evidenced in Richard Doner *et al.*, 'Systemic Vulnerability and the Origins of Development States: Northeast and Southeast Asia in Comparative Perspective' (2005); Helen Milner and Kubota Keiko, 'Why the Move to Free Trade? Democracy and Trade Policy in Developing Countries' (2005); and Marc Busch, 'Overlapping Institutions, Forum Shopping, and Dispute Settlement in International Trade' (2007). The *International Studies Review* forum on 'The North–South Divide and International Studies' (2007) is a useful primer.

For the new forces in IPE, particularly instructive/entertaining is the 'debate' between Stephen Krasner, 'International Political Economy: Abiding Discord' and Susan Strange, 'Wake up Krasner! The World *Has* Changed' (1994). Robert Gilpin, *The Challenge of Global Capitalism: The World Economy in the 21st Century* (2000) presents a wide-ranging, more orthodox, but by no means uncritical, account of the forces and ideas discussed in this chapter and offers another way into this material. Specifically on the multinational corporation, Kenichi Ohmae, *The Borderless World* (1990), and Robert Reich, *The Work of Nations* (1992), promote globalist accounts of the MNC, as do Richard Barnet and John Cavanagh in *Global Dreams: Imperial Corporations and the New World Order* (1994). Andrew Baker *et al.* (eds), *Governing Financial Globalization* (2005) address the importance of finance to the global economy. More conventional accounts of MNCs would include Raymond Vernon, *Sovereignty at Bay* (1971); see also the *Millennium* special issue 'Sovereignty at Bay, 20 Years After' (1991); and Robert Gilpin, *US Power and the Multinational Corporation* (1975). The approach adopted in this book is heavily influenced by John Stopford and Susan Strange, *Rival States, Rival Firms: Competition for World Market Shares* (1991) – see also Strange, 'States, Firms and Diplomacy' (1992); and Louis Turner and Michael Hodges, *Global Shakeout* (1992). A valuable study of the state in the age of multinational economic actors is Philip Cerny, *The Changing Architecture of Politics* (1990).

For general studies of the changes in the global economy summarized by the term globalization, see the further reading specified in Chapter 9.

The gap between 'structuralism' and new approaches to Southern poverty is partially bridged by works such as Immanuel Wallerstein, *Unthinking Social Science: The Limits of Nineteenth-Century Paradigms* (1991b); and Caroline Thomas, *In Search of Security: The Third World in International Relations* (1987). Other works here would include Paul Ekins, *A New World Order: Grassroots Movements for Global Change* (1992); Amartya Sen, *Poverty and Famine* (1982); John Cavanagh, Daphne Wysham and Marcos Arruda, *Beyond Bretton Woods: Alternatives to the Global Economic Order* (1994); and Barry Gills *et al.*, *Low Intensity Democracy: Political Power in the New World Order* (1993). Neil Harvey, *The Chiapas Rebellion* (1998), is the best account of that particular anti-systemic movement. Caroline Thomas and Peter Wilkin (eds), *Globalization and the South* (1999) is a useful collection. The *Review of International Political Economy* is a useful source of heterodox work on Southern poverty. The debate over global poverty continues with a volume of publicity unusual in academic publishing, but the most notable recent work is Paul Collier's *The Bottom Billion: Why the Poorest Countries are Failing and What Can Be Done About It* (2007). Similarly disillusioned with foreign aid are William Easterly's *The White Man's Burden: Why the West's Efforts to Aid the Rest Have Done So Much Ill and So Little Good* (2007), and Robert Calderisi's *The Trouble with Africa: Why Foreign Aid Isn't Working* (2007). Ha-Joon Chang, *Bad Samaritans: The Myth of Free Trade and the Secret History of Capitalism* (2007) takes the dissenting view that state control and intervention are the keys to economic growth both for the West and for the development success stories such as South Korea.

Chapter 9

Globalization

Introduction

There is no subject in contemporary international relations that attracts more nonsense than the notion of globalization. Much of this nonsense comes from the pen of theorists of 'hyperglobalization', many of whom work in business schools and write for a particular class of high-flying business executives (Held *et al.* 1999). Only such a person, for example, could write of the emergence of a 'borderless world' (Ohmae 1990). The world may seem borderless to people who turn left when they board an airliner, but one would not want to have to explain -- much less defend – the notion to the millions of refugees, displaced persons and asylum-seekers who find themselves shunted from one holding facility to another while their fate is determined. In fact, since 9/11, new security arrangements have meant that even top business executives are mildly inconvenienced when they cross borders, though passengers to the UK who land in private jets at Northolt Airport still have an easier time of it than the rest of us who use nearby Heathrow. This 'globaloney' is extremely irritating, but almost equally misleading is the characteristic professional deformation of the IR scholar, which is to deny that anything ever changes, or indeed could change this side of the Apocalypse. It may well be that certain things about human beings do not change, and so, say, Thucydides or Hobbes are still useful guides to the darker side of social life – but it would be truly extraordinary if the momentous changes in the way ordinary people live throughout the world did not have some impact both on international relations and on the theories that are developed to understand these relations. The task, then, is to keep a cool head; that is, to acknowledge change but also to recognize continuity, and all the time to remember that this is an unequal and divided world – things that seem very important to the rich and powerful are unlikely to be read in the same way by the poor and weak, and any account of globalization that does not place this fact continually before us will be radically deficient.

Bearing all this in mind, this chapter will fall into four parts. First, the political economy of globalization needs to be examined; the evolution of the world economy is central to any reasonable account of globalization, a fact that the hyperglobalizers got right, even though they got so much else wrong. Second, the impact of this evolution on the theories of political economy discussed in the previous chapter needs to be assessed. Third, an account needs to be given of the problems thrown up by the processes of global change, problems that the old Westphalian system cannot cope with; international environmental degradation is an obvious, but not exclusive, focus here. Finally, the putative emergence of a global civil society needs to be examined; is it really the case that global media and common consumption patterns are creating a new, genuinely global, social order?

A new economy?

Towards the end of the previous chapter some important changes in the world economy that have taken place since the early 1980s were described, most particularly the growing salience of giant corporations operating as 'multinationals' and integrating production on a global scale; and the emergence of a 24-hour, integrated, global capital market created by the fusion of national capital markets. These changes – in short, the emergence of an integrated global economy – are central to any account of globalization, but what has really made the difference has been the force behind these changes, which has been the runaway growth of the information technology industries. The rate of change in the area of information technology (IT) is staggering. 'Moore's Law' – named after the co-founder of Intel, Gordon Moore – states that the performance of processors will double every 18–24 months; physical limitations as to what can be done with silicon may end this process within the next decade, but the possibility of 'molecular electronics' could extend exponential growth into the 2050s (Overton 2000). Numbers of personal computers (PCs) and mobile phones, and the use of e-mail and the internet has been increasing exponentially, and as saturation point is reached with one technology, another takes its place. The 'runaway world' seems a reasonably sober characterization of this rate of change (Giddens 1999).

It should be noted that this progress is, for the most part, *not* being driven by need. For word-processing, e-mail and internet access, and the use of spreadsheets – that is, for the things that many, if not most, people buy PCs for – high processing speeds are more-or-less irrelevant, and large memories are only necessary because of the existence of complicated programs that contain features most people do not need, and because of continual upgrades of operating systems – the benefits of which for ordinary users are, again, doubtful. Interestingly, in response to this, a recent trend has been growth in the market for lightweight, solid-state, Linus-based machines; these mini-laptops began life as toys but have found a market with both business people

and students. In any event, it is not without significance that the single individual who is still the most potent symbol of the new technology – Bill Gates
of Microsoft – is at root a businessman rather than a scientist or technologist.
It is international business that drives forward this technology, though,
arguably, it has now reached the point where the dynamic is self-sustaining.

The new technologies have already revolutionized the way people in the
advanced industrial world live. Most of the readers of this book will be
involved in education in one way or another, and the majority will have first-
hand experience of the way in which the internet can be used for the trans-
mission of knowledge. Researchers exchange findings by e-mail and the World
Wide Web, international collaboration is easier than it has ever been, and
Wikipedia is a regularly used source of (often unreliable) knowledge. Current
events can be followed via YouTube as well as via online journals, newspapers
and blogs. But it is not simply the intellectual proletariat whose lives have been
transformed; the worker who reads your gas meter or repairs your refrigera-
tor will download the results via a laptop, modem and mobile phone, and
order spares in the same way. De-skilling and re-skilling takes place in a great
many professions and occupations: some things become easier, requiring fewer
skills – shop assistants no longer have to work their cash registers, and bank
clerks no longer have to total-up manually at the end of the day; and others
more difficult – it is unlikely that fridge repairers in the 1990s would have
needed basic IT skills. And all this has taken place in the last decade; even such
basic technologies as the photocopier, fax and word processor have only been
in general usage since the 1970s. Describing to today's students how mimeos
were 'run off' in the 1970s generates stares of blank incomprehension; equally,
explaining to a jazz fan in the 1970s how I am able to write this while listen-
ing to KJazz 88 Los Angeles on an internet radio would be next to impossible.

All this is in the rich world; the increasing importance of IT has had a major
effect on rich–poor relations – on the whole, heightening differences between
nations and continents, but not in the kind of systematic way that would re-
legitimate talk of the South as a coherent entity. The rich world still possesses
nearly three-quarters of the world's telephone lines – the single most important indicator of the ability to use the new technologies – and is home to the
majority of internet users, but Chinese websites and surfers proliferate, albeit
trapped behind the 'great firewall of China'. Thailand is not yet part of the
rich world, but is estimated to have more mobile telephones in use than the
whole of sub-Saharan Africa. Even the comparatively wealthy inhabitants of
African cities cannot reliably access the internet via the unreliable telephone
systems available to them, though this section of the population will eventually benefit from the availability of inexpensive satellite phones. On the other
hand, there have been some clear gainers on the periphery of the world
economy. India's 'silicon valley' in and around Bangalore has benefited greatly
from the presence of a well-educated, English-speaking population a conven-

ient number of time-zones away from the United States; software problems can be passed at the end of the American working day from New York and Los Angeles to Indian programmers, in the hope that solutions can be found overnight – and many Indian programmers have made successful careers in the US as valued migrants. If the computer you bought in the UK develops a fault, it is a safe bet that the service centre that answers your call for help will be in South India – the telephone call having been re-routed via the internet. And, speaking of peripheries, internet use in New Zealand is just about the highest in the world.

Put the impact of IT together with the trend towards an integrated global economy, and the central features of the political economy of globalization become apparent. They are the *dematerialization* and *disembedding* of production. Dematerialization refers to the fact that the cutting edge of contemporary capitalism is not about the production of physical goods – which increasingly takes place in the more politically stable parts of the old South – but rather the manipulation of symbols. American global dominance used to be symbolized by US Steel and General Motors; now it is Microsoft, Intel, Time-Warner and Disney that symbolize this dominance. The actual physical products they are still involved with – for example, Intel's Pentium chips – are largely made outside the USA. In the early 1980s, Bill Gates turned Microsoft into a world leader by realizing that there was more money to be made from producing the operating systems used by computers than by producing the computers themselves. Once-mighty IBM allowed him to dominate the software market and nearly went under. In the 1990s, Gates himself nearly made the same mistake, allowing the emergence of an independent internet browser; Microsoft's subsequent attempt to destroy Netscape led it directly into an anti-trust suit that almost produced the downfall of the firm. Meanwhile, in August 2004, Google, a search engine that can use Netscape, Safari (the Apple Mac browser) or Internet Explorer, was launched as a public company and initially valued at around US$25 billion.

Disembedding follows from dematerialization. When what was being produced were *things*, *where* they were produced was crucial, and one could still plausibly think about a national economy. Is this still the case? The extent to which national economies have disappeared can be exaggerated. There are still a lot of material things being produced in the advanced industrial world – though often as top-of-the-range, niche products rather than as genuine mass market goods, and even then your new BMW, Mercedes or Saab will be made out of a large number of components imported from lower-wage economies – and, as Paul Hirst and Grahame Thompson (1999) have eloquently and persuasively argued, the statistical evidence on capital creation suggests that the national economy remains far more central than one might have expected. Still, the integration of global production and the emergence of global capital markets, combined with the impact of the new technologies, does suggest that it is more difficult than it once was to conceptualize the idea of a national economy. The next question is, what are the implications of these trends for the theories of political economy set out in the previous chapter?

Neoliberalism and its critics

The most influential response to these trends since the 1980s has been the revival of liberal political economy, now often described as 'neoliberalism' (not to be confused, though it often is, with the liberal institutionalism described in Chapter 3 above). The neoliberal position is that many of the options that appeared to be available to governments in the post-1945 era are no longer on offer. In that immediate post-1945 era a variety of different models of the economy coexisted; setting aside the communist command model, even within capitalism there was great variation, with different levels of planning and welfare provision in different countries or groups of countries; Keynesian ideas of demand management were accepted with varying degrees of enthusiasm. Social democratic and quasi-corporatist politics dominated many European polities. The majority of developing countries adopted socialist models of one kind or another, albeit usually with a substantial role for the private sector.

Since the late 1970s, with the rise of the integrated global economy described above, the range of possible economic systems seems to have narrowed quite substantially. The biggest single change has been the complete collapse of the communist model post-1989, at least in part because of its failure to keep up with the West, but, more generally, social democratic and welfarist economies have come under great pressure. The point about social democracy is that it relies on the ability of the state to control key economic variables, such as interest rates and the level of employment, and this involves an ability to isolate particular countries from global trends, an ability that is being undermined by the forces discussed above. Unified capital markets and the control of key areas of production by giant firms make even the limited autonomy required by social democracy difficult to achieve. States can exclude foreign competition and limit the capacity of foreigners to own domestic corporations, but they do so at a very high cost. In technology-driven areas, local national firms will only be able to survive if they enter into R&D arrangements with foreign corporations, the alternative being that their products will be increasingly out-of-date and unattractive even to domestic customers – the fate of car manufacturers in the UK and the USA. Openness to external investment, on the other hand, brings dividends in terms of jobs, tax revenues and exports – witness the revived Anglo-Japanese car industry – but in order to be attractive to foreign firms, unwelcome changes may be needed domestically.

In the English-speaking countries and in Scandinavia, welfare states have been under extreme pressure as a result of these factors, and demand-management has been abandoned almost completely as a strategy. The economics profession has come to be dominated by neoclassical economic liberalism, and the political expressions of the latter, Thatcherism in Britain and 'Reagonomics' in the USA to the fore, have established a firm footing. In effect, the New Labour (1997–) and New Democrat (1993–2000) administrations in the UK and the USA have accepted a great deal of the economic thought of their Conservative/Republican predecessors, as have social democrat governments in most of the rest of the world. Only in France, Belgium and, to a much lesser extent, Germany, is neoliberalism seriously resisted at a government level – and even in those countries it is doubtful whether the costs of an extremely expensive welfare state will be politically bearable for much longer; certainly, President Sarkozy and Chancellor Merkel would like to bring about reform in France and Germany, respectively, but whether the vested interests that do so well out of the present system, largely at the expense of a very large, excluded underclass, will let them, is still moot.

In short, it is increasingly the case that it is accepted as part of the common sense of the age that markets should be as free as possible, that physical controls, price controls and planning do not and will not work, and that economies should be as open to the rest of the world as possible. This 'neoliberal' position was dominant in the major economic international organizations in the first half of the 1990s, and in that context became known as the 'Washington Consensus', which provided the intellectual backbone for the programmes recommended by the IMF and the World Bank for developing countries requiring the assistance of those bodies, programmes that mandated the prioritization of low inflation, the ending of price controls, the cutting of government spending and a general opening-up to the world economy. Also part of this package was and is the notion of 'good governance', which essentially meant the adoption of Western modes of government in order to make these developing countries attractive to foreign investors. In some respects this has been a progressive move – non-corrupt democratic government and the rule of law are not only valuable for MNCs, they are also welcomed by most local citizens, though the occasional attempt to impose US accounting standards and patent law has been less welcome. In any event, it is worth noting that this programme of policies is widely regarded as having failed even within the community of IMF/World Bank/US Treasury officials who created it in the fist place. There have been very few success stories for the Washington Consensus and plenty of examples of increased suffering for ordinary people; cuts in government spending were usually targeted on the poor, and the ending of price controls on basic foodstuffs added to the misery. Figures such as Joseph Stiglitz, until 1999 Chief Economist at the World Bank, have acknowledged that this is so and become very critical of neoliberal ideas (Stiglitz

2004). However, there has been no swing back towards socialist or social democratic approaches to the economy, and in a strong sense neoliberal ideas have come to dominate the political economy of globalization –though it is a moot point whether the trend towards de-regulation will survive the credit crunch; the re-regulation of financial markets at least seems on the cards.

Neo-Gramscian critics argue that this is an example of the establishment of a new kind of hegemony. This is hegemony in a different sense from that discussed in Chapter 7, in the context of 'hegemonic stability'. There, hegemony meant a certain kind of domination exercised by a particular actor, albeit with the tacit consent of others. Here, hegemony refers to the way in which certain kinds of ideas become seen as so much part of the common sense of a society that they cease to be seen as 'ideas' at all, but rather become part of 'how things really are'. This notion of hegemony was developed by Gramsci in the 1920s, building on Marx's notion of ideology, but it is not necessarily tied to Marxist – as opposed to radical – accounts of the world.

Neoliberal ideas are hegemonic on a global scale in so far as they have genuinely captured the common sense of the age about economic matters. This hegemony is discernable in the behaviour of the opponents of neoliberalism; it is striking that, while a great many groups have presented strong critiques of economic globalization, positive alternatives are fewer on the ground. Thus, for example, the demonstrators on the streets in the 'Battle of Seattle' at the major WTO conference in November 1999 and on many subsequent occasions agreed that they were opposed to the WTO and 'world capitalism', but were much less clear about what they favoured – and when alternatives were mooted they tended to be mutually contradictory. The opponents included economic nationalists, socialists, and 'deep-green' opponents of industrial society as well as more moderate environmentalists and human rights activists, and their inability to find even the elements of a common programme seriously hampers their effectiveness as pressure groups. One May Day demonstrator in London in 2001 held aloft a banner reading 'Replace Capitalism with Something Nicer' – even if this was meant as a joke, it is as straightforward an illustration of the inability to present a coherent alternative to neoliberalism as one could ask for, and a clear sign of the latter's hegemony.

In the above discussion, neoliberalism has been treated as a set of ideas, but, of course, it is far more than that; it is not necessary to be a Marxist to think that the triumph of neoliberalism represents the triumph of certain kinds of interests – though, clearly, Marxists will have a particular account of the kinds of interests that will shape systems of thought. One of the forces driving neoliberalism has been the emergence of giant corporations in whose interests many of the precepts of neoliberalism work, while the rise of the giant corporation is itself partly shaped by the rise of neoliberal ideas. There is a dialectic at work here that makes it difficult, if not impossible, to say that one of these forces created the other. The spread of neoliberal ideas has been hastened by the restructuring of the world production system that has taken place since the 1980s, *and vice versa.*

Before accepting the hegemonic status of neoliberalism, however, it might be as well to ask whether the options available to states are quite as limited as both the neoliberals and their Gramscian opponents argue. The role of the state may have changed, but it has not disappeared; certainly, globalization has made some forms of state intervention ineffective, but the political challenge posed by globalization has encouraged states to develop new techniques, and, perhaps most of all, new attitudes. What we may be seeing is the emergence of a new kind of diplomacy involving firms and states (Strange 1992, 1996). As technology comes to dominate production processes, so firms in advanced sectors come to find that their long-run survival depends on their ability to conduct the R&D that will keep them in the forefront of their sector. Absolute size is crucial here, which means that access to markets is crucial, either directly or via arrangements with other firms. Since states can, at a pinch, control access to markets – and can sanction or forbid franchising arrangements or take-overs – the desire that firms have to expand gives states a degree of leverage over their activities. On the other hand, states want successful, technologically-advanced firms to be located on their territories – inward investment generates employment, supports regional policy, provides a tax base and contributes to the export capacity of a country. This means that firms have something to offer states, and thus a good bargaining position.

Put another way, both states and firms are concerned with 'market share'; firms want the largest market share they can get, and states want firms with the largest market share they can get on their territories. The new diplomacy is about the ways in which firms and states achieve their ends. It is a triangular diplomatic system. States negotiate and bargain with other states – about access to each other's markets and, within the European Union, for example, about the crucial rules governing what degree of 'local content' is required for, say, a Toyota Corolla constructed in Britain to count as a British as opposed to a Japanese car. States negotiate and bargain with firms – about the terms and conditions upon which the latter are allowed to operate on the territory of the former, the tax concessions that new investment will attract, the location of this investment, the employment it will provide, and, currently in the case of the UK, the impact of joining or not joining the single European currency. Firms negotiate and bargain with other firms – about co-production, about pooling R&D, about franchising, sometimes about co-ownership. Each of the three sides of this diplomacy affects the other two. The attractiveness of one state over another as a location for new investment (state–firm diplomacy) will often depend on its ability to guarantee access to the markets of other states (state–state diplomacy) and the degree to which incoming firms are able to negotiate deals with at least some of those already in the market (firm–firm diplomacy).

This new diplomacy changes the agenda on MNCs; much of the past literature on MNCs paid great attention to the repatriation of profits, the implication being that foreign corporations exploited the local economy for the benefit of *rentiers* back home. Nowadays any corporation, local or global, that does not invest most of its profits in R&D will not be around very long to pay out dividends to its shareholders. Perhaps most of all, the notion of 'sovereignty at bay' is highly misleading (Vernon 1971). On the one hand, as we have seen, sovereignty in the old sense of complete control of a territory probably never existed, and, in any event, is now long gone; on the other hand, the ability to be effectively sovereign today – to meet the welfare needs of one's population, to promote economic growth – depends crucially on getting into a healthy relationship with international business. A strong state is a state that is able to use MNCs for its own ends, not one that excludes them or prevents them from making a profit. It is here that the 'good governance' referred to above with respect to developing countries becomes crucial – corrupt, undemocratic, irresponsible local elites will not be successful in using MNCs for national ends, although they may be very successful at filling their own offshore bank accounts.

New global problems – 'Westfailure' and the environment

This is a discussion that could be continued more or less indefinitely, but it is necessary to move on and look at some of the specific problems raised by globalization. The central issue here is the apparent inability of our present global political system to cope with the problems created by globalization. Although she hated the latter term, the British scholar Susan Strange provided a good account of the dilemma here in her last, posthumously published, article, 'The Westfailure System' (1999). She begins by arguing, uncontroversially, that sovereign states claiming the monopoly of legitimate violence within a territory grew up in symbiosis with a capitalist market economy, but then argues that the latter now poses problems that cannot be solved within the terms set by the former. Specifically, these problems concern the global credit/finance system, which is a source of recurrent crises that are irresolvable because states are unwilling to give power to an international central bank; the inability of the sovereignty system to cope with environmental degradation because the absence of authoritative decision-making and effective enforcement undermines collective action; and the humanitarian failures generated both by global inequalities, which are widening and increasingly unmanageable, and by the inability of the state to protect its citizens from global economic forces. In short, she argues, the system has failed to satisfy the long-term conditions for sustainability: Westphalia is 'Westfailure'.

This is a strong argument – and a rather pessimistic one, since Strange offers no solution here. Humanitarian failings have been addressed somewhat already and will be returned to later in the context of 'humanitarian intervention' in Chapter 11, and the issue of a global central bank – a particular interest of Strange's – would require an excessively technical discussion, so the focus here will be on the environment, which is both deeply serious as an issue, and highly revealing in terms of what it tells us about contemporary IR. One of the first principles of traditional international law is that state sovereignty involves control over natural resources and local economic activity. Some such principle is implied by the very nature of the modern state – unlike, for example, some medieval institutions, contemporary political forms have been territorial since at least the seventeenth century, and territoriality involves a claim of ownership over natural resources. Moreover, the nature of capitalist economies as they have developed over the same time period has been such that it was inevitable that in the advanced industrial countries 'ownership' would not be interpreted as 'stewardship' but as 'dominion'. Natural resources were there to be exploited for gain by landowners, the state, and perhaps, at least in modern welfare capitalist societies, the people. However, even in the latter case, 'the people' means 'citizens of the state in question' and not people generally: until comparatively recently, the idea that a state might be held globally accountable for economic activities conducted on its territory would have seemed incompatible with the first principles of the system.

This attitude began to change in the late 1960s and early 1970s. In the first place it became clear that certain kinds of economic activity could have quite dramatic effects beyond the borders of the state in question: the phenomenon of 'acid rain' is paradigmatic here, with deforestation in, for example, Scandinavia or Canada caused by industrial pollution originating in Britain, Germany or the United States. However, while these are serious issues, they pose no particularly interesting theoretical problems. In principle, cross-border pollution is much the same as intra-border pollution; cleaning up the Rhine (which flows through several states) is more complicated than cleaning up the Thames, but poses the same sorts of problems – in particular, how to cost what economists call 'externalities', whether to regard pollution control as a general charge on taxation or something that can be handled on the basis that the polluter pays, and so on. Once the problem is recognized, capitalist economies have fewer problems dealing with this sort of question than one might expect. Private ownership cuts both ways – it can hinder collective action, but it also means that it is, in principle, possible to identify and hold accountable the agents of environmental degradation. An interesting contrast here is with the far greater difficulties in controlling direct pollution experienced by communist industrial powers, where 'public ownership' provided a reason for not tackling similar problems, as the post-communist states that have inherited dead rivers and urban industrial nightmares have reason to be aware.

Of greater long-term significance was the second reason for the increased salience of environmental issues in the early 1970s, namely a growing consciousness that there might be 'limits to growth' (Meadows *et al.* 1974). It was argued that industrial civilization depended on the ever-faster consumption of materials, the supply of which was, by definition, finite. Hydrocarbon-based fuels that had been created over millions of years were being consumed in decades. Demand for resources that were, in principle, renewable – such as wood or agricultural products – was growing faster than matching supplies, creating other potential shortages further down the line. The point about these rather doom-laden predictions was that, unlike phenomena such as acid rain, they challenged the prospects of continued and sustained economic growth, the central driving force and legitimating principle of contemporary industrial society. If sustained, such a challenge would bring about a dramatic reshaping of the politics of the advanced industrial countries, but it would pose far greater problems for the 'developing' world which was, if anything, even more reliant on the beneficial effects of general economic growth than the rich world.

In fact, these problems were put on hold for a few years. The downturn in economic activity in the 1970s reduced demand for raw materials, and new technological advances such as the microchip revolution were less dependent on material input than the old technologies. The 'limits to growth' predictions were, in any event, probably excessively pessimistic, and, moreover and quite fortunately, self-defeating, since they concentrated minds to a far greater extent on energy conservation, recycling, and the development of new resources. In the sense in which the term was used then, we are, clearly, still a long way away from reaching the limits of growth. None the less, the debates of the 1970s were a useful rehearsal for the problems that have emerged in the 1980s and 1990s and, a fortiori in the 2000s. Climatic changes such as the depletion of the ozone layer and global warming, rising water levels, deforestation, loss of biodiversity and the desertification of large parts of Africa pose similar sorts of challenges to the civilization of productivity to those posed by the idea of limits to growth – with the significant difference that these challenges are rather better supported by scientific opinion, and rather less amenable to piecemeal responses. This time it really does seem possible that 'we', all of us, may have to change the way we live – if we, or 'our' states, can summon the willpower so to do.

The case of chlorofluorocarbons (CFCs), which attack the ozone layer, is instructive. The Vienna Convention for the Protection of the Ozone Layer in 1985, protocols on the same subject from Montreal 1987 and London 1990, and discussion at the United Nations Conference on Environment and Development (UNCED) in Rio in 1992 and in a number of subsequent forums

– especially Kyoto 1998 – bear witness to the perceived importance of ozone depletion and the need to cut the emission of CFCs. An interesting question is: how did this perception arise? It is clear that there are quite good, albeit short-sighted, reasons why states might not want to take up this issue. CFCs are created by the employment of technologies which, while they are polluting, are undoubtedly cheaper than the alternatives. Developing states that wish to foster the increased use of refrigeration want to employ the cheapest technology available, which creates CFCs; developed countries are equally disinclined to cease using technologies on which they have come to depend. Everyone has a long-term interest in avoiding the stripping away of the earth's protective shield, but everyone equally has a short-term interest in not leading the way in this matter. This is a classic problem of collective action, notoriously difficult to address; however, while few would describe the response of the international community as wholly adequate, the issue is, at least, on the agenda. Why? How did it get there?

The answer seems to be that it got there because of the emergence of a consensus among scientists that it was a problem that could no longer be avoided; on the basis of this consensus, governments were lobbied and, often reluctantly, convinced that they had to act. This is an example of an interesting new phenomenon in international relations – the emergence of international 'pressure' groups, the source of whose influence is the possession of highly specialized technical knowledge rather than more conventional political resources. Peter Haas (1989) has introduced the term *epistemic communities* into the literature to describe such groups. It is clear that, in the right circumstances, they can be very effective; governments can be made to feel that they have no alternative other than to act in the way that the scientific consensus indicates. There may often be a scarcely concealed political threat here – act or we shall reveal to the public your willingness to expose them to life-threatening risk – but the basic influence exerted by epistemic communities arises simply from their ability, or at least the public's belief in their ability, to provide a dominant interpretation of the nature of the problem.

Yet the significance of epistemic communities should not be overestimated. They require the right conditions to be effective; such conditions include a near-consensus among the relevant knowledge holders, and an issue that does not touch the core interests of states. One interesting feature of epistemic communities is their lack of democratic legitimacy. Greenpeace International is a salient case here, because it is often seen as the paradigm of a pressure group that employs scientific expertise to make its case in global civil society. Greenpeace scientists are highly regarded, and their opinions are taken very seriously by large parts of Western public opinion. They have been capable of scoring quite important political successes – the Brent Spar affair of 1995 is a case in point, when a Greenpeace campaign involving a public relations blitz and consumer boycotts succeeded in reversing a decision by Shell and the

British government to scuttle the redundant Brent Spar oil platform in the Atlantic Ocean. As it turns out, there were mistakes in Greenpeace's calculations, and it is still a matter of dispute whether disposal at sea might not have been the most environmentally sound strategy, but what is interesting, and might in some circumstances be rather sinister, is that the unelected, unaccountable Greenpeace scientists were able to manipulate public opinion and override the will of a democratically elected government and its scientific advisers. There is an added irony here – many of Greenpeace's supporters have a very sceptical view of the authority of science in general, and yet it is precisely the public's lack of scepticism on this issue that gives the organization its clout.

Moving away from epistemic communities, environmental politics have had a major impact on the normative issue of global justice, most importantly by highlighting the tensions between approaches to justice that focus on the rights of communities and those that focus on global concerns. A generation or so ago, the issue of global inequality was relatively easy to comprehend, and the remedy for world poverty appeared equally unproblematic – though, of course, action to relieve poverty was another matter. Poor states were 'underdeveloped' and thus needed to 'develop'; there were intense debates as to whether development was possible under the current world economic system, but the goal itself was less at issue – the consensus in favour of 'development' ranged from free-market liberals to dependency theorists via old-style Marxists. The Washington Consensus was simply the most recent expression of this developmentalist perspective. But it is clear that in one crucial respect this consensus was fundamentally wrong: the one thing we can be sure about the future is that it will *not* involve a global industrial civilization in which the developing nations become developed and possess advanced industrial economies following the model of the West in the 1950s and 1960s – or, at least, if such a future does come into existence, the price paid will be intolerable unless some quite extraordinary technological advances change the calculations fundamentally. If the dream of development has become a nightmare, where does this leave those countries whose current situation is such that even the scenario of a raped and pillaged environment might count as an improvement?

The contrast between the needs and interests of the world as a whole and those of particular countries seems acute. On the one hand, it is clear that industrial development on the Western model, if generalized to China, the Indian sub-continent, Africa and Latin America, would be a disaster for everyone, including the peoples of those regions, but it is equally clear that the governments of the South will wish to go down this route unless they are presented with sufficient incentives to do otherwise. No such incentive scheme is likely to work if the end result is a world in which the peoples and governments of the North are allowed to preserve the undoubted benefits of an industrial civilization denied to the South. On the other hand, it is equally clear that something has to be done to cut carbon emissions in the United States, which has refused to sign or ratify the Kyoto Accords, and which persists in refusing to tax gasoline for power generation and transport at rates that would discourage waste – and indeed allows the ubiquitous sport utility vehicle (SUV) to flout those controls on waste materials from auto exhausts that do exist (not that the Europeans have a much better record, though they do talk a better game). What is striking about both these cases is that the problems are not created by special interests or political elites; it is ordinary people who want cheap refrigeration in China, and cheap gasoline, central heating and air-conditioning in the USA – certainly in the latter case some of the oil companies have lobbied against Kyoto, but the failure to ratify that treaty is largely a function of the fact that no Senator wants to face his or her electorate after endorsing major increases at the petrol pump.

A kind of stalemate seems to have developed here; the USA is unwilling to envisage major changes in its policies on CO_2 emissions, while China is building two new coal-fired power stations every week, but China is, understandably, unwilling to slow down its drive for prosperity and leave the present inequalities between nations intact. However, there are some signs that this log-jamming may be breaking up; the Bush Administration in the USA has finally acknowledged that climate change does pose a real problem, which might not seem much comfort, but is a distinct shift in attitudes, and attitudes are likely to shift even further when President Obama takes office. Meanwhile, the extraordinary measures that were taken to ensure that athletes did not experience problems at the Beijing games in the Summer of 2008 illustrated to everyone, including the Chinese leadership, how serious a problem is air pollution in Chinese cities.

In any event, this is an issue that strikes at the heart of the settled norms of the current international order. The ruling assumption of this order is that individual states have the right to pursue their own conception of the Good without external interference; the norms of the system are designed to promote coexistence rather than problem-solving. The challenge posed by the destruction of the environment is one of the ways in which this ruling assumption is under threat, one example of the way in which the emergence of a global industrial civilization has, apparently, outstripped the political forms available to us – a classic example of 'Westfailure'.

One response to this situation has been, perhaps ironically, to widen the scope of one of the key concepts of the old Westphalian system – security. As concern over military security became less pressing in the post-Cold War period, so a wider conception of security has come to the fore, promoted by the 'Copenhagen School', whose leading members are Barry Buzan and Ole Waever, and the critical security studies movement, many of whose most prominent members are to be found at the University of Wales, Aberystwyth. The basic thought for both groups is that, whether the referent object of security is an individual, group, state or nation, 'security' is an ontological status, that of feeling secure, which at any one time may be under threat from a number of different directions. Clearly, one such is external military threat, but it is also the case that depletion of the ozone layer, mass unemployment, large-scale drug trafficking, crime and the arrival on its borders of large numbers of refugees can each threaten the security of a state. Moreover, the security of individuals is also bound up with these threats, both in so far as individuals are members of communities, but also, and perhaps more importantly, in circumstances where the security of the individual may be threatened by the state itself. Denial of human rights, ill-treatment and persecution for reasons of gender or sexual orientation, the deprivations of famine and poverty are all factors that threaten the security of individuals and fall within the purview of the new security studies.

As both Copenhagen and Aberystwyth are aware, there is clearly an issue here as to whether it is appropriate to 'securitize' these issues; it might well be held that securitization induces highly inappropriate reactions to some of these problems – for example, the way in which asylum-seekers have been demonized as 'bogus' in a great deal of recent political discourse in Britain may reflect the view that these harmless individuals are represented as posing some kind of threat to the security of the nation. In the case of the main subject matter of this section, it could well be argued that the impact of securitizing the environment is to make the problem of environmental degradation more difficult to solve – instead of treating this as a common problem for humanity as a whole, the tendency might be to regard other people's behaviour as a threat to oneself, and thus, mentally and perhaps physically, to throw the cost of change on others. It might also be argued that, in our modern 'risk society', too much emphasis on security is inappropriate; learning to live creatively with insecurity may be more to the point than excessive concern with the kind of stable identities that can no longer be sustained (Beck 1999). This is an interesting potential starting-point for a discussion of the wider social impact of globalization.

Global civil society?

As the notion of Beck's Risk Society illustrates, some sociologists have addressed the extent to which globalization has changed our conceptions of society but, for the purposes of this book, a more important question is whether there is emerging some kind of genuinely global society, and, if so, what is its nature? A number of individual writers and schools of thought have answered the first of these questions in the affirmative, and there is now a burgeoning literature on the notion of 'global civil society', including a very useful annual, the *Global Civil Society Yearbook*.

The notion of 'civil society' emerged in eighteenth-century thought and denoted the idea of a social space organizing itself separately from, and potentially set against, both the state and the extended family, the two social institutions that previously dominated human existence. This notion – developed by Adam Ferguson, Adam Smith and, in a different way, G. W. F. Hegel – was revived in the 1980s and early 1990s in response to the fall of communism, which, many argued, had been deficient precisely because it systematically denied the possibility of the existence of such a space. The idea of a 'global civil society' developed in parallel with the institutions of global governance described in Chapter 7. The institutions act as a substitute for the state, while global civil society itself is partly signified by the existence of informal, non-state, transnational pressure groups (often in the area of the environment, but also encompassing human rights, animal rights, the anti-global-capitalist movement, pro-capitalist groupings such as Davos and Bilderberg, religious movements, transnational political parties and so on), and reinforced as a global phenomenon by cross-cultural global trends in consumption, entertainment and 'infotainment'. This latter point is very important; the existence of global branding and global media is one of the most striking features of our world. McDonald's arches have become symbols of one world brand, though nowadays Starbucks has replaced McDonald's as a more sophisticated example of global branding, and the Nike 'swoosh' is equally well-known – Michael Jordan, the basketball-playing symbol of Nike, has some claim to be the most recognizable man on the planet, except, as it happens, in the UK, where basketball has not yet become a mass television sport (LaFeber 1999).

There are several features of this account of global civil society that are worthy of note. First, it should be noted that nearly all of the global brands, and most of the transnational pressure groups, originate from a very small number of countries in the advanced industrial world – over time, India and China may produce such brands, but for the moment the generalization holds. As to the former, the notion of a globalization of world culture has certainly become fused with the idea that the world is becoming 'Americanized'. Certainly, most of the global brands are American in origin, as are most of the players in the infotainment business (though in the Arab world the Al Jazeera network has eclipsed both CNN and the BBC) and it has become customary for opponents of globalization to regard these forces as the instruments of American cultural imperialism; trashing a McDonald's or a Starbucks has become the twenty-first-century equivalent of the traditional protest of attacking the local American Embassy. On the other hand, globalization is, if anything, more of a threat to American culture than to that of the rest of the world; French bistros and cafés will remain, but the American roadside diner is rapidly disappearing. Also, in parenthesis, the extent to which global brands actually extend choice and improve quality ought not to be forgotten; the success of McDonald's in many parts of the world rests precisely on the standardization of quality disapproved of by gourmets – the certainty that the hamburgers they are eating are made of materials that pass stringent health tests is a major attraction for many consumers in parts of the world where this cannot always be guaranteed. Similarly, Britons and Americans who enjoy good coffee have every reason to be grateful for the existence of franchises such as Starbucks and the Seattle Coffee Company, even if nowadays we frequent their local competitors. There is a wider point here; the success of global brands rests ultimately on the consumer, and even when the consumer acts for reasons that are not as rational as that imputed here to British coffee-lovers, there is no justification for failing to respect their choices.

Of perhaps greater long-run significance is the generally Western origin of the transnational groups that are at the heart of the notion of global civil society. Very frequently, these groups claim to act on behalf of the poor and dispossessed of the world, and, in many cases, do important and necessary work – but there is, none the less, an element of *de haut en bas* about this activity: Lady Bountiful distributing charity to the peasants. This feeling is amplified by the fact that these groups are different in kind from their immediate predecessors. Transnational groups such as the Red Cross made a point of their neutrality and non-judgemental approaches to conflict – sometimes taking this attitude to extremes, as in the Red Cross's refusal to comment on the Nazi death-camps in the Second World War, focusing instead on the conditions of regular prisoners of war. New groups such as Médecins Sans Frontières (MSF) – formed by French doctors as a breakaway from the Red Cross during the Biafra conflict of the late 1960s – are explicitly political and aim to act as advocates internationally for those who are suffering, which inevitably involves interfering in local politics.

This raises a second set of questions about global civil society. The groups of which it is composed are, in a literal sense, irresponsible – that is, not that they behave irresponsibly, but that they are responsible to no one. One of the features of the original idea of civil society was that it presumed the existence of an effective state, which would prevent any one group in civil society from exercising too much power – such a constraint is much hazier at the global level. Groups such as MSF and Greenpeace International exercise as much power as they can by appealing directly to (Western) public opinion, often over the heads of democratically elected governments. Progressively-minded people of good will might not be too worried about the activities of these particular groups – though, as we have seen, Greenpeace International is as capable of getting the science wrong as anyone else – but, of course, global civil society is not simply composed of progressive groups; fascists, paedophiles, drug-dealers, and religious extremists also form transnational groups and are rather less benign, while it is not only groups like Greenpeace that can use 'direct action' in support of their policies. When French farmers block roads throughout France in order to preserve agricultural subsides that are against the interests of the developing world, they too are part of global civil society, as are the British truck-drivers who blockaded power stations in the autumn of 2000 in opposition to environmentally-friendly taxes on petrol consumption. Sauce for the goose is also sauce for the gander, and well-meaning demonstrators who gaily break the law in the interest, as they see it, of the wider good ought not to be surprised when others use the same tactics for different ends.

Still, the fact that global civil society can be profoundly anti-democratic and patronizing to the poor, while interesting in view of the progressivist credentials of most of its promoters, does not address the core issue, which is how significant this phenomenon actually is. Does the notion of global civil society have real explanatory power? The 'Stanford School' of sociologists argues that nation-state identities, structures and behaviours are increasingly shaped by world society, and that 'world culture celebrates, expands, and standardizes strong but culturally somewhat tamed national actors' (Meyer *et al.* 1997: 173). This is quite a strong claim – though it ought to be noted that English School writers on the idea of International Society also talk about the 'taming' of national actors. In the nineteenth century this was known as imposing the 'standards of civilization' on regimes that did not practice the rule of law, or respect property rights in ways that the members of the, then predominantly European, society of states considered adequate; 'cultural taming' is a rather good, albeit somewhat euphemistic, term to describe this process (Gong 1984).

Before global civil society can do much work, however, there are three features of the current world order that need to be taken on board, and these will be the subjects of the next three chapters. First, globalization creates uniformity, but it also creates resistance to uniformity – a new international politics of identity is emerging; the subject of Chapter 10. Second, if a global civil society is to emerge, it must be on the basis of some kind of normative foundation, possibly in international law and the international human rights regime; the subject of Chapter 11. Finally, global civil society must be read in the context of the general structure of the international system – the subject of the final chapter of this book. Before moving on, though, a question dodged throughout this chapter can be avoided no longer – what, exactly, is globalization? Jan Aart Scholte offers the following as the first of his core theses on the subject: 'globalization is a transformation of social geography marked by the growth of supraterritorial spaces *but* globalization does not entail the end of territorial geography; territoriality and supraterritoriality coexist in complex interrelations' (Scholte 2000: 8) and, as we have seen, both the initial definition and the qualifier get to the heart of the issue.

Further reading

General studies of the economic dimension of globalization include David Held *et al.*, *Global Transformations* (1999), and *The Global Transformations Reader* (2nd edn 2003), and Jan Aart Scholte, *Globalization 2nd ed* (2005). David Held and Andrew McGrew return once more with *Globalization Theories: approaches and controversies* (2007). Earlier valuable works from a variety of positions include Anthony McGrew *et al.*, *Global Politics: Globalization and the Nation State* (1992); Christopher Chase-Dunn, *Global Formation: Structures of the World Economy* (1989); P. Dicken, *Global Shift: The Internationalization of Economic Activity* (2004); Paul Kennedy, *Preparing for the Twenty-first Century* (1993); Kenichi Ohmae, *The Borderless World* (1990); and Michael Veseth, *Selling Globalization: The Myth of the Global Economy* (1998). Paul Hirst and Grahame Thompson, *Globalization in Question: The International Economy and the Possibilities of Governance* (2000) is a thoroughly researched and compellingly argued rebuttal of, at least, extreme versions of the thesis. The relationship between liberalism and globalization is explored in the Millennium special issue, 'The Globalization of Liberalism' (1995). On the general debate on globalization, two characteristic papers by the late Susan Strange cover a great deal of the debate – the review essay 'Globaloney' (1998a) expresses one point of view, but the posthumous 'The Westfailure System' (1999) shows the reverse of the medal.

On globalization as a social and cultural phenomenon, there is a vast amount of literature. Manuel Castells, *The Information Age: Economy, Society and Culture*, 3 vols (1996/7), is a monumental study; with Martin Albrow, *The Global Age: State and Society Beyond Modernity* (1996), equally ambitious, if on a smaller canvas. Zygmund Bauman, *Globalization: The Human Consequences* (1998); Ulrich Beck, *World Risk Society* (1999); Saskia Sassen, *Globalization and its Discontents* (1998), and Leslie Sklair, *The Sociology of the Global System* (1995), offer further sociological perspectives. Anthony Giddens' Reith Lecture, *The Runaway World* (1999), is aimed at a wider, non-academic market, but is none the less highly thought-provoking. John Tomlinson, *Globalization and Culture* (1999), pulls together a great deal of material on this subject. Justin Rosenberg, *Follies of Globalization Theory* (2001) is a sceptical response.

From within the world of IR theory, there have been a number of excellent contributions from different perspectives. Without relying on the term globalization, J. N. Rosenau, *Along the Domestic–Foreign Frontier: Exploring Governance in a Turbulent World* (1997), is a valuable contribution to this literature. Richard Falk's *Predatory Globalization: A Critique* (1999) is a useful corrective to the over-enthusiasm of hyperglobalizers from the doyen of World Order Modelling; Ian Clark's *Globalization and International Relations Theory* (1999) represents the classical tradition at its best, and Martin Shaw (ed.), *Politics and Globalization: Knowledge, Ethics and Agency* (1999) is a very useful collection representing what may come to be known as the 'Sussex School'. It should be stressed that these references are only a small selection of the available material; David Held *et al.* (2003) and Jan Aart Scholte (2000) have excellent bibliographies. Niall Ferguson, 'Sinking Globalization' (2005), and Mathias Albert, '"Globalization Theory": Yesterday's Fad or More Lively than Ever?' (2007), are useful overviews.

The lack of material on IR and the new technologies is (still) striking. For a broadly positive account of the future, see Thomas Friedman, *The Lexus and the Olive Tree* (1999). For a more unsettling account of the possible impact of the new technologies, see Bill Joy, 'Why the Future Doesn't Need Us' (2000). The latter, which appeared in the magazine *Wired* – which is an important source of ideas on the new world that is emerging – is particularly disturbing because of Joy's position as co-founder and chief scientist at Sun Microsystems, and co-chair of the presidential commission on the future of IT research. The 1999 *Human Development Report* of the UNDP devotes a great deal of space to global inequalities in access to IT. The *Millennium* Special Issue on 'International Relations in the Digital Age' (2003) contains interesting pieces by, *inter alia*, James Der Derian and Ronald Deibert.

The term 'Washington Consensus' to refer to the neoliberal position articulated by IMF and the US Treasury Department was coined by John Williamson – 'What Washington Means by Policy Reform' (1990); for discussion, see Richard Higgott, 'Economic Globalization and Global Governance: Towards a Post Washington Consensus' (2000). The evolution of official thinking is traceable in quasi-official publications by the agencies, for example, for the IMF, Jahangir Aziz and Robert F. Wescott, *Policy Complementarities and the Washington Consensus* (1997), and for the World Bank, Shih Javed Burki and Guillermo E. Perry, *Beyond the Washington Consensus: Institutions Matter* (1998).

Joseph Stiglitz, *Globalization and its Discontents* (2004), portrays the doubts of one leading liberal; Jagdish Bhagwati, *In Defence of Globalization* (2004), shows that not all liberals have lost their nerve, while Meghnad Desai, *Marx's Revenge* (2002), illustrates the connections between classical Marxism and liberalism.

The neo-Gramscian approach to IPE is well represented in the *Review of International Political Economy*. Texts taking this broad approach include Gill and Law (1988). The leading neo-Gramscian theorist is Robert W. Cox; see his *Production, Power and World Order: Social Forces in the Making of History* (1987) and his collected papers (with Timothy Sinclair), *Approaches to World Order* (1996). Stephen Gill (ed.), *Gramsci, Historical Materialism and International Relations* (1993) is still the best general collection on Gramsci and IR. Other important studies include Kees Van der Pijl, *Transnational Classes and International Relations* (1998); and Ronen Palan and Jason Abbott, *State Strategies in the Global Political Economy* (1996).

On good governance and the Washington consensus, G. C. Gong, *The Standard of 'Civilisation' in International Society* (1984), is the classic study of nineteenth-century theory and practice of the 'standards of civilization'. Robert Jackson, *Quasi-States: Sovereignty, International Relations and the Third World* (1990), is a modern classic bringing the story of good governance into the late twentieth century.

Andrew Hurrell and Benedict Kingsbury (eds), *The International Politics of the Environment* (1992) is a very valuable collection, with essays on institutions, standard-setting and conflicts of interest. Wolfgang Sachs (ed.), *Global Ecology: A New Arena of Political Conflict* (1993), and John Vogler and Mark Imber (eds), *The Environment and International Relations* (1995), are equally useful. See also Garth Porter and Janet Welsh Brown, *Global Environmental Politics* (1991); and Caroline Thomas, *The Environment in International Relations* (1992). Thomas (ed.), 'Rio: Unravelling the Consequences', a Special Issue of *Environmental Politics* (1994), is the best single source on UNCED. Early warning of environmental problems ahead was given in Richard Falk, *This Endangered Planet* (1971). Peter Haas (ed.), 'Knowledge, Power and International Policy Coordination', a Special Issue of *International Organization* (1992), is the best source for epistemic communities. Oran Young *et al.* (eds), *Global Environmental Change and International Governance* (1996), is an important study. John Vogler, *The Global Commons: Environmental and Technological Governance* (2000), is a useful overview. There is a new edition of Lorraine Elliot's excellent *The Global Politics of the Environment* (2004). Robyn Eckersley, *The Green State* (2004), develops a theory of a green states system, and Andrew Dobson and Robyn Eckersley (eds), *Political Theory and the Ecological Challenge* (2006), examines the role of the environment from different theoretical perspectives. Eva Lövbrand and Johannes Stripple, 'The Climate as Political Space: On the Territorialisation of the Global Carbon Cycle' (2006); Peter Newell, 'The Political Economy of Global Environmental Governance' (2008); and Karen Backstrand, 'Democratizing Global Environmental Governance? Stakeholder Democracy after the World Summit on Sustainable Development' (2006), access the impact of environmental concerns in global politics.

On new notions of security and securitization, for the Copenhagen School, see Barry Buzan, *People, States and Fear* (1990), Buzan *et al.*, *The European Security Order Recast: Scenarios for the Post-Cold War Era* (1990), and, especially, Buzan, Waever and de Wilde, *Security: A New Framework for Analysis* (1998). An informative debate on the Copenhagen School can be found in the pages of the *Review of International Studies:* Bill McSweeney, 'Identity and Security: Buzan and the Copenhagen School' (1996); Barry Buzan and Ole Waever, 'Slippery? Contradictory? Sociologically Untenable? The Copenhagen School Replies' (1997); and McSweeney, 'Durkheim and the Copenhagen School' (1998). For critical security studies, see Ken Booth (ed.) *New Thinking about Strategy and International Security* (1991a), 'Security and Emancipation' (1991c), and, especially, *Theory of World Society* (2007); and Keith Krause and Michael C. Williams (eds) *Critical Security Studies: Concepts and Cases* (1997). Steven Walt, 'The Renaissance of Security Studies' (1991), is apparently unconvinced by redefinitions. Sean M. Lynn-Jones and Steven Miller (eds), *Global Dangers: Changing Dimensions of International Security* (1995) give the view from the pages of *International Security.* Mikkel Rasmussen, *The Risk Society At War: Terror, Technology and Strategy in the Twenty-First Century* (2006) reflects on the risk society and current global politics. Mohammed Nuruzzaman, 'Paradigms in Conflict: The Contested Claims of Human Security, Critical Theory and Feminism' (2006) is a good critical appraisal of recent thinking on security. The recent trend towards the privatization of security forces is examined in a number of works, including Sarah Percy, *Mercenaries: The History of a Norm in International Relations* (2007), and 'Mercenaries; Strong Norm, Weak Law,' (2007); Deborah Avant, *The Market for Force: The Consequences of Privatizing Security* (2005); Rita Abrahamsen and Michael C. Williams (eds), Special Issue of *International Relations*, 'The Privatisation and Globalisation of Security in Africa' (2007).

On global civil society, the annual *Global Civil Society Yearbook* is an excellent source of both data and opinion; approximately the same team have recently produced Marlies Glasius *et al.*, *International Civil Society* (2004). The contributors to Michael Walzer (ed.), *Toward a Global Civil Society* (1997), are rather less convinced that one is on the way than is Mary Kaldor, *Global Civil Society: An Answer to War* (2003). John Keane, *Global Civil Society?* (2003), has a sensible question mark in its title; and David Chandler, *Constructing Global Civil Society* (2004), probably should have. Chris Brown, 'Cosmopolitanism, World Citizenship and Global Civil Society' (2001), is highly critical of the notion. Mathias Albert *et al.* (eds), *Civilising World Politics: Society and Community Beyond the State* (2000), is a good collection with mainly German contributors. Albert *et al.* (eds), *Identities, Borders, Orders: Rethinking International Relations Theory* (2001), is another useful collection. Donatella Della Porta (ed.), *Social Movements: An Introduction* (2006), is a good recent introduction; Della Porta and Sidney Tarrow (eds), *Transnational Protest and Global Activism* (2005), is also valuable. The debate over what exactly global civil society means is carried on in Jens Bartelson, 'Making Sense of Global Civil Society' (2006), and Vivien Collingwood's 'Non-governmental Organisations, Power and Legitimacy in International Society' (2006). The *Millennium* special issue on 'Power in International Relations' includes Ronnie Lipschutz, 'Power, Politics and Global Civil Society' (2005), and Doris Fuchs, 'Commanding Heights? The Strength and Fragility of Business Power in Global Politics' (2005). Noret Gotz, 'Reframing NGOs: The Identity of an International Relations Non-Starter' (2008) seeks to clarify the working conception of NGOs.

On the anti-globalization movement, popular studies include Naomi Klein, *No Logo* (2001), and Thomas Frank, *One Market under God* (2001). *Millennium* has published a very valuable set of brief essays (2000) on the 'Battle for Seattle' at the WTO Conference in November 1999, with contributions from Steven Gill, Fred Halliday, Mary Kaldor and Jan Aart Scholte (2000). Chris Brown, *Sovereignty, Rights and Justice* (2002), ch. 12, discusses the movement.

Chapter 10

The International Politics of Identity

Introduction

The next two chapters offer a somewhat different approach to International Relations theory from the previous nine. The emphasis will remain on theory, on developing a conceptual understanding of the subject, but the context will no longer be quite so dependent on the development of the discourse itself as in the earlier chapters. From now on, the driving force will come from events in the world rather than the academy – arguably, this has always been the case with International Relations theory, but here the relationship between theory and practice is much clearer. The agendas of these two chapters are set by international politics since the 1980s and will be readily recognizable by practitioners as well as scholars, and by informed members of the public as well as students of the social sciences.

The two aspects of contemporary international politics that these chapters will focus on appear at first sight to point in different directions and to contradict each other. First impressions may be correct here. There is an old joke connected with unreliable television reception in the early days of the medium that may be apposite here – do not adjust your sets, reality is at fault. There is no guarantee that the most salient features of contemporary international relations will hang together in a coherent way. On the one hand, we live in a world undergoing change at an unprecedented rate, while on the other we live in a world whose basic institutions are inherited from another age; in the circumstances, a certain amount of dissonance is to be expected. The dissonant features of contemporary international relations to be examined in these chapters are, first, the rise of identity politics, that is, the increasing salience of nationhood, ethnicity and religion and, second, the increasing importance of the individual as an international actor, as expressed through the international human rights regime and changing conceptions of international law. Groups and individuals do not necessarily gel easily to present one neatly packaged account of how the world is, but they clearly are related one to

199

another. Faced with the occasionally unwelcome demands of group loyalty, and the dangers of unchecked power, it is not surprising that some individuals have looked to strengthen their positions via the notion of universal human rights, while the increasing salience of rights may be seen by some as reflecting an external challenge that requires stronger group loyalty. There are complicated dialectics at work here, and it is difficult to discern a clear path through the various contradictions.

Chapter 11 will examine the rise of the individual as an international actor; this chapter will focus on the new international politics of identity. One way of framing this latter issue is to ask whether there is today a model of politics and the political process that can reasonably be seen as universal, at least in the weak sense that most countries over time will gravitate towards it? To ask this question nowadays is to invite the immediate answer 'no' – in spite of, or perhaps because of, the spread of globalization and the emergence of a 'human rights culture', it is clear at the time of writing that political forces driven by nationalism, ethnicity and religion are incredibly powerful and act as an influential counterpoint to these universal categories. A generation ago, however, it would not have been unreasonable to assume that uniformity rather than diversity would be the dominant motif of twenty-first-century politics. The shift from an assumption of uniformity to one of increasing diversity, and the implications of this shift for international politics, is one way of looking at the subject matter of this chapter. Before embarking on this discussion, it is worth noting that this is not simply a forward-looking question – it also relates to the origins of the contemporary international order. We live today in a world in which almost 200 states are members of the United Nations; the international community of the twenty-first century must accommodate Christians, Muslims, Buddhists, Hindus and Jews, as well as millions of people with no religious affiliations. All races and ethnicities have a claim to be part of this international community. And yet the core institutions and practices of the international community, the sovereign state, diplomacy and international law, are the product of one particular part of the world, one particular cultural heritage – that of Europe, or, to be more specific, that part of Europe whose cultural heritage was shaped by Catholic Christianity and the Western Roman Empire. The contrast between the cultural specificity of the current international order, and the cultural diversity demonstrated by its members, provides a backdrop to the following discussion.

Politics in industrial societies

Of course, this diversity might be on the wane, and in the 1970s, the advanced industrial capitalist countries did indeed seem to be settling down into a kind of common pattern shaped by the process of industrialization itself. Most of the industrial societies had been through a nationalist phase, a period of nation-building, but in most cases nationalism was no longer the dominant force in domestic politics, though it could still be powerful in particular regions. In many European countries, political identity had in the past been associated with religion, but, again, these associations were, in the main, weakening; thus, for example, the post-1945 Christian Democratic parties in Europe had become moderate conservative parties, no longer based on the Catholic Church, while in Britain the association of Anglicanism with conservatism, and Nonconformity with radicalism, though still statistically significant, was nowhere near as strong as it once had been. The few places, such as Northern Ireland, where national and religious identities reinforced each other, seemed to be the exception rather than the rule. Instead, politics revolved around notions of 'left' and 'right', progressive and conservative, that essentially related to economic issues, and in particular, to property relations. Most of the advanced industrial countries had political parties that claimed to represent the interests of industry, commerce and the middle classes, and parties that claimed to represent the interests of organized labour; these parties operated in a world of cross-cutting social pluralism that prevented the division between them from becoming too extreme. Depending on the voting system and social structure, one might find multi-party systems, where different interests were represented by different parties, or two-party systems where the two parties in question were themselves coalitions of interests, but, in any event, politics in the advanced industrial world had become a matter of compromise, adjustment and accommodation. In contrast with the immediate past, there were very few mass political movements or parties whose aims involved large-scale social or economic change; even in France and Italy, where large-scale communist parties had survived, they had largely lost interest in revolution.

This is a snapshot of how politics was conceived in the advanced industrial world, but the general assumption was that the developing world would, in the longer run, take the same path. The international system into which these new nations had been born or, in the case of older polities that had not been subjected to direct imperial rule, into which they had now been admitted, was, in its origins, clearly European, and the expectation was that they would adapt to it by becoming themselves, in their politics at least, rather more European. Notions of state- and nation-building, and models of development all pretty much assumed that the aim of the exercise was to make the non-industrial world look a lot like the industrial one. Whether this could be achieved within the capitalist system was a serious issue – the 'structuralists' discussed in Chapter 8 thought not – but most of the alternatives to capitalism looked increasingly implausible. The critics of capitalist development models usually had in mind some kind of Marxist alternative, but those Marxist regimes that did exist looked less and less plausible as alternatives to the capitalist West. In the 1940s and 1950s, there were many observers who genuinely believed that communist planning methods had solved the problems posed by the boom and bust pattern commonly observed under capitalism, but by the 1970s it had become increasingly difficult to believe that this was the case – the regimes of 'really-existing socialism' were very obviously not providing the kind of material success to be found in the capitalist West. Neither was it possible to argue that these societies were more socially just than their competitors in the West; the terrifying repression of the Stalinist totalitarian era may have passed in Eastern Europe by the 1970s and 1980s, but personal freedom was still very limited and the regimes were widely perceived by their own citizens as lacking legitimacy.

In any event, in the course of the 1980s and 1990s, communist regimes in Europe unravelled and were replaced by political systems that aspired to be like the political systems of the advanced capitalist world. The reasons for this collapse are complex and inevitably disputed; the impact of Western, especially American, pressure, the internal dynamics of a process of change that got out of hand, the role of particular individuals (Mikhail Gorbachev, Pope John Paul II, Ronald Reagan), the role of ideas: the list of candidates for the role of prime agent of change is long, and debates will continue, but the key point is that communism as a system of rule fell apart. The kind of convergence between East and West that many had envisaged as the probable outcome of the Cold War did not take place. Instead, the East adopted the ideas of the West. The significance of this was noted immediately by some of the more perceptive thinkers of the period. A key text here is 'The End of History', a much misunderstood piece by the American political philosopher and policy analyst Francis Fukuyama (1989).

This was a Hegelian analysis of the consequences of the end of the Cold War, which temporarily captured the *Zeitgeist,* attracted immense media interest and led to a major book, *The End of History and the Last Man* (1992). In this book, in essence, Fukuyama argues that in vanquishing Soviet communism, liberal democracy removed its last serious competitor as a conception of how an advanced industrial society might be governed. In the early nineteenth century, the shape of liberal democracy emerged as a combination of a market-based economy, representative institutions, the rule of law and constitutional government. Since then there have been a number of attempts to go beyond this formula, but each has failed. Traditional autocracy, authoritarian capitalism, national socialism and fascism each failed in wars against liberal societies. Liberalism's most powerful enemy (and also one of its earliest) was Marxian socialism, which held that the freedoms liberalism offered were insufficient and could be transcended – specifically that political freedoms were undermined by economic inequality, and that ways of running industrial society without the market and via the rule of the Party rather than representative government were viable.

The events of the 1980s demonstrated the falsity of this claim. The societies of 'really-existing socialism' proved unable to keep up with liberal capitalist societies in the provision of consumer goods, and their citizens became increasingly unwilling to accept that party rule could substitute for genuinely representative government. Eventually these regimes collapsed and have been replaced by political systems that are, at least in principle, liberal democratic. Fukuyama describes the victory of these principles as 'the end of history', employing Hegelian categories suggesting that the triumph of 'liberalism' amounts to the firm establishment of the only kind of human freedom that is possible. Since 'history' was about the shaping and development of human freedom, and since this task is now complete, 'history' is over (indeed, Hegel believed that history ended in 1807, so we have been living in post-historical time for over two centuries). This piece of Hegelian language is perhaps unfortunate and certainly off-putting; the key point is that Fukuyama argues that there is not now (and, more importantly, will not be in the future) any *systematic* alternative to liberalism: non-liberal regimes will persist on an ad hoc, contingent basis, but without being able to mount a coherent challenge to liberalism. It should be noted that this is *not* the triumphalist position it is often taken to be – Fukuyama regrets the emergence of a politics in which all the big issues have been solved.

History ends, according to Fukuyama, but this does not mean that there will be no future events; international relations will continue but will no longer involve the big issues, which are now settled. Others argue that while international relations will continue, they will do so on a different basis. The 'democratic peace' thesis states that democratic states, while as war-prone in general as any other kind of state, do not fight each other – an argument we have already met in Chapter 4, in the context of a more general discussion of the relationship between domestic and international structures, but an argument that seemed likely to take on a new salience in the post-Cold War era. Major research projects in the 1980s and 1990s found the basic hypothesis to be remarkably 'robust' – which is to say that whatever definition of democracy is employed, and however war is defined, the result comes out in much the same way. Constitutionally stable democracies do not fight each other, though they do engage in as much war as other states with non-democracies – and, worryingly, during the process of democratization the core generalization might not hold. Clearly, the more sophisticated and sensitive the indicators, the more likely it is that there will be minor exceptions to the proposition, or 'near-misses' as Russett (1993) puts it, and it may be that the law-like statement that democracies never fight one another will not stand. None the less, the research suggests that the general proposition is perhaps the best supported empirical hypothesis that contemporary International Relations can offer.

A statistically well-supported hypothesis is not the same thing as an explanation; how do we account for the democratic peace? Russett offers two possible explanations. First, there is the *cultural-normative* model. In stable democracies, decision-makers will expect to be able to resolve internal conflicts by compromise and without violence, and, hypothetically, they will carry over this expectation when dealing with decision-makers in other stable democracies that have similarly non-violent conflict-resolving mechanisms. Conversely, decision-makers in non-democratic systems are more likely to use and threaten violence in domestic conflict resolution, and this attitude is also likely to spill over internationally. Knowing this, and to avoid being exploited, democracies will adopt non-democratic norms in dealing with non-democracies. A second model stresses *structural-institutional* factors. Systems of checks and balances, and the need to generate public consent, will slow down decisions to use large-scale violence, and reduce the likelihood that such decisions will be taken. Recognizing this, leaders of other democratic states will not fear surprise attacks, and will allow peaceful conflict-resolution methods to operate. Leaders of non-democratic states, on the other hand, are less constrained, and can more easily initiate large-scale violence. Being aware that democratic leaders do not have this option, they may be tempted to exploit what they see as a weakness – but being aware that this is so, leaders of democracies may set aside institutional constraints when dealing with non-democracies in order to avoid being exploited. These two models are not the only explanations for the democratic peace that could be offered – though others, such as that of David Lake (1992), can be assimilated to one or the other – and neither are they entirely separable; as Russett remarks, norms underlie and are buttressed by institutions. A later account will probably merge the two.

In any event, what is striking about the thesis is the support it gives (or, perhaps, gave) to the idea that a universal *liberal internationalist* world order might now be possible. From the vantage point of 1989 it looked as if the history of ideological conflicts was coming to an end, and if the now-dominant liberal capitalist states are unlikely to engage in violent conflict with each other, then it was not unreasonable to expect that an era of relative peace and security would dawn. Instead, of course, the period since 1989 has seen the wholesale revival of political identities based on ethnicity and religion, and not simply in the developing world – the hopes for a new kind of international relations post-1989 have largely been dashed. What happened, and why?

Identity politics post-1989

Most of the post-communist regimes of the former Soviet Union and former Yugoslavia declared a determination to become, as their people often put it, 'normal' polities, which they understood to mean the kind of pluralist political systems found in Western Europe. Some have succeeded, more or less; in

2004, Poland, the Czech Republic, Slovakia, Hungary, Slovenia and the Baltic Republics all entered the European Union as full members whose political systems had passed the necessary tests; while somewhat less plausibly, Bulgaria and Romania joined in 2007. The Ukraine is also a relative success story, but elsewhere the picture has been less encouraging. The Russian Federation has survived as a quasi-democratic presidential regime but with many violent ethnic conflicts among its southern republics, and the new states to the south of Russia that emerged on the collapse of the Soviet Union have been riven with national, ethnic and religious conflicts. In the Balkans, of the Republics carved out of the Yugoslav Federation, only Slovenia has been more-or-less peaceful, and Croatia, Bosnia-Herzegovina and Kosovo have been sites of major conflicts that have involved the UN, the EU and NATO. Even in the People's Republic of China, where a form of 'market Stalinism' has emerged based around capitalist economic forms combined with firm party-rule, nationalism remains a serious issue in China's 'Wild West' region of Xingjian with its Muslim Uighur population, and in Tibet; also, despite fierce persecution, religious movements such as Falun Gong simmer in the background as a latent threat.

Many of these ethnic/national conflicts could be seen as hangovers from an earlier era, actually preserved by communism. The kind of national conflicts that were resolved elsewhere in Europe by the operation of pluralistic politics were frozen in place by communist dictatorship; to use a common if rather unpleasant metaphorical representation, whereas in the West ethnic divisions were healed by the need for different groups to co-operate in the political process, in the East, similar divisions were simply covered over by the bandage provided by authoritarian communist rule – take away the bandage and the sores re-emerged, unhealed and festering. Moreover, there are features of communism and nationalism that make it relatively simple for communist leaders to translate themselves into nationalist leaders (as has happened so frequently in the Balkans – most strikingly perhaps in Croatia, where a wartime communist partisan, Franjo Tudjman, used fascist, wartime Ustache symbols to lever himself into power, roughly the equivalent of a Zionist adopting the swastika as a motif). Both doctrines involve thinking in monolithic terms (whether of class or nation), which undermines the legitimacy of the intermediate, cross-cutting groups that make pluralism work, and both provide seemingly compelling reasons to override individual rights in the name of the collectivity (Puhovski 1994).

All this may be true, but what it does not explain is why the 1990s also saw a revival of this kind of politics in Western as well as Eastern Europe. With the exception of the conflict in Northern Ireland, which has become marginally less violent, other identity-based conflicts in the West have persisted and their numbers have increased, with, for example, the addition of a more virulent form of regionalism in Italy demonstrated by the rise of the Northern

League. More generally, conflicts have arisen in most of these societies, revolving around immigration, refugees and asylum-seeking, and such conflicts have been cast increasingly in religious as well as ethnic terms, with particular reference to the problems posed by the integration of large numbers of Muslims into Western societies. Alongside these conflicts has emerged, in many advanced industrial countries, a strategy of conflict-avoidance based on the politics of multiculturalism and group rights; whereas the politics of industrial society described in the first section of this chapter worked to lessen conflict by creating overlapping groups, this new politics takes for granted the existence within a given society of a multiplicity of groups whose identities will not weaken over time – and the ethos of this politics is that conflict can be avoided if each group is recognized as having its own distinctive contribution to make to the wider society (Kymlicka 1995). Old-style egalitarians and socialists regret this development (Barry 2000).

Returning to the general issue, the revival of identity politics has not simply rested on ethnicity or nationalism, and neither has it been confined to Europe or Eurasia. A striking feature of politics since the 1980s has been the increasing number of people who have adopted a political identity based on religion, and in particular on 'fundamentalist' religious movements; this convenient term has somewhat misleading Christian connotations, but the phenomenon of radical religious movements is very widespread. The rise of radical Islam is an obvious reference point here; Islamicist politics have posed threats to most Muslim-majority political systems since around the mid-1990s, and Islamic terrorism has become a major concern for the world as a whole – the events of 9/11 in the USA are simply the most extreme manifestation of this issue. However, radical Hindu movements have been equally powerful in the relevant context, going a long way to reshape the politics of approximately one-sixth of humanity in India, and it should not be forgotten that the rise of fundamentalist Christianity in the USA is having a major impact on that political system. In the latter case, there are very direct foreign policy implications; evangelical Christian support for Israel on the basis that the establishment of the Jewish state is a forerunner of the Second Coming has added a new factor into the US–Arab–Israeli relationship, a factor making that relationship more difficult to manage than ever before. Equally, in Latin America, the rise of evangelical Protestantism as a genuine challenge to the Roman Catholic Church has been a striking feature since the 1980s. Meanwhile, in Africa, the contest between Christian and Islamic missionaries continues – but a striking feature since the 1990s has been the rising political significance of witchcraft and other traditional animist religious beliefs, which have proved surprisingly capable of adapting themselves to the changing circumstances of their constituencies.

It is important to note that, when we examine the rise of religious movements of this kind, we are observing a phenomenon that is simultaneously domestic and international. Consider, for example, the aforementioned rise of evangelical Protestant Christianity in Latin America. This clearly reflects the very well-financed missionary work of North American evangelicals, but it also reflects features of the domestic societies in question. It has been noted, for example, that in many of these societies Protestantism has been particularly attractive to women because, it is argued, it is less tolerant of male domestic violence and drunkenness than traditional Catholicism; it is also the case that as Catholic Christianity has become more left-wing in these societies, so the political right has looked to the evangelicals. The point is that the international and the domestic interact and cannot readily be separated. The same is even more obviously true of the rise of radical Islam. The importance of Saudi money in financing Islamic education based on their particular, rather austere, version of Islam is clear, and radical groups such as Al Qaeda clearly operate as international non-governmental institutions – albeit of a particular, postmodern kind, as networks without a formal, hierarchical command structure – but the impact of these international movements is also dependent on local conditions. The attractions of radical Islam in Britain and France owe a great deal to the sense of alienation felt by Muslim youth in these countries – what Al Qaeda and other, less radical, international groups provide is a way for these young people to make sense of their situation that is superior to that provided by the dominant society or by older Muslim networks. Similarly the attraction of radical Islam in countries such as Indonesia lies in its apparently offering an alternative to the corruption of local elites. There is always a dialectic between the international and the domestic at work in these situations.

In short, Fukuyama may be right to think that there is no *systematic* alternative to liberal democracy on the horizon – and none of the movements mentioned above offer the kind of globally relevant systematic conception of society characteristic of communist ideology – but the number of non-systematic, local and particularist alternatives is very striking, and cannot be explained away in terms of the short-run impact of the end of communism. There does genuinely seem to be a new kind of politics emerging, with considerable implications for international relations.

Globalization and postindustrial society

Nationalists and the fervently religious explain their commitments in simple terms. In the first case, the nation (or ethnie) is taken to be a pre-existent phenomenon – it is simply a fact about the world that it is composed of nations that shape the political identities of their members, and once this is recognized it follows (for the nationalist) that it is natural for each of us to orientate our political actions towards 'our' nation or ethnic group. The so-called revival of nationalist politics, on this account, is simply the re-assertion of a truth that ideologies such as communism and liberalism suppressed. Religiously-minded people take a similar view; the truth about the world is to be found revealed in the Koran or the Bible (or in the Hindu scriptures and so on); these books tell us how to behave towards our fellow believers and towards others, and what needs to be explained is why most people do not follow the word of God, not why some people do. Again, the increased salience of religion is not to be explained in terms of social factors but in its own terms, terms that have been de-legitimated by the Enlightenment and post-Enlightenment secular politics of the last two hundred years but whose relevance is constantly being re-asserted by witnesses to the faith. As social scientists, students of International Relations may wish to contest these self-understandings; after all, contrary to the claims of nationalists, it is quite impossible to identify any objective characteristics of a nation, and, contrary to the claims of religious fundamentalists, it is clear that the holy scriptures on which they rely do not interpret themselves – the word of God never comes through *en clair.* It is, however, important to recognize that the interpretations that social scientists offer for the revival of identity politics are not those that the individuals concerned would usually accept. We are not obliged to accept the explanations of the true believers, but we are obliged to try not to patronize them by 'explaining away' their beliefs. Still, and bearing this proviso in mind, it is possible to identify one clear explanation for the revival of identity politics, or, better, a family of explanations – namely that the kind of political identities described above are a reaction to the new social/economic/political forces conveniently summarized by the term 'globalization'.

The central argument here is simple: globalization potentially creates a uniform world with global production and consumption patterns gradually ironing out the differences between peoples and societies – slowly but surely we are all coming to do the same kinds of jobs, wear the same kinds of clothes, eat the same kinds of food, watch the same kinds of television programmes and so on. But, so the argument goes, people need meaning in their lives as well as material goods; generally, we have interpreted our social world precisely through the kinds of differences that are now being removed or undermined. National stereotypes were (and sometimes still are) a crude illustration of the point – very few Englishmen have ever worn bowler hats, and roast beef was always expensive; the beret was equally unusual across the Channel, and the French diet does not consist of frogs' legs and snails – but the sense that Englishmen were genuinely different from Frenchmen, crudely expressed by these caricatures, was ingrained in both societies and has been an important part of their respective self-understandings. In so far as global brands eliminate difference – tee-shirts, denims and hamburgers being universally consumed by English and French alike – many people feel that something important has been lost. This feeling potentially creates the social basis for a reaction in favour of an exaggerated version of difference, and this is where the new identity politics comes into its own, assuring us that we are not simply the product of global branding, but can control our own destinies by asserting ourselves as Christians, Scots, Sikhs or whatever.

Benjamin Barber captures this nicely in his amusingly (but misleadingly) titled *Jihad vs. McWorld* (1996). McWorld is a convenient way of expressing the rise of an unimaginative and somewhat bland sameness, but 'Jihad' is less well chosen, since its Islamic connotations may seem to limit its applicability – in fact, Barber intends this word to summarize all the reactions to McWorld of whatever faith or region. His jihadists could as easily be American or Indian as Saudi or Iranian, Christian or Hindu as Shia or Sunni. The central point is that globalization creates its own antibodies. People do not want to become cogs in a global machine so they look for ways of asserting themselves. Sometimes this involves taking part in global movements against globalism (redefined for the purposes as 'global capitalism' by the anti-globalization campaign) but, equally, faced by the challenge of homogenizing external forces, some individuals and groups have responded by returning to their roots – national or religious – or at least to a sanitized version of the roots they imagine themselves to possess. Often, it should be said, these roots are preserved or propagated by the very technology that allegedly threatens them; satellite television and the internet are now widely used by nationalist and religious groups. Whereas once diaspora communities grew apart from their original culture, often exaggerating some features, understating others – so that, for example, the average Dubliner nowadays has very little in common with a Boston Irish-American whose forefathers left at the time of the famine – nowadays communications between new and old homelands is so easy that this sort of gap does not emerge so readily; though, probably because they do not have to live with the consequences, diasporas are often more orientated towards radical identity politics than their stay-at-home cousins. In any event, the gap between a nationalist and an anti-capitalist reaction to McWorld is sometimes very narrow. It is striking how many prominent individuals seem to straddle this gap – the classic case being the French farmer Jose Bové, who has himself become almost a global brand on the basis of his opposition to McDonald's in France, but whose own politics are dedicated to protecting the interests of French farmers, which often directly contradict the interests of farmers in Africa or Asia. In the new politics of identity, old-style economic interests are played down – Bové opposes 'McDo' and that is good enough for the anti-globalization coalition.

It is plausible to suggest that part of the reason for the revival of identity politics lies in this opposition between the global and the local, but there may be deeper causes involved, especially when it comes to the post-industrial world. As noted above, what we think of as modern politics revolved around the production process, taking the form of a contest over the distribution of the gains from the increases in productivity that capitalist industrialization created, a contest in which the rights of property-owners were contrasted with the needs of the poor, and the power of the vote was, eventually, set against the power of money and capital. Postmodern politics, corresponding to post-industrialism, does not take this shape, largely because the oppositions that shaped the old politics no longer exist in the same, politically-relevant, form. Of course, in the advanced industrial world, the poor still exist in large numbers – especially if poverty is defined in relative terms, as ultimately it has to be – but they are not employed in the kinds of jobs where unionization is relatively easy, and neither are they unemployed and pushed towards the breadline and potential support for extremist parties. Instead they answer telephones in call-centres or flip burgers, making enough to get by but not enough to build much of a stake in society. Very importantly, often they are not citizens but illegal immigrants or guest workers, but even when they are entitled to vote they tend not to – the percentage of the electorate that turns out on election day has been declining in all the advanced industrial countries.

Political parties of the left who have not acknowledged this change, and have tried to mobilize on the old basis, have tended to lose out, while those who have reshaped themselves – Bill Clinton's New Democrats, Tony Blair's New Labour and other 'third way' groups – have done well by de-emphasizing the old ideological divides and emphasizing managerial competence. However, while such policies may be electorally effective they do not heighten the emotions; 'The workers' flag is deepest red, It shrouded oft our martyred dead;' sang the members of the old Labour Party – these are extreme sentiments perhaps, and not many workers have been murdered by the forces of reaction in Britain since the Trafalgar Square riot of 1886 which inspired the song, but they used to reach out to people in a way that the anodyne pop songs (McMusic?) which have replaced the Red Flag do not. And so people look elsewhere than to the regular political parties to make sense of their lives and to give meaning to the rapidly changing social context in which they are situated – hence the rise of political identities based on ascribed characteristics such as ethnicity rather than ideology, or on religious beliefs.

Approached from another angle, politics is always and essentially oppositional; that is, about division, about who's in and who's out – or about 'friends' and 'enemies' as Carl Schmitt (1932/1996) more formally defined the process. If class position and the economy no longer shape these oppositions, then something else will, and political entrepreneurs concerned to increase their own influence will look for and promote that 'something else', be it a religious, an ethnic or a national identity. This is not wholly new; the mid-nineteenth-century belief that conservative, pro-capitalist political parties would not survive the impact of universal suffrage was proved wrong precisely because many of these parties realized that working men would not define themselves simply by their class interests and could be persuaded to support patriotic, imperialist parties. Political entrepreneurs such as Benjamin Disraeli and Otto von Bismarck were very successful employers of this strategy. Today, though, things have gone much further. In the USA, where the process has gone further than in other industrial societies, elections seem to be fought largely around 'values' and lifestyle issues. Hollywood stars, who benefited massively from President Bush's tax cuts for the rich, campaign almost exclusively for the Democrats, while the rural poor of the American mid-West, who have been hit hard by his policies, vote Republican. These are positions that make little sense in terms of economic interest, but perfect sense in terms of the new divisions in American society. A leaked document from Bush's leading strategist Karl Rove summarized things nicely; the Democrats, he is said to have written, have the labour unions, but we have the Christians – and he did not need to say that the 40 per cent of Americans who describe themselves as 'born-again' Christians are a far more powerful voting bloc than the unions, if, that is, they can be persuaded to vote as a bloc. In short, in any political order there will be some basis for division; if it is not economic interest then it will be something else. Think of this process happening on a world scale and not just in America, and the shape of international politics in the twenty-first century starts to look easier to explain – but not necessarily easier to manage.

Democracy promotion, Asian values and the 'clash of civilizations'

Since the 1980s there has been a revival of the politics of identity – but there has also been movements in the other direction, some of which will be traced in Chapter 11. Under the influence of Western Europeans and liberal North Americans, a serious attempt has been made to strengthen the international human rights regime, to develop a doctrine of humanitarian intervention, and, more generally, to establish the individual as an international actor, and both the object and subject of international law. Needless to say, this trend goes against much of what has been discussed above. In the realm of religion, both Islam and Christianity are, in principle, universal movements, but in practice they oppose fully-developed notions of universal rights because such notions usually involve legitimating practices that are anathema to religious fundamentalists, such as abortion, gender equality and the right to change religion. Nationalists begin from a perspective where individual rights are understood as being generated by the group, which, goes against the kind of universalism to be discussed in the next chapter. There is a clear tension here, but whether it is made manifest has been a matter of practical politics; in practice, the key issue has become whether the West would attempt to generalize from its victory over communism and promote its values on a global scale.

It is fair to say that, in the early post-Cold War years, the answer to this question was 'no'. In the late 1980s and early 1990s, some aid agencies began to insist that aid recipients carried out reforms to promote human rights and good government, Western-style, but this version of 'conditionality' received little support from the USA or the other major Western powers. Indeed, when President George H. W. Bush attempted to promulgate a 'New World Order', pluralism was built into his thinking (Bush 1990). The essence of the New World Order was to be: the sovereign state as the key unit of international relations; respect for the norms of non-aggression and non-intervention; and support for international law and institutions. This is, in effect, the *liberal internationalist* position of the immediate post-First World War era, restated for the post-Cold War world, but with one important difference. In 1919, a crucial element of Wilson's vision was that peace-loving states would be liberal-democratic. Bush, on the other hand, offered a New World Order in which all states of whatever political complexion would receive the protection of the norms of non-intervention and non-aggression if they were themselves prepared to endorse these norms. There is no sense here that the USA or any other state ought to engage in the promotion of democratic politics, and neither is there any suggestion of an elaborated doctrine of humanitarian intervention.

In any event, with the ambiguous end of the 1990–1 Gulf War – Kuwait liberated, but Saddam still in power and massacring his own people – the reaction of most commentators to Bush's formula was, perhaps predictably, somewhat jaundiced. 'The New World gives the Orders' was a characteristic jibe – and it did indeed seem that the New World Order was simply a slogan designed to give international legitimacy to US policy preferences. The incoming Clinton Administration did not endorse Bush's vision, but instead promised to take the idea of 'democracy promotion' seriously. Anthony Lake, Clinton's leading foreign policy adviser seemed particularly taken with the idea that 'democracies do not fight democracies' – the 'democratic peace' thesis discussed above – and seemed to be looking forward to an era in which the USA would actively push to promote Western/American values in the world, and, in particular, getting behind moves to strengthen the international human rights regime. A major UN Conference in the summer of 1993 in Vienna was designed to do just that. But before this conference, a number of regional conferences were held, and from one of these the Bangkok Declaration emerged, which expressed the desire of many Asian leaders to call a halt to this process and to resist the idea of a drive towards universalism. The Bangkok Declaration did not explicitly reject the idea of universal values, but it circumscribed them quite sharply in the interests of allowing regional and religious distinctiveness to dominate – the so-called 'Asian values' perspective, a position that was largely recognized in the final declaration of the Vienna Conference, much to the chagrin of many human-rights activists.

Asian values is a misnomer, because many Asians do not share the preference for authoritarianism expressed by proponents such as Singapore's elder
statesman Lee Kwan Yew (while many non-Asians do), and since the mid-
1990s the salience of this position has risen and fallen in accordance with the
shifting politics of the era – in particular, the Asian Crash of 1997 undermined
the strength of many Asian governments, and with it their ability to push their
vision of the world. Moreover, perhaps predictably, the commitment of the
Clinton Administration to the promotion of democracy proved fickle at best.
But the general issue raised by this controversy has remained of interest and
was given a scholarly focus by the American political scientist, Samuel
Huntington, in his influential paper, and later book, 'The Clash of
Civilizations' (1993a and 1996). The burden of Huntington's thesis is that,
with the end of the Cold War, a new basis of division has emerged in the
world; the ideological conflicts of the past will be replaced by conflicts
between 'cultures' or civilizations. Huntington identifies as the major contemporary civilizations the Sinic (*sic*), Japanese, Hindu, Islamic and Western, with
Orthodox and Latin American civilizations as possible derivations of Western
civilization with identities of their own, and Africa (perhaps) making up the
list. In any event, on his account, there are three civilizations that are likely to
generate serious potential problems in the near future – the declining West; the
rising Sinic; and the unstable Islamic.

As this formulation might suggest, the first two components go together –
economically, demographically and, ultimately, militarily, the West is losing
power to the Asian civilizations and in particular to China (Huntington anticipated that China would come to dominate Japan, and that the Japanese are
likely to accept, tacitly, a subordinate status). An increasingly successful and
powerful China will not accept a world in which its values are regarded as
inferior to those of the West, and will not accept global socio-economic institutions that limit its possibilities – and Huntington acknowledges that the
existing structure of international institutions is indeed a product of
Western/American hegemony and reflects Western values. Only by the West
adopting a policy of coexistence and recognizing the legitimacy of the Chinese
way will violent conflict be avoided between these two civilizations.

Chinese civilization will pose – indeed *is* posing – problems (particularly for
the West but also for Japan) because of its success; the world of Islam will
pose – and similarly *is* posing – problems for all its neighbours because of its
failure. Demographic pressures in Islam and the lack of any core Islamic state
with the potential of China, or even the 'baby tigers' of South East Asia, will
lead to frustrations; moreover, Islam is a proselytizing religion and Islamic
civilization has borders with most of the other world civilizations. These
borders ('fault-lines') will be, and indeed already are, the site of many cross-
civilizational conflicts, from Bosnia and Chechnya to Kashmir and the Sudan.
Ending such conflicts may be virtually impossible, certainly far more difficult

than the daunting enough task of promoting coexistence between Chinese and Western civilizations.

It is easy to pick holes in Huntington's work; from the outset his account of 'civilization' is ad hoc and muddled; civilizations are systems of ideas, and, as such, it is difficult to see how they could clash, though individuals and groups claiming to represent these ideas certainly can. Moreover, these systems of ideas are not now, nor have they ever been, self-contained or impermeable, a fact that Huntington acknowledges, but the significance of which he perhaps underplays. On the other hand, he deserves considerable credit for attempting to break up what was becoming in the early 1990s a rather sterile debate about the post-Cold War world. In his response to critics, 'If not Civilizations, What?', Huntington suggests that the only alternative models for what he is interested in are the old statist paradigm and a new 'un-real' vision of one world united by globalization (1993b). In effect, Huntington is providing a non-statist, but none the less realist, account of the world, which is an interesting addition to the conceptual toolkit of contemporary international relations theory. Moreover, the attack on the World Trade Center of September 2001 seemed to many to vindicate his pessimism. The deep sense of solidarity with the people of New York that was felt throughout Europe contrasted sharply with the scenes of rejoicing in Palestine and the general satisfaction expressed in street and bazaar elsewhere in the Middle East. Huntington's original article was widely referenced, and, indeed, reprinted in the London *Sunday Times* (14 October 2001), where it was described as 'uncannily prescient'. On the other hand, again, there are some who argue that Huntington's work amounted to an attempt to identify a new 'other' to take the place of Soviet communism, and that the desire to see the world in these terms actually increased the tensions out of which 9/11 emerged (Connolly 2000).

One of the reasons for the general academic rejection of Huntington's thesis is that, while not statist, it remains spatial/territorial. His prevailing metaphor is of the physical 'fault-lines' between civilizations. There are two problems with this notion; first, the analysis underplays the extent to which key dividing lines are made by humans, and recent – in the former Yugoslavia, for example, the recurrent crises of the 1990s owe more to the success of Slobodan Milošević in mobilizing political support behind the nationalist cause of Greater Serbia than they do to, largely spurious, ethnic and religious differences, much less historical divides that go back to the Middle Ages or earlier. Such differences and divides certainly exist and have always existed, but their current political significance is the result of contingency rather than some inevitable process – in effect, Huntington takes the self-interpretations of nationalists too much on their own terms. Second, and rather more important, the 'tectonic' notion of civilizations does not recognize sufficiently the extent to which civilizations are already interpenetrated. The clash of civilizations, in so far as it exists at all, is as likely to take the form of the politics of identity, multiculturalism and recognition in the major cities of the world as violent clashes on the so-called 'fault-lines'; policing problems in London or Los Angeles are, thankfully, more characteristic of this kind of politics than the violence of Kosovo or Chechnya, horrifying though the latter may be.

Pluralism and international society

Huntington's work is best seen as a reaction to two bodies of contemporary International Relations theory – on the one hand, the work of neo- and classical realists who argue that, one way or another, the state remains at the heart of IR and will continue to act in terms of ends–means rationality, and, on the other, the work of theorists of globalization, who see the emergence of a borderless world, in which legal structures will no longer be dominated by the state. Plausibly enough, Huntington argues that both are mistaken, but both have caught hold of one aspect of the emerging world order – realists are right that intergroup conflict will continue to be a central feature of that order, while globalizers are right to doubt that the state will remain the most important actor within that conflict. Instead, conflict will persist but be intercivilizational – unless, that is, the West gives up its attempt to impose its values on the rest of the world, in which case the basis may exist for a, somewhat uncomfortable, modus vivendi.

In fact, there is a body of work that comes close to addressing the question that Huntington poses, while remaining statist in inclination – namely the work of the English School and theorists of international society, encountered in Chapter 3 above, in the context of the constructivist critique of neorealism. As noted there, English School writers focus on the state rather than sub-state or universal categories, but – in contrast to neorealists – they argue that when states interact they may form a *society*, a norm-governed relationship whose members accept that they have at least limited responsibilities towards one another and to society as a whole. These responsibilities are summarized in the traditional practices of international law and diplomacy. The international society that these writers describe was, in its origins at least, a firmly European phenomenon, but there are at least two reasons to think that it could be made to work in a largely non-European world. First, though as we have seen, the modern world is incontestably and increasingly multicultural in social terms, the Western invention of the nation-state has proved remarkably attractive to a great many different cultures – even those societies that are very critical of allegedly Western notions (such as human rights) are strong promoters of the equally Western notion of the sovereign state. Whether because they genuinely meet a need, or because, given the existing order, sovereign territorial political units are more or less unavoidable, nation-states seem to be desired everywhere – at least by political elites. The only part of the world where the institution is under serious threat from an alternative form of political organization is at its place of origin in Western Europe, in the form of the European Union.

A more fundamental reason for the possible relevance of notions of inter-national society in a multicultural world is that, on some accounts, the very rationale of the idea is precisely its ability to cope with cultural diversity. An important writer here is Terry Nardin, whose account of international society as a 'practical association' has been highly influential (Nardin 1983). Nardin's point is that, unlike a 'purposive association' such as NATO or the WTO, which is built around a concrete project (collective defence or the expansion of trade) and assumes common purposes among its members (all of whom have voluntarily joined the organization in question), international society is an all-inclusive category whose practices are authoritative on every state precisely because they do *not* involve common purposes or a concrete project. The only common purpose is to live together in peace and with justice, and in this context justice is a procedural rather than a substantive notion. It is clear that, if these distinctions hold, the origins of the practices of international society in the European states system are irrelevant to their authority in the twenty-first century. These practices are authoritative precisely because they do not privilege any one conception of the 'Good', and this means that they are ideally suited to a world in which many and various such practices are to be found.

This 'pluralist' conception of international society has received a good deal of attention in recent years, most noticeably via a major book by Robert Jackson (2000), and does, on the face of it, appear to offer a way to cope with the new politics of identity that is, in certain respects, superior to Huntington's call for a modus vivendi between civilizations, or the frequent suggestion that the world should engage in a large-scale inter-civilizational dialogue to iron out our differences (Parekh 2000). Rather than relying on the hazy and controversially essentialist notion of a 'civilization', the pluralist account rests on an institution – the state – that is concrete and widely accepted. Still, pluralism does seem to rule out the very notion of an interna-tional human rights regime – it would be difficult to argue that respect for human rights is a necessary practice for international society on a par with, for example, diplomatic immunity – and many people would be reluctant to abandon this notion altogether, even if they are conscious of how the pursuit of universal human rights could indeed create the kinds of clashes that Huntington describes. There is a genuine dilemma here, one response to which has been offered by 'solidarist' theorists of international society, in particular Nicholas Wheeler and Tim Dunne (Wheeler 2000; Dunne and Wheeler 1996).

Their point is that while an international society constitutes a rational polit-ical order for humanity taken as a whole (because problems of scale make global government impossible, laws lose their effectiveness at a distance, and tyranny is less likely if political society occurs on a human scale), the ultimate referent object of international society ought to be individual human beings rather than states as such. The *telos* of international society is not, in the last resort, simply to preserve a multiplicity of separate states, but ultimately to promote human flourishing; thus, although theorists of international society from Grotius, Pufendorf and Burke through to Bull and Nardin have argued that this goal is best achieved via a society of legally autonomous, sovereign states, sovereign rights cannot be employed to justify conduct that clearly prevents human flourishing, such as large-scale human rights violations.

It should be noted that this solidarist version of international society cannot drift too far away from the pluralism more normally associated with the idea of a society of states without losing contact with the tradition as a whole. Gross violations of human rights may be regarded as a modern version of 'gross violations of human dignity', justifying external intervention on the part of anyone who can prevent them, but this is a long way away from the cosmo-politan notion that universal standards in all areas of human life should supplant the local. Adherents to the idea of a society of states may agree that there are some things that ought not to be tolerated, but they are coming at matters from a different angle from human rights activists, and alliances between these two groups will always be uneasy and unstable. The solidarist account of international society amounts to a *reimagining* of what is involved in a society of states, an amendment to pluralist accounts rather than an alter-native to them. These matters will be addressed in further detail in Chapter 11.

Conclusion

To summarize a rather complex discussion; in the twenty-first century we are seeing the emergence, at both the international and the domestic level, of a new politics of identity. A feature of twenty-first-century life in many of the advanced industrial societies is the demand for respect and esteem made by groups of one kind or another who consider themselves to have been margin-alized and undervalued by the dominant, patriarchal, heterosexualist, white culture. 'Multiculturalism' is one response to this situation, as is a politics based on uniting the fragments in a 'Rainbow Coalition' that would challenge the status quo on behalf of all oppressed groups. The problem with this latter strategy is clear. While each of the fragments opposes the dominant culture, this does not mean that their demands are compatible with each other; Quebecois nationalists routinely deny that aboriginal Bands would have the right to secede from Quebec, while popular cultural representatives of African-American men, such as rap artists, routinely spread misogynist and homophobic attitudes. 'Multi-faith' education in schools attempts to instil respect for all religions, but while some liberal Christians may be happy with the thought that their faith is one among many valid possibilities, few other religions take such a relaxed attitude towards the truth of their basic tenets.

If the issue domestically has been the challenge of handling a shift from a politics based on universal categories to a politics based on identity, at the international level problems have been generated in the other direction. As the theorists of international society have argued, the old international order was based on an 'ethic of coexistence', in which political, social and cultural differences are preserved, if not positively valued; this order increasingly faces the challenge of movements that seek to impose common standards world-wide, most obviously in connection with human rights. The international politics of this process, which has attempted increasingly to make the individual, and not the state, the focus of international law, is the subject of the next chapter.

Further reading

Globalization, the English School and the democratic peace thesis are referenced elsewhere in this book – in Chapters 9, 3 and 4, respectively.

Raymond Garthoff, *The Great Transition: American–Soviet Relations and the End of the Cold War* (1994), and Don Oberdorfer, *The Turn: How the Cold War Came to an End* (1991), are useful histories of the end of the Cold War. On the wider meaning of this event, see the essays in Michael Hogan (ed.), *The End of the Cold War: Its Meaning and Implications* (1992), and Alex Danchev (ed.), *Fin De Siècle: The Meaning of the Twentieth Century* (1995). Cynthia Enloe's *The Morning After: Sexual Politics at the End of the Cold War* (1993) also places these events in perspective. Richard Ned Lebow and Thomas Risse-Kappen (eds), *International Relations Theory and the End of the Cold War* (1995) – part of which appeared in *International Organization*, vol. 48, Spring 1994 – is the best collection on its subject. Václav Havel, 'What I Believe', in *Summer Meditations on Politics, Morality and Civility in a Time of Transition* (1993), is a moving account of what the end of communist rule could have meant, and perhaps does still mean, for some.

Of Will Kymlicka's many works on multiculturalism, *Politics and the Vernacular: Nationalism, Multiculturalism and Citizenship* (2001), is very useful, as is, with a more limited reference point, Kymlicka and M. Opalski (eds), *Can Liberal Pluralism Be Exported? Western Political Theory and Ethnic Relations in Eastern Europe* (2001). On the impact of globalization on diasporas, Arjun Appadurai, *Modernity at Large: Cultural Dimensions of Globalization* (1996) is outstanding. Bhikhu Parekh, *A New Politics of Identity: Political Principles for an Interdependent World* (2008) continues the multiculturalism debate.

James Mayall, *Nationalism and International Society* (1990), is a valuable overview of the subject; F. H. Hinsley, *Nationalism and the International System* (1974), still usefully provides the historical framework. E. H. Carr, *Nationalism and After* (1968), represents the 'nationalism is outmoded' viewpoint, now itself outmoded. Of A. D. Smith's many books, *Nationalism and Modernity* (1998) is perhaps the most relevant. Benedict Anderson, *Imagined Communities*, 2nd edn (1991), is a much-misunderstood modern classic – imagined is not the same as imaginary. Michael Brown *et al.* (eds), *Nationalism and Ethnic Conflict* (1997), collects mainstream US essays on the subject; Yosef Lapid and Friedrich Kratochwil (eds), *The Return of Culture and Identity in International Relations Theory* (1996), is more eclectic. Kevin Dunn and Patricia Goff (eds), *Identity and Global Politics* (2004), is an interesting recent collection. Recent work on the changing understanding of identity and nationalism includes Erik Gartzke and Kristian Skrede Gleditsch, 'Identity and Conflict: Ties that Bind and Differences that Divide' (2006); Fiona Adamson and Madeleine Demetriou, 'Remapping the Boundaries of "State" and "National Identity": Incorporating Diasporas into IR Theorizing' (2007); Brian Greenhill, 'Recognition and Collective Identity Formation in International Politics' (2008); and Susanne Buckley-Zistel, 'Dividing and Uniting: The Use of Citizenship Discourses in Conflict and Reconciliation in Rwanda' (2006), which makes clear the importance and complexity of identity and membership in volatile political times. Friedrich Kratochwil's 'Religion and (Inter-)National Politics: On the Heuristic of Identities, Structures, and Agents' (2005) is also useful.

There is a shortage of good work on the general subject of religion and IR, but increasing attention is being paid to the topic. The *Millennium* Special Issue on 'Religion and International Relations' (2000) is an uneven collection, but useful for an extended bibliography. Charles Taylor's massive *A Secular Age* (2007) will be an influential reference, assuming anyone makes it to the end. Other macro-level reflections on religion and secularism include the Daniel Philpott *et al.*, *God's Century* (forthcoming); Elizabeth Hurd, *The Politics of Secularism in International Relations* (2007); and Maia Carter Hallward, 'Situating the "Secular": Negotiating the Boundary between Religion and Politics' (2008). Eva Bellin, 'Faith in Politics: New Trends in the Study of Religion and Politics' (2008) is a good summary. Timothy Byrnes and Peter Katzenstein (eds), *Religion in an Expanding Europe* (2006), examines the challenges religion presents to European expansion and integration. John Micklethwait and Adrian Wooldridge, *The Right Nation* (2004), is very good and non-polemical on the Christian right in the USA. Holly Burkhalter, 'The Politics of AIDS' (2004), demonstrates the influence of evangelical Christianity on US policy towards AIDS in Africa. Ellis and Ter Haar give a good overview of African religion in *Worlds of Power: Religious Thought and Political Practice in Africa* (2004). Peter Geschiere, *The Modernity of Witchcraft: Politics and the Occult in Postcolonial Africa* (1997), is a useful anthropological study. Post-9/11, studies of Islam have, predictably, multiplied. Bernard Lewis, *What Went Wrong? The Clash between Islam and Modernity in the Middle East* (2002), is the most useful of his recent volumes. Malise Ruthven, *A Fury for God: The Islamicist Attack on America* (2004), is excellent, and his *Islam: A Very Short Introduction* (2000) does what it says. Paul Berman, *Terror and Liberalism* (2004), traces the link between radical Islam and fascism. Roger Scruton, *The West and the Rest: Globalization and the Terrorist Threat* (2003), and John Gray, *Al Qaeda and What it Means to be Modern* (2004), are stimulating think-pieces.

Fukuyama's works are cited in the text. For a very hostile liberal reaction, see Ralf Dahrendorf, *Reflections on the Revolution in Europe* (1990). Critical, but less outraged, are Fred Halliday, 'An Encounter with Fukuyama' (1992), and Chris Brown, 'The End of History?' in Danchev (1995). Huntington's essays are referenced in the text: his book *The Clash of Civilizations and the Remaking of World Order* (1996) is less convincing than the original shorter pieces. His later work, *Who Are We?* (2004) takes up the theme of identity in a US context, arguing that the American Anglo-Protestant core identity is under threat from the refusal of Hispanic immigrants to assimilate. Kishore Mahbubani, 'The West and The Rest' (1992), and Eisuke Sakakiba, 'The End of Progressivism: A Search for New Goals' (1995), offer not dissimilar reflections on the same theme. Chris Brown, 'History Ends, World Collide' (1999), is a more extended discussion of some of the themes of this chapter. Amitai Etzioni, *From Empire to Community* (2004), is a response to Fukuyama and Huntington, as well as communitarian conception of global politics. Kimberly Hutchings' work *Time and World Politics* (2008) is very relevant, both as a conceptualization of politics today and a critique of post-Cold War theorizing. Larry Diamond, 'The Democratic Rollback' (2008), points to the advance of autocratic states.

Joanne Bauer and Daniel A. Bell (eds), *The East Asian Challenge for Human Rights* (1999), judiciously presents the 'Asian values' debate. Daniel Bell, *East Meets West: Democracy and Human Rights in East Asia* (2000), is the best single volume on the subject, engagingly written as a series of dialogues. F. Zakaria, 'Culture is Destiny: A Conversation with Lee Kwan Yew' (1994), is a good source for the thinking of the most respectable and articulate spokesman for the Asian case. Mahathir Bin Mohamed and Shintaro Ishihara's modestly titled *The Voice of Asia: Two Leaders Discuss the Coming Century* (1996) gives the case against the West. Arlene Tickner (2003) provides a valuable examination of concepts such as nationalism, the state and sovereignty from a non-Western perspective in 'Seeing International Relations Differently: Notes from the Third World'. See also Chris Brown, 'Cultural Diversity and International Political Theory' (2000b). Ian Buruma and Avishai Margalit, *Occidentalism: The West in the Eyes of Its Enemies* (2004), turns the mirror on Western 'civilization' to reveal its complicity in anti-Western radicalism.

Chapter 11

International Relations and the Individual: Human Rights, Humanitarian Law and Humanitarian War

Introduction

Up until now this book has been largely concerned with what could be called the structural factors of international relations: the state system, power, economics and war, and where we have considered agents as opposed to structure, it has been the agency of institutions such as the state. This, as discussed in Chapter 4, is in line with the progression of International Relations as an academic discipline. Both neorealism and neoliberal institutionalism see the international system level as the most productive level of analysis – the only one that can generate succinct and useful insights into the most important issues that we study. Constructivists have shown a little more concern with 'agency' as opposed to 'structure', but still focus predominantly on the state as the most significant actor. This chapter, in common to some extent with the last, will look inside and across states at the individuals who populate them.

It is not easy to see at first why we should be concerned with individuals in International Relations. After all, there are many other disciplines that can provide insights about humans within political boundaries. Surely, our concern is for how those aggregates of people – states, and also increasingly intergovernmental organizations and multinational corporations – react to the constraints of the international system and to each other? Indeed, if states were sovereign according to the traditional criteria then this argument would hold. However, the Westphalian system of legend may now be just that. States increasingly recognize legal superiors, so undermining their juridical sovereignty, plus the capacities of many if not all states are limited by the processes of globalization described in Chapter 9. This leaves individuals both more vulnerable (they cannot rely on a strong state to protect their interests) and potentially more powerful (they can demand certain rights not as a result of their status as citizen of a particular state but because of their identity as a human being). The most critical theoretical implication of this shift is that it supports normative thinking in IR. The dominant theories of International Relations, traced in Chapters 2 and 3, claim to be explanatory and value-free rather than normative. Theorizing about ethics in the international system has been seen as utopian and even irrelevant. States in an anarchy make the decisions they must, based on national-interest calculations and (for the neorealist and neoliberal institutionalist) systemic imperatives. Morality exists only within the borders of the sovereign state, which protects and promotes the values of its citizens and thereby makes morality possible, and as such it is of no concern to IR theorists. Post-positivist thinkers dispute the first claim – that the dominant theories are value-free; while normative theorists take on the second claim – about the relationship between morality and state borders. As the Westphalian system is challenged, so the question of whether the state makes morality possible, or hinders it, becomes more relevant. The ethical relationships between individual and state, and between individuals across state borders, are being studied today with a new vigour, and normative theorists feel vindicated in their claim that it is as critical to study how agents *should* behave as how they *do* behave if we are to make sense of a fast-changing world.

Is the individual really more consequential in contemporary international relations? In this chapter it will be argued that there was a shift in power distribution among actors in three linked areas during the 1990s: in the rapid expansion of the human rights regime, and in attempts to enforce these rights through law and through war; and that this shift in power has indeed led to the increased importance of the individual at the international level. The focus here is not on particular, named, individuals, but on the new concern for individual welfare and rights that will be documented below.

Universal human rights

Following the collapse of the Berlin Wall, there was a surge of activity in the development of the human rights regime. The idea that individuals have rights as human beings which they ought to be able to claim against their own governments was established in the 1948 Universal Declaration on Human Rights, but little progress was made towards claiming these rights for all people until relatively recently. During the Cold War, human rights were often treated as a strategic bargaining tool, to be used to gain concessions from or to embarrass the states of the East. After 1989, the political barriers to the universal spread of human rights came down, plus advances in technology enabled non-governmental organisations (NGOs) concerned with the promotion of human rights to exert more influence than before.

Perhaps the most concrete example of this increased activity is the number of states ratifying the six main human rights conventions and covenants, which has risen dramatically since 1990. Ratifications of the International Covenant on Economic, Social and Cultural Rights, and the International Covenant on Civil and Political Rights grew from around 90 to nearly 150 during the 1990s, and at the time of writing stand at 159 and 162, respectively. Broad support for the goals of the regime was also demonstrated by the participation of over 170 countries in the 1993 World Conference on Human Rights, which met in Vienna to reaffirm their commitment to protect human rights. This was the first time in twenty-five years that such a meeting had taken place. Following discussions at the Conference, the UN General Assembly voted unanimously to create the post of UN High Commissioner for Human Rights, charged with co-ordinating the UN human rights programme and promoting universal respect for human rights.

The 1990s and early years of the twenty-first century also saw a considerable increase in the number of human rights activities in UN field operations, including the monitoring of human rights violations, education, training and other advisory services. This was in part a result of prolonged pressure from NGOs promoting the 'mainstreaming' of human rights in UN operations, stemming from the belief that conflict prevention and reduction efforts need to be combined with measures aimed at reducing human rights abuses. Thus, UN missions in El Salvador, Cambodia, Guatemala, Haiti, Burundi, Rwanda, the former Yugoslavia and the Democratic Republic of the Congo have all prioritized the establishment of a framework of respect for human rights as an integral part of post-conflict peace building.

NGOs have been a crucial factor in the recent spread of human rights ideas. The number of registered international NGOs grew during the 1990s, to reach 37,000 by 2000, many claiming to act as a 'global conscience', representing broad human interests across state boundaries, and focusing on human rights issues. NGOs have an impact the human rights regime in various ways. Organizations such as the International Committee of the Red Cross (ICRC), Médecins Sans Frontières (MSF) and Oxfam work directly in the field to relieve suffering, but they also campaign on behalf of those they treat, to promote the observance of human rights treaties and humanitarian law. The work of organizations such as Human Rights Watch and Amnesty International is principally to monitor the behaviour of governments and businesses, and to publicize human rights abuses. They apply pressure by gaining media coverage (at which they have grown particularly adept since 1990, with media mentions for human rights NGOs growing exponentially) and have achieved some notable successes.

A key achievement has been to force private actors into the discourse of human rights: to make human rights the 'business of business'. Prior to the 1990s, multinational corporations (MNCs) asserted that their correct role in global trade was to stay neutral and avoid getting involved in the politics of the regimes of the states within which they were operating. Western firms sourced cheap raw materials and labour from states ruled by unpleasant regimes, with no real criticism from the governments who collected tax on the corporations' profits. By the mid-1990s, major campaigns by Amnesty International in the UK and Human Rights Watch in the USA were under way, to persuade big business to assume economic and social responsibility commensurate with their power and influence, especially in the field of human rights. These campaigns, and the consumer pressure that accompanied them, resulted in firms such as Gap, Nike, Reebok and Levi Strauss drastically improving working conditions in their overseas factories, and incorporating internationally recognized human rights standards into their business practices. Pressure has also been applied to oil firms, with more limited success. In 1993, the Movement for the Survival of the Ogoni People in Nigeria mobilized tens of thousands of people against Shell, and succeeded, through the creative use of the internet, in making the situation an international issue. They forced the world's leading oil company to stop production temporarily; however, the Nigerian government responded by arresting, imprisoning and, in some cases, executing Ogoni activists. Campaigns have also highlighted the activities of British Petroleum (BP) in Colombia, Mobil Oil in Indonesia, Total and Unocal in Myanmar, and Enron in India, all of which were said to be contributing to serious human rights abuses. These campaigns have resulted more often than not in a flurry of press releases from the firms concerned and some well orchestrated public relations exercises, but little substantive change. The most significant results were gained in the UK at the end of the decade, when a group of multinationals, including Shell, BP-Amoco and the Norwegian state oil company, Statoil, announced policies that included a focus on human rights.

Other achievements for NGOs have involved pressurizing governments and inter-governmental organizations (IGOs). The International Campaign to Ban Land Mines, a coalition of more than 1,400 NGOs in ninety states that was awarded the Nobel Peace Prize in 1998, was instrumental in the Mine Ban Treaty of 1997. The Jubilee 2000 Campaign for developing world debt relief collected 25 million signatures across the world, and influenced Western governments and international financial institutions so heavily that US$30bn in debt was cancelled. The Coalition for an International Criminal Court was in large part responsible for the success of the 1998 Rome Conference and Treaty that established the International Criminal Court (ICC), which will be covered in the next section of this chapter. Because of their success in galvanizing public opinion and applying pressure, human rights groups have won a leading role in influencing many IGO activities. They help to design and often to staff the human rights operations that now accompany UN missions, and monitor the implementation of peace agreements or UN Security Council resolutions in the field.

NGOs have also been the driving force behind the expansion of the idea of human rights to include both social and economic rights, and women's rights, but it is in these areas that the criticisms of the human rights regime are most eloquently expressed. The human rights regime is grounded on ideas of substantive justice, of what we can claim from others, and what we owe to others by virtue of our common humanity, but there is a tendency in Western theorizing about human rights to elevate civil and political rights above social and economic rights. This has been noted and criticized by socialist states, by the Asian leaders who signed the Bangkok Declaration (discussed in Chapter 10) and increasingly by Western NGOs and thinkers such as Henry Shue, Charles Beitz and Thomas Pogge, who question the separation of global distributive justice from the broader goal of global justice. Can human freedom be promoted adequately when so many of the world's people are desperately poor? Shue argues that only by having the essentials for a reasonably healthy and active life, such as unpolluted air and water, adequate food, clothing and shelter and some basic health care (or subsistence rights) can a person cannot enjoy any other rights. He contends that these economic rights are inherently necessary to the idea of rights – not an optional extra (Shue 1980). Similarly, both Beitz (1999) and Pogge (2002) argue that the distribution of material resources is significant for justice, and wealth differentials cannot be justified by morally arbitrary criteria such as the borders of nations. Thus the issue of global inequality should have a place in any discussion of human rights. This notion has met with a great deal of resistance in the West, partly because of the reasonable fear that, if economic rights prove very difficult to achieve, then the entire human rights regime may suffer; and partly, one suspects, because of the much less defensible fear that to admit the importance of economic rights in achieving human flourishing would mean giving up some of the resources people in the West have long enjoyed.

Critiques of the human rights regime are not limited to a discussion of the priority of particular rights; they are also concerned with the nature of the rights holder himself (with the gendered term being intentional here). The idea of a human right implies a kind of universal human identity that transcends the national, ethnic and religious identities that were focused on in the previous chapter. Supporters of human rights see the individual as having those rights simply by virtue of his or her humanity, and regardless of the community or nation of which he or she is a member. This position is generally regarded as 'cosmopolitan', and is supported by the intuition that humans have so much in common that what they share must be politically significant. A counter-argument, one that motivates the criticisms of commentators from both West and East, posits that humans have very little of consequence in common *qua* humans. Rather, human identities stem from their embeddedness in social relations, and are not established prior to them. The idea of human rights on this account has no legitimate claim to universal validity.

This argument is fundamental to many feminist critiques of the universal human rights regime. The 1948 Universal Declaration was designed to cover the rights of all human beings, male and female, and stipulates in Article 2 that human rights apply to all equally 'without distinction of any kind such as race, colour, sex, language ... or other status'. However, feminist critics charge that the conception of the individual at the heart of the regime is gendered: the archetypal rights holder is male, head of his family, and the principal wage earner. Jean Bethke Elshtain finds that the roots of this characterization of the rights holder can be traced back to the Classical Greek distinction between the private and the public realm (Elshtain 1981 & 1987). The rights outlined in the Declaration are designed to protect the individual from arbitrary state interference while he acts in his public capacity as a citizen of the polity or a unit of labour, without impinging upon his activities in the private sphere. As women have been confined traditionally to the private sphere, where the protection they need is from other individuals rather than the state, their experiences of violation (justified by family, religion or culture) are not covered by the human rights regime. Rape within marriage, domestic violence and unequal property rights remain legal within many states, and too frequent in all. Even in the context of war, the public/ private split seems to have had an effect. The Fourth Geneva Convention of 1949 does require that women be protected against any attack on their 'honour', including rape, however sexual violence, enforced prostitution and trafficking in women have long been regarded as weapons, spoils or unavoidable consequences of conflict.

Feminist scholars and campaigners are divided on how best to promote the welfare of women within the international framework. Theorists such as Catherine MacKinnon (1993) contend that the regime itself is so heavily gendered that minor adjustments around the edges will never be enough to properly incorporate the experiences of women. They argue that rights language has no resonance for many women as they are marginalized or excluded from the public sphere, or do not enjoy the social and economic conditions and freedom from the threat of violence that make meaningful the status of citizen. Concepts such as empowerment and a 'capabilities approach', supposedly more egalitarian and sensitive to the differing needs of individuals under divergent social structures, have been suggested to replace the idea of human rights entirely. Others, for instance Hilary Charlesworth (1994), argue that the current human rights regime can be (and to a large extent has been) altered to better reflect feminist concerns. They see a commitment to the idea of a universal humanity, and to the equal status of persons inherent within it, as being necessary in order to change long held assumptions of the inferior status of women, and point to achievements such as the criminalization of gender and sexual violence in the Rome Statute, and the ratification of the Convention on the Elimination of All Forms of Discrimination Against Women (CEDAW) by 185 states by 2008 as examples of the human rights regime becoming genuinely gender neutral.

The remarkable number of states that have ratified international human rights instruments such as CEDAW and the Mine Ban Treaty (156 as of the summer of 2008), combined with the dominance of human rights discourse in the day-to-day workings of not just the UN and its agencies, but international financial organizations such as the IMF and the World Bank, and MNCs, and the unprecedented spread of human-rights-based NGOs would suggest that a global consensus has emerged. Certainly, the view of many states and international organizations at the end of the 1990s was that the human rights regime was unassailable. However, the attacks on the USA on 9/11 have had effects that question this conclusion. Amnesty International reported in 2004 that human rights and international humanitarian law were under their most sustained attack in fifty years, as a result of violence by armed groups, and the responses to these groups by governments. The USA (and to a lesser extent the EU) have been criticised heavily in Amnesty's 2008 Annual Report for double standards in supporting allies in the 'War on Terror' who also happen to have terrible human rights records, and for failing to uphold fundamental protections such as the prohibition on torture. The War on Terror forced domestic security much higher on the Bush Administration's agenda, and the USA, a prime mover in the advancement of human rights since the 1940s, has been condemned repeatedly for its 'pick and choose' attitude to international humanitarian law. Cited as evidence are its treatment of 'enemy combatants' at detention centres in Guantanamo Bay and Iraq, abrogation of the Convention against Torture if necessary for national security, and turning a blind eye to abuses committed abroad in the name of anti-terrorism. The USA, along with many other states, has introduced legislation since 2001 that allows the detention without charge of foreign terrorist suspects, extensive 'stop and search' and surveillance powers, and significant limits to political and religious dissent. It is unlikely that these recent changes in law and policy will lead to a longer-term global rejection of human rights standards, and it should be noted that many of the new measures are being justified in terms of the (human) right to security. That said, playing fast and loose with international standards may well have damaged goodwill towards the USA to the extent that it will find it much harder in future to require particular standards of other states in the treatment of either their own citizens or American citizens and service personnel.

Rights and international law

The idea of human rights was made concrete in the 1948 Universal Declaration; the Preamble to the Declaration states that human rights should be protected by the rule of law, but it was not until the 1990s that major shifts towards the emergence of a legal regime that was genuinely capable of protecting those rights took place. The emerging regime concentrates on protecting civilians from the gross breaches of rights involved in genocide, crimes against humanity and war crimes, and includes a variety of treaties, ad hoc tribunals, regional courts and the new International Criminal Court.

The human rights regime suggests that there may be some actions, such as torture, slavery and arbitrary detention, that are prohibited regardless of their status in domestic law, and regardless of the official status of the perpetrator. The enforcement of this position is a severe challenge to the sovereignty of states, and to the 'sovereign immunity' from prosecution conventionally enjoyed by heads of state and other state officials. This is a challenge opposed by major powers including the USA, Russia and China, yet Slobodan Milošević, former President of Yugoslavia, was arrested in 2001 and put on trial at the International Criminal Tribunal for the former Yugoslavia, on sixty-six counts of genocide, crimes against humanity and war crimes (he died in custody during the trial), and the trial of Charles Taylor, former President of Liberia, at the Special Court of Sierra Leone, on eleven counts of crimes against humanity, war crimes and other serious violations of international humanitarian law, is continuing as this book is being written. These are the first instances in history of the prosecution of former heads of state by international courts for such crimes. This section will trace critical developments in international law and ideas of responsibility through the twentieth century to understand how the apparent revolution in the 1990s came about.

War crimes prosecutions themselves are not new. There are records of such trials dating back as far as Ancient Greece, but, until the twentieth century, suspected war criminals were tried under domestic law in national courts (meaning, in practice, that the perpetrators were safe from prosecution if they held senior positions within the state). In 1872, Gustav Moynier, one of the founders of the International Committee of the Red Cross, called for the creation of a permanent international criminal court. The process of its creation took more than 100 years, and most moves towards it coincided with the end of important conflicts.

During both the First and Second World Wars there were calls for the international prosecution of leaders of belligerent states for acts of aggression and gross violations of the laws of war. The 1919 Treaty of Versailles provided for an ad hoc international court to try the Kaiser and German military officials. No prosecutions ever took place, as the Netherlands granted asylum to the Kaiser (this is ironic, given that the International Criminal Court is now based in the Hague) and Germany refused to hand over suspects, but the demand marked a shift in thinking in favour of holding individuals internationally responsible for war crimes. During the Second World War an international criminal court was proposed, but rejected by the Allies, who instead established ad hoc International Military Tribunals at Nuremburg and Tokyo. These tribunals began the process of the international criminalization of acts constituting serious human rights violations, rejected the principle of sovereign immunity and began to target *individuals* as the relevant actors rather than states or groups.

The Cold War led to deep divisions in the UN and its various bodies, and work on international criminal law lay almost dormant for more than thirty years. Only after 1989 did demands for a permanent, centralized system grow again. Perhaps surprisingly, given the charges made by various scholars that the international institutional system is a tool of Western hegemony, it was not the West who instigated the campaign for an international criminal court, but Trinidad and Tobago, who were struggling to control activities related to the international drugs trade taking place on their soil, and in 1989 requested that the UN reconvened the International Law Commission to establish a permanent institution.

Reports of ethnic cleansing in the former Yugoslavia overtook the work of the Commission, and in 1993, the Security Council established the International Criminal Tribunal for the former Yugoslavia (ICTY). A year later, the International Criminal Tribunal for Rwanda (ICTR) was established, this time in response to the deaths of an estimated 800,000 Tutsis and moderate Hutus, but also as a subsidiary organ of the Security Council. Questions remain over whether the tribunals were an appropriate response to these atrocities or a more cynical, low-cost way of responding to the demand that 'something be done'. Still, the tribunals have set a number of important precedents for both the situations and the people over which the jurisdiction of international criminal law extends. Previous war crimes trials had all been concerned with acts that took place in the context of inter-state war; however, the ICTY has jurisdiction to prosecute individuals responsible for crimes against humanity whether these were committed in an international or an internal armed conflict, while the ICTR Statute makes no reference to armed conflict at all, implying that these crimes can take place in peacetime, within a state. This is a highly significant step in the enforcement of human rights, but also a challenge to state sovereignty. The trial of Milošević at the ICTY was the first time that a former head of state had been prosecuted for international crimes, and the conviction of Jean Kambanda, former prime minister of Rwanda, marked the first time that a head of government was convicted for the crime of genocide. The ICTY will continue to make headlines now that Radovan Karadžić, former leader of the Bosnian Serbs, has finally been arrested and is standing trial at the Hague – leaving only two suspects still at large out of the 161 people indicted by the ICTY. This level of success suggests that impunity for high-ranking statesmen and women for gross abuses of human rights may be a thing of the past.

Despite the will of the international community to bring the perpetrators of atrocities in Rwanda and the former Yugoslavia to justice, the tribunals soon demonstrated major drawbacks. Principal among these is the enormous cost and slow speed of the proceedings. The monies paid to the ICTY since 1993 total more than US$1.2bn, and the ICTR has received more than US$1bn since 1996. Yet the number of trials completed is astonishingly low. These sums of money have paid for 111 trials in fourteen years at the ICTY, and 32 trials in thirteen years at the ICTR.

The conflicts in former Yugoslavia and in Rwanda made two distinct contributions to the campaign for an ICC. They re-focused attention on large-scale human rights violations during times of conflict, and they highlighted the significant practical difficulties encountered in setting up and running ad hoc tribunals, so showing the benefits to be gained from a permanent international body dedicated to the administration of criminal justice. William Schabas argues that the tribunals provided a valuable 'laboratory' for international justice that drove the agenda for the creation of an ICC forward (Schabas 2004: vii).

In 1998, delegates from 160 states plus 33 IGOs and a coalition of 236 NGOs met in Rome at the UN Diplomatic Conference of the Plenipotentiaries on the Establishment of an International Criminal Court. A draft Statute was drawn up, and was adopted by majority vote at the final session; 120 states voted in favour of the Rome Statute, 21 abstained (including India and a range of Islamic, Arab and Caribbean states), and 7 voted against. The votes were not recorded, but the USA, China, Israel, Libya, Iraq, Qatar and Yemen are widely reported to have voted against. After 60 states ratified the Statute, it came into force on 1 July 2002. The Court is now up and running, with investigations opened into alleged war crimes taking place in the Democratic Republic of Congo, Northern Uganda, the Central African Republic and the Darfur region of Sudan, and the first trial proceedings are now under way.

The Rome Statute established a Court with broad-ranging powers to prosecute acts of genocide, crimes against humanity, war crimes and, potentially, aggression (though the Court will only have jurisdiction over crimes of aggression if a definition can be agreed upon, which looks unlikely). The Court is an independent organization and not an arm of the UN. It is funded by state parties (those states that have ratified the Rome Statute – 108 at the time of writing), voluntary contributions and the UN. The Court can prosecute for crimes committed after the Statute came into force, and committed either on the territory of a state party, or by a national of a state party. It follows the jurisprudence of the ICTY and ICTR in establishing that prosecutable genocide and crimes against humanity can take place both in the context of internal armed conflict, and in times of peace. Prosecutable war crimes can take place in internal armed conflict, but not in times of peace. Also following the tribunals, individuals are treated equally before the Court, and exceptions are not made for people who hold positions in the government, bureaucracy, parliament or the military.

Cases can be brought before the court in three ways. They can be referred by State parties or the Security Council, or instigated by the Prosecutor (non-state parties, NGOs and individuals have access to the process by petitioning the Prosecutor to start an investigation). When a matter is referred by the Security Council, as in the case of the Darfur region of Sudan, the territory of the offence and the nationality of the offender are irrelevant: the Court has jurisdiction as a result of the superior legal status of the Council. This final point is of particular concern to non-state parties, as it establishes automatic jurisdiction: thus jurisdiction no longer depends on state consent. Both non-state and state parties have the option to try cases in their domestic courts. Under the principle of complementarity, the Court will only exercise its juris-diction when the states that would normally have national jurisdiction are either unable or unwilling to exercise it. If a national court is willing and able to exercise jurisdiction in a particular case, the ICC cannot intervene.

The role of the Security Council in the Rome Statute is highly controversial, and the relationship worked out between the Court and the Council may be the deciding factor in the success of the Court. The UN Charter gives the Security Council primary responsibility for the maintenance of international peace and security, and as such its decisions under Chapter VII of the UN Charter are binding and legally enforceable in all states. A critical concern at the Rome Conference was the ability of the Council to interfere with the work of the Court. States that were not Permanent Members of the Council did not want the international legal process to be politicized. Permanent Members argued that decisions over possible criminal prosecutions should not be taken at a time when negotiations to promote international peace and security were under way. The compromise reached allows the Council to prevent the Court from exercising jurisdiction by passing a positive resolution, renewable annu-ally, which has the effect of deferring investigations for a year at a time. The Council must be acting pursuant to Chapter VII in order to defer, and crucially, any member of the Permanent Five can veto a deferral, but they cannot veto an investigation or prosecution. The relationship between the Court and the Council could in principle be mutually beneficial; the Court, through its role in investigating and prosecuting war criminals, could assist the Council in its task of maintaining international peace and security. The Council, in turn, could help the ICC to enforce international criminal law more broadly, through its ability to grant effective universal jurisdiction to the Court when it refers a case. The more likely scenario appears to be continual clashes, in large part a result of the animosity towards the Court by the most powerful member of the Council: the USA.

The US is not alone in its opposition to the ICC. Of the Permanent Five, only the UK and France – the least powerful members – have ratified the Rome Statute. Not one of the nuclear powers outside Europe has ratified the treaty, and the Court is dominated by European, Latin-American and African states. Still, while the USA is not alone, its lack of support is the most worrying. Without the USA, it is very difficult to see how any major international institution can be a success. One only needs to think back to the fortunes of the League of Nations, which collapsed in large part because of a lack of US backing. In terms of international justice, US help was imperative in bringing Milošević to trial: the USA made the extradition of Milošević a condition before Serbia could receive a significant economic aid package, plus American intelligence technology enabled him to be tracked and arrested. The American position on the Court is therefore worth examining in some detail. From 1995 to 2000, the US government supported the establishment of an ICC, but always argued for a Court that could be controlled through the Security Council, or that provided exemption from prosecution for US officials and nationals. On the final day of the Clinton Administration, the USA signed the Rome Statute, signalling its desire to stay in the debate. At that time, President Clinton stated the treaty was fundamentally flawed and would not be forwarded to the Senate for ratification. The Bush Administration took an altogether more aggressive approach. It renounced the US signature on the Statute and any legal implications that followed from it, and since then has passed the American Service Members Protection Act, which authorizes the president to take 'all means necessary' to free Americans taken into custody by the court, presumably including invading the Netherlands. It also states that US military assistance to ICC states parties that do not sign bilateral immunity agreements (BIAs) with the USA will be cut off. These agreements provide that neither party to the agreement will transfer the other's current or former government officials, military and other personnel, or nationals to the jurisdiction of the ICC. The USA aims to get all states to sign BIAs, and over 100 states had reportedly done so by the summer of 2008, including forty-six state parties to the ICC. The USA also threatened to veto all future peacekeeping operations in order to gain support for UNSC resolution 1422, which guaranteed that non-state parties contributing to UN forces were exempt from the Court. This resolution was passed, and renewed in 2003, but the Abu Ghraib prisoner abuse scandal in 2004 resulted in insufficient support on the Council for a further renewal. The USA is now relying on BIAs to prevent US personnel from being prosecuted.

So why is the USA, a state known for its long-standing support for human rights and commitment to promoting them throughout the world, so vehemently opposed to the Court? There are two main aspects to their opposition: pragmatic concern over risks to US military personnel; and doubts over the scope and nature of international law. The pragmatic concerns focus on the fact that as the USA is the world's sole remaining superpower, it is expected to deploy its military to 'hot spots' more often than other countries. This makes it more vulnerable to politically motivated accusations and prosecutions. This argument is well grounded, but does not explain why the USA is not prepared to take the British position, which is to ratify the Statute but commit to investigating all accusations within its domestic court system, thus preventing British nationals appearing before the Court.

The US position is more concerned with the emerging structure of international society. A 'new sovereigntist' critique, expounded by politicians – for instance Jesse Helms (2000/01) – and lawyers – such as Lee A. Casey and David B. Rivkin, Jr (2000/01) – alike argues that the Court is a grave threat to state sovereignty because of its potential jurisdiction over US nationals even if the US does not ratify the treaty, which is seen as fundamentally in breach of both customary treaty practice and UN Charter protections of national sovereignty. The critique also takes a position on global ethics, arguing that the move from state to individual responsibility is flawed and should be reversed as there is no world consensus on moral issues. Without such a consensus it is both illegitimate and an invasion of national sovereignty for an international body to usurp national legislatures and assign duties to individuals. This view is shared by China and India – both countries view the ICC as a Western project, dominated by Western moral understandings and state power.

These issues are not easily resolved. Supporters of the Court argue that the Statute is entirely in line with US law and the provisions of the US Constitution, but this is not the point. The US objects to losing its rights as sole legislator, bound only by laws it consents to. The doubts over a global moral consensus are also widely appealing. The Court at present looks very much like a European project, supported by relatively minor players on the world stage, from Canada, South America and Africa. If the Europeans push too fast to establish a dominant Court, the beginnings of a global consensus mentioned in the first part of this chapter could be destroyed, along with the idea that international relations can be managed within a legal framework. This seems to be a very real danger at present, as the ICC is coming under heavy criticism for interference in conflicts, and is accused of making the situations in Darfur and Uganda worse. The ICC's search for justice is seen by its opponents as threatening peace, through its politically-motivated interference and intransigence. The Chief Prosecutor, Luis Moreno-Ocampo, has been accused by the African Union – which is staffing a grossly underfunded and under-resourced UN Peacekeeping Force in Darfur (UNAMID) – of 'pouring oil on the fire' in the conflict by seeking an arrest warrant for President Bashir of Sudan on charges that include genocide. The AU wants to negotiate with Bashir to bring about a ceasefire, and regards pressure from the ICC as destructive to such efforts and as endangering peacekeepers and humanitarian workers by angering the ruling regime. The situation in Northern Uganda is equally grave: President Museveni of Uganda referred the conflict in Northern Uganda to the ICC in 2003, in a supposed bid to bring peace and justice to a region that has experienced civil war for more than twenty years. It seems now that this referral may have backfired. The ICC was quick to take up the case, and issued arrest warrants for five of the commanders of the chief rebel group, the Lord's Resistance Army, for war crimes and crimes against humanity. Then, in 2007, movement was finally made towards peace talks in the region – Sudan offered to host the talks and the Ugandan government and the LRA signed a truce. However, the talks failed because Joseph Kony, head of the LRA and therefore a key figure in making sure that any peace deal is carried through, refused to sign the proposed deal in April 2008 without assurances that the ICC would lift its arrest warrant on him. The conflict continues, and the refusal of the ICC to suspend its activities is blamed by many for the lack of peace.

It is tremendously difficult to know what the Court should do in these circumstances. Should justice ever be pursued at the expense of peace? While this is a serious question, it is not impossible to suggest answers. The Security Council has a crucial role to play in supporting the Court – it may be that the Court should continue to pursue justice aggressively, and rely on the UNSC to defer cases if peace talks appear to be threatened (though this would not solve the problem of indictees such as Kony, who may still disrupt peace negotiations out of fear of prosecution). We may yet discover that the ICC encourages peace as well as justice, in so far as the threat of legal proceedings incentivizes warring factions to negotiate for peace – there is evidence to suggest that the LRA was only willing to attend peace talks out of fear of the Court. More controversially, it is yet to be established whether the Court is simply a political tool of the West. But again, this is not an insoluble situation. If the Court makes serious efforts to widen its geographical appeal, is willing to engage with views of powerful non-Western discontents as well as of the USA, and can build up a store of sensible judgments, it may be able to establish itself as a very valuable part of the international system.

The ICC is still young, and any assessment of its impact on the protection of human rights can only be tentative. By contrast, the European Court of Human Rights, set up to enforce the 1950 European Convention for the Protection of Human Rights and Fundamental Freedoms, is a long-standing institution, argued to be the world's most effective international tool for the protection of human rights, and may provide a model for the ICC. The European Convention is formally and legally binding on signatories (unlike the Universal Declaration, which is a resolution of the General Assembly, and as such not binding) and the jurisprudence of the Court, built on over 1,000 judgments and drawing both from the Convention and from international human rights law, has had a profound influence on the laws and practices of the forty-seven member states. During the 1990s, two factors caused the growth of the Court. First, as the Cold War ended and the Council of Europe enlarged to the East, the Court gained jurisdiction over an increasing number of states, including Russia. Second, in 1994, the Council of Europe concluded an additional protocol to the 1950 Convention, which allowed individual applicants to bring cases before the Court. Prior to this, individuals only had access to the Commission, which produced non-binding reports. Now, individuals and non-state groups have access to the Court alongside states, and states found to have breached the Convention are required to take corrective action, usually by amending national law. There is little that can be done to enforce the decisions of the Court, but the carrot of EU membership and the stick of trade and commercial sanctions for states whose record at the Court is poor have produced a system where the norm is compliance.

Of course, the high level of integration in Europe is an exception rather than the rule in international politics, but the success of the ECHR is almost impossible for a realist to explain, and suggests that the nature of sovereignty is indeed changing as individual welfare becomes more highly valued in IR. Why would self-interested actors in an international anarchy choose freely to give up sovereignty, bind themselves to international institutions, and allow their citizens to become subject to laws that originate above the level of the nation state? The same question can be asked of states that have ratified the Rome Statute, as the ICC has the potential to become every bit as powerful over its state parties as the ECHR.

Even more challenging to the realist is explaining why states would risk their own resources and security to intervene militarily in the affairs of others when human rights are being abused. The next section of the chapter will examine the issue of humanitarian intervention.

Humanitarian intervention

As well as seeing changes in the promotion of human rights and their protection in international law, the 1990s also saw the birth of a new, more violent, phenomenon of rights protection: 'humanitarian intervention'. The decade started and finished with innovative international action: in 1991, 'Safe Areas' were created for Kurds in Northern Iraq; and in 1999, NATO intervened in Kosovo. What are we to make of these actions? This section will examine whether humanitarian intervention was a temporary phenomenon, made possible by the relative peace of the 1990s and now seen to be floundering after the US invasion of Iraq in 2003, or whether it is a permanent fixture of twenty-first-century international society.

Humanitarian intervention is a more comprehensive challenge to the sovereign state than either the idea of human rights or the expansion of international law, as it involves the invasion of sovereign territory using military force. According to English School and International Society theorists, the Westphalian system can only work if states recognize each other's sovereignty. Rulers understand that the only way they can enjoy the rights they wish to have, principally the right to sole jurisdiction within their territory, is to recognize similar rights in others. Thus one of the principal norms of the system is that of non-intervention; each state must respect the borders of other states to ensure that its own borders remain secure. This is not to say that states *do* always respect borders: since the Peace of Westphalia in 1648, there have been countless invasions, incursions and threats to territorial borders (see Krasner 1999). The point is that there is a 'settled norm' of non-intervention – that is, a principle that all members of international society agree is in force even if they do not apply it all of the time (Frost 1996). When the norm appears to be breached, the wrongdoers are called upon by others to explain why they did not act according to the norm, or to show that they did. This norm is not an arcane remnant of an old system: it was reaffirmed as a principle of the international order, alongside universal self-determination and the promotion of human rights, in the UN Charter.

The norm was radically unsettled during the 1990s by the birth of humanitarian intervention – the forcible invasion of sovereign territory by one or more states, with or without the backing of international bodies, motivated supposedly to alleviate suffering within that state. Such action appears to be entirely in contradiction to the principles of the sovereign state system. Its emergence can be linked to the increasing strength of the human rights regime, particularly the regime's conception of legitimate state sovereignty as flowing from the rights of individuals.

The growth of the human rights regime in the 1990s meant that states were held to new standards of legitimacy, based on their observance of international human rights laws and norms. State sovereignty and non-intervention began to be seen as privileges, conditional upon observance of international standards. A logical implication of the view that human rights rank higher than state rights to sovereignty is that intervention in support of human rights becomes legitimate and maybe even required. This view can be traced back to the 1960s, or perhaps earlier, but fear of superpower involvement and commitment to traditional views of sovereignty meant that interventions in Bangladesh, Cambodia and Uganda in the 1970s, which could have been seen as humanitarian, were not. The end of the Cold War simultaneously removed the risk of superpower conflict, and created many more candidates for humanitarian action as protectorates collapsed and nationalism spread through former socialist states.

After the Second World War, the UN outlawed imperialism and decreed that all states should be self-governing as quickly as possible. The capacity of states to govern – what Robert Jackson would call their 'positive sovereignty' (Jackson 1990) – was not taken into account, and states without sufficient capacity, but with strategic value, frequently became informal protectorates of the superpowers. When the Cold War ended, these states were often abandoned by their sponsors and effectively became the well-armed and volatile responsibility of the international community. This was not the case with the first humanitarian action of the 1990s in Northern Iraq (which was brought about partly by Western concerns about the persecution of the Shias and Kurds by the Iraqi force just defeated in Kuwait, but also by more traditional concerns about international peace and security), but was certainly the case with the second. Somalia had allied itself with the Soviet Union until 1977, then switched allegiance to the USA in return for substantial military aid, but in 1989, the USA withdrew its support on the basis of human rights viola-tions. Authority within the state collapsed, warlords took over the control of food distribution, famine spread and UNISOM I, a small UN mission already on the ground, was unable to intervene. In December 1993, the UN Security Council approved the insertion into Somalia of a much bigger, US-led, UN mission to assist in aid deliveries (UNITAF). This intervention was explicitly humanitarian, and did not have the approval of the target state (as the state had collapsed). The intervention appeared successful at first, but the scaling down of the force in early 1993 and its replacement by UNISOM II, along with disagreement over mission objectives, frittered away this success and the advantage swung back to the warlords. After the murder of twenty-four Pakistani UN peacekeepers, UN/US forces engaged in fighting a more conven-tional war; and eighteen US Rangers were killed in October 1993 (along with hundreds of Somalis) in the famous 'Black Hawk Down' incident. The UN/US mission withdrew soon afterwards, having learnt the hard way that the inter-national community did not have the requisite co-ordinated military strategy, intelligence, experience at nation-building or commitment from member states to fulfil the goal it had set itself. More tragically, the failure in Somalia, and the casualty-aversion shown by the USA when pursuing a mission not judged to be in its national interest, contributed to the inaction of the international community in the face of the genocide that took place in Rwanda in 1994.

The international community did act in the case of the breakdown of the former Yugoslavia. After the fall of communism, the institutions that had bound the six republics of Yugoslavia together as a state disappeared, and political elites began to mobilize support along nationalist lines. Fear of the dominance of Serbia, under the leadership of Slobodan Milošević, led to Slovenia, Croatia and Bosnia-Herzegovina declaring their independence. Serbia cared little for Slovenia, but had substantial Serb populations in the other republics, so resisted their secession and civil war broke out. Reports began to reach the international community about ethnic cleansing being carried out by Serb forces, but the community was torn over how to react. The Security Council initially imposed an arms embargo on all parties, which perpetuated Serb dominance, then the UN recognized the three republics as being independent in June 1992 and began mediation efforts. Heeding calls for assistance from the recognized governments of Croatia and Bosnia, the Security Council established the UN force UNPROFOR in the same year, but its mandate was limited to protecting humanitarian aid. In 1993, this was extended to include the guarantee of 'safe areas' in Bosnia where Muslims could gather and be protected from Serb forces. This policy was a disaster, resulting most notoriously in the fall of Srebrenica and the murder of thousands of men and boys who had travelled there to gain UN protection. Again, the UN had acted on principle to alleviate suffering, but its actions may have led to greater harm because of its delayed response to the reported atrocities and its lack of commitment to using substantial military force.

The 1990s ended with the most controversial of all cases of humanitarian intervention – the NATO action in Kosovo. Kosovo was an autonomous region within the republic of Serbia until Milošević revoked its autonomy in 1989 in an attempt to defend Serbs who were being oppressed within the territory. Elements of the majority Kosovo Albanian population formed the Kosovo Liberation Army (KLA), which launched an extensive campaign against the Serbs in 1998. They succeeded in provoking Serbian atrocities, which led to the situation being debated in the Security Council. Council members were divided over how to deal with it, with Russia and China asserting that domestic oppression was not a threat to international peace and security, and as such the Council could not authorize an armed intervention against the wishes of the recognized government. Nevertheless, NATO decided to act, and began to bomb the Serbian army and Serbian infrastructure in March 1999. The intervention was carried out without ground troops as NATO member states were unwilling to risk casualties. The results of this decision were the deaths of an estimated 500 civilians as a result of the bombing, and the speeding-up of the Serbian policy of ethnic cleansing. NATO did succeed in ending Serbian control of Kosovo and brought back many refugees, but was forced to establish a long-term unofficial protectorate in the province until Kosovo declared independence in February 2008.

The international community is still deeply divided over whether NATO's actions in Kosovo were legal or just. Other 1999 interventions in Sierra Leone and East Timor were much less controversial (as the recognized Sierra Leonean government invited intervention to assist in its fight against rebels, and the UN had never recognized the Indonesian right to East Timor), and it is the action in Kosovo that remains the test case for the legitimacy of humanitarian action. Politicians from the USA and UK spoke at the time of the emergence a new world order, where foreign policy decisions are motivated by a fundamental belief in universal human rights. In a speech in April 1999 to the Chicago Economic Club, Tony Blair argued that that a new 'doctrine of the international community' was evolving, based on the idea of a 'just war': a war based not on any territorial ambitions but on stopping or preventing humanitarian disasters. The Chinese and Russians reject this grand idea of a new type of 'just war', maintaining that NATO had no right to interfere in the affairs of a sovereign state, and acted illegally in intervening without Security

Council authorization. They argue that humanitarian intervention is a breach of the right of self-determination, motivated by a desire to impose Western standards on other states, and, perhaps, to covertly pursue Western interests.

The motives of interveners have received a great deal of attention in this debate. Many campaigners who oppose human rights abuses support the idea of humanitarian intervention, but by a force constituted and controlled by the UN, on the basis that states tend to act only when it is in their national interest to do so. Putting aside the question of whether the UN, itself a coalition of states, is the benevolent body it is imagined to be by those who take this position, we should ask whether it is wrong for states to intervene for reasons of national interest. It may be that we would prefer that they *also* intervene in situations of gross human rights violations that are not in their interest – for example, in Rwanda – but it is not surprising that states are most willing to risk the lives of their troops in situations where they perceive some possible national gain. In addition, international crises tend to be so complex and involve so many actors that motives to act are bound to be mixed. Some will be self-regarding, and others may be humanitarian, but if we prevent every state that might have some interest in the outcome from intervening in situations of atrocity, it is unlikely that there will be any interveners left.

Linked to this argument about motives are the problems of legitimacy and authority thrown up by intervention. Who should intervene, under whose orders and with what level of force? If the Security Council is not recognized as the final arbiter in such questions, then who has the authority to decide? Equally, if action can only be authorized by the Council, is it right that the protection of individuals is left to the whim of the veto-wielding Permanent Five? In 2001, a report entitled 'The Responsibility to Protect' (R2P), published by the International Commission on Intervention and State Sovereignty, attempted to answer some of these questions. The ICISS was set up by the Canadian government in 2000 after Kofi Annan challenged the international community to build a consensus around the basic principles and processes of intervention. The report argues that sovereign states have primary responsibility for the protection of their citizens, but that when they are unwilling or unable to provide this protection, the international community must take responsibility. The report supports the use of military force to prevent human rights abuses, even without explicit Security Council approval, but only if force is used as a last resort. It also sets out guidelines for intervention in some detail. The UN World Summit debated the R2P principles in 2005, and endorsed a more limited version of the report in which the authority of the Security Council was reestablished. It is not yet clear how influential the R2P principles will be – they are criticized (predictably) by some for being just another tool of Western imperialism, but are being taken very seriously by NGOs campaigning for international action in conflict-ridden states.

A particularly problematic issue, not dealt with adequately in the R2P process, is the fact that humanitarian interventions usually fail. Nearly two decades after the intervention, Somalia is still unstable and has become home to fundamentalist Islamic groups, making it a potential target in the War on Terror. NGOs regard the post-conflict efforts in Bosnia as only recently starting to make headway, and violence in the region of the former Yugoslavia is by no means over. In taking sides in the Kosovo struggle and backing the KLA, NATO effectively gave legitimacy and power to an organization that has continued to promote anti-Serb violence. In March 2004, NATO had to reinforce its troops in Kosovo after the worst clashes between Serbs and ethnic Albanians since 1999 took place in Mitrovica. Other interventions in Sierra Leone and East Timor have had reasonable success, but UN troops were still present in both states until 2005. Humanitarian interventions are more problematic to 'win' than traditional wars, as the criteria for success include bringing about a stable peace. This requires long-term focus and resources as well as sufficient military force. Few of the world's militaries are structured to enable an easy transition from war-fighting to peace-keeping, and the nation-building that is necessary to prevent future atrocities is extremely difficult to do. The attention of interveners tends to return quickly to their national projects, leaving under-resourced UN/NGO teams to piece together states that may never be viable. These problems can also be seen after the recent conflicts in Afghanistan and Iraq, the implications of which will be considered at the end of this section.

The Chinese and Russian arguments against intervention do not turn on practical issues such as motivation, decision-making and the likelihood of success. They are based on a different theoretical conception of the international system, and reject the idea that a state's right to sovereignty stems from the rights of the individuals within it. On this view, the rights to sovereignty and national self-determination are necessary conditions of order in the international system, and it is not the business of any other body to pass judgement on what happens within the borders of a recognized state. Universal human rights are rejected as being a Western liberal project, and the use of military might to force weaker states to behave according to subjective and self-serving standards is viewed as aggression. Realists argue a similar point. They see humanitarian intervention as either the pursuit of self-interest dressed up as ethical action, or as mistaken policy made possible by the temporary absence of a balance of power. Such intervention is regarded as dangerous because it threatens international order, plus it carries an inherent risk of escalation because interventions tend to be justified using ideas of good and evil, thus legitimating disproportionate force to be used to combat 'evil'. Some liberals have related concerns – they believe in the universal applicability of human rights, but argue that the principle of non-intervention is necessary either to support the right to liberty or to promote peace. The most prominent liberal theorist to support non-intervention is Michael Walzer – though, in recent years, his position has wavered somewhat (Walzer 2004). Like many supporters of humanitarian intervention, he links state rights to individual rights, but his conclusions differ. He argues that states have a moral right to autonomy, which derives, via an implied social contract, from the rights of the individual citizens of a state. State rights to territorial integrity and political sovereignty can therefore be defended morally in the same way as the individual's rights to life and liberty. He sees humanitarian intervention as being theoretically justifiable, but only in very rare cases, when acts are taking place that 'shock the moral conscience of mankind'; sadly, he acknowledges that such cases may be becoming more frequent. In general, according to Walzer, we should assume that states do represent the interests of their citizens, and therefore respect their right to autonomy. This differs markedly from proponents of intervention, who regard the state as a principal threat to the welfare of its citizens, and advocate intervention in any situation where basic human rights are not being respected. For David Luban, the concept of sovereignty (and by extension the rights of states) is 'morally flaccid' as it is indifferent to the question of legitimacy, a point missed by Walzer as he confuses, according to Luban, the political community or nation (which may have a right of non-intervention derived from the rights of its members) with the state (Luban 1985: 201). The existence of a nation does not prove the legitimacy of its corresponding state, and therefore interventions in support of an oppressed nation may be not just morally permissible, but morally required. This position, however, rests on notions of universal humanity rejected by the opponents discussed above, so offers little to those not already disposed to reject absolute rights to non-intervention.

The preceding paragraphs outline the significant practical and theoretical obstacles faced by supporters of humanitarian intervention. But is the debate already dead? Since the terrorist attacks of 9/11, 'coalitions of the willing' have deposed regimes in Afghanistan and Iraq, with far-reaching consequences. These wars were justified by the leaders of the coalitions, first and foremost on grounds of national security, but humanitarian motives have been cited increasingly in post hoc defences of their actions. The war to depose the Taliban was presented as an opportunity to support the human rights of the people of a failed state, and particularly to benefit oppressed women. The USA and UK have both justified the war in Iraq to some extent, on the basis that removing Saddam Hussein's government and restoring democracy has benefited the Iraqi people, and the relative weight of these justifications increased as more time passed without finding the weapons of mass destruction that were the initial reason cited for war. This is perceived by many as cynical exploitation of the idea of humanitarian intervention, and the failure of the coalition to live up to their own standards evidenced at Guantanamo Bay and the Abu Ghraib prison in Iraq, alongside the shaky commitment of coalition forces to provide the troops and financing necessary to genuinely improve conditions in Afghanistan, are used to suggest that coalition members' support for human rights is nothing more than a cover for the pursuit of their own gain.

The coalitions recognized that being seen to act in a humanitarian way was necessary to earn or retain international support for their actions, and so engaged their militaries in the kind of reconstruction projects for which the UN and NGOs have traditionally been responsible. This has had devastating and unforeseen effects. Military, UN and NGO activities are being confused by the populations they are aiming to assist, and aid organizations have lost the reputation for neutrality that kept them safe in combat zones. Humanitarian workers have increasingly become the target of violence, with the Baghdad headquarters of the UN and the ICRC being targeted by massive car bombs, and scores of aid workers being murdered in Afghanistan since March 2003. The UN and the ICRC were both forced to pull out of Iraq, and Médecins Sans Frontières and the International Rescue Committee judged the risk to their staff in Afghanistan to be too great, so suspended all operations there. The 'good offices' function of the UN and organizations such as the Red Cross and major NGOs has been crucial to post-conflict reconstruction in the past, and their perceived loss of neutrality will make them less able to fulfil those roles in the future. This, combined with the high cost and low success rates of past interventions, and the profound loss of trust in Western motivation following the Iraq war, means that humanitarian intervention is a much more problematic option for the international community to consider. The UN response to the genocidal conflict in Darfur, in which 300,000 people are estimated to have died and 2,000,000 to have been displaced since 2003, has been pitifully slow, despite the supposed agreement on the Responsibility to Protect principles. A peacekeeping force (UNAMID) was finally deployed in 2007, but it still has less than half of the troops and only a fraction of the equipment it needs to have any real effect. If this force is allowed to fail, as appears likely at the time of writing, it may signal the end of international willingness to intervene with force to protect human lives and human rights, less than five years after the R2P was endorsed at the World Summit.

Conclusions

Have we come full circle, from the emergence of realism out of the ashes of the pre-war liberal internationalism that marked the beginning of this discipline, to the triumph of liberal beliefs in universal values, human rights and the role of international law in making the world a better place? Some of the evidence of this chapter might point in that direction, but such a conclusion would contradict many of the findings of Chapter 10 and would not reflect current fears about the death of intervention as a viable option in the face of gross violations of human rights. The notion of human rights does have a central and seemingly secure place in contemporary debates on international relations. Certainly, most states speak in the language of human rights, but whether they mean the same things by it, and the extent to which they prioritize the human rights of their own citizens and of foreigners is up for debate. The increasing importance of the individual in international relations is borne out both in increasing protection for individuals from their states, and in increasing individual accountability. As the legal regime for protecting human rights has grown, so accountability for gross breaches of human rights has shifted towards the individual. Prior to the wars of the twentieth century, states were accorded principal rights in controlling their own territory, but were also held responsible for violations of international law during wars. At the start of the twenty-first century, individuals can make claims to courts beyond their national boundaries if they feel their rights have been breached, but the defences of 'superior orders' and position of state are no longer available to them if they participate in human rights abuses. Does this mean that states have lost power? The ICC and the ECHR are substantial challenges to the sovereign state, as they bind states and individuals in times of war and peace, for their future actions as well as for what they have done in the past. Humanitarian intervention, should it survive as part of the international toolkit to deal with conflict, is an even more direct breach of sovereignty. However, states remain tremendously powerful actors, and power is currently shifting away from those states that traditionally support human rights promotion, and towards those who are a great deal more wary, and more defensive of traditional notions of sovereignty. The final chapter of this book documents this shift, and assesses its likely implications for global politics.

Further reading

On human rights, Tim Dunne and N. J. Wheeler (eds), *Human Rights in Global Politics* (1999), is the best single-volume collection; R. J. Vincent, *Human Rights and International Relations: Issues and Responses* (1986), and Jack Donnelly, *International Human Rights* (1993) are useful studies. H. J. Steiner and P. Alston, *International Human Rights in Context: Law, Politics, Morals: Texts and Materials*, 3rd ed (2007), contains a great deal of commentary on human rights law along with links to an Online Resource Centre with the texts of all the major HR documents, and most of the minor ones. Richard Rorty, 'Human Rights, Rationality and Sentimentality' (1993), outlines a case for universal human rights that does not rely on Western liberal foundations. The role of NGOs in forcing rights on to the agenda of MNCs is examined in Rebecca DeWinter, 'The Anti-Sweatshop Movement: Constructing Corporate Moral Agency in the Global Apparel Industry' (2003). NGO action in the field of rights more generally is best understood by browsing the extensive resource and publications sections on the websites of the major organizations. The 2008 Amnesty report referenced in the text is available from http://thereport.amnesty.org. Michael Ignatieff, *The Warrior's Honour: Ethnic War and the Modern Consciousness* (1999), contains interesting material on the 'new moral interventionism' of NGOs in conflict zones. The journals *Human Rights Quarterly* and *International Journal of Human Rights* are reliable sources of reading material on all human rights issues. Two recent collections that stand above the mass of writing on human rights are Mark Goodale and Sally Engle Merry, *The Practice of Human Rights: Tracking Law Between the Global and the Local* (2007); and Lynn Hunt, *Inventing Human Rights* (2007), which is a very readable intellectual history of human rights. Jack Donnelly gives his customary clear and sympathetic account of human rights foundations in 'The Relative Universality of Human Rights' (2007) in *Human Rights Quarterly*, which also feature a civil but illuminating exchange with critics. Finally, Eric Neumayer, 'Do International Human Rights Treaties Improve Respect for Human Rights?', sceptically answers the eponymous question.

For a flavour of the global justice literature, see Thomas Pogge, *World Poverty and Human Rights* (2002); Ian Shapiro and Lea Brilmayer (eds), *Global Justice* (1999); Charles Beitz *et al.*, *International Ethics* (1985); Shue, *Basic Rights: Subsistence, Affluence and U.S. Foreign Policy* (1980). More recent worthwhile works include Simon Caney, *Justice Beyond Borders* (2006), and Christian Barry and Thomas Pogge (eds), *Global Institutions and Responsibilities: Achieving Global Justice* (2005). Closer to the discipline of IR, the *Review of International Studies* forum, 'Reading Charles Beitz: Twenty-five Years of Political Theory and International Relations', (2005) is an excellent introduction to an important writer, but not one that should overshadow the seminal *Political Theory and International Relations* (1999).

The best collection exploring the feminist critique of human rights is J. S. Peters and A. Wolper (eds), *Women's Rights, Human Rights: International Feminist Perspectives* (1995). See also Catherine Mackinnon's Amnesty Lecture, 'Crimes of War, Crimes of Peace' (1993); and Rebecca Cook, *Human Rights of Women: National and International Perspectives* (1994) – particularly the chapters by Coomaraswamy and Charlesworth. For feminist argument in favour of universalism, read Martha Nussbaum, 'The Professor of Parody: The Hip Defeatism of Judith Butler' (1999).

The Law of War Crimes: National and International Approaches, edited by Timothy McCormack and Gerry Simpson (1997) is an excellent introduction to international criminal law, offering both theoretical and historical insight. Yves Beigbeder, *Judging War Criminals: The Politics of International Justice* (1999), looks in more detail at the development of individual responsibility. Christopher Rudolph, 'Constructing an Atrocities Regime: The Politics of War Crimes Tribunals' (2001); Frederic Megret, 'The Politics of International Criminal Justice' (2002); Elizabeth Dauphinee, 'War Crimes and Ruin of Law' (2008) are good recent theoretical pieces. Tim Kelsall, 'Politics, Anti-politics, International Justice: Language and Power in the Special Court for Sierra Leone' (2006), is a critical look at the often neglected Sierra Leone case. William Schabas, *An Introduction to the International Criminal Court* (2004), and Antonio Cassese *et al.*, *The Rome Statute of the International Criminal Court: A Commentary* (2002), are the best general texts on the ICC; and the *American Journal of International Law* (1999) is the best collection of papers on the Court. The official website of the ICC is at http://www.icc-cpi.int/home.html&l=en. All relevant documents can be found on the website of the Rome Statute: http://www.un.org/law/icc/. The most broad-ranging internet resource in this area is www.iccnow.org (a website run by the Coalition for the ICC, a group of NGOs), which contains updates on ratifications and investigations, a good Q&A section and much more. To understand the US critique of the ICC, see Jason Ralph, 'International Society, the International Criminal Court and American Foreign Policy' (2005), and Peter Spiro 'The New Sovereigntists' (2000); Jessie Helms, 'American Sovereignty and the UN' (2000/1); David Rivkin and Lee Casey 'The Rocky Shoals of International Law' (2000/1) on the 'new sovereign-tist' critique. Linda Bishai takes a broader view of America's position on international law in 'Leaving Nuremberg: America's Love/Hate Relationship with International Law' (2008). Christian Reus-Smit (ed.), *The Politics of International Law* (2005), is a useful recent collection.

On humanitarian intervention N. J. Wheeler, *Saving Strangers* (2000), is indispensable. Wide-ranging collections include Terry Nardin and Melissa Williams, *Humanitarian Intervention* (2006); Deen K. Chatterjee and Don E. Scheid (eds), *Ethics and Foreign Intervention: Kosovo and Beyond* (2004); Anthony Lang (ed.), *Just Interventions* (2003); Jeff Holzgrefe and Robert Keohane, *Humanitarian Intervention: Ethical, Legal, and Political Dilemmas* (2003); Jonathon Moore (ed.), *Hard Choices: Moral Dilemmas in Humanitarian Intervention* (1998). Michael Walzer, *Just and Unjust Wars* (2000), sets out a liberal position inimical to humanitarian intervention, which some of the later essays in his *Arguing About War* (2004) modify somewhat. The journal *Ethics and International Affairs*, published by the Carnegie Council for Ethics and International Affairs, is a valuable source of material on this subject.

The Further reading section of Chapter 7 lists texts on specific interventions. See also: Mohamed Sahnoun, 'Mixed Intervention in Somalia and the Great Lakes: Culture, Neutrality and the Military' (1998); Mark Bowden, *Black Hawk Down* (1999); Philip Gourevitch, *We Wish to Inform You that Tomorrow We Will Be Killed with Our Families: Stories from Rwanda* (1998); Gérard Prunier, *The Rwanda Crisis 1959–94: History of a Genocide* (1995); James Gow, *Triumph of the Lack of Will: International Diplomacy and the Yugoslav War* (1997); Ken Booth, *The Kosovo Tragedy: the Human Rights Dimensions* (2001); Tony Blair, 'Doctrine of International Community' (1999). The journals *International Affairs* and *Foreign Affairs* also routinely publish articles of interest.

Noam Chomsky, *The New Military Humanism* (1999), and John Pilger, *New Rulers of the World* (2002), attack the motives of Western interveners. Samantha Power, *A Problem from Hell: America and the Age of Genocide* (2002), looks at US policy and genocide. *Harvard Human Rights Journal*, vol. 17 (2004) examines the relations between NGOs and the US military in recent conflicts. Chris Brown, 'Do Great Powers Have Great Responsibilities? Great Powers and Moral Agency' (2004), and Toni Erskine '"Blood on the UN's Hands"? Assigning Duties and Apportioning Blame to an Intergovernmental Organisation' (2004) look at issues of moral responsibility and authority. A recent theme is the connection between intervention and democracy; see Bruce Bueno de Mesquita, 'Intervention and Democracy' (2006), and Christopher Finlay, 'Reform Intervention and Democratic Revolution' (2007). Sceptical, though not wholly hostile, work includes Alan Kuperman, 'The Moral Hazard of Humanitarian Intervention: Lessons from the Balkans' (2008), and Roberto Belloni, 'The Trouble with Humanitarianism' (2007). Finally, the continuing debate over the responsibility to protect can be tracked in Louise Arbour, 'The Responsibility to Protect as Duty of Care in International Law and Practice' (2008), and Alex Bellamy, 'The Responsibility to Protect and the Problem of Military Intervention' (2008).

Chris Brown, *Sovereignty, Rights, and Justice: International Political Theory Today* (2002), covers much of the subject matter of this chapter, and readers are referred to both the text and the bibliography.

Chapter 12

The Shape of Things to Come

Introduction

As was established at the outset, *Understanding International Relations* sets out to provide an introduction to the discipline of International Relations, and is certainly not intended as a guide to current affairs. On the other hand, it would be unfortunate in the extreme if the kinds of theoretical debates presented in the main body of the book were to be understood as having no impact on the way the world is; we are entitled to ask of any social science that it illuminates the real-world subject matter it purports to theorize, and International Relations is no exception to this rule. In recent years, International Relations theory – in both its conventional, 'positivist' guise as well as in explicitly post-positivist work – has become increasingly abstract, but the intention is, or at least should be, to be 'action-guiding' rather than simply 'world-revealing', to use Stephen White's distinction (White 1991). Accordingly, in this final chapter, the aim is to try to apply some of the ideas set out in earlier chapters to the current world order, and to identify – albeit tentatively – some trends we expect to come to fruition in the years ahead.

As a first step, it may be instructive to look back at what was said in the final chapters of the previous three editions of *Understanding International Relations*, each of which ended in a similar way. The first edition, published in 1997, but written in the summer of 1996 (such a delay is, of course, normal, and applies equally to the other two editions, and to this one) ended with two chapters in a Part IV entitled 'New Agendas'. The first of these chapters was, in fact, rather backward-looking – it was dominated by the end of the Cold War and the theorizing this provoked. Various formulas and slogans of the early 1990s were rehearsed and discussed – 'back to the future' (Mearsheimer 1990), the 'end of history' (Fukuyama 1989), the 'democratic peace thesis' and President George H. W. Bush's announcement of a 'New World Order' (but, interestingly and strangely, not the 'clash of civilizations' announced by Samuel Huntington in 1993). These positions are still set out in later editions of the book, but with much less prominence. The second 'final chapter' was on the genuinely new agendas of the period, new not in the sense that the problems they addressed had only just arrived, but new in the sense

247

that they were just in the process of being addressed by International Relations theorists – new notions of security, international environmental politics, gender, refugees and migration, and more generally the turn towards emancipation in IR theory. Most of these issues have been 'mainstreamed' in later editions of *Understanding International Relations*, more or less as predicted.

In the second edition, published in 2001, there are, again, two 'final' chapters. In the penultimate chapter, the Cold War is finally put to rest, and US hegemony is the order of the day. William Wohlforth's 1999 article on the stability of a unipolar world is central (Wohlforth 1999); US military superiority is taken to be more-or-less unchallengeable in conventional terms for the foreseeable future, and the 'bandwagoning' behaviour of US allies is noted, as is the discomfort of those who argued that attempts would be made to balance the power of the USA. More attention is paid to the way in which US power had been used in the 1990s, and in particular to the humanitarian interventions of the period; this discussion led naturally to the final chapter, where globalization was the theme. That chapter picked up and expanded some of the material introduced in a cursory way in the first edition – humanitarianism, gender issues, securitization, border issues, and, in particular, the economic and technological forces that were allegedly creating a new global economy, society and polity. The prediction that the third edition would be dominated by globalization was offered.

Instead, of course, the third edition, published in 2005, was dominated by 9/11 and its aftermath, the 'War on Terror' and the coalition wars in Afghanistan and Iraq. The conventional military superiority of the USA remained intact, but nineteen men with Stanley knives (or 'box cutters' as they are known in the USA) had shown how to turn a jetliner into a very effective guided missile, while others had utilized improvised explosive devices (IEDs) to demonstrate that while US warplanes were more-or-less invulnerable, the foot soldiers who would always be needed to control territory certainly were not. Most US allies were still bandwagoning rather than balancing US power, but the extreme lack of enthusiasm for the Iraq expedition shown by continental Europeans, much less Russians and Chinese, suggested things might be different in the longer run. A related feature of the post-9/11 world was the confirmation of the importance of identity politics. It remained *de rigueur* for scholars to criticize Huntington's 'clash of civilizations' thesis, but the wider public were more impressed by his ideas, whichever crudely defined civilization they might be taken to belong to. Theorists of globalization continued to proclaim the importance of global socio-economic trends, and in areas such as international criminal law and the emergence of a putative 'responsibility to protect' (R2P) it did indeed seem that the shift towards a 'global' as opposed to an 'international' politics was continuing to take place in spite of the 'War on Terror' – and, indeed, it was noted that, just as the USA does not epitomize a conventional empire (even though the term has some descriptive value) so Al Qaeda is not a conventional terrorist organization, but rather a network, franchise even, whose structure mirrored some of the changes that were taking place in the world economy.

If this brief survey of three editions of the same book over twelve years demonstrates nothing else, it illustrates the pace and unpredictability of change in the modern world – which makes the current exercise particularly challenging, and perhaps unwise. On the other hand, the aim here is not to predict the precise course of events over the next few years, but rather to try to identify some underlying trends; a 'surprise-free' future would be genuinely surprising, but even apparently world-defining moments such as 9/11, or the Rwanda genocide, rarely do more than speed up the processes of change, or bring to the surface problems that had long existed – Islamist terrorism pre-dated 9/11 by some years, decades even; and Rwanda did little more than illustrate the obvious inability of the so-called international community to prevent terrible atrocities being conducted by governments against their own peoples. There is, then, some point in picking up the narrative four years on from the previous edition and producing some further thoughts that will probably be outdated in another four years, though one hopes they will not be completely useless. So, what trends can we identify? In brief, with changes in leadership and direction in most of the major European countries, and, of course, in the USA, it seems that the Western alliance is in rather better shape than seemed likely four years ago. But the increasing assertiveness of an economically powerful People's Republic of China, in de facto alliance with an authoritarian Russian nationalism, fuelled, literally, by high energy prices, does suggest that some of the other major powers are no longer content just to bandwagon. Chinese economic growth is a key feature of contemporary world politics – as is the almost equally impressive growth of the Indian economy (although India, as well as being a potential new economic super-power is allied quite closely with the USA – one of President George W. Bush's few foreign policy successes). In short, while the USA remains in conventional military terms the world's sole superpower, something resembling a new balance of power does seem to be taking place. Much of this chapter will examine this rather unusual set of relationships. The rest will be devoted to an attempt to reconcile the re-emergence of these very traditional, pre-1914 patterns of international politics with the continued, and indeed amplified, development of social, economic and political trends that seem to defy this return to conventional international relations. A key question here is whether the woes that are besetting the world economy at the time of writing will develop into the kind of economic depression that is likely to reverse these trends.

A return to multipolarity?

In the immediate post-Cold-War world it really did appear that a kind of convergence of domestic political and economic systems was taking place, at least among the major powers. The successor states of the old Soviet Union were all, in formal terms, democratic; a wave of democracy struck in Latin America and Africa; and while China remained a single-party autocracy, the expectation was that, as its economy grew, the pressure to liberalize its political system would grow as well. As we have seen in earlier chapters, there is much debate as to whether 'regime type' determines foreign policy, and 'democratic peace' theory is hotly contested, but still it was not an unreasonable assumption that a world composed of democracies would find it easier to solve problems peacefully. Hard-line neorealists assume that capabilities are all that matters, and predicted that a new balance of power would emerge (Waltz 1993), but the majority of scholars believed that intentions matter as well as capabilities, and on that basis it seemed reasonable to assume that the major powers would bandwagon with the USA, rather than attempt to balance American power, since the latter was not being used in ways that threatened their core interests. In the 1990s, dictators such as Saddam Hussein and Slobodan Milošević felt the sharp edge of US military superiority, but those powers that might conceivably have adopted a balancing strategy did not do so, presumably because they did not feel threatened. Whether this period of relative great-power harmony should be attributed to regime convergence or to some other factor was debatable, but the harmony itself, and the ideological convergence, seemed to be incontestable.

In the twenty-first century, things have been rather different, for a combination of two reasons. In the first place, the use of its power by the USA in pursuit of the 'War on Terror', and in Afghanistan and Iraq, seemed less consensus-orientated than had been its actions in the 1990s, but also, and more important, the assumption of ideological convergence began to look eminently contestable. The obvious attraction of anti-democratic versions of Islam in the Muslim world, and the return of Peronist leaders such as Hugo Chavez in Latin America, shook the earlier complacency somewhat, but more significant has been the continued success of China's autocracy, and the increasingly authoritarian nature of the Russian political system. China's economic growth has been amazing since the mid-1990s, and while it may be true that in the long run individual private property rights will prove to be incompatible with the state's monopoly of political power, there is no sign of this happening in the foreseeable future. Perhaps more interesting is the shift that has taken place in Russia. The corrupt crony capitalism of the 1990s appears to have poisoned the minds of ordinary Russians against liberal democratic institutions, and the authoritarian turn of recent years appears to be genuinely popular, albeit helped along by the wealth that Russia's energy resources have bestowed on the Russian government. In short, both societies appear to be refuting the proposition that there is something natural about a progression towards market capitalism and liberal democracy. In the West, the market-states analysed by Philip Bobbitt do seem firmly embedded, but elsewhere other models dominate (Bobbitt 2003, 2008). Moreover, and here again debates over regime-type and foreign policy come into play, it does seem that these powerful autocracies have adopted a more hostile approach to the use of American power than in the past, precisely because of their own political nature; Robert Kagan makes a plausible case that, for these authoritarian regimes, the Kosovo Campaign of 1999, largely seen as a humanitarian action in the West, was a kind of wake-up call, suggesting a general desire on the part of the USA to destabilize authoritarian regimes such as themselves – and US foreign policy post-9/11 has reinforced this perception (Kagan 2008).

Of course, it is not only authoritarian regimes that have had doubts about US policy – democratic India opposed the Kosovo intervention, and France and Germany took action to prevent the USA from gaining UN Security Council support for the Iraq invasion in 2003. In response to these moves, some scholars suggested that these countries were actually engaged in 'soft balancing' against the United States (Pape 2005). Rather more plausibly, Stephen Brooks and William Wohlforth (2005) argued that what these states were doing was engaging in conventional diplomacy; that is, attempting to influence US policy via diplomatic means, and that this is not seen as balancing at all. In any event, the disagreements that were so visible within the Western Alliance in 2003 have now largely disappeared; President Sarkozy and Chancellor Merkel are on much better personal terms with the US president than their predecessors Chirac and Schroeder ever were, and in any event the departure of President Bush in January 2009 removed one potent source of tension. Equally, India's opposition to the Iraq war does not extend to the wider 'War on Terror', and US–Indian relations are generally good (albeit at least in part because of the willingness of the USA to legitimize India's breaches of the Nuclear Non-Proliferation Regime).

Russia and China, on the other hand, have hardened their opposition to the USA. The Shanghai Cooperation Organisation, which was set up in 1996 as a confidence-building measure by China and the five bordering former Soviet Republics, including Russia, is now being used as a way of bringing the authoritarian regimes closer together, and in particular to resist what they see as US encroachments in Central Asia. Further, both countries strongly oppose the continuing US attempt to develop effective ballistic missile defences, and both are modernizing and scaling up their conventional and nuclear arsenals. Does this mean that a new balance of power is emerging, as predicted so often by realist scholars? Up to a point. There is an interesting paradox here. Realists do indeed believe that balancing behaviour is likely to emerge whenever one country becomes over-powerful – but realists also believe that the key indicator of relative power between states is military might, and, *pace* Russian and Chinese rearmament plans, this is the one area where the USA remains superior and is likely to hold this superiority for the foreseeable future. It is true that, for the time being at least, these two countries have put aside their own quite considerable differences, and it is also true that they are both much wealthier than they ever have been in the past, both in real terms and in comparison to the USA, but this does not mean that either of them, or both together, will be in a position to challenge the USA militarily any time soon.

Non-realists, on the other hand, though not wedded to balance of power theory, may be more willing to discount the importance of military force, and to look to the wider picture when it comes to the exercise of power. The nuclear dimension of contemporary military force is particularly interesting in this respect, and again somewhat paradoxical. The last few years have in fact seen a revival of the old idea that nuclear weapons make national governments and international anarchy a luxury the world can no longer afford; works by Campbell Craig (2003), Daniel Deudney (2007) and Alexander Wendt (2003) have presented different arguments as to why a world state is either desirable or inevitable, and these and many other writers have stressed that the use of nuclear weapons would be self-destructive and wholly immoral. But no nuclear weapon state has any intention of giving them up, and a number of states, especially those that feel threatened by the conventional power of the USA, are very keen to acquire them. The rulers of North Korea and Iran have every reason to believe that Saddam Hussein would still be alive and in power in Baghdad had he been able to continue the nuclear weapons programme he began in the 1980s. In short, while logicians and ethicists deconstruct and condemn the idea of nuclear deterrence, many, perhaps most, governments remain wedded to the doctrine – but if nuclear deterrence is perceived to be effective, then as between nuclear states, military force becomes less of a factor, *pace* the nuclear war-fighting notions of some hardline strategists. It certainly is just about *possible* to imagine modern great-power war – between China and the USA over Taiwan, for example – but it is, fortunately, quite difficult to imagine the chain of circumstances that would lead to decision-makers in any major nuclear-weapons power resorting to using military force against each other.

If this discounting of military force is correct, there are many areas where changes towards a more multipolar decision-making environment are evident. Global economic decision-making is increasingly having to take into account the sheer size of the Chinese and Indian economies – the days when the EU, Japan and the USA could deal with such matters among themselves, regarding the rest of the world as a minor nuisance, are past. European countries are only too conscious of their increasing dependence on Russian oil and natural gas, and of the willingness of the Russian government to use this dependence for political ends – something Ukraine has already experienced beyond doubt.

Russian power is being exercised in the Caucasus, especially against Georgia, in ways that are reminiscent of the bad old days, and the possibility that anyone will intervene on behalf of the latter, or that Russia will be deterred by international disapproval, is receding. China is less immediately belligerent than Russia, although Chinese anger at Western criticism of its policy in Tibet is manifest, as was their fury at attempts to, as they saw it, politicize the Beijing Olympics of 2008.

So, in a period when the West is rediscovering a willingness to co-operate – and this even extends militarily to encompass the campaign in Afghanistan – the spectre arises of a new 'West versus the Rest' pattern of power. Some journalists have described this as a 'New Cold War', but few scholars have followed them in this; the Cold War was far more complex than the new configuration of power; if anything, the historical analogy that makes more sense is with the old, non-ideological, European states-system of the nineteenth century, though this is hardly comforting, given the nature of the end of that system in 1914. In fact, of course, because of the clear conventional military superiority of the USA, the pre-1914 system is not a good analogy either; it was a feature of that system that no state had the kind of dominant military presence that the USA has at the time of writing – much of the actual international politics of the period stemmed precisely from this absence. Perhaps rather surprisingly, a better analogy for the emerging system can be found from the 1970s, not so much from the politics of that decade but from the theoretical resources it produced in International Relations. The theory of 'complex interdependence', described in Chapter 2 above, was designed specifically to cope with a situation in which there were multiple layers of power, and where military and 'civilian' sources of power did not necessarily coincide with or complement each other. Complex interdependence was, of course, largely generated in response to changes in the world economy, and so the task of developing the analogy between today and the 1970s will be left for the final section of this chapter. The next stage in this chapter is to examine some of the current problems in the world economy, but before moving on it would be helpful to address a little more thought to the current situation *vis-à-vis* American power – this is the 800lb gorilla that is always in the room when the architecture of the emerging international system is discussed.

In the previous edition of this book, much space was given to a discussion of the USA as an imperial power. The imperial America thesis has not disappeared completely in the years since 2004 – few ideas in International Relations ever disappear completely – but it is much less prominent today than it was then. Why is this so? The Iraq War, and especially its aftermath, is at the heart of this story. The inability of the USA to reconstruct Iraqi society in the desired direction is now difficult to deny; the situation in the summer of 2008 in Iraq was better than it had been since 2003, with lower levels of violence generally, and some signs of the re-emergence of civil society, but this has not been achieved in the desired way. The incumbent Iraqi government is mildly authoritarian, and worryingly sectarian; the only part of Iraq that is governed in the way that the USA had hoped would be the case generally is the Kurdish region – but this region was de facto independent prior to 2003. It is necessary to be clear about one point: this Iraqi government is considerably less oppressive than that of Saddam Hussein, and a mildly authoritarian but stable regime would constitute genuine progress for that country – but this is not what the USA set out to achieve in 2003.

The result of this failure, and the dwindling level of support for the war effort in the US itself, has been a reassertion in the American political system of the value of multilateralism. The current Administration has been far more multilateralist than its rhetoric might suggest, but it is striking that both the candidates who competed to replace President Bush endorsed multilateralism. Consider the following text (from the *Financial Times*, 18 March 2008):

> [Our] great power does not mean we can do whatever we want whenever we want, nor should we assume we have all the wisdom and knowledge necessary to succeed. We need to listen to the views and respect the collective will of our democratic allies. When we believe that international action is necessary, whether military, economic or diplomatic, we will try to persuade our friends that we are right. But we, in return, must also be willing to be persuaded by them.

The author was Senator John McCain, but could just as easily have been Senator Barack Obama. There can be little doubt that President George W. Bush's Texan rhetoric and general manner has been deeply unpopular with the rest of the world more-or-less since the beginning of his presidency – what is different is that, whereas the majority of Americans were initially indifferent to this hostility, now there is a great desire to reconnect with friends and allies, and the new leadership of both Republican and Democrat parties recognizes this new mood.

But what exactly does 'multilateralism' mean to the US political elite? In Europe, it is sometimes felt that it means a European veto on the exercise of US power; but this, it is safe to say, is not what Americans mean by the term. Multilateralism certainly means taking the UN more seriously than was the case in the early years of the Bush Administration, but no responsible US leader is suggesting that the UN as presently constituted can be more than a sounding board for global discussions. Two of the 'Permanent Five' members of the UN Security Council are the new authoritarian challengers to Western power, and while the USA and the West more generally favour expanding the number of permanent members to include countries such as Japan, India and Brazil, it is recognized that this will make that body less effective than it is currently, and less likely to, for example, find the will to end the massacres in the Darfur region of Sudan. President Obama will take more seriously than his predecessor the issue of climate change, and may even make a symbolic gesture, such as signing up to the largely redundant targets in the Kyoto Protocol – but it is unlikely that he will be able to bring about an end to the US love of the automobile and air-conditioning. Similarly, a more multilateral approach is unlikely to involve a shift towards accepting the International Criminal Court; a majority could not be constructed in the Senate for ratification of the Rome Treaty, even if President Bush's bizarre 'unsigning' of the treaty were to be reversed.

So, what will be the forum for US multilateralism? The key to the desired forum is embedded in John McCain's speech, quoted above – the reference to democratic allies. McCain has called for a 'League of Democracies', a proposal set out in a recent book by his adviser, Robert Kagan (Kagan 2008), and endorsed by some key Obama aides, most notably Ivo Daalder and Anthony Lake. This League or 'Concert' would include the European allies of the USA, but it would also include Australia, Japan, India, South Korea and the Latin-American democracies. Part of the thinking here is clearly that some of these countries – in particular India, Japan and South Korea – share with the USA a view of the dangers of Chinese power, and are deemed more likely than the Europeans to take a robust approach to the problems faced over the next decade. The suggestion is not to give the proposed League a veto power over action, but rather to provide a forum within which like-minded countries can co-ordinate action should they so desire. For the more historically minded supporters of the notion, a Kantian 'Pacific Union' is what they have in mind – and it should be recalled that Kant's 'Federation' of Republican States did not boast an executive arm.

Is this proposal likely to come to fruition over the next few years? It is not impossible that if President Obama pushes hard enough, some kind of framework may emerge, but it has to be said that, at the time of writing, the potential non-American members of the League are more-or-less universally unimpressed. The Europeans see little need for such a body, and recognize the intent to weaken their own influence in Washington, and while the Indian political elite does indeed desire good relations with the USA, and is conscious of a commonality of interests over China, there is little support for a new institution to formalize this informal alliance. For the present, this looks like a non-starter – but the possibility that in the medium-run some such body will emerge cannot be discounted.

One of the reasons for not discounting this possibility is the extraordinary popularity of the new President in the world outside the US. The effect of his election in undermining popular anti-Americanism can hardly be exaggerated - he is a living refutation of the crude idea that all Americans are obese, ignorant and racist. Still, it remains to be seen whether this favourable sentiment will produce a deeper change in political attitudes - for example, however

much the Europeans may admire President Obama it is clear that most of
them will want to refuse his request for extra troops in a combat role in
Afghanistan, and European leaders are already fearful that he will find it difficult to resist Congressional pressures for protectionism, if indeed he wishes to
do so. He begins his Presidency with more global goodwill than virtually any
of his predecessors, at least since John F. Kennedy in 1960, but he also faces
more daunting problems than any of his predecessors since Franklin Delano
Roosevelt in 1933, and time will tell whether that goodwill will be vindicated,
or whether 'buyer remorse' will be experienceed by those who have placed
such high hopes in the new political order in Washington.

To summarize this section, the post-Cold War 'holiday from history' (in
Charles Krauthammer's felicitous formulation) is usually seen as having been
brought to an abrupt conclusion on 9/11 (Krauthammer 2003). In fact, while
Al Qaeda and its associates would undoubtedly like to constitute an existential threat to the West, subsequent events suggest that they do not in fact have
anything like the power to do so, unless, paradoxically, the West co-operates
by betraying its own ideals. Even a series of successful terrorist attacks of the
kind that we have seen since 9/11 would not constitute an existential threat
in the way that, say, a nuclear exchange between the USA and the USSR would
have done – but 'existence' is about more than physical survival, and if the
West undermines its own commitment to constitutional government and the
rule of law in order to combat the threat from terrorism, then terrorism would
have to be seen as a kind of existential threat. But, to return to Krauthammer's
phrase, in another sense the holiday is indeed over. In the 1990s, it seemed
that a new kind of international order might emerge, one in which the political values of the West would become dominant in societies everywhere. The
opponents of this new order, the Miloševićs, the Saddams and so on were
essentially small fry, capable of testing the will of the West, but not of with-
standing genuine pressure – when Milošević went too far he lost Bosnia, and
when he repeated the mistake he lost Kosovo; most humanitarian interventions were either failures or ambiguous successes, but still some progress was
made, democracy did spread, and the 'long 1990s' (1989–2001) ended with
the qualified optimism of the 'Responsibility to Protect' Report. At the time
of writing (late 2008), the picture looks rather different. The presence at the
top table of Russia, China and India suggests that the period of Western hegemony is going to be much shorter than expected, and indeed may already have
ended. But there are some reasons to be cheerful; we are unlikely to see a third
Cold War, or even a pre-1914 balance-of-power system. Instead, what is
happening looks rather more like an intensification of the complex kinds of
interdependence modelled quite successfully in the 1970s (Keohane and Nye
1977, 2000). The new 'great powers' will often try to behave like traditional
great powers, but, because of these interdependencies, 'outlaw' behaviour will
be very costly, and the new system will look more like the world of the English

School's pluralism than the contest of rational egoists envisaged by the neorealists. In short, the holiday may be over, but the new workplace is not likely to be quite as bleak and unforgiving as the old. But does this optimism rest on false assumptions about the fate of the international economy?

Crisis in the global economy

As is often observed, and is noted above, two key features of the modern international order are Chinese economic growth and Russian energy wealth. What is noted less often is that, in the medium to long run, these two factors contradict each other. Chinese growth is based on its ability to export (in fact, usually to re-export goods that are imported in an incomplete state) to the rest of the world, especially to the USA and Europe – but soaring prices of oil and natural gas had it continued may well have come to limit the ability of the rest of the world to continue to import Chinese goods. To add to the potentially vicious circle, one of the reasons why energy prices rose so steeply is because of increased Chinese demand stimulated by the growth of manufacturing in that country. Clearly, this is a worrying set of relationships – and there are other worries of a similar magnitude in the world economy. It has become clear since mid-2007 that the expansion of credit in the US (and, to a lesser extent European) markets in recent years has been most unwise. Too many mortgages in the USA and the UK have been 'sub-prime' – so-called 'ninja' mortgages, given to people with no income and no job – and, what is in some ways more damaging, these poor-quality mortgages have been bundled in with soundly based loans, with the result that banks have been very unwilling to lend to each other on the basis of the normal security. If, say, one in ten loans is of poor quality but it is not known which one, the tendency will be not to accept any loans as security for inter-bank lending. The result has been the failure of some very high profile financial institutions in the USA, and mergers between others, the first run on a major bank for 150 years in the UK, and the suspension of competition rules to allow the UK's largest provider of mortgages to be taken over by another bank. As is always the case in these circumstances, even good credit risks now find it difficult to borrow money, and the result has been a slowdown in the housing market on both sides of the Atlantic, with falling house prices and unemployment slowly creeping up. But, more generally, prices overall are rising everywhere, especially prices of basic foodstuffs, causing real problems in parts of the non-industrial world, with food riots and political unrest becoming common. To add to the sense that things are coming together and not in a good way, rising food prices are, at least in part, an unanticipated consequence of measures taken to alleviate environmental degradation – the use of land for growing bio-fuels has certainly contributed to rising food prices.

Add all this together and it certainly seems that the period of expansion in the world economy that has lasted, with one or two hiccups, since the early 1990s, appears to be coming to an end. A recession, and perhaps worse, seems to be on the way. If this pessimism is justified, then a great many of the assumptions upon which policy, and academic analysis, has been based since the 1990s will have to be revised. Consider, for example, the extensive literature – both popular and academic – on globalization, the anti-globalization movement, neo-liberalism and the critique of neo-liberalism reviewed in earlier chapters of this book. Much of this work is highly critical of the structure and institutions of the contemporary world economy, but, equally, most of it assumes, tacitly or explicitly, that the goods will continue to be delivered by this imperfect economy. It is not difficult to rehearse the many failings of neo-liberalism, but it is difficult to deny that since the 1980s there has been real progress on virtually all fronts. The extraordinary success of the Chinese and Indian economies offers the promise that within a generation more than 2 billion people will be lifted out of poverty, and in Latin America and South-East Asia there are a great many similar stories to be told. Certainly, critics of neo-liberal policies are entitled to point out that inequalities remain in the successful countries, and the 'bottom billion' have not shared the general spread of prosperity (Collier 2007) – but it is difficult to believe that these disadvantaged peoples, the new 'wretched of the earth', will benefit in any way from a collapse of the world economy. The WTO may, or may not, be an agent of global capitalism, but it is difficult to see how the poor will benefit if the current Doha Round of trade negotiations collapses, as seems likely. The net result of such a collapse is pretty well certain to be the reinforcement of already-existing protectionist tendencies in the West – 2008 saw a marked shift towards protectionism in the USA; whether or not the new president goes with the trend, the Democrat majority in the new Congress will ensure that any attempt to further liberalize trade will get a rough ride – which will make it more difficult for those in poverty to escape their fate by exporting to the developed world, and, setting aside the autarchic fantasies of some of the anti-global capital movement, export-led growth has been the engine of success for those economies that have managed to grow since the 1990s.

Consider the position of the Chinese economy. Chinese growth rests not on technological innovation or the newer information-based industries – India has a far more developed IT sector – but on the import of unfinished manufactures, and their re-export as finished goods. This has been an extraordinarily successful strategy, and has allowed the Chinese economy to grow at a fast rate, and to build up a very substantial trading surplus with the developed economies, especially the USA. It has used this surplus to buy US Treasury Bonds and the like, thereby sustaining a relatively high dollar, and improving the competitiveness of its goods, leading to even higher surpluses. The figures here are staggering; according to the US General Administration of Customs, the Chinese trade surplus with the USA was US$20 billion in May 2008 (imports from the USA, US $100bn, 28 per cent higher than in May 2007; exports to the US US$120bn, 40 per cent higher than in May 2007); and for the first five months of 2008 trade volume stood at US$1,012bn, a year-on-year rise of 26 per cent. The World Bank's China Quarterly Update of June 2008 describes China's expected GDP growth as moderating to a more sustainable pace – but the figure is still projected to be 9.8 per cent, which in any other context would certainly not be seen as moderate. The point is that, whatever the circumstances, it is difficult to see how this situation could continue without a crisis-point being reached very soon, but if it is indeed the case that the world economy is looking at a recession, the crisis is likely to arrive very suddenly, and have an extremely deleterious effect on the Chinese economy, bringing the current extended boom to a full-stop, if not reversing some of the gains of recent years.

What would be the political consequences of such a reversal? Here, we return to the subject of multipolarity, discussed in the previous section of this Chapter. It was noted there that the Chinese and Russian regimes have been adopting a somewhat more aggressive stance *vis-à-vis* the West in recent years, but that China was rather less belligerent than Russia. A sudden downturn in the world economy is unlikely to dampen their hostility, and may actually intensify it. The Russian case here is the most disturbing; Russia's new assertiveness has been based on the wealth and political leverage that rising energy costs have given it, and Russian public opinion has rallied to the nationalist programme of President (now Prime Minister) Putin largely because this wealth has enabled him to raise the standard of living of ordinary Russians. If that wealth were to disappear because of falling energy prices brought about by a collapse in demand as a result of a global recession – and prices have already fallen dramatically since their peak in the Autumn of 2008 - it is likely that Russian nationalism would become more aggressive – the tendency to blame the foreigner for lack of progress is always present in Russia, as elsewhere, but is likely to be amplified in these circumstances. Wealth brings a degree of confidence, which can turn to adventurism, but it also brings a desire not to kill the goose that lays the golden eggs – if the goose stops laying there is likely to be trouble ahead. Similarly, Chinese hostility to some trends in US policy has been muted by the obvious interconnectedness of the two economies – but if this interconnectedness were to be broken, the consequences could be very worrying.

Of course, it is not only in authoritarian regimes that economic distress can shift state behaviour and public opinion in a nationalist direction. It was noted above that, as hard times begin to set in, US public and elite opinion has turned away from the kind of free trade thinking epitomized by the North Atlantic Free Trade Area (NAFTA) and towards increased protectionism. Similar pressures can be identified in Europe – while the EU Commission, and especially former Trade Commissioner Peter Mandelson (now returned to a cabinet post in the UK) have been working hard to keep Doha alive, many politicians closer to their electorates have been critical of this stance. Equally, on both sides of the Atlantic, a general tightening of the belt has led to anti-immigrant sentiments being expressed. The UK situation is particularly interesting here; as a result of a combination of EU and domestic rules (and the widespread knowledge of basic English) the UK has become an attractive destination for many workers from the new EU member countries in Eastern Europe, symbolized by the iconic figure of the 'Polish plumber' (though most Polish plumbers work in the building trade rather than in the domestic repairs market). In 2006, nearly 600,000 people immigrated to the UK (with approximately 400,000 moving in the other direction, half of them being British citizens). Such workers have a negative impact on the wages of the low-paid in the UK, and may have contributed to the rise in house prices, but in a time of prosperity the general need for labour cancels out such disadvantages. Once unemployment starts to rise, however, hostility to foreign workers taking 'our' jobs becomes much more general, and is more likely to be pandered to by vote-seeking politicians.

There are some signs at the time of writing that this is happening in the UK – and the UK is an interesting case, because in the UK the new migrants present relatively few cultural problems. A migrant workforce consisting largely of young, single men will not be universally welcomed in any city, but Poles and other East Europeans are not 'visible minorities' in the way that early immigrants in the 1950s and 1960s were, and share many cultural traits with the native British. When times are good, their impact is neutral or positive (in Southampton, for example, it is estimated that some 10 per cent of the population are Polish – my own Sikh newsagent stocks *Newsweek* in a Polish edition, and buying good quality bread has become easier, but otherwise the estimated 20,000 Poles in the town seem to have had markedly little impact). In other countries, cultural problems loom larger. In the USA, most immigrants are Spanish-speaking, and from south of the Rio Grande, which is definitely a source of concern to some of the native population. *Who Are We?* is the title of a book by Samuel Huntington, in which the 'clash of civilizations', which he posited a decade or more earlier is brought home to the USA itself (Huntington, 2005). According to the US Census Bureau in 2006, Spanish was the language spoken at home by 34 million peoples in the USA, approximately half of whom live in three states – California, Texas and Florida – but this certainly understates the number of Spanish speakers, many of whom are illegal immigrants who steer clear of census, or any other, officials. Whether this constitutes a problem or not is, of course, contestable – without such workers, the agricultural industries of the states named above would collapse, and while the framers of the US Constitution were largely Protestant English-speakers, it is not immediately apparent why Catholic Spanish-speakers could not be equally committed to American values. Huntington makes the interesting point that these immigrants are able, because of modern communications technology, to continue to think of themselves as Mexicans, Colombians or whatever, and that this will limit their willingness to become genuinely American. Most academic critics think he overstates his case – but members of the general public in the USA, while most have never heard of Huntington, are more sympathetic to this kind of argument. Just as NAFTA has become very unpopular with US voters, and therefore with many US politicians, so immigration has become an issue –though the candidate of the most anti-immigrant party in the recent election, the Republican, John McCain, himself had a very strong pro-immigrant reputation. In 2005, he co-sponsored a bill on Immigration with Senator Edward Kennedy that was regarded with horror by many members of his own party, something he had to finesse once he became their candidate.

Of course, even though anti-immigrant sentiment is real, it is important not to put too much stress on its novelty – native-born workers have never enjoyed competition from foreigners, even in good times, and an economic downturn simply exaggerates trends that were always present. There is a more general point here. In laying emphasis on the negative consequences of the current economic crisis, it is important not to make false comparisons. In our discussion of the globalization literature in earlier chapters of this book, we were duly sceptical of some of the wilder claims made, and it is important that we should not forget this scepticism when we come to examine present difficulties. *Pace* Thomas Friedman, the world has never been flat, and, a fortiori, *pace* Kenichi Ohmae, we have never lived in a borderless world. Still, there will be changes if current problems do indeed turn into a recession, much less a depression.

Consider the example at the heart of Friedman's thesis – the development of outsourcing on a large scale, where numerous factories in many countries are involved in producing the components that are ultimately brought together in yet another location to produce, say, a Dell computer. Friedman suggests that a plausible rule of thumb would be that no two countries that are part of the Dell production chain would ever go to war with one another, which, if true, would be comforting, since a number of apparently bitter political rivals are so enmeshed. In fact, of course, the decision to go to war is rarely made on the basis of the kind of rational weighing of consequences that this would imply, and Friedman's new law may go the same way as earlier rules of this kind – most recently, the proposition that no two countries with branches of McDonalds would ever go to war with each other was refuted in 1999, when the Belgrade branch of McDonalds did not perform its expected magic. Still, one does not have to buy into the more extravagant claims made by Friedman to see some merit in the case he is making, and if one of the consequences of an economic crisis would be for the chains of production he describes to contract somewhat, this would increase inter-state tensions. There is a familiar process that is likely to be seen here – in times of economic hardship and rising unemployment it is usual for states to try to shift the adverse costs of change away from their own nationals. The familiar critique that multinational firms export jobs from the industrial heartlands will always be heard, but has far greater political force when the economy as a whole is in trouble and with unemployment rising. Economists will tell us that the rise in protectionist sentiment that usually accompanies recessions is the product of economic illiteracy; that keeping trade as free as possible is the way out of crisis; and attempting to resist changes in the international division of labour is self-defeating, but people are no more likely to listen to economists in the future than they have in the past.

Bad times, good times

The various trends and projections discussed above seem to add up to a rather grim picture; the return of something like an old-fashioned balance of power, increasing influence for authoritarian regimes, and signs of a recession. Many writers have looked forward to a 'post-American world', to borrow the title of Fareed Zakaria's new book, but not *this* post-American world (Zakaria 2008); similarly, those who called for an end to the dominance of neoliberalism were not anticipating a return to protectionism and crude forms of economic nationalism. So, a depressing picture – but, as the cliché has it, if things are so bad, how come things are so good? Prices of basics are rising everywhere, but most people – and not simply most people in the developed world – seem to be taking the bad news in their stride. Consumption levels remain very high; the major corporations continue to chase profits via technological innovation, with great success. The cover of this book was adorned with, *inter alia*, a compact disc for the first two editions; for the third edition the very old-hat technology of the CD (introduced in the dark ages of 1982) was replaced by an up-to-the-minute iPod – but this time the iPod has gone the way of the CD and we now have an iPhone (after a debate on whether a Wii controller might not be cooler, decided by the fact that, while students would know what it was, their teachers might not!). Sales of such new technology, and of SatNav, plasma and HD TVs, Blue Ray DVDs and so on continue to rise.

Part of the message here is that capitalism is enormously resilient and adaptable. Particular forms of production may disappear, but new products, and new forms of production, will take their place. The age of Web 2.0 is orientated towards 'wikis' – pieces of software that enable users to create and edit their own content (Wikipedia is the most famous example) – and hostile to 'broadcast' entertainment media; there is still a place for mass entertainment (cinema blockbusters, for example), but the future seems orientated towards niche products. However, this does not mean that conventional capitalist profit-making cannot continue. An example from the classical music industry occurs to one of the authors: the acerbic critic Norman Lebrecht has announced the end of the classical music industry, and a cursory glance at the output from the giants in the field – Universal (which includes DG, Decca and Philips), Sony BMG, EMI and so on – would seem to confirm this (Lebrecht 2007). These companies seem so desperate that they have taken to the equivalent of dumping their product – for example, box sets containing all of EMI's Callas recordings, and all its Karajan recordings, for less than a pound a disc – and yet there is more recording of classical music taking place now than there has ever been. The difference is that this recording is being undertaken by small, niche labels, sometimes owned by the performers, rather than by the giants, and often 'live'; costs are relatively low, no one is making a lot of money, but, apparently no one is going bankrupt either. It is striking that, whereas recording a Beethoven symphony cycle was something that the big labels used to do for their star performers, at great expense as a prestige project, the two most critically acclaimed recent cycles were recorded on an own-brand label (Bernard Haitink with the London Symphony Orchestra) and an independent (Charles Mackerras with the Scottish Chamber Orchestra at the Edinburgh Festival, recorded live by Hyperion). The one recent attempt at a star cycle – Mikhail Pletnev on DG – was a critical failure and almost certainly lost money. All this may seem a digression, and perhaps it is, but it also illustrates the principle of the 'long tail', as set out by Chris Anderson (Anderson 2006). With modern, customized production methods, and the kinds of information available via the internet, 'endless choice creates unlimited demand', to quote Anderson's sub-title. Anderson estimates that 25 per cent of Amazon's book sales come from items that are not in the 100,000 top selling books; businesses can make a lot of money by selling a very wide range of products in small packages to niche markets.

The resilience and adaptability of capitalism is certainly part of the reason why things don't seem as bad as perhaps they should, but there may also be wider forces at work that will damp down the potentially negative effects of both the economic downturn and the rather depressing political environment. It could be that some features of global civil society have become sufficiently embedded that they act as a constraint on the kinds of developments that can take place. As noted earlier in this book, there are difficulties with the very notion of global civil society, most obviously the absence of a global state; the classic notion of civil society was designed precisely to carve out a public space between the state and private life, and such a model is difficult to reconcile with the global political order that is still, at root, anarchic. None the less, some of the changes that have been identified as being connected to the notion of global civil society do seem to have developed a life of their own. Consider, for example, the changes that have taken place in the perceived nature of international law, documented in Chapter 11 above, particularly the shift towards making the individual the subject and object of international law, as opposed to the state, and the concomitant development of international criminal law and an International Criminal Court (ICC), all in the service of attempting to develop an evolving international humanitarianism. There have always been serious conceptual problems with this shift, some of them being set out in Chapter 11 – most obviously, the apparent absence of universal global standards of criminality, and the absence of an executive branch to enforce international criminal law, or a legislative branch to make it. These are compelling points, and virtually everything that has happened in the world since 2003 would seem to reinforce them. Trials involving Slobodan Milošević and Saddam Hussein have illustrated the absence of consensus – neither the defendants nor their supporters accepted the legitimacy of the courts (admittedly, a domestic court in Saddam's case, but established under some international pressure, and using the Rome Statute – which established the ICC to provide the definitions of the crimes against humanity for which Saddam was eventually hanged). The use of humanitarian justifications for the Iraq War have not been widely accepted and have largely discredited the notion of humanitarian intervention, as has the inability of the UN Security Council to agree on measures to stop the genocide in the Darfur region of Sudan. These are contingent factors, it might be argued, but more significant is the rise in power and status in the world of China and Russia, and for that matter, India. Moscow, Beijing and New Delhi have all expressed their commitment to very traditional notions of sovereignty, their hostility to the notion of humanitarian intervention, and their opposition to the development of international criminal law. These problems are reinforced by the fact that, in this area as in virtually no other, the USA agrees substantially with the rising nations.

So, in these circumstances, one might have expected that the drive towards the developments noted above would slow down, if not go into reverse. And yet, as Chapter 11 elaborates, this has simply not happened. Since the previous edition of this book, the notion a 'Responsibility to Protect' (R2P) proposed by an International Commission of the great and the good, which reported in 2001, has been adopted by the UN General Assembly (albeit in a rather weak form). The ICC is now up and running, has handed down eleven indictments (all of Africans, rather embarrassingly) and is preparing for its first trials. US opposition to the Court remains in place, but has softened somewhat – against its earlier position, the USA did not veto a UNSC resolution to refer the Darfur problem to the ICC, and no longer threatens to end UN peacekeeping operations unless they are exempt from the jurisdiction of the Court. Despite the world becoming a more hostile environment for its operations, the Court is pressing on. The major Asian countries and the USA give no indication that they are about to change tack and support its work, but this does not seem to be slowing things down.

The main point all this is intended to illustrate is not the rather Panglossian view that, contrary to appearances, we live in the best of all possible worlds, but rather to suggest that we actually live in many worlds at the same time, worlds dominated by increasing great-power rivalry and where recession may be just around the corner, but also where our mobile phones contain more computing power than was used to send the Apollo missions to the moon, and where murderers and tyrants are obliged to keep at least one eye open to the possibility that they might be held to account for their crimes. All these worlds, and many others with them, are real, and which one is the most relevant will vary over time. In the immediate post-Cold War world there was a search for the right formula to describe the new era that was opening up with the fall of the Soviet Union – as noted above, this search took up a great deal of space in the first edition of this book. Clearly, we could regard the search as still being on, and this chapter has touched on one or two slogans or formulas that might bear further thought – a 'league of democracies', the 'post-American world', the 'responsibility to protect' and so on – but it may well be that such a search would miss the important point, which is that no single slogan can capture the current complexity. This is as true of the work of globalization theorists, with their vision of one world, as it is of their critics from the left who speak of a rich world and a poor world, and their neorealist critics who deny the reality of anything that contradicts their model of great power conflict.

Or perhaps there is one motto that is worth repeating: students of international relations should never surrender their capacity to be surprised by the turn of events. As pointed out at the very beginning of this text, the international system is always capable of throwing up some new problem – the context there (see page 5) was the arrival, apparently from out of the blue, of wars in the Falklands/Malvinas in 1982, and over Kuwait in 1990–1, but the point applies equally to the non-military-strategic end of the discourse. Who would have predicted in December 2007 that the US presidential election of 2008 would be fought out between candidates who were not part of the 'boomer' generation: a young African-American Democrat, and a Republican who, it seemed, had been written out of the script by George Bush in 2000? In fact, the scriptwriters of the TV Series *The West Wing* had envisaged something similar (their Democrat candidate was actually modelled on Barack Obama) but even they failed to anticipate Sarah Palin, Senator McCain's choice of running mate. More to the point – although we have not heard the last of Governor Palin – no-one anticipated the kind of campaign Obama would run, nor the enthusiasm with which it was greeted, in the US and abroad, to the point that, for a short while, even his domestic opponents were congratulating themselves on the strengths of American democracy.

We began this chapter by reviewing the agendas that its equivalents had addressed in 1997, 2001 and 2005 – it is in the nature of the discourse of International Relations, and its subject matter, that predicting the agenda of a hypothetical fifth edition in 2113 is quite impossible. We find this strangely reassuring, and hope that other students of our discipline will share our pleasure at its unpredictability.

Further reading

Given the aim of this chapter, to apply IR theory to contemporary world politics, much of the reading highlighted in previous chapters will be relevant and worth returning to, particularly Chapters 5, 8 and 11. For contemporary political coverage, journals that combine research, politics and journalism are a good source – *Foreign Affairs* is the paradigm publication; other good sources include *Ethics & International Affairs*; *Foreign Policy*; *The World Today*; and *International Affairs*; the *Economist* and *Financial Times* provide the best up-to-the-moment coverage. Apart from the print media, it is also well worth becoming acquainted with the world of blogs. Most newspapers and major media outlets have an online presence, which often has in-depth material that has not been broadcast or published; apart from the obvious sources (BBC, CNN), 'Bill Moyers' Journal', with material from Public Broadcasting Service television in the USA, is well worth a look http://www.pbs.org/moyers/journal/index-flash.html. The journal *Foreign Policy* runs a blog that is one good source of opinion on international affairs (http://www.foreignpolicy.com/). Another, UK-based, dedicated site is http://www.opendemocracy.net/. The online magazine http://www.slate.com/ has good coverage of international affairs, while the Huffington Blog is becoming essential: http://www.huffingtonpost.com/. Everyone will have their favourite opinion formers; ours include Norm Geras at Normblog: http://normblog. typepad.com/ and *Dissent* magazine, especially when Michael Walzer opines: http://www.dissentmagazine.org/. In the interest of balance, see http://www. guardian.co.uk/commentisfree. *The Onion* might not quite live up to its masthead as 'America's Finest News Source' but its spoof stories and TV news clips often get closer to the heart of a story than its legitimate counterparts: http://www. theonion.com/content/index.

There is no lack of speculation on the future of both events and research in international relations, what follows is only a summary. Georg Sørensen, 'What Kind of World Order? The International System in the New Millennium' (2006) investigates the significance of contemporary events for the various approaches in IR. In the same issue of *Cooperation and Conflict* there is a 'Symposium on World Order' (2006), which collects a number of useful responses. For mainstream reflections on the changing international order, see Richard Haass, 'The Age of Nonpolarity: What Will Follow U.S. Dominance' (2008); *Harvard International Review*'s special issue entitled, 'A Tilted Balance: Who Will Rise?' (2007); C. Dale Walton, *Geopolitics and the Great Powers in the Twenty-first Century: Multipolarity and the Revolution in Strategic Perspective* (2007); and Charles

Doran, *Systems in Crisis: New Imperatives of High Politics at Century's End* (2008). Constructivist responses to current events is more diverse: intriguing contributions include Richard Ned Lebow, *A Cultural Theory of International Relations* (2008), which focuses on the role of identity and the human need for self-esteem; and Emmanuel Adler, *Communitarian International Relations: The Epistemic Foundations of International Relations* (2005) offers a constructivism that focuses on overlapping epistemic communities. Brian Rathbun's 'Uncertain about Uncertainty: Understanding the Multiple Meanings of a Crucial Concept in International Relations Theory' (2007) makes the case successfully for its relevance in the title. Less obviously relevant is Nermeen Shaikh (ed.), *The Present as History: Critical Perspectives on Global Power* (2007), yet it takes the sensible approach of considering our current moment as rather unexceptional, and a number of sober contributions by high quality authors make it worthwhile.

For those inclined either to celebrate or to fret over the waning of American power, there is Joseph Nye, 'Recovering American Leadership' (2008); Stephen Brooks and William Wohlforth, *World Out of Balance: International Relations and the Challenge of American Primacy* (2008); and Fareed Zakaria, *The Post-American World* (2008).

Given that the West only seems to match Chinese productivity in the writing of books about the rise of China, what follows is a sample of relevant titles, both academic and popular. G. John Ikenberry, 'The Rise of China and the Future of the West: Can the Liberal System Survive?' (2008); Richard Rosecrance, 'Power and International Relations: The Rise of China and Its Effects' (2006); David Lake, 'American Hegemony and the Future of East–West Relations' (2006); Yong Deng, *China's Struggle for Status: The Realignment of International Relations* (2008); Robyn Meredith, *The Elephant and the Dragon: The Rise of India and China and What It Means for All of Us* (2008); Will Hutton, *The Writing on the Wall: China and the West in the 21st Century* (2007); and Bill Emmott, *Rivals: How the Power Struggle Between China, India and Japan Will Shape Our Next Decade* (2008).

The number of books concerning Russia's rise is less, but that is made up for with much scarier titles. See Robert Legvold, *Russian Foreign Policy in the 21st Century & the Shadow of the Past* (2007); Edward Lucas, *The New Cold War: How the Kremlin Menaces Both Russia and the West* (2008); and finally, Yuri Felshtinksy and Vladimir Pribylovsky's sublimely titled, *The Age of Assassins: The Rise and Rise of Vladimir Putin* (2008).

Current work on human rights, international law and humanitarian intervention continues to be important to the discipline, but recent events have proved sobering, a fact reflected in more restrained reflection on the possibility of ethical politics. Richard Price, *Moral Limit and Possibility in World Politics* (2008) captures the less naïve mood. Recent discussion of tragedy as metaphor in international politics is also relevant here; the best of the bunch include Richard Ned Lebow, *The Tragic Vision of Politics: Ethics, Interests and Orders* (2003); Mervyn Frost, 'Tragedy, Ethics and International Relations' (2003); and Chris Brown, 'Tragedy, "Tragic Choices" and Contemporary International Political Theory' (2007). Other references include Brooke Ackerly, *Universal Human*

Rights in a World of Difference (2008); Jack Goldsmith and Eric Posner, *The Limits of International Law* (2005); Toni Erskine, *Embedded Cosmopolitanism: Duties to Strangers and Enemies in a World of 'Dislocated Communities'* (2008); and Urfan Khaliq, *Ethical Dimensions of the Foreign Policy of the European Union* (2008).

On the financial crisis current at the time of writing, Robert J. Shiller, *The Subprime Solution: How Today's Global Financial Crisis Happened and What to Do About It* (2008), and George Soros, *The New Paradigm for Financial Markets: The Credit Crisis of 2008 and What It Means* (2008) are ahead of the pack. On the ever useful nature of economics, Cass Sunstein and Richard Thaler, *Nudge: Improving Decisions About Health, Wealth, and Happiness* (2008), praises behavioural economics. As a final underline for the imperative that we should always expect the unexpected is Nassim Taleb, *The Black Swan: The Impact of the Highly Improbable* (2007).

Bibliography

Ackerly, B. (2008) *Universal Human Rights in a World of Difference* (Cambridge: Cambridge University Press).

Ackerly, B., M. Stern and J. True (eds) (2006) *Feminist Methodologies for International Relations* (Cambridge: Cambridge University Press).

Adamson, F. B. and M. Demetriou (2007) 'Remapping the Boundaries of "State" and "National Identity": Incorporating Diasporas into IR Theorizing', *European Journal of International Relations* (13) 489–526.

Adler, A. (1997) 'Seizing the Middle Ground', *European Journal of International Relations* (3) 319–64.

Adler, E. (2005) *Communitarian International Relations: The Epistemic Foundations of International Relations* (London: Routledge).

Albert, M. (2007) '"Globalization Theory": Yesterday's Fad or More Lively than Ever?', *International Political Sociology* (1) 165–182.

Albert, M., L. Brock and K-D. Wolf (eds) (2000) *Civilising World Politics* (Lanham, MD: Rowman & Littlefield).

Albert, M., D. Jacobson and Y. Lapid (eds) (2001) *Identities, Borders, Orders: Rethinking International Relations Theory* (Minneapolis, MN: Minnesota University Press).

Albrow, M. (1996) *The Global Age: State and Society Beyond Modernity* (Cambridge: Polity Press).

Aldcroft, D. H. (1977) *From Versailles to Wall Street 1919–1929* (Harmondsworth: Penguin).

Alexander, Jason (2007) *The Structural Evolution of Morality* (Cambridge: Cambridge University Press).

Alkopher, T. D. (2005) 'The Social (and Religious) Meanings that Constitute War: The Crusades as Realpolitik vs. Socialpolitik', *International Studies Quarterly* (49) 715–38.

Allison, G. T. (1971) *Essence of Decision* (Boston, MA: Little, Brown).

Allison, G. T. and G. F. Treverton (eds) (1992) *Rethinking America's Security: Beyond Cold War to New World Order* (New York: W. W. Norton).

Allison, G. T. and P. Zelikow (1999) *Essence of Decision: Explaining the Cuban Missile Crisis,* 2nd edn (New York: Longman).

American Journal of International Law (1999) 'Developments in International Criminal Law' (93) 1–123.

American Political Science Review (1997) 'Forum on Neo-Realism' (91) 899–936.

American Political Science Review (2005) 'Forum on Democratic Peace' (99) 452–72.

Amin, S. (1974) *Accumulation on a World Scale,* Vols I and II (New York: Monthly Review Press).

Amin, S. (1977) *Imperialism and Unequal Development* (New York: Monthly Review Press).

Anderson, B. (1991) *Imagined Communities,* 2nd edn (London: Verso).

Anderson, C. (2006) *The Long Tail* (New York: Random House)

Angell, N. (1909) *The Great Illusion* (London: Weidenfeld & Nicolson).

Appadurai, A. (1996) *Modernity at Large: Cultural Dimensions of Globalization* (Minneapolis, MN: Minnesota University Press).

Arbour, L. (2008) 'The Responsibility to Protect as a Duty of Care in International Law and Practice', *Review of International Studies* (34) 445–58.

Archibugi, D. and D. Held (eds) (1995) *Cosmopolitan Democracy* (Cambridge: Polity Press).

Aron, R. (1967) *Peace and War: A Theory of International Relations* (London: Weidenfeld & Nicolson).

Arrighi, G., T. Hopkins and I. Wallerstein (1989) *Anti-systemic Movements* (London: Verso).

Art, R. and K. Waltz (eds) (1993) *The Use of Force: Military Power and International Politics* (Lanham, MD: University Press of America).

Ash, T. G. (2004) *Free World: Why A Crisis of the West Reveals an Opportunity of our Time* (London: Allen Lane).

Ashley, R. K. (1984) 'The Poverty of Neorealism', *International Organization* (38) 225–86.

Ashley, R. K. (1989a) 'Imposing International Purpose: Notes on a Problematic of Government', in Czempial and Rosenau, *Global Changes.*

Ashley, R. K. (1989b) 'Living on Borderlines: Man, Poststructuralism and War', in Der Derian and Shapiro, *International/Intertextual.*

Ashley, R. K. (1989c) 'Untying the Sovereign State: A Double Reading of the *Anarchy Problematique*', *Millennium* (17) 227–86.

Ashley, R. K. and R. B. J. Walker (eds) (1990) 'Speaking the Language of Exile: Dissidence in International Studies', Special Issue, *International Studies Quarterly* (34) 259–417.

Ashworth, L. (2006) 'Where Are the Idealists in Interwar International Relations?', *Review of International Studies,* (32) 291–308.

Avant, D. (2005) *The Market for Force: The Consequences of Privatizing Security* (Cambridge: Cambridge University Press).

Axelrod, R. (1984) *The Evolution of Cooperation* (New York: Basic Books).

Axelrod, R. and R. O. Keohane (1985) 'Achieving Cooperation under Anarchy: Strategies and Institutions', *World Politics* (38) 226–54.

Aziz, J. and R. F. Wescott (1997) *Policy Complementarities and the Washington Consensus* (Washington, DC: The International Monetary Fund).

Bacevich, A. (2004) *American Empire: The Realities and Consequences of US Diplomacy* (Cambridge, MA: Harvard University Press).

Bachrach, P. and M. P. Baratz (1970) *Power and Poverty* (New York: Oxford University Press).

Backstrand, K. (2006) 'Democratizing Global Environmental Governance? Stakeholder Democracy after the World Summit on Sustainable Development', *European Journal of International Relations* (12) 467–98.

Baker, A., D. Hudson and R. Woodward (eds) (2005) *Governing Financial Globalization* (London: Routledge).

Balaam, D. and M. Veseth (2004) *Introduction to International Political Economy*, 3rd edn (New York: Prentice Hall).

Balakrishnan, G. (2000) 'Virgilian Visions', *New Left Review*, September/October, 142–8.

Baldwin, D. A. (1985) *Economic Statecraft* (Princeton, NJ: Princeton University Press).

Baldwin, D. A. (1989) *Paradoxes of Power* (New York: Basic Books).

Baldwin, D. A. (ed.) (1993) *Neorealism and Neoliberalism: The Contemporary Debate* (New York: Columbia University Press).

Baldwin, D. A. (1997) 'The Concept of Security', *Review of International Studies* (23) 5–26.

Baldwin, D. A. (1998) 'Correspondence Evaluating Economic Sanctions', *International Security* (23) 189–98.

Baldwin, D. A. (1999/2000) 'The Sanctions Debate and the Logic of Choice', *International Security* (24) 80–107.

Balzacq, T. (2005) 'The Three Faces of Securitization: Political Agency, Audience and Context', *European Journal of International Relations* (11) 171–201.

Baran, P. (1957) *The Political Economy of Growth* (New York: Monthly Review Press).

Barber, B. (1996) *Jihad vs. McWorld* (New York: Ballantine Books).

Barber, B. (2004) *Fear's Empire* (New York: W. W. Norton).

Barkawi, T. (2005) *Globalization and War* (London: Rowman & Littlefield).

Barkawi, T. and M. Laffey (1999) 'The Imperial Peace: Democracy, Force and Globalization', *European Journal of International Relations* (5) 403–34.

Barkawi, T. and M. Laffey (eds) (2001) *Democracy, Liberalism and War* (Boulder, CO: Lynne Rienner).

Barkawi, T. and M. Laffey (2002) 'Retrieving the Imperial: *Empire* and International Relations', *Millennium* (31) 109–27.

Barkawi, T. and M. Laffey (2006) 'The Postcolonial Moment in Security Studies', *Review of International Studies* (32) 329–52.

Barnard, F. M. (ed.) (1969) *J. G. Herder on Social and Political Culture* (Cambridge: Cambridge University Press).

Barnet, R. and J. Cavanagh (1994) *Global Dreams: Imperial Corporations and the New World Order* (New York: Simon & Schuster).

Barnett, M. (2003) *Eyewitness to Genocide: The UN and Rwanda* (Ithaca, NY: Cornell University Press).

Barnett, M. and R. Duvall (2005a) 'Power in International Politics', *International Organization* (59) 39–75.

Barnett, M. and R. Duvall (2005b) *Power in Global Governance* (Cambridge: Cambridge University Press).

Barnett, M. and M. Finnemore (2004) *Rules for the World* (Ithaca, NY: Cornell University Press).

Barry, B. (1989) 'The Obscurities of Power', in *Democracy, Power and Justice* (Oxford: Oxford University Press).

Barry, B. (2000) *Culture and Inequality* (Cambridge: Polity).

Barry, B. and R. E. Goodin (eds) (1992) *Free Movement* (Hemel Hempstead: Harvester Wheatsheaf).

Barry, C. and T. Pogge (eds) (2005) *Global Institutions and Responsibilities: Achieving Global Justice* (Oxford: Wiley-Blackwell).

Bartelson, J. (2006) 'Making Sense of Global Civil Society', *European Journal of International Relations* (12) 371–95.

Bauer, J. and D. A. Bell (eds) (1999) *The East Asian Challenge for Human Rights* (Cambridge: Cambridge University Press).

Bauer, P. (1981) *Equality, The Third World and Economic Delusion* (London: Weidenfeld & Nicolson).

Bauman, Z. (1998) *Globalization: The Human Consequences* (Cambridge: Polity Press).

Beck, U. (1999) *World Risk Society* (Cambridge: Polity Press).

Beigbeder, Y. (1999) *Judging War Criminals: The Politics of International Justice* (New York: St. Martin's Press).

Beitz, C. R. (1999) *Political Theory and International Relations* (Princeton, NJ: Princeton University Press).

Beitz, C. R., M. Cohen, T. Scanlon and J. Simmons (1985) *International Ethics* (Princeton, NJ: Princeton University Press).

Bell, D. (2000) *East Meets West: Democracy and Human Rights in East Asia* (Princeton, NJ: Princeton University Press).

Bellamy, A. (ed.) (2004) *International Society and Its Critics* (Oxford: Oxford University Press).

Bellamy, A. (2008) 'The Responsibility to Protect and the Problem of Military Intervention', *International Affairs* (84) 615–39.

Bellin, E. (2008) 'Faith in Politics: New Trends in the Study of Religion and Politics', *World Politics* (60).

Belloni, R. (2007) 'The Trouble with Humanitarianism', *Review of International Studies* (33) 451–74.

Bender, J. and T. H. Hammond (1992) 'Rethinking Allison's Models', *American Political Science Review* (86) 301–22.

Bentham, J. (1789/1960) *Principles of Morals and Legislation* (Oxford: Basil Blackwell).

Berdal, M. (1996) 'The United Nations in International Relations', *International Affairs* (22) 95–106.

Berdal, M. (2003) 'The UN Security Council: Ineffective but Indispensable', *Survival* (45) 7–30.

Berenskoetter, F. and M. J. Williams (2007) *Power in World Politics* (London: Routledge).

Berman, P. (2004) *Terror and Liberalism* (New York: W. W. Norton).

Bernstein, B. J. (2000) 'Understanding Decisionmaking, US Foreign Policy and the Cuban Missile Crisis: A Review Essay', *International Security* (25) 1134–64.

Berridge, G. R. (2002) *Diplomacy: Theory and Practice*, 2nd edn (Basingstoke/New York: Palgrave Macmillan).

Best, G. (1994) *War and Law since 1945* (Oxford: Oxford University Press).

Bhagwati, J. (2004) *In Defence of Globalization* (Oxford: Oxford University Press).

Bhaskar, R. (1979) *The Possibility of Naturalism: A Philosophical Critique of the Contemporary Human Sciences* (Atlantic Highlands, NJ: Humanities Press).

Bhaskar, R. (2008) *A Realist Theory of Science* (London: Verso Books).

Binmore, K. (2005) *Natural Justice* (Oxford: Oxford University Press).

Bishai, L. (2008) 'Leaving Nuremberg: America's Love/Hate Relationship with International Law', *Review of International Studies* (34) 425–44.

Blainey, G. (1988) *The Causes of War* (New York: Free Press).

Blair, T. (1999) 'Doctrine of the International Community', Speech in Chicago, 24 April; available at: http://www.number-10.gov.uk/output/Page1297.asp.

Blake, D. H. and R. S. Walters (1991) *The Politics of Global Economic Relations* (London: Prentice Hall).

Block, F. (1977) *The Origins of International Economic Disorder* (Berkeley, CA: University of California Press).

Bluth, C. (2004) The British Road to War: Blair, Bush and the Decision to Invade Iraq', *International Affairs* (80) 871–92.

Bobbitt, P. (2003) *The Shield of Achilles* (Harmondsworth: Penguin).

Bobbitt, P. (2008) *Terror and Consent* (New York: Penguin)

Bohas, A. (2006) 'The Paradox of Anti-Americanism: Reflection on the Shallow Concept of Soft Power', *Global Society* (20) 395–414.

Bohman, J. and M. Lutz-Bachmann (eds) (1997) *Perpetual Peace: Essays on Kant's Cosmopolitan Ideal* (Cambridge, MA: MIT Press).

Boot, M. (2002) 'What the Heck Is a "Neo Con"?', *Wall St Journal Online*, 30 December.

Booth, K. (ed.) (1991a) *New Thinking about Strategy and International Security* (London: HarperCollins).

Booth, K. (1991b) 'Security in Anarchy: Utopian Realism in Theory and Practice', *International Affairs* (67) 527–45.

Booth, K. (1991c) 'Security and Emancipation', *Review of International Studies* (17) 313–26.

Booth, K. (1997) 'A Reply to Wallace', *Review of International Studies* (23) 371–7.

Booth, K. (ed.) (2000) 'The Kosovo Tragedy: The Human Rights Dimension', Special Issue of *International Journal of Human Rights* (4) 1/2; reprinted as Booth (2001).

Booth. K. (ed.) (2001) *The Kosovo Tragedy: The Human Rights Dimension* (London: Frank Cass).

Booth, K. (2007) *Theory of World Security* (Cambridge: Cambridge University Press).

Booth, K. and T. Dunne (eds) (2002) *Worlds in Collision* (Basingstoke: Palgrave Macmillan).

Booth, K. and S. Smith (eds) (1995) *International Relations Theory Today* (Cambridge: Polity Press).

Booth, K. and N. Wheeler (2007) *The Security Dilemma: Fear, Cooperation and Trust in World Politics* (Basingstoke: Palgrave).

Boucher, D. (1998) *Political Theories of International Relations* (Oxford: Oxford University Press).

Boulding, K. (1962) *Conflict and Defense* (New York: Harper & Row).

Bowden, M. (1999) *Black Hawk Down* (New York: Bantam Books).

Bozeman, A. B. (1960) *Politics and Culture in International History* (Princeton, NJ: Princeton University Press).

Brahimi Report (2000) *Report of the Panel on UN Peace Operations* (United Nations); available at: http://www.un.org/peace/reports/peace_operations/.

Brecher, M. (1993) *Crises in World Politics: Theory and Reality* (Oxford: Pergamon Press).

Brenner, R. (1977) 'The Origins of Capitalist Development', *New Left Review* (104) 25–92.

Bretherton, C. and J. Vogler (2005) *The European Union as a Global Actor* (London: Routledge).

Brett, E. A. (1985) *The World Economy since the War* (Basingstoke/New York: Palgrave Macmillan).

Brewer, A. (1990) *Marxist Theories of Imperialism: A Critical Survey* (London: Routledge).

British Journal of Politics and International Relations (2007) Special Issue 'Beyond Being Marginal: Gender and International Relations in Britain (9) 183–325.

Brooks, S. G. (1997) 'Duelling Realisms', *International Organization* (51) 445–77.

Brooks, S. G. and W. Wohlforth (2002) 'American Primacy in Perspective', *Foreign Affairs* (81) 20–33.

Brooks, S. G. and W. Wohlforth (2005) 'Hard Times for Soft Balancing' *International Security* (30) 72–108.

Brooks, S. G. and W. Wohlforth (2008) *World Out of Balance: International Relations and the Challenge of American Primacy* (Princeton, NJ: Princeton).

Brown, C. (1992a) *International Relations Theory: New Normative Approaches* (Hemel Hempstead: Harvester Wheatsheaf).

Brown, C. (1992b) '"Really-Existing Liberalism", and International Order', *Millennium* (21) 313–28.

Brown, C. (1994a) 'Critical Theory and Postmodernism in International Relations', in Groom and Light, *Contemporary International Relations*.

Brown, C. (ed.) (1994b) *Political Restructuring in Europe: Ethical Perspectives* (London: Routledge).

Brown, C. (1994c) '"Turtles All the Way Down": Antifoundationalism, Critical Theory, and International Relations', *Millennium* (23) 213–38.

Brown, C. (1995) 'The End of History?', in Danchev, *Fin de Siècle*.

Brown, C. (1999) 'History Ends, Worlds Collide', *Review of International Studies,* Special Issue, 'The Interregnum' (25) 45–57; also in M. Cox, K. Booth and T. Dunne (eds), *The Interregnum* (Cambridge: Cambridge University Press).

Brown, C. (2000a) 'On the Borders of (International) Political Theory', in N. O'Sullivan (ed.), *Political Theory in Transition* (London: Routledge).

Brown, C. (2000b) 'Cultural Diversity and International Political Theory', *Review of International Studies* (26) 199–213.

Brown, C. (2001) 'Cosmopolitanism, World Citizenship and Global Civil Society', in Jones and Caney, *Human Rights*.

Brown, C. (2002) *Sovereignty, Rights and Justice: International Political Theory Today* (Cambridge: Polity Press).

Brown, C. (2004) 'Do Great Powers Have Great Responsibilities? Great Powers and Moral Agency', *Global Society* (18) 21–42.

Brown, C. (2007) 'Tragedy, "Tragic Choices" and Contemporary International Political Theory', *International Relations* (21) 5–13.

Brown, C., T. Nardin and N. J. Rengger (eds) (2002) *International Relations in Political Thought* (Cambridge: Cambridge University Press).

Brown, M. E., S. M. Lynn-Jones and S. E. Miller (eds) (1995) *The Perils of Anarchy: Contemporary Realism and International Security* (Cambridge, MA: MIT Press).

Brown, M. E., S. M. Lynn-Jones and S. E. Miller (eds) (1996) *Debating the Democratic Peace* (Cambridge, MA: MIT Press).

Brown, M. E., O. R. Coté, Jr., S. M. Lynn-Jones and S. E. Miller (eds) (1997) *Nationalism and Ethnic Conflict* (Cambridge, MA: MIT Press).

Brown, M. E., O. R. Coté, Jr., S. M. Lynn-Jones and S. E. Miller (eds) (2004a) *New Global Dangers: Changing Dimensions of International Security* (Cambridge, MA: MIT Press).

Brown, M. E., O. R. Coté, Jr., S. M. Lynn-Jones and S. E. Miller (eds) (2004b) *Offense, Defense and War* (Cambridge, MA: MIT Press).

Brzezinski, Z. (2004) *Choice: Global Domination or Global Leadership* (New York: Basic Books).

Buckley-Zistel, S. (2006) 'Dividing and Uniting: The Use of Citizenship Discourses in Conflict and Reconciliation in Rwanda', *Global Society* (20) 101–13.

Bueno de Mesquita, B. (2006) 'Intervention and Democracy', *International Organization* (60) 627–49.

Bull, H. (1976) 'Martin Wight and the Theory of International Relations', *British Journal of International Studies* (2) 101–16.

Bull, H. (1977/1995/2002) *The Anarchical Society* (London/Basingstoke: Palgrave Macmillan; New York: Columbia University Press).

Bull, H. (1984) *Justice in International Relations: The Hagey Lectures* (Waterloo, Ontario: University of Waterloo).

Bull, H. and A. Watson (eds) (1984) *The Expansion of International Society* (Oxford: Clarendon Press).

Burchill, S., A. Linklater, R. Devetak, J. Donnelly, T. Nardin, M. Paterson, C. Reus-Smit and J. True (2009) *Theories of International Relations,* 4th edn (Basingstoke/New York: Palgrave Macmillan).

Burkhalter, H. (2004) 'The Politics of Aids', *Foreign Affairs* (83) 8–14.

Burki, S. J. and G. E. Perry (1998) *Beyond the Washington Consensus: Institutions Matter* (Washington, DC: The World Bank).

Burton, J. W. (1968) *Systems, States, Diplomacy and Rules* (Cambridge: Cambridge University Press).

Burton, J. W. (1972) *World Society* (Cambridge: Cambridge University Press).

Buruma, I. and A. Margalit (2004) *Occidentalism: The West in the Eyes of Its Enemies* (New York: Penguin).

Busch, M. L. (2007) 'Overlapping Institutions, Forum Shopping, and Dispute Settlement in International Trade', *International Organization* (61) 735–61.

Bush, President G. H. W. (1990) 'Towards a New World Order', Address before a joint session of Congress, 11 September, *US Department of State Dispatch,* 17 September 1990, 91–4.

Butterfield, H. (1953) *Christianity, Diplomacy and* War (London: Epworth).

Butterfield, H. and M. Wight (eds) (1966) *Diplomatic Investigations* (London: George Allen & Unwin).

Buzan, B. (1990) *People, States and Fear,* 2nd edn (London: Harvester Wheatsheaf).

Buzan, B. (1993) 'From International System to International Society: Structural Realism and Regime Theory Meet the English School', *International Organization* (47), 327–52.

Buzan, B. (1999) 'The English School as a Research Programme', BISA Conference, Manchester; available at: http://www.ukc.ac.uk/politics/englishschool/.

Buzan, B. (2004) *From International to World Society: English School Theory and the Social Structure of Globalization* (Cambridge: Cambridge University Press).

Buzan, B. (2005) 'Not Hanging Separately: Responses to Dunne and Adler', *Millennium: Journal of International Studies* (34) 183–94.

Buzan, B. and O. Waever (1997) 'Slippery? Contradictory? Sociologically Untenable? The Copenhagen School Replies' [to McSweeney 1996], *Review of International Studies* (23) 241–50.

Buzan, B., M. Kelstrup, P. Lemaitre and E. Tromer (eds) (1990) *The European Security Order Recast: Scenarios for the Post-Cold War Era* (London: Pinter).

Buzan, B., C. Jones and R. Little (1993) *The Logic of Anarchy: Neorealism to Structural Realism* (New York: Columbia University Press).

Buzan, B., O. Waever and J. de Wilde (1997) *Security: A New Framework for Analysis* (Boulder, CO: Lynne Rienner).

Byman, D. A. and K. M. Pollack (2001) 'Let Us Now Praise Great Men: Bringing the Statesman Back In', *International Security* (25/4) 107–46.

Byman, D. A. and M. C. Waxman (2000) 'Kosovo and the Great Air Power Debate', *International Security* (24) 5–38.

Byrnes, T. and P. Katzenstein (eds) (2006) *Religion in an Expanding Europe* (Cambridge: Cambridge University Press).

Calderisi, R. (2007) *The Trouble with Africa: Why Foreign Aid Isn't Working* (London: Palgrave Macmillan).

Callinicos, A. (2007) 'Does Capitalism Need the State System?', *Cambridge Review of International Affairs* (20) 533–49.

Campbell, D. (1993) *Politics without Principle: Sovereignty, Ethics, and the Narratives of the Gulf War* (Boulder, CO: Lynne Rienner).

Campbell, D. (1998) *National Deconstruction: Violence, Identity and Justice in Bosnia* (Minneapolis, MN: University of Minnesota Press).

Caney, S. (2006) *Justice beyond Borders: A Global Political Theory* (Oxford: Oxford University Press).

Caporaso, J. (ed.) (1978) 'Dependence and Dependency in the Global System', Special Issue of *International Organization* (32) 1–300.

Cardoso, F. and E. Faletto (1979) *Dependency and Development in Latin America* (Berkeley, CA: University of California Press).

Carlsnaes, W. (1992) 'The Agent–Structure Problem in Foreign Policy Analysis', *International Studies Quarterly* (36) 245–70.

Carlsnaes, W., Risse, T. and Simmonds, B. (eds) (2004) *Handbook of International Relations* (London: Sage).

Carr, E. H. (1939/2001) *The Twenty Years' Crisis,* ed. Michael Cox (London/Basingstoke/New York: Palgrave Macmillan).

Carr, E. H. (1968) *Nationalism and After* (London: Macmillan).

Carr, E. H. and R. W. Davies (1978) *A History of Soviet Russia* (London/New York: Palgrave Macmillan).

Carver, T., M. Cochran and J. Squires (1998) 'Gendering Jones', *Review of International Studies* (24) 283–97.

Cassese, A., P. Gaeta and J. R. W. D. Jones (eds) (2002) *The Rome Statute of the International Criminal Court: A Commentary* (Oxford: Oxford University Press).

Castells, M. (1996/7) *The Information Age: Economy, Society and Culture,* 3 vols (Oxford: Basil Blackwell).

Cavanagh, J., D. Wysham and M. Arruda (1994) *Beyond Bretton Woods: Alternatives to the Global Economic Order* (London: Pluto Press).

Cerny, P. (1990) *The Changing Architecture of Politics* (London: Sage).

Chalmers, A. F. (1999) *What Is This Thing Called Science?,* 3rd edn (Milton Keynes: Open University Press).

Chandler, D. (2004) *Constructing Global Civil Society* (Basingstoke/New York: Palgrave Macmillan).

Chang, H. (2007) *Bad Samaritans: The Myth of Free Trade and the Secret History of Capitalism* (London: Bloomsbury Press).

Charlesworth, H. (1994) 'What Are "Women's International Human Rights"?', in Cook (ed.), *Human Rights of Women.*

Charlesworth, H. and C. Chinkin (2000) *The Boundaries of International Law: A Feminist Analysis* (Manchester: Manchester University Press).

Chase-Dunn, C. (1989) *Global Formation: Structures of the World Economy* (Oxford: Basil Blackwell).

Checkel, J. (ed.) (2007) *International Institutions and Socialization in Europe* (Cambridge: Cambridge University Press).

Chatterjee, D. K. and D. E. Scheid (eds) (2004) *Ethics and Foreign Intervention: Kosovo and Beyond* (New York: Cambridge University Press).

Chernoff, F. (2005) *The Power of International Theory: Reforging the Link to Foreign Policy-Making through Scientific Inquiry* (London: Routledge).

Chojnacki, S. (2006) 'Anything New or More of the Same? Wars and Military Interventions in the International System, 1946–2003', *Global Society* (20) 25–46.

Chomsky, N. (1994) *World Orders, Old and New* (London: Pluto Press).

Chomsky, N. (1999) *The New Military Humanism* (London: Pluto Press).

Chomsky, N. (2004) *Hegemony or Survival: America's Quest for Global Dominance* (London: Penguin).

Chryssochoou, D. (2001) *Theorizing European Integration* (London: Sage).

Clark, G. and L. B. Sohn (1966) *World Peace through World Law* (Cambridge, MA: Harvard University Press).

Clark, I. (1999) *Globalization and International Relations Theory* (Oxford: Oxford University Press).

Clark, I. (2005) *Legitimacy in International Society* (Oxford: Oxford University Press).

Clark, I. (2007) *Legitimacy in World Society* (Oxford: Oxford University Press).

Clarke, M. and B. White (eds) (1989) *Understanding Foreign Policy: The Foreign Policy Systems Approach* (Aldershot: Edward Elgar).

Claude, I. L. (1962) *Power and International Relations* (New York: Random House).

Claude, I. L. (1971) *Swords into Plowshares* (New York: Random House).

Clausewitz, K. von (1976) *On War* (trans. and ed. by Michael Howard and Peter Paret) (Princeton, NJ: Princeton University Press).

Cochran, M. (2000) *Normative Theory in International Relations* (Cambridge: Cambridge University Press).

Cohen, B. (1990) 'Review Article: The Political Economy of International Trade', *International Organization* (44) 261–78.

Cohen, B. (2007) 'The Transatlantic Divide: Why Are American and British IPE so Different?' *Review of International Political Economy* (14) 197–219.

Cohen, R. (1994) 'Pacific Unions: A Reappraisal of the Theory that "Democracies Do Not Go To War With Each Other"', *Review of International Studies* (20) 207–23.

Coker, C. (1994) *War in the Twentieth Century* (London: Brassey's).

Coker, C. (1998) *War and the Illiberal Conscience* (Boulder, CO: Westview Press).

Coker, C. (2001) *Humane Warfare: The New Ethics of Post-Modern War* (London: Routledge).

Collier, P. (2007) *The Bottom Billion: Why the Poorest Countries are Failing and What Can Be Done About It* (Oxford: Oxford University Press).

Collingwood, V. (2006) 'Non-governmental Organisations, Power and Legitimacy in International Society', *Review of International Studies* (32) 439–54.

Connolly, W. E. (1993) *The Terms of Political Discourse*, 2nd edn (Oxford: Martin Robertson).

Connolly, W. E. (1991) *Identity/Difference: Democratic Negotiations of Political Paradox* (Ithaca, NJ: Cornell University Press).

Connolly, W. E. (1995) *The Ethos of Pluralization* (Minneapolis, MN: University of Minnesota Press).

Connolly, W. E. (2000) 'Speed, Concentric Circles and Cosmopolitanism', *Political Theory* (28) 596–618.

Connolly, W. E. (2002) *Neuropolitics: Thinking, Culture, Speed* (Minneapolis, MN: University of Minnesota Press).

Constantinou, C. (1994) 'Diplomatic Representation, or, Who Framed the Ambassadors?', *Millennium* (23) 1–23.

Constantinou, C. (1996) *On the Way to Diplomacy* (Minneapolis, MN: University of Minnesota Press).

Cook, R. (ed.) (1994) *Human Rights of Women: National and International Perspectives* (Philadelphia: University of Pennsylvania Press).

Coomaraswamy, R. (1994) 'To Bellow Like a Cow: Women, Ethnicity and the Discourse', in Cook (ed.), *Human Rights of Women*.

Cooperation and Conflict (2006) Symposium on World Order (41) 341–402.

Cooper, R. (2003) *The Breaking of Nations* (London: Atlantic Books).

Cottam, M. (1986) *Foreign Policy Decision-Making: The Influence of Cognition* (Boulder, CO: Westview Press).

Cox, M. (2003) 'The Empire's Back in Town: Or America's Imperial Temptation – Again', *Millennium* (32) 1–29.

Cox, M. (2005) 'Beyond the West: Terrors in Transatlantia', *European Journal of International Relations* (11) 203–33.

Cox, M. (2006) 'Let's Argue about the West: Reply to Vincent Pouliot', *European Journal of International Relations* (12) 129–34.

Cox, M., K. Booth and T. Dunne (eds) (1999), *The Interregnum* (Cambridge: Cambridge University Press).

Cox, M., T. Dunne and K. Booth (eds) (2002) *Empires, Systems and States: Great Transformations in International Politics* (Cambridge: Cambridge University Press).

Cox, R. (1981) 'Social Forces, States, and World Orders: Beyond International Relations Theory', *Millennium* (10) 126–55.

Cox, R. (1987) *Production, Power and World Order: Social Forces in the Making of History* (New York: Columbia University Press).

Cox, R. and H. K. Jacobson (eds) (1973) *The Anatomy of Influence* (New Haven, CT: Yale University Press).

Cox, R. (with T. Sinclair) (1996) *Approaches to World Order* (Cambridge: Cambridge University Press).

Craig, C. (2003) *Glimmer of a New Leviathan: Total War in the Realism of Niebuhr, Morgenthau, and Waltz* (New York: Columbia University Press).

Craig, G. C. and A. L. George (eds) (1983) *Force and Statecraft* (New York: Oxford University Press).

Crane, G. T. and A. M. Amawi (eds) (1999) *The Theoretical Evolution of International Political Economy: A Reader* (New York: Oxford University Press).

Creasy, E. (1902) *Fifteen Decisive Battles* (London: Macmillan).

Czempial, E.-O. and J. N. Rosenau (eds) (1989) *Global Changes and Theoretical Challenges* (Lexington, MA: Lexington Books).

Daalder, I. and M. Hanlon (2001) *Winning Ugly* (Washington, DC: The Brookings Institute).

Daalder, I. and J. M. Lindsay (2003) *America Unbound: The Bush Revolution in Foreign Policy* (Washington, DC: The Brookings Institute).

Dahl, R. (1961) *Who Governs?* (New Haven, CT: Yale University Press).

Dahl, R. (1970) *Modern Political Analysis* (New York: Prentice Hall).

Dahrendorf, R. (1990) *Reflections on the Revolution in Europe* (London: Chatto & Windus).

Dallaire, R. (2003) *Shake Hands with the Devil* (Montreal: Random House of Canada).

Dallmayr, F. (2002) *Dialogue Among Civilizations* (Basingstoke: Palgrave Macmillan).

Danchev, A. (ed.) (1995) *Fin de Siècle: The Meaning of the Twentieth Century* (London: I. B. Tauris).

Dauphinee, E. (2008) 'War Crimes and the Ruin of Law', *Millennium* (37) 49–67.

Dawkins, R. (1989) *The Selfish Gene* (Oxford: Oxford University Press).

Dean, K., J. Joseph, J. Roberts and C. Wight (2006) *Realism, Philosophy and Social Science* (Basingstoke: Palgrave).

De Goede, M. (2008) 'The Politics of Preemption and the War on Terror in Europe', *European Journal of International Relations* (14) 161–85.

Dehio, L. (1965) *The Precarious Balance* (New York: Knopf).

Della Porta, D. and M. Diani (eds) (2006) *Social Movements: An Introduction* (Oxford: Blackwell).

Della Porta, D. and S. G. Tarrow (eds) (2005) *Transnational Protest and Global Activism* (Lanham, MD: Rowman & Littlefield).

Deng, Y. (2008) *China's Struggle for Status: The Realignment of International Relations* (Cambridge: Cambridge University Press).

Der Derian, J. (1987) *On Diplomacy: A Genealogy of Western Estrangement* (Oxford: Basil Blackwell).

Der Derian, J. (1992) *Antidiplomacy: Spies, Terror, Speed and War* (Oxford: Basil Blackwell).

Der Derian, J. (1998) *The Virilio Reader* (Oxford: Basil Blackwell).

Der Derian, J. (2001) *Virtuous War: Mapping the Military–Industrial–Media–Entertainment Network* (Boulder, CO: Westview Press).

Der Derian, J. and M. Shapiro (eds) (1989) *International/Intertextual: Postmodern Readings in World Politics* (Lexington, MA: Lexington Books).

Desai, M. (2002) *Marx's Revenge* (London: Verso).

Dessler, D. (1989) 'What's at Stake in the Agent–Structure Debate'. *International Oranization* (43) 441–73.

Deudney, D. (2000) 'Geopolitics as Theory: Historical Security Materialism', *European Journal of International Relations* (6) 77–108.

Deudney, D. (2007) *Bounding Power* (Princeton, NJ: Princeton University Press).

Deudney, D. and G. J. Ikenberry (1999) 'The Nature and Sources of Liberal International Order', *Review of International Studies* (25) 179–96.

Devetak, R. (2009) 'Critical Theory' and 'Postmodernism', in Burchill *et al.*, *Theories of International Relations*.

DeWinter, R. (2003) 'The Anti-Sweatshop Movement: Constructing Corporate Moral Agency in the Global Apparel Industry', in Erskine (ed.), *Can Institutions Have Responsibilities?*

Diamond, L. (2008) 'The Democratic Rollback', *Foreign Affairs* (87) 2, 36–48.

Dicken, P. (2004) *Global Shift: The Internationalization of Economic Activity* (London: Chapman & Hall).

Dillon, M. and L. Lobo-Guerrero (2008) 'Biopolitics of Security in the 21st Century: An Introduction', *Review of International Studies* (34) 265–92.

Dingwerth, K. and P. Pattberg (2006) 'Global Governance as a Perspective on World Politics', *Global Governance* (12) 185–204.

Dobson, A. and R. Eckersley (eds) (2006) *Political Theory and the Ecological Challenge* (Cambridge: Cambridge University Press).

Donegan, B. (2006) 'Governmental Regionalism: Power/Knowledge and Neoliberal Regional Integration in Asia and Latin America', *Millennium* (35) 23–51.

Doner, R. F., B. K. Ritchie and D. Slater (2005) 'Systemic Vulnerability and the Origins of Developmental States: Northeast and Southeast Asia in Comparative Perspective', *International Organization* (59) 327–61.

Donnelly, J. (1993) *International Human Rights* (Boulder, CO: Westview Press).

Donnelly, J. (2000) *Realism and International Relations* (Cambridge: Cambridge University Press).

Donnelly, J. (2006) 'Sovereign Inequalities and Hierarchy in Anarchy: American Power and International Society', *European Journal of International Relations* (12) 139–70.

Donnelly, J. (2007) 'The Relative Universality of Human Rights', *Human Rights Quarterly* (29) 281–306.

Doran, C. (2008) *Systems in Crisis: New Imperatives of High Politics at Century's End* (Cambridge: Cambridge University Press).

Doty, R. L. (1997) 'Aporia: A Critical Exploration of the Agent-Structure Prolematique in International Relations Theory', *European Journal of International Relations* (3) 365–92.

Dowty, A. (1987) *Closed Borders* (New Haven, CT: Yale University Press).

Doyle, M. (1983) 'Kant, Liberal Legacies and Foreign Policy', Parts I and II, *Philosophy and Public Affairs* (12) 205–35; 323–53.

Doyle, M. (1986) 'Liberalism and World Politics', *American Political Science Review* (80) 1151–70.

Doyle, M. (1997) *Ways of War and Peace: Realism, Liberalism and Socialism* (New York: W. W. Norton).

Doyle, M. (2008) *Striking First: Preemption and Prevention in International Conflict* (Princeton, NJ: Princeton University Press).

Doyle, M. and N. Sambanis (2006) *Making War and Building Peace: United Nations Peace Operations* (Princeton, NJ: Princeton University Press)

Dunn, K. C. and P. M. Goff (eds) (2004) *Identity and Global Politics* (Basingstoke/New York: Palgrave Macmillan).

Dunne, T. (1995) 'The Social Construction of International Society', *European Journal of International Relations* (1) 367–89.

Dunne, T. (1998) *Inventing International Society* (Basingstoke/New York: Palgrave Macmillan).

Dunne, T. (2003) 'Society and Hierarchy in International Relations', *International Relations* (17) 303–20.

Dunne, T. (2005) 'System, State and Society: How Does It All Hang Together?', *Millennium* (34) 157–70.

Dunne, T. and N. Wheeler (1996) 'Hedley Bull's Pluralism of the Intellect and Solidarism of the Will', *International Affairs* (72) 91–107.

Dunne, T. and N. Wheeler (eds) (1999) *Human Rights in Global Politics* (Cambridge: Cambridge University Press).

Dunne, T., M. Kurki and S. Smith (eds) (2007) *International Relations Theories: Discipline and Diversity* (Oxford: Oxford University Press).

Durkheim, E. (1982) *The Rules of Sociological Method* (New York: Free Press).

Easterly, W. (2007) *The White Man's Burden: Why the West's Efforts to Aid the Rest Have Done So Much Ill and So Little Good* (New York: Penguin).

Eberwein, W. and B. Badie (2006) 'Prevention and Sovereignty: A Vision and a Strategy for a New World Order?' *Global Society* (20) 1–24.

Eckersley, R. (2004) *The Green State: Rethinking Democracy and Sovereignty* (Cambridge, MA: MIT Press).

Edkins, J. (1999) *Poststructuralism and International Relations: Bringing the Political Back In* (Boulder, CO: Lynne Rienner).

Edkins, J. (2003) *Trauma and the Memory of Politics* (Cambridge: Cambridge University Press).

Edkins, J., N. Persram and V. Pin-Fat (eds) (1999) *Sovereignty and Subjectivity* (Boulder, CO: Lynne Rienner).

Eilstrup-Sangiovanni, M. (ed.) (2006) *Debates on European Integration* (Basingstoke: Palgrave).

Ekins, P. (1992) *A New World Order: Grassroots Movements for Global Change* (London: Routledge).

Elliot, L. (2004) *The Global Politics of the Environment*, 2nd edn (Basingstoke: Palgrave Macmillan; New York: New York University Press).

Ellis, S. and G. Ter Haar (2004) *Worlds of Power: Religious Thought and Political Practice in Africa* (London: C. M. Hurst).

Elman, C. (1997) 'Horses for Courses: Why Not Neorealist Theories of Foreign Policy?', *Security Studies* (6) 7–53.

Elshtain, J. B. (ed.) (1981) *Public Man, Private Woman* (Oxford: Martin Robertson).

Elshtain, J. B. (1987) *Women and War* (Brighton: Harvester Wheatsheaf).

Elshtain, J. B. (1998) '*Women and War* Ten Years After', *Review of International Studies* (24) 447–60.

Elshtain, J. B. (2004) *Just War Against Terror: The Burden of American Power in a Violent World* (New York: Basic Books).

Emmanuel, A. (1972) *Unequal Exchange* (London: New Left Books).

Emmott, B. (2008) *Rivals: How the Power Struggle Between China, India and Japan Will Shape Our Next Decade* (New York: Harcourt).

Enloe, C. (1993) *The Morning After: Sexual Politics at the End of the Cold War* (Berkeley, CA: University of California Press).

Enloe, C. (2000) *Bananas, Beaches and Base: Making Feminist Sense of International Politics*, 2nd edn (Berkeley, CA: University of California Press).

Enloe, C. (2004) *The Curious Feminist: Searching for Women in a New Age of Empire* (Berkeley, CA: University of California Press).

Erskine, T. (ed.) (2003) *Can Institutions Have Responsibilities? Collective Moral Agency and International Relations* (Basingstoke/New York: Palgrave Macmillan).

Erskine, T. (2004) '"Blood on the UN's Hands"? Assigning Duties and Apportioning Blame to an Intergovernmental Organisation', *Global Society* (18) 21–42.

Erskine, T. (2008) *Embedded Cosmopolitanism: Duties to Strangers and Enemies in a World of 'Dislocated Communities'* (Oxford: Oxford University Press)

Ethics and International Affairs (2002) Roundtable: 'New Wars: What Rules Apply?' (16) 1–26.

Ethics and International Affairs (2003a) Roundtable: 'Evaluating the Pre-Emptive Use of Force' (17) 1–35.

Ethics and International Affairs (2003b) Special Section, 'The Revival of Empire' (17).

Etzioni, A. (2004) *From Empire to Community* (Basingstoke: Palgrave).

Evans, G. (1975) 'E. H. Carr and International Relations', *British Journal of International Studies* (1) 77–97.

Evans, M. (ed.) (2005) *Just War Theory: A Reappraisal* (Edinburgh: Edinburgh University Press).

Evans, P., D. Rueschemeyer and T. Skocpol (eds) (1985) *Bringing the State Back In* (Cambridge: Cambridge University Press).

Evans, P. B., H. K. Jacobson and R. D. Putnam (eds) (1993) *Double-Edged Diplomacy: International Diplomacy and Domestic Politics* (Berkeley, CA: University of California Press).

Falk, R. (1971) *This Endangered Planet* (New York: Vintage).

Falk, R. (1999) *Predatory Globalization: A Critique* (Cambridge: Polity Press).

Fawn R. and R. Hinnebusch (eds) (2006) *The Iraq War: Causes and Consequences* (Boulder, CO: Lynne Rienner).

Felshtinsky, Y. and V. Pribylovsky (2008) *The Age of Assassins: The Rise and Rise of Vladimir Putin* (London: Gibson Square Books).

Ferguson, N. (2004) *Colossus; The Rise and Fall of the American Empire* (London: Allen Lane).

Ferguson, N. (2005) 'Sinking Globalization', *Foreign Affairs* (84).

Finlay, C. J. (2007) 'Reform Intervention and Democratic Revolution', *European Journal of International Relations* (13) 555–81.

Forsyth, M. G., H. M. A. Keens-Soper and P. Savigear (eds) (1970) *The Theory of International Relations* (London: Allen & Unwin).

Fox, W. R. T. (1985) 'E. H. Carr and Political Realism: Vision and Revision', *Review of International Studies* (11) 1–16.

Frank, A. G. (1971) *Capitalism and Underdevelopment in Latin America* (Harmondsworth: Penguin).

Frank, A. G. and B. Gills (eds) (1993) *The World System: Five Hundred Years or Five Thousand?* (London: Routledge).

Frank, T. (2001) *One Market Under God* (New York: Random House).

Freedman, L. (ed.) (1994) *War* (Oxford: Oxford University Press).

Freedman, L. (2000) 'Victims and Victors: Reflections on the Kosovo War', *Review of International Studies* (26) 335–58.

Freud, S. (1985) *Civilisation, Society and Religion* (Harmondsworth: Penguin).

Friedberg, A. L. (2005) 'The Future of U.S.–China Relations: Is Conflict Inevitable?', *International Security* (30) 7–45.

Frieden, J. A. and D. A. Lake (eds) (1999) *International Political Economy: Perspectives on Global Power and Wealth*, 4th edn (Belmont, CA: Wadsworth; London: Routledge).

Friedman, M. (1966) *Essays in Positive Economics* (Chicago: Chicago University Press).

Friedman, T. (1999) *The Lexus and the Olive Tree* (New York: HarperCollins).

Frost, M. (1996) *Ethics in International Relations* (Cambridge: Cambridge University Press).

Frost, M. (2003) 'Tragedy, Ethics and International Relations', *International Relations* (17) 477–95.

Fuchs, D. (2005) 'Commanding Heights? The Strength and Fragility of Business Power in Global Politics', *Millennium* (33) 771–801.

Fukuyama, F. (1989) 'The End of History', *The National Interest* (16) 3–16.

Fukuyama, F. (1992) *The End of History and the Last Man* (New York: Free Press).

Gaddis, J. L. (2004) *Surprise, Security and the American Experience* (Cambridge, MA: Harvard University Press).

Galtung, J. (1971) 'A Structural Theory of Imperialism', *Journal of Peace Research* (13) 81–94.

Gardner, R. N. (1980) *Sterling–Dollar Diplomacy in Current Perspective: The Origins and Prospects of our International Economic Order* (New York: Columbia University Press).

Garthoff, R. (1994) *The Great Transition: American–Soviet Relations and the End of the Cold War* (Washington, DC: Brookings Institute).

Gartzke, E. and K. S. Gleditsch, (2006) 'Identity and Conflict: Ties that Bind and Differences that Divide', *European Journal of International Relations* (12) 53–87.

Gat, A. (2005) 'The Democratic Peace Theory Reframed: The Impact of Modernity', *World Politics* (58) 73–100.

Gellman, P. (1988) 'Hans Morgenthau and the Legacy of Political Realism', *Review of International Studies* (14) 247–66.

Gellner, E. (1988) *Plough, Sword and Book: The Structure of Human History* (London: Collins Harvill).

George, A. L. (1971) *The Limits of Coercive Diplomacy* (Boston, MA: Little, Brown).

George, J. (1994) *Discourses of Global Politics: A Critical (Re) Introduction to International Relations* (Boulder, CO: Lynne Rienner; Basingstoke: Palgrave Macmillan).

George, S. (1988) *A Fate Worse than Debt* (Harmondsworth: Penguin).

Germain, R. and M. Kenny (1998) 'Engaging Gramsci: International Relations Theory and the New Gramscians', *Review of International Studies* (24) 3–21.

Gerner, D. J. (1991) 'Foreign Policy Analysis: Exhilarating Eclecticism, Intriguing Enigmas', in Howell, 'International Studies'.

Geschiere, P. (1997) *The Modernity of Witchcraft: Politics and the Occult in Postcolonial Africa* (Richmond, VA: University of Virginia Press).

Giddens, A. (1985) *The Nation-State and Violence* (Cambridge: Polity Press).

Giddens, A (1986) *The Constitution of Society* (Cambridge: Polity Press)

Giddens, A. (1999) *The Runaway World* (Cambridge: Polity Press).

Gill, S. (ed.) (1993) *Gramsci, Historical Materialism and International Relations* (Cambridge: Cambridge University Press).

Gill, S. and D. Law (1988) *The Global Economy: Prospects, Problems and Policies* (London: Harvester).

Gills, B., J. Rocamora and R. Wilson (1993) *Low Intensity Democracy: Political Power in the New World Order* (London: Pluto Press).

Gilpin, R. (1975) *US Power and the Multinational Corporation* (New York: Basic Books).

Gilpin, R. (1981) *War and Change in World Politics* (New York: Cambridge University Press).

Gilpin, R. (1984) 'The Richness of the Tradition of Political Realism', *International Organization* (38) 287–304.

Gilpin, R. (1992) *The Political Economy of International Relations* (Princeton, NJ: Princeton University Press).

Gilpin, R. (2000) *The Challenge of Global Capitalism: The World Economy in the 21st Century* (Princeton, NJ: Princeton University Press).

Gilpin, R. (2001) *Global Political Economy: Understanding the International Economic Order* (Princeton, NJ: Princeton University Press).

Glasius, M., D. Lewis and H. Seckinelgin (eds) (2004) *International Civil Society* (London: Routledge).

Gleditsch, N. P. and T. Risse-Kappen (eds) (1995) 'Democracy and Peace', Special Issue, *European Journal of International Relations* (1) 429–574.

Global Civil Society Yearbook, annual (Oxford: Oxford University Press).

Global Governance (2006) Special Issue on the International Monetary Fund (12) 343–523.

Global Governance (2007) Special Issue on the World Bank (12) 461–581.

Goldsmith, J. and E. Posner (2005) *The Limits of International Law* (Oxford: Oxford University Press).

Goldstein, J. and R. O. Keohane (eds) (1993) *Ideas and Foreign Policy* (Ithaca, NY: Cornell University Press).

Gong, G. C. (1984) *The Standard of 'Civilisation' in International Society* (Oxford: Oxford University Press).

Goodale, M. and S. E. Merry (2007) *The Practice of Human Rights: Tracking Law Between the Global and the Local* (Cambridge: Cambridge University Press).

Gordon, P. and Shapiro, J. (2004) *Allies at War* (New York: McGraw-Hill Higher Education).

Gotz, N. (2008) 'Reframing NGOs: The Identity of an International Relations Non-Starter', *European Journal of International Relations* (14) 231–58.

Gourevitch, P. (1998) *We Wish to Inform You that Tomorrow We will be Killed with our Families: Stories from Rwanda* (New York: Farrar, Straus & Giroux).

Gow, J. (1997) *Triumph of the Lack of Will: International Diplomacy and the Yugoslav War* (London: C. Hurst).

Gowa, J. (1983) *Closing the Gold Window: Domestic Politics and the End of Bretton Woods* (Ithaca, NY: Cornell University Press).

Gowa, J. (1999) *Ballots and Bullets: The Elusive Democratic Peace* (Princeton, NJ: Princeton University Press).

Grant, R. and K. Newland (eds) (1991) *Gender and International Relations* (Milton Keynes: Open University Press).

Gray, C. (1999) 'Clausewitz Rules OK! The Future Is the Past with GPS', *Review of International Studies,* Special Issue 'The Interregnum' (25) 161–82; also in Cox *et al.* (1999).

Gray, J. (2004) *Al Qaeda and What it Means to Be Modern* (London: Faber & Faber).

Greenhill, B. (2008) 'Recognition and Collective Identity Formation in International Politics', *European Journal of International Relations* (14) 343–68.

Grieco, J. M. (1988) 'Anarchy and the Limits of Cooperation: A Realist Critique of the Newest Liberal Institutionalism', *International Organization* (42) 485–508.

Griffiths, M. (1992) *Realism, Idealism and International Politics: A Reinterpretation* (London: Routledge).

Groom, A. J. R. and M. Light (eds) (1994) *Contemporary International Relations: A Guide to Theory* (London: Pinter).

Groom, A. J. R. and P. Taylor (eds) (1975) *Functionalism: Theory and Practice in World Politics* (London: University of London Press).

Groom, A. J. R. and P. Taylor (eds) (1984) *The Commonwealth in the 1980s* (London: Macmillan).

Groom, A. J. R. and P. Taylor (eds) (1994) *Frameworks for International Co-operation* (London: Pinter).

Gulick, E. V. (1955) *Europe's Classical Balance of Power* (Ithaca, NY: Cornell University Press).

Guzzini, S. (2000) 'A Reconstruction of Constructivism in International Relations', *European Journal of International Relations* (6) 147–82.

Guzzini, S. and A. Leander (eds) (2006) *Constructivism and International Relations: Alexander Wendt and his Critics* (London: Routledge).

Haas, E. B. (1964) *Beyond the Nation State* (Stanford, CA: Stanford University Press).

Haas, P. (1989) 'Do Regimes Matter: Epistemic Communities and Mediterranean Pollution Control', *International Organization* (43) 377–403.

Haas, P. (ed.) (1992) 'Knowledge, Power and International Policy Coordination', Special Issue, *International Organization* (46) 1–390.

Haass, R. (2008) 'The Age of Nonpolarity,' *Foreign Affairs* (87), 3.

Habermas, J. (1994) *The Past as Future* (Cambridge: Polity Press).

Habermas, J. (1997) 'Kant's Idea of Perpetual Peace, with the Benefit of Two Hundred Years' Hindsight', in Bohman and Lutz-Bachmann, *Perpetual Peace*.

Habermas, J. (1999) 'A War on the Border Between Legality and Morality', *Constellations* (6) 263–72.

Habermas, J. (2002) *The Inclusion of the Other: Studies in Political Theory* (Cambridge: Polity Press).

Hall, R. B. (1999) *National Collective Identity: Social Constructs and International System* (New York: Columbia University Press).

Halliday, F. (1992) 'An Encounter with Fukuyama', *New Left Review* (193) 89–95.

Halliday, F. (1994) *Rethinking International Relations* (London: Macmillan).

Hallward, M. C. (2008) 'Situating the "Secular": Negotiating the Boundary between Religion and Politics', *International Political Sociology* (2) 1–16.

Halper, S. and J. Clarke (2004) *America Alone: The Neo-Conservatives and Global Order* (Cambridge: Cambridge University Press).

Hamilton, K. and R. T. B. Langhorne (1995) *The Practice of Diplomacy* (London: Routledge).

Hanson, V. D. (1989) *The Western Way of War: Infantry Battle in Classical Greece* (New York: Knopf).

Harding, S. (1986) *The Science Question in Feminism* (Milton Keynes: Open University Press).

Hardt, M. and A. Negri (2001) *Empire* (Cambridge, MA: Harvard University Press).

Hardy, D. T. and J. Clarke (2004) *Michael Moore Is a Big Fat Stupid White Man* (London: HarperCollins).

Harris, N. (1986) *The End of the Third World* (Harmondsworth: Penguin).

Harvard Human Rights Journal, vol. 17 (2004).

Harvard International Review (2007) Special Issue, 'A Titled Balance: Who Will Rise?' (29).

Harvey, N. (1998) *The Chiapas Rebellion* (Durham, NC: Duke University Press).

Hasenclever, A., P. Mayer and V. Rittberger (1997) *Theories of International Regimes* (Cambridge: Cambridge University Press).

Hasenclever, A., P. Mayer and V. Rittberger (2000) 'Integrating Theories of International Regimes', *Review of International Studies* (26) 3–33.

Haslam, J. (2002) *No Virtue like Necessity: Realist Thought in International Relations since Machiavelli* (New Haven, CT: Yale University Press).

Hassner, P. (2002) *The United States: The Empire of Force or the Force of Empire* (Chaillot Papers, No. 54), Paris.

Havel, V. (1993) *Summer Meditations on Politics, Morality and Civility in a Time of Transition* (New York: Vintage).

Hay, C., M. Lister and D. Marsh (eds) (2006) *The State: Theories and Issues* (Basingstoke/New York: Palgrave Macmillan).

Hegel, G. F. W. (1821/1991) *Elements of the Philosophy of Right* (Cambridge: Cambridge University Press).

Held, D. (1995) *Democracy and the Global Order* (Cambridge: Polity Press).

Held, D. and A. McGrew (eds) (2003) *The Global Transformations Reader*, 2nd edn (Cambridge: Polity Press).

Held, D. and A. McGrew (eds) (2007) *Globalization Theory: Approaches and Controversies* (Cambridge: Polity Press).

Held, D, A. McGrew, D. Goldblatt and J. Perraton (1999) *Global Transformations* (Cambridge: Polity Press).

Helms, J. (2000/1) 'American Sovereignty and the United Nations', *The National Interest* (62) 31–4.

Hendrickson, D. C. (2002) 'Towards Universal Empire: The Dangerous Quest for Absolute Security', *World Policy Journal* (19) 2–10.

Hermann, C. E., C. W. Kegley and J. N. Rosenau (eds) (1987) *New Directions in the Study of Foreign Policy* (London: Allen & Unwin).

Herz, J. (1956) 'Rise and Demise of the Territorial State', *World Politics* (9) , 4, pp. 473 – 493,

Heuser, B. (2002) *Reading Clausewitz* (London: Pimlico).

Higgott, R. (1994) 'International Political Economy', in Groom and Light, *Contemporary International Relations*.

Higgott, R. (2000) 'Economic Globalization and Global Governance: Towards a Post Washington Consensus', in Rittberger and Schnabel, *The UN Global Governance System in the Twenty-First Century.*

Hill, C. (1989) '1939: The Origins of Liberal Realism', *Review of International Studies* (15) 319–28.

Hill, C. (2002) *The Changing Politics of Foreign Policy* (Basingstoke/New York: Palgrave Macmillan).

Hill, C. (2003) 'What Is to Be Done? Foreign Policy as a Site for Political Action', *International Affairs* (79) 233–55.

Hinsley, F. H. (1963) *Power and the Pursuit of Peace* (Cambridge: Cambridge University Press).

Hinsley, F. H. (1966) *Sovereignty* (London: Hutchinson).

Hinsley, F. H. (1974) *Nationalism and the International System* (London: Hodder & Stoughton).

Hirst, P. and G. Thompson (2000) *Globalization in Question: The International Economy and the Possibilities of Governance* (Cambridge: Polity Press).

Hitchens, C. (2003) *The Long Short War: The Postponed Liberation of Iraq* (London: Plume Books).

Hobbes, T. (1946) *Leviathan* (ed. with an introduction by M. Oakeshott) (Oxford: Basil Blackwell).

Hobson, J. A. (1902/1938) *Imperialism: A Study* (London: A. Constable).

Hobson, J. M. (2000) *The State and International Relations* (Cambridge: Cambridge University Press).

Hobson, J. M. (2001) 'The "Second State Debate" in International Relations: Theory Turned Upside Down', *Review of International Studies* (27) 395–414.

Hodges, M. (ed.) (1972) *European Integration* (Harmondsworth: Penguin).

Hoffmann, S. (1977) 'An American Social Science: International Relations', *Daedalus* (106) 41–61.

Hogan, M. (ed.) (1992) *The End of the Cold War: Its Meaning and Implications* (Cambridge: Cambridge University Press).

Holbraad, C. (1970) *Concert of Europe* (London: Longman).

Hollis, M. (1995) *The Philosophy of the Social Sciences* (Cambridge: Cambridge University Press).

Hollis, M. and S. Smith (1991) *Explaining and Understanding International Relations* (Oxford: Clarendon Press).

Holsti, O., R. Siverson and A. George (1980) *Change in the International System* (Boulder, CO: Westview Press).

Holzgrefe, J. L. and R. O. Keohane (eds) (2003) *Humanitarian Intervention: Ethical, Legal, and Political Dimensions* (New York: Cambridge University Press).

Houghton, D. P. (2007) 'Reinvigorating the Study of Foreign Policy Decision Making: Toward a Constructivist Approach,' *Foreign Policy Analysis* (3) 24–45.

Howard, M. (1983) *Clausewitz* (Oxford: Oxford University Press).

Howell, L. D. (ed.) (1991/2) 'International Studies: The State of the Discipline', Special Issue, *International Studies Notes* (16/17) 1–68.

Hume, D. (1987) *Essays: Moral, Political and Literary* (Indianapolis, IN: Liberty Classics).

Hunt, K. and K. Rygiel (eds) (2006) *(En)Gendering the War on Terror: War Stories and Camouflaged Politics* (London: Ashgate).

Hunt, L. (2007) *Inventing Human Rights* (New York: W. W. Norton).

Huntington, S. (1993a) 'The Clash of Civilizations', *Foreign Affairs* (72) 22–49.

Huntington, S. (1993b) 'Response: If Not Civilizations, What?', *Foreign Affairs* (72) 186–94.

Huntington, S. (1996) *The Clash of Civilizations and the Remaking of World Order* (New York: Simon & Schuster).

Huntington, S. (2005) *Who Are We?* (New York: Free Press).

Hurd, E. S. (2007) *The Politics of Secularism in International Relations* (Princeton, NJ: Princeton University Press).

Hurrell, A. (2007) *On Global Order: Power, Values and the Constitution of International Society* (Oxford: Oxford University Press)

Hurrell, A. and B. Kingsbury (eds) (1992) *The International Politics of the Environment* (Oxford: Oxford University Press).

Hutchings, K. (2008) *Time and World Politics* (Manchester: Manchester University Press).

Hutton, W. (2007) *The Writing on the Wall: China and the West in the 21st Century* (London: Little, Brown).

Ignatieff, M. (1999) *The Warrior's Honour: Ethnic War and the Modern Consciousness* (New York: Vintage).

Ignatieff, M. (2000) *Virtual War* (New York: Metropolitan Books).

Ignatieff, M. (2003) *Empire Lite* (London: Minerva).

Ikenberry, G. J. (1998) 'Constitutional Politics in International Relations', *European Journal of International Relations* (4) 147–77.

Ikenberry, G. J. (1998/99) 'Institutions, Strategic Restraint and the Persistence of American Post-War Order', *International Security* (23) 43–78.

Ikenberry, G. J. (2001) *After Victory* (Princeton, NJ: Princeton University Press).

Ikenberry, J. G. (ed.) (2002a) *America Unrivalled: The Future of the Balance of Power* (Ithaca, NY: Cornell University Press).

Ikenberry, J. G. (2002b) 'America's Imperial Ambition', *Foreign Affairs* (81) 5–52.

Ikenberry, J. G. (2008)'The Rise of China and the Future of the West; Can the Liberal System Survive', *Foreign Affairs* (87).

International Affairs (2007) 'Forum: Europe at 50' (83) 227–317.

International Commission on Intervention and State Sovereignty, The (2002) *The Responsibility to Protect*; available at: http://www.dfait-maeci.gc.ca/iciss-ciise/pdf/Commission-Report.pdf.

International Feminist Journal of Politics (2002) 'Forum: The Events of 11 September and Beyond' (4) 95–113.

International Organization (1998) Special Issue: '*International Organization*' at Fifty', P. Katzenstein, R. O. Keohane and S. Krasner (eds) (52) 645–1012.

International Relations (2005) Roundtable: The Battle Rages On (19) 337–60.

International Relations (2006) Forum: Rethinking the Rules (20) 273–349.

International Relations (2007) Special Issue: 'The Privatisation and Globalisation of Security in Africa' (2) 131–256.

International Security (2001/2) Special Section, 'The Threat of Terrorism: US Policy after September 11th' (26) 5–78.

International Security (2005) Forum: Balancing Acts (30) 7–45.

International Studies Perspectives (2005) 'Policy and the Poliheuristic Theory of Foreign Policy Decision Making: A Symposium' (6) 94–150.

International Studies Review (2006a) Forum: The Changing Face of Europe: European Institutions in the Twenty-First Century (8) 139–97.

International Studies Review (2006b) Forum: Moving Beyond the Agent–Structure Debate (8) 355–81.

International Studies Review (2007) 'The North–South Divide and International Studies: A Symposium' (9) 556–710.

Jackson, R. (1990) *Quasi-States: Sovereignty, International Relations and the Third World* (Cambridge: Cambridge University Press).

Jackson, R. (2000) *The Global Covenant* (Oxford: Oxford University Press)

Jackson, R. and G. Sorensen (2006) *Introduction to International Relations,* 3rd edn (Oxford: Oxford University Press).

Janis, I. (1972) *Victims of Groupthink* (Boston, MA: Houghton Mifflin).

Jarvis, A. (1989) 'Societies, States and Geopolitics', *Review of International Studies* (15) 281–93.

Jervis, R. (1976) *Perception and Misperception in World Politics* (Princeton, NJ: Princeton University Press).

Jervis, R. (1999) 'Realism, Neoliberalism and Co-operation: Understanding the Debate', *International Security* (24) 42–63.

Jessop, Bob (2002) *The Future of the Capitalist State* (Cambridge: Polity Press).

Jessop, Bob (2007) *State Power* (Cambridge: Polity Press).

Joll, J. (1984) *The Origins of the First World War* (London: Longman).

Jones, A. (1996) 'Gendering International Relations', *Review of International Studies* (22) 405–29.

Jones, A. (1998) 'Engendering Debate', *Review of International Studies* (24) 299–303.

Jones, P. and S. Caney (eds) (2000) *Human Rights and Global Diversity* (London: Frank Cass).

Jones, R. W. (1999) *Security, Strategy and Critical Theory* (Boulder, CO: Lynne Rienner).

Jones, R. W. (ed.) (2001) *Critical Theory and World Politics* (Boulder, CO: Lynne Rienner).

Joseph, J. (2008) 'Hegemony and the Structure–Agency Problem in International Relations: A Scientific Realist Contribution,' *Review of International Studies* (34) 109–29.

Joy, B. (2000) 'Why the Future Doesn't Need Us', *Wired* (8 April) 238–62.

Kagan, R. (2004) *Paradise and Power: America and Europe in the New World Order* (London: Atlantic Books).

Kagan, R (2008) *The Return of History and the End of Dreams* (NY: Atlantic Books).

Kaher, M. (ed.) (1986) *The Political Economy of International Debt* (Ithaca, NY: Cornell University Press).

Kaldor, M. (2003) *Global Civil Society: An Answer to War* (Cambridge: Polity Press).

Kaplan, M. (1957) *System and Process in International Politics* (New York: Wiley).

Katznelson, I. and H. Milner (eds) (2002) *Political Science: The State of the Discipline* (New York: W. W. Norton).

Katzenstein, P, R.O. Keohane, and S. Krasner (1999) *Exploration and Contestation in the Study of World Politics* (Cambridge, MA: MIT press)

Kaufman, S., R. Little and W. Wohlforth (2007) *Balance of Power in World History* (London: Palgrave).

Keane, J. (2003) *Global Civil Society?* (Cambridge: Cambridge University Press).

Keegan, J. (1978) *The Face of Battle* (London: Jonathan Cape).

Keegan, J. (2004) *The Iraq War* (London: Hutchinson).

Kegley, C. W. Jr (ed.) (1995) *Controversies in International Relations Theory: Realism and the Neoliberal Challenge* (Belmont, CA: Wadsworth; London: Macmillan).

Kegley, C. W. Jr and E. Wittkopf (2004) *World Politics: Trend and Transformation,* 9th edn (Belmont, CA: Wadsworth).

Kelsall, T. (2006) 'Politics, Anti-Politics, International Justice: Language and Power in the Special Court for Sierra Leone', *Review of International Studies* (32) 587–602.

Kennan, G. (1952) *American Diplomacy* (New York: New American Library).

Kennedy, P. (1981) *The Realities Behind Diplomacy* (London: Allen & Unwin).

Kennedy, P. (1988) *The Rise and Fall of the Great Powers* (London: Unwin, Hyman).

Kennedy, P. (1993) *Preparing for the Twenty-First Century* (New York: Random House).

Keohane, R. O. (1980) 'The Theory of Hegemonic Stability and Changes in International Economic Regimes, 1967–1977', pp. 132–62 in Holsti *et al., Change in the International System*; also in Keohane (1989).

Keohane, R. O. (1984) *After Hegemony* (Princeton, NJ: Princeton University Press).

Keohane, R. O. (ed.) (1986) *Neorealism and its Critics* (New York: Columbia University Press).

Keohane, R. O. (1988) 'International Institutions: Two Approaches', *International Studies Quarterly* (32) 379–96; also in Keohane (1989).

Keohane, R. O. (1989) *International Institutions and State Power* (Boulder, CO: Westview Press).

Keohane, R. O. and S. Hoffmann (eds) (1991) *The New European Community* (Boulder, CO: Westview Press).

Keohane R. O. and J. S. Nye (eds) (1971) *Transnational Relations and World Politics* (Cambridge, MA: Harvard University Press).

Keohane, R. O. and J. S. Nye (1977/2000) *Power and Interdependence, 1st/3rd* edn (Boston, MA: Little, Brown).

Kerr, D. (2005) 'The Sino-Russian Partnership and US Policy toward North Korea: From Hegemony to Concert in Northeast Asia', *International Studies Quarterly* (49) 411–38.

Keylor, W. (2005) *The Twentieth Century World and Beyond: An International History since 1900* (New York: Oxford University Press).

Keynes, J. M. (1919) *The Economic Consequences of the Peace* (London: Macmillan).

Khaliq, U. (2008) *Ethical Dimensions of the Foreign Policy of the European Union* (Cambridge: Cambridge University Press).

Kiely, R. (2006) 'US Hegemony and Globalisation: What Role for Theories of Imperialism?', *Cambridge Review of International Affairs* (19) 205–21.

Kiely, R. (2007) 'Poverty Reduction through Liberalisation? Neoliberalism and the Myth of Global Convergence', *Review of International Studies* (33) 415–34.

Kiely, R. (2007) *The New Political Economy of Development* (Basingstoke: Palgrave).

Kindleberger, C. (1973) *The World in Depression 1929–1939* (Harmondsworth: Penguin).

King, G., R. O. Keohane and S. Verba (1994) *Designing Social Enquiry: Scientific Inference in Qualitative Research* (Princeton, NJ: Princeton University Press).

Kissinger, H. (1994) *Diplomacy* (London: Simon & Schuster).

Klein, N. (2001) *No Logo* (London: Flamingo).

Knorr, K. and J. N. Rosenau (eds) (1969) *Contending Approaches to International Politics* (Princeton, NJ: Princeton University Press).

Koch, H. (ed.) (1972) *The Origins of the First World War* (London: Longman).

Krasner, S. D. (1972) 'Are Bureaucracies Important? (Or Allison Wonderland)', *Foreign Policy* (7) 159–79.

Krasner, S. D. (ed.) (1983) *International Regimes* (Ithaca, NY: Cornell University Press).

Krasner, S. D. (1985) *Structural Conflict: The Third World Against Global Liberalism* (Berkeley, CA: University of California Press).

Krasner, S. D. (1994) 'International Political Economy: Abiding Discord', *Review of International Political Economy* (1) 13–19.

Krasner, S. D. (1999) *Sovereignty: Organized Hypocrisy* (Princeton, NJ: Princeton University Press).

Kratochwil, F. (1989) *Rules, Norms and Decisions* (Cambridge: Cambridge University Press).

Kratochwil, F. (1995) 'Sovereignty as *Dominium:* Is There a Right of Humanitarian Intervention?', in Lyons and Mastanduno, *Beyond Westphalia?*

Kratochwil, F. (2000) 'Constructing a New Orthodoxy? Wendt's *Social Theory of International Politics* and the Constructivist Challenge', *Millennium: Journal of International Studies* (29) 73–101.

Kratochwil, F. (2005) 'Religion and (Inter-)National Politics: On the Heuristic of Identities, Structures, and Agents', *Alternatives* (30) 113–40.

Kratochwil, F. and E. Mansfield (eds) (2005) *International Organization and Global Governance: A Reader* (New York: Pearson).

Kratochwil, F. and J. G. Ruggie (1986) 'International Organization: the State of the Art or the Art of the State', *International Organization* (40) 753–75.

Krause, K. and M. C. Williams (eds) (1997) *Critical Security Studies: Concepts and Cases* (Minneapolis, MN: University of Minnesota Press).

Krauthammer, C. (2003) 'The Unipolar Moment Revisited', *The National Interest* (Winter 2002/3) 5–17.

Krugman, P. (1994) *Rethinking International Trade* (Cambridge, MA: MIT Press).

Krugman, P. (1996) *Pop Internationalism* (Cambridge, MA: MIT Press).

Krugman, P. (1998) *The Accidental Theorist and Other Despatches from the Dismal Science* (Cambridge, MA: MIT Press).

Krugman, P. (2004) *The Great Unravelling* (New York: W. W. Norton).

Krugman, P. and M. Obstfeld (2002) *International Economics: Theory and Policy* (New York: HarperCollins).

Kubalkova, V., N. Onuf and P. Kowert (1998) *International Relations in a Constructed World* (Armonk, NY: M. E. Sharpe).

Kuperman, A. J. (2008) 'The Moral Hazard of Humanitarian Intervention: Lessons from the Balkans', *International Studies Quarterly* (52) 49–80.

Kurki, M. (2006) 'Causes of a Divided Discipline: Rethinking the Concept of Cause in International Relations Theory', *Review of International Studies* (32) 189–216.

Kurki, M. (2008) *Causation in International Relations: Reclaiming Causal Analysis* (Cambridge: Cambridge University Press).

Kymlicka, W. (ed.) (1995) *The Rights of Minority Cultures* (Oxford: Oxford University Press).

Kymlicka, W. (2001) *Politics and the Vernacular: Nationalism, Multiculturalism and Citizenship* (Oxford: Oxford University Press).

Kymlicka, W. and M. Opalski (eds) (2001) *Can Liberal Pluralism be Exported? Western Political Theory and Ethnic Relations in Eastern Europe* (Oxford: Oxford University Press).

Laclau, E. (1976) *Politics and Ideology in Marxist Theory* (London: New Left Books).

LaFeber, W. (1999) *Michael Jordan and the New Global Capitalism* (New York: W. W. Norton).

Lakatos, I. and A. Musgrave (eds) (1970, reprinted 2008) *Criticism and the Growth of Knowledge* (Cambridge: Cambridge University Press).

Lake, D. (1988) *Power, Protection and Free Trade: International Sources of US Commercial Strategy, 1887–1939* (Ithaca, NY: Cornell University Press).

Lake, D. (1992) 'Powerful Pacifists: Democratic States and War', *American Political Science Review* (86) 24–37.

Lake, D. (1993) 'Leadership, Hegemony and the International Economy: Naked Emperor or Tattered Monarch with Potential', *International Studies Quarterly* (33) 459–89.

Lake, D. (2006) 'American Hegemony and the Future of East–West Relations', *International Studies Perspectives* (7) 23–30.

Lake, D. (2007) 'Escape from the State of Nature: Authority and Hierarchy in World Politics', *International Security* (32) 47–79.

Lal, D. (1983) *The Poverty of 'Development Economics'* (London: Institute of Economic Affairs).

Lang, A. F. (ed.) (2003) *Just Interventions* (Washington, DC: Georgetown University Press).

Lapid, Y. (1989) 'The Third Debate: On the Prospects of International Theory in a Post-Positivist Era', *International Studies Quarterly* (33) 235–54.

Lapid, Y. and F. Kratochwil (eds) (1996) *The Return of Culture and Identity in International Relations Theory* (Boulder, CO: Lynne Rienner).

Layne, C. (1994) 'Kant or Cant: the Myth of the Democratic Peace', *International Security* (19) 2; 5–49.

Lebow, R. N. (1981) *Between Peace and War: The Nature of International Crisis* (Baltimore, MD: Johns Hopkins University Press).

Lebow, R. N. (2003) *The Tragic Vision of Politics: Ethics, Interests and Orders* (Cambridge: Cambridge University Press).

Lebow, R. N. (2008) *A Cultural Theory of International Relations* (Cambridge: Cambridge University Press).

Lebow, R. N. and T. Risse-Kappen (eds) (1995) *International Relations Theory and the End of the Cold War* (New York: Columbia University Press).

Lebow, R. N. and J. Stein (1994) *We All Lost the Cold War* (Princeton, NJ: Princeton University Press).

Lebrecht, N. (2007) *Maestros, Masterpieces and Madness: The Secret Life and Shameful Death of the Classical Record Industry* (London: Allen Lane)

Legro, J. W. and A. Moravcsik (1999) 'Is Anybody Still a Realist?', *International Security* (24) 25–55.

Legvold, R. (2007) *Russian Foreign Policy in the 21st Century & the Shadow of the Past* (New York: University of Columbia Press).

Levi-Faur, D. (1997) 'Economic Nationalism: From Friedrich List to Robert Reich', *Review of International Studies* (23) 359–70.

Levit, K. (2005) 'Keynes and Polanyi: The 1920s and the 1990s', *Review of International Political Economy* (13) 152–77.

Levy, M. A., O. R. Young and M. Zürn (1995) 'The Study of International Regimes', *European Journal of International Relations* (1) 267–330.

Lewis, B. (2002) *What Went Wrong? The Clash between Islam and Modernity in the Middle East* (Oxford: Oxford University Press).

Lieber, R. (2007) *The American Era: Power and Strategy for the 21st Century* (Cambridge: Cambridge University Press)

Light, M. and A. J. R. Groom (eds) (1985) *International Relations: A Handbook in Current Theory* (London: Pinter).

Linklater, A. (1990) *Beyond Realism and Marxism* (Basingstoke/New York: Macmillan).

Linklater, A. (1992) 'The Question of the Next Stage in International Relations Theory: A Critical-Theoretic Approach', *Millennium* (21) 77–98.

Linklater, A. (1998) *The Transformation of Political Community* (Cambridge: Polity Press).

Linklater, A. and H. Suganami (2006) *The English School of International Relations: A Contemporary Reassessment* (Cambridge: Cambridge University Press)

Lipschutz, R. (2005) 'Power, Politics and Global Civil Society', *Millennium* (33) 747–69.

Liska, G. (1990) *The Ways of Power: Patterns and Meanings in World Politics* (Oxford: Basil Blackwell).

List, F. (1966) *The National System of Political Economy* (London: Frank Cass).

Little, I. M. D. (1982) *Economic Development: Theory, Policy, and International Relations* (New York: Basic Books).

Little, R. (1994) 'International Relations and Large Scale Historical Change', in Groom and Light, *Contemporary International Relations.*

Little, R. (2007) *The Balance of Power in International Relations: Metaphors, Myths and Models* (Cambridge: Cambridge University Press).

Little, R. and M. Smith (eds) (2006) *Perspectives on World Politics: A Reader* (London: Routledge).

Loescher, G. (1993) *Beyond Charity: International Co-operation and the Global Refugee Crisis* (New York: Oxford University Press).

Lomas, P. (2005) 'Anthropomorphism, Personification and Ethics: A Reply to Alexander Wendt', *Review of International Studies* (31) 349–56.

Long, D. and B. Schmidt (eds) (2005) *Imperialism and Internationalism in the Discipline of IR* (New York: State University of New York Press).

Long, D. and P. Wilson (eds) (1995) *Thinkers of the Twenty Years' Crisis: Interwar Idealism Reassessed* (Oxford: Clarendon Press).

Lövbrand, E. and J. Stripple (2006) 'The Climate as Political Space: On the Territorialisation of the Global Carbon Cycle', *Review of International Studies* (32) 217–35.

Lucas, E. (2008) *The New Cold War: How the Kremlin Menaces Both Russia and the West* (London: Bloomsbury).

Lukes, S. (1974/2004) *Power: A Radical View,* 2nd edn (London/Basingstoke/New York: Palgrave Macmillan).

Lynn-Jones, S. M. and S. E. Miller (eds) (1995) *Global Dangers: Changing Dimensions of International Security* (Cambridge, MA: MIT Press).

Lyons, G. M. and M. Mastanduno (eds) (1995) *Beyond Westphalia?* (Baltimore, MD: Johns Hopkins University Press).

MacKinnon, C. (1993) 'Crimes of War, Crimes of Peace', in Shute and Hurley, *On Human Rights.*

MacMillan, J. (1996) 'Democracies Don't Fight: A Case of the Wrong Research Agenda', *Review of International Studies* (22) 275–99.

MacMillan, J. and A. Linklater (eds) (1995) *Boundaries in Question* (London: Pinter).

Macridis, R. C. (ed.) (1992) *Foreign Policy in World Politics* (London: Prentice-Hall).

Mahbubani, K. (1992) 'The West and The Rest', *The National Interest* (28) 3–13.

Mann, J. (2004) *The Rise of the Vulcans* (New York: Viking Books).

Mann, M. (1986/1993) *The Sources of Social Power,* Vols I and II (Cambridge: Cambridge University Press).

Mann, M. (1988) *States, War and Capitalism* (Oxford: Basil Blackwell).

Mann, M. (2003) *Incoherent Empire* (London: Verso).

Mannheim, K. (1936/1960) *Ideology and Utopia* (London: Routledge & Kegan Paul).

Mansfield, E and R. Snyder (2005) *Electing to Fight: Why Emerging Democracies go to War* (Cambridge, MA: MIT Press)

Martel, G. (ed.) (1986) *The Origins of the Second World War Reconsidered: The A. J. P. Taylor Debate after Twenty-Five Years* (Boston, MA: George Allen & Unwin).

Marx, K. (1973) *Political Writings,* Vol. 1 (London: Penguin).

Mayall, J. (1990) *Nationalism in International Society* (Cambridge: Cambridge University Press).

Mayall, J. (ed.) (1996) *The New Interventionism: 1991–1994* (Cambridge: Cambridge University Press).

McCormack, T. L. H. and G. J. Simpson (eds) (1997) *The Law of War Crimes: National and International Approaches* (The Hague: Kluwer Law International).

McGrew, A. and P. Lewis (1992) *Global Politics: Globalization and the Nation State* (Milton Keynes: Open University Press).

McSweeney, B. (1996) 'Identity and Security: Buzan and the Copenhagen School', *Review of International Studies* (22) 81–94.

McSweeney, B. (1998) Durkheim and the Copenhagen School', *Review of International Studies* (24) 137–40.

Mead, W. R. (2002) *Special Providence* (London: Routledge).

Mead, W. R. (2004) *Power, Terror, Peace and War* (New York: Alfred A. Knopf).

Meadows, D., J. Randers, D. L. Meadows and W. W. Behrens (1974) *Limits to Growth* (London: Pan).

Mearsheimer, J. (1990) 'Back to the Future: Instability in Europe after the Cold War', *International Security* (15) 5–56; and collected in M. E. Brown, Lynn-Jones and Miller, *The Perils of Anarchy* (1995).

Mearsheimer, J. (1994/5) 'The False Promise of International Institutions', *International Security* (19) 5–49; and collected in M. E. Brown, Lynn-Jones and Miller, *The Perils of Anarchy* (1995).

Mearsheimer, J. (2001) *The Tragedy of Great Power Politics* (New York: W. W. Norton).

Mearsheimer, J. (2005) 'E.H. Carr vs. Idealism: The Battle Rages On', *International Relations* (19) 139–52.

Mearsheimer, J. and S. Walt (2006) 'The Israel Lobby,' *London Review of Books* (28) 3–12.

Mearsheimer, J. and S. Walt (2007) *The Israel Lobby and U.S. Foreign Policy* (New York: Straus and Giroux).

Megret, F. (2002) 'The Politics of International Criminal Justice', *European Journal of International Law* (13) 1261–84.

Meinecke, F. (1957) *Machiavellism: The Doctrine of Raison d'Etat and Its Place in Modern History* (London: Routledge & Kegan Paul).

Meredith, R. (2008) *The Elephant and the Dragon: The Rise of India and China and What It Means for All of Us* (New York: W. W. Norton).

Meyer, J., J. Boli, G. Thomas and F. Ramirez (1997) 'World Society and the Nation State', *American Sociological Review* (62) 171–90.

Micklethwait, J. and A. Wooldridge (2004) *The Right Nation* (London: Allen Lane).

Miliband, R. (1973) *The State and Capitalist Society* (London: Quartet Books).

Millennium (1988) 'Women and International Relations', Special Issue (17) 419–598.

Millennium (1991) 'Sovereignty at Bay, 20 Years After', Special Issue (20) 198–307.

Millennium (1995) 'The Globalization of Liberalism', Special Issue (24) 377–576.

Millennium (1998) 'Gender and International Relations', Special Issue (27) 809–1100.

Millennium (2000a) 'Seattle December 1999' (29) 103–40.

Millennium (2000b) 'Religion and International Relations', Special Issue (29) 565–89.

Millennium (2002) 'Exchange: "What Empire: Whose Empire?"' (31) 318–45.

Millennium (2003) 'International Relations in the Digital Age', Special Issue (32) 441–672.

Millennium (2005) 'Facets of Power in International Relations', Special Issue (33) 477–961.

Millennium (2007a) 'Forum: Scientific and Critical Realism in International Relations', (35) 343–407.

Millennium (2007b) 'Theory of the International Today', Special Issue (35) 495–817.

Millennium (2008a) 'Exchange: Pluralism in IR', (36) 105–20.

Millennium (2008b) 'Forum: Reflections on the Past, Prospects for the Future in Gender and International Relations' (37) 97–179.

Mills, K. (2005) 'Neo-Humanitarianism: The Role of International Humanitarian Norms and Organizations in Contemporary Conflict,' *Global Governance* (11) 161–83.

Milner, H. V. and K. Keiko (2005) 'Why the Move to Free Trade? Democracy and Trade Policy in the Developing Countries', *International Organization* (59) 107–43.

Mitrany, D. (1966) *A Working Peace System* (Chicago: Quadrangle Books).

Mitrany, D. (1975) *The Functional Theory of Politics* (London: Martin Robertson).

Modelski, G. (1987) *Long Cycles in World Politics* (London: Macmillan).

Mohamed, M. Bin and S. Ishihara (1996) *The Voice of Asia: Two Leaders Discuss the Coming Century* (Tokyo: Kodansha International).

Moore, J. (ed.) (1998) *Hard Choices: Moral Dilemmas in Humanitarian Intervention* (Lanham, MD: Rowman & Littlefield).

Moore, M (2004a) *Dude, Where's My Country* (London: Penguin).

Moore, M. (2004b) *Stupid White Men* (London: Penguin).

Moravcsik, A. (1997) 'Taking Preferences Seriously: The Liberal Theory of International Politics', *International Organization* (51) 513–53.

Moravcsik, A. (1998) *The Choice for Europe: Social Purpose and State Power from Messina to Maastricht* (Ithaca, NY: Cornell University Press).

Morgenthau, H. J. (1948) *Politics Among Nations: The Struggle for Power and Peace* (New York: Alfred P. Knopf) (5th edn 1978).

Morton, A. D. (2007) 'Waiting for Gramsci: State Formation, Passive Revolution and the International', *Millennium* (35) 597–621.

Murphy, C. (1994) *International Organization and Industrial Change: Global Governance since 1850* (Cambridge: Polity Press).

Murphy, C. and R. Tooze (eds) (1991) *The New International Political Economy* (Boulder, CO: Lynne Rienner).

Murray, A. J. (1996a) 'The Moral Politics of Hans Morgenthau', *The Review of Politics* (58) 81–107.

Murray, A. J. H. (1996b) *Reconstructing Realism* (Edinburgh: Keele University Press).

Nardin, T. (1983) *Law, Morality and the Relations of States* (Princeton, NJ: Princeton University Press).

Nardin, T. (ed.) (1996) *The Ethics of War and Peace* (Princeton, NJ: Princeton University Press).

Nardin, T. and D. Mapel (eds) (1992) *Traditions of International Ethics* (Cambridge: Cambridge University Press).

Nardin, T. and M. S. Williams (2006) *Humanitarian Intervention* (London/New York: New York University Press).

National Commission on Terrorist Attacks, 'The 9/11 Commission Report' (2004) *The Full Final Report of the National Commission on Terrorist Attacks Upon the United States* (New York: W. W. Norton).

National Interest, The (2003) Special Issue on Empire (71) 2–62.

National Interest, The (2004) Forum on Iraq (76) 5–56.

Navari, C. (2007) 'States and State Systems: Democratic, Westphalian or Both?' *Review of International Studies* (33) 577–95.

Navon, E. (2001) 'The "Third Debate" Revisited', *Review of International Studies* (27) 611–25.

Neufeld, M. (1995) *The Restructuring of International Relations Theory* (Cambridge: Cambridge University Press).

Neumann, I. B. and O. J. Sending (2007) '"The International" as Governmentality', *Millennium* (35) 677–701.

Neumayer, E. (2005) 'Do International Human Rights Treaties Improve Respect for Human Rights?', *Journal of Conflict Resolution* (49) 925–53.

Newell, P. (2008) 'The Political Economy of Global Environmental Governance', *Review of International Studies* (34) 507–30.

Nicholas, H. G. (1985) *The United Nations as a Political System* (Oxford: Oxford University Press).

Nicholson, M. (1996) *Causes and Consequences in International Relations: A Conceptual Survey* (London: Pinter).

Niebuhr, R. (1932) *Moral Man and Immoral Society* (New York: Charles Scribner's Sons).

Nuruzzaman, M. (2006) 'Paradigms in Conflict: The Contested Claims of Human Security, Critical Theory and Feminism', *Cooperation and Conflict* (41) 285–303.

Nussbaum, M. (1999) 'The Professor of Parody: The Hip Defeatism of Judith Butler', *The New Republic*, 22 February, 37–45.

Nye, J. (1971) *Peace in Parts* (Boston, MA: Little, Brown).

Nye, J. S. (1988) Neorealism and Neoliberalism', *World Politics* (40) 235–51.

Nye, J. S. (1990) *Bound to Lead: The Changing Nature of American Power* (New York: Basic Books).

Nye, J. S. (2002) *The Paradox of American Power* (New York: Oxford University Press).

Nye, J. S. (2005) *Soft Power* (New York: PublicAffairs).

Nye, J. S. (2008) 'Recovering American Leadership', *Survival* (50) 55–68.

Oberdorfer, D. (1991) *The Turn: How the Cold War Came to an End* (London: Jonathan Cape).

O'Brien, R. and M. Williams (2007) *Global Political Economy*, 2nd edn (Basingstoke/ New York: Palgrave Macmillan).

Odysseos, L. and H. Seckinelgin (2002) *Gendering the International* (London: Palgrave).

O'Hanlon, M. E. (2002) 'A Flawed Masterpiece', *Foreign Affairs* (81) 47–63.

Ohmae, K. (1990) *The Borderless World* (London: Collins).

Olson, W. C. and A. J. R. Groom (1992) *International Relations Then and Now* (London: Pinter).

Onuf, N. (1989) *World of Our Making* (Columbia, SC: University of South Carolina Press).

Onuf, N. (1995) 'Levels', *European Journal of International Relations* (1) 35–58.

Overton, R. (2000) 'Molecular Electronics will Change Everything', *Wired* (8 July) 240–51.

Palan, R. and J. Abbott (1996) *State Strategies in the Global Political Economy* (London: Pinter).

Pape, R. A. (1997) 'Why Economic Sanctions Do Not Work', *International Security* (22) 90–136.

Pape, R. A. (1998) 'Why Economic Sanctions *Still* Do Not Work', *International Security* (23) 66–77.

Pape, R. A. (2005) 'Soft Balancing against the United States' *International Security* (30) 7–45

Parekh, B. (2000) *Rethinking Multiculturalism* (Basingstoke: Palgrave Macmillan; Cambridge, MA: Harvard University Press).

Parekh, B. (2008) *A New Politics of Identity: Political Principles for an Interdependent World* (London: Palgrave).

Paret, P. (ed.) (1986) *Makers of Modern Strategy from Machiavelli to the Nuclear Age* (Princeton, NJ: Princeton University Press).

Patomaki, H. (2002) *After International Relations: Critical Realism and the (Re)Construction of World Politics* (London: Routledge).

Patomäki, H. and C. Wight (2000) 'After Postpositivism: The Promise of Critical Realism', *International Studies Quarterly* (44) 213–37.

Pederson, T. (2002) 'Co-operative Hegemony: Power, Ideas and Institutions in Regional Integration', *Review of International Studies* (28) 677–96.

Percy, S. (2007a) *Mercenaries: The History of a Norm in International Relations* (Oxford: Oxford University Press).

Percy, S. (2007b) 'Mercenaries; Strong Norm, Weak Law', *International Organization* (61) 367–97.

Peters, J. S. and A. Wolper (eds) (1995) *Women's Rights, Human Rights: International Feminist Perspectives* (New York: Routledge).

Peterson, V. S. (ed.) (1992) *Gendered States: Feminist (Re)Visions of International Relations Theory* (Boulder, CO: Lynne Rienner).

Philpott, D. *et al* (forthcoming) *God's Century* (New York: W. W. Norton)

Pijl, K. Van der (1998) *Transnational Classes and International Relations* (London: Routledge).

Pilger, J. (2002) *New Rulers of the World* (London: Verso).

Pin-Fat, V. (2005) 'The Metaphysics of the National Interest and the "Mysticism" of the Nation-State: Reading Hans J. Morgenthau', *Review of International Studies* (31) 217–36.

Pinker, S. (2003) *The Blank Slate: The Modern Denial of Human Nature* (Harmondsworth: Penguin).

Pogge, T. (2002) *World Poverty and Human Rights* (Cambridge: Polity Press).

Polanyi, K. (1975) *The Great Transformation* (Boston, MA: Beacon Books).

Porter, B. (ed.) (1969) *The Aberystwyth Papers* (Oxford: Oxford University Press).

Porter, G. and J. Welsh Brown (1991) *Global Environmental Politics* (Boulder, CO: Westview Press).

Posen, B. (2000) 'The War for Kosovo: Serbia's Political Military Strategy', *International Security* (24) 39–84.

Poulantzas, N. (1978/2001) *State, Power, Socialism* (London: Verso Books).

Pouliot, V. (2006) 'The Alive and Well Transatlantic Security Community: A Theoretical Reply to Michael Cox', *European Journal of International Relations* (12) 119–27.

Pouliot, V. (2008) The Logic of Practicality: A Theory of Practice of Security Communities', *International Organization* (62) 257–88.

Powell, R. (1991) 'Absolute and Relative Gains in International Relations Theory', *American Political Science Review* (85) 1303–20.

Powell, R. (1994) 'Anarchy in International Relations: The Neoliberal–Neorealist Debate', *International Organization* (48) 313–34.

Power, S. (2002) *A Problem from Hell: America and the Age of Genocide* (London: Flamingo).

Prebisch, R. (1950) *The Economic Development of Latin America and Its Principal Problems* (New York: United Nations).

Price, M. (2008) *Moral Limit and Possibility in World Politics* (Cambridge: Cambridge University Press).

Price, R. and C. Reus-Smit (1998) 'Dangerous Liaisons: Critical International Theory and Constructivism', *European Journal of International Relations* (4) 259–94.

Prunier, G. (1995) *The Rwanda Crisis, 1959–94: History of a Genocide* (New York: Columbia University Press).

Puhovski, Z. (1994) 'The Moral Basis of Political Restructuring', in C. Brown (ed.), *Political Restructuring in Europe*.

Quirk, J. and V. Darshan (2005) 'The Construction of an Edifice: The Story of a First Great Debate', *Review of International Studies* (31) 89–107.

Rai, S. and G. Waylen (eds) (2008) *Global Governance: Feminist Perspectives* (Basingstoke: Palgrave).

Ralph, J. (2005) 'International Society, the International Criminal Court and American Foreign Policy', *Review of International Studies* (31) 27–44.

Ramsbotham, O. and T. Woodhouse (1996) *Humanitarian Intervention in Contemporary Conflict* (Cambridge: Polity Press).

Rasler, K. and W. Thompson (eds) (2005) *Puzzles of the Democratic Peace* (Basingstoke: Palgrave).

Rasmussen, M. (2006) *The Risk Society at War: Terror, Technology and Strategy in the Twenty-first Century* (Cambridge: Cambridge University Press).

Rathbun, B. (2007) 'Uncertain about Uncertainty: Understanding the Multiple Meanings of a Crucial Concept in International Relations Theory', *International Studies Quarterly* (51) 533–57.

Reich, R. (1992) *The Work of Nations* (New York: Vintage).

Reiss, H. (ed.) (1970) *Kant's Political Writings* (Cambridge: Cambridge University Press).

Reus-Smit, C. (ed.) (2004) *The Politics of International Law* (Cambridge: Cambridge University Press).

Review of International Studies (1999a) Special Issue: *The Interregnum* (25) (also published as M. Cox, K. Booth and T. Dunne (eds) (1999), *The Interregnum* (Cambridge: Cambridge University Press).

Review of International Studies (1999b) Forum on Andrew Linklater's *The Transformation of Political Community* (25) 139–75.

Review of International Studies (2000) Forum on Alexander Wendt's *Social Theory of International Politics* (26) 123–80.

Review of International Studies (2001) Forum on the English School (27) 465–513.

Review of International Studies (2003a) Forum on American Realism (29) 401–60.

Review of International Studies (2003b) Forum on Chomsky (29) 551–620.

Review of International Studies (2004a) Forum on the State as a Person (30) 255–316.

Review of International Studies (2004b) Forum on the American Empire (30) 583–653.

Review of International Studies (2005a) Forum on Habermas and International Relations (31) 127–209.

Review of International Studies (2005b) Forum on Charles Beitz: Twenty-five Years of Political Theory and International Relations (31) 361–423.

Review of International Studies (2006) Special Issue on Force and Legitimacy in World Politics (31) 3–263.

Review of International Studies (2007) Special Issue: Critical International Relations Theory after 25 years (33) 3–174.

Ricardo, D. (1971) *Principles of Political Economy and Taxation* (Harmondsworth: Penguin).

Richardson, J. L. (1994) *Crisis Diplomacy* (Cambridge: Cambridge University Press).

Rieff, D. (2002) *A Bed for the Night: Humanitarianism in Crisis* (New York: Vintage).

Ripsman, N. M. and T.V. Paul (2005) 'Globalization and the National Security State: A Framework for Analysis', *International Studies Review* (7) 199–227.

Risse, T. (2000) 'Let's Argue', *International Organization* (54) 1–39.

Risse-Kappen, T. (ed.) (1995) *Bringing Transnational Relations Back In: Non-State Actors, Domestic Structures and International Institutions* (Cambridge: Cambridge University Press).

Rittberger, V. (ed.) (1993) *Regime Theory and International Relations* (Oxford: Oxford University Press).

Rittberger, V. and A. Schnabel (eds) (2000) *The UN Global Governance System in the Twenty-first Century* (Tokyo: United Nations University Press).

Rivkin, D. B. and L. A. Casey, (2000/1) 'The Rocky Shoals of International Law', *The National Interest* (62) 35–46.

Roberts, A. and R. Guelff (eds) (2000) *Documents on the Laws of War* (Oxford: Oxford University Press).

Roberts, A. and B. Kingsbury (eds) (1993) *United Nations, Divided World: The UN's Role in International Relations* (Oxford: Oxford University Press).

Robertson, E. M. (ed.) (1971) *The Origins of the Second World War: Historical Interpretations* (London: Macmillan).

Rodney, W. (1983) *How Europe Underdeveloped Africa* (London: Bogle-Louverture).

Rorty, R. (1993) 'Human Rights, Rationality and Sentimentality', in Shute and Hurley, *On Human Rights*.

Rorty, R. (1998) 'The End of Leninism, Havel, and Social Hope', in *Truth and Progress: Philosophical Papers, Vol. 3* (Cambridge: Cambridge University Press).

Rosamond, B. (2000) *Theories of European Integration* (Basingstoke/New York: Palgrave Macmillan).

Rose, G. (1998) 'Neoclassical Realism and Theories of Foreign Policy', *World Politics* (51) 144–72.

Rosecrance, R. (2006) 'Power and International Relations: The Rise of China and Its Effects', *International Studies Perspectives* (7) 31–35.

Rosen, S. P. (2005) *War and Human Nature* (Princeton, NJ: Princeton University Press).

Rosenau, J. N. (ed.) (1967) *Domestic Sources of Foreign Policy* (New York: Free Press).

Rosenau, J. N. (ed.) (1969) *International Politics and Foreign Policy: A Reader* (New York: Free Press).

Rosenau, J. N. (1997) *Along the Domestic–Foreign Frontier: Exploring Governance in a Turbulent World* (Cambridge: Cambridge University Press).

Rosenau, J. N. and E.-O. Czempiel (eds) (1992) *Governance without Government: Order and Change in World Politics* (Cambridge: Cambridge University Press).

Rosenberg, J. (1994) *The Empire of Civil Society* (London: Verso).

Rosenberg, J. (2001) *Follies of Globalization Theory* (London: Verso).

Rosenthal, J. (1991) *Righteous Realists* (Baton Rouge: University of Louisiana Press).

Rubin, J. (2003) 'Stumbling into War', *Foreign Affairs* (82) 46–66.

Rudolph, C. (2001) 'Constructing an Atrocities Regime: The Politics of War Crimes Tribunals', *International Organization* (55) 655–92.

Ruggie, J. G. (1982) 'International Regimes, Transactions and Change: Embedded Liberalism in the Postwar Economic Order', *International Organization* (36) 379–415.

Ruggie, J. G. (1983) 'Continuity and Transformation in the World Polity: Towards a NeoRealist Synthesis', *World Politics* (35) 261–85.

Ruggie, J. G. (1998) *Constructing the World Polity* (London: Routledge).

Russett, B. (1993) *Grasping the Democratic Peace: Principles for a Post-Cold War World* (Princeton, NJ: Princeton University Press).

Russett, B., J. L. Ray and R. Cohen (1995) 'Raymond Cohen on Pacific Unions: A Response and a Reply', *Review of International Studies* (21) 319–25.

Ruthven, M. (2000) *Islam: A Very Short Introduction* (Oxford: Oxford University Press).

Ruthven, M. (2004) *A Fury for God: The Islamicist Attack on America* (Cambridge: Granta Books).

Sachs, W. (ed.) (1993) *Global Ecology: A New Arena of Political Conflict* (London: Zed Books).

Sagan, S. D. and K. Waltz (1995) *The Spread of Nuclear Weapons* (New York: W. W. Norton).

Sagarin, R. D. and T. Taylor (eds) (2008) *Natural Security: A Darwinian Approach to a Dangerous World* (Berkeley, CA: University of California Press).

Sahnoun, M. (1998) 'Mixed Intervention in Somalia and the Great Lakes: Culture, Neutrality and the Military', in Moore, *Hard Choices*.

Sakakiba, E. (1995) 'The End of Progressivism: A Search for New Goals', *Foreign Affairs* (74) 8–15.

Sassen, S. (1998) *Globalization and its Discontents* (New York: New Press).

Sassen, S. (2000) *Cities in a World Economy* (Thousand Oaks, CA: Pine Forge Press).

Schabas, W. (2004) *An Introduction to the International Criminal Court*, 2nd edn (Cambridge: Cambridge University Press).

Schelling, T. (1960) *The Strategy of Conflict* (Cambridge, MA: Harvard University Press).

Schmidt, B. (1998) *The Political Discourse of Anarchy: A Disciplinary History of International Relations* (Albany, NY: State University of New York Press).

Schmitt, C. (1932/1996) *The Concept of the Political* (Chicago: University of Chicago Press).

Scholte, J. A. (2005) *Globalization*, 2nd edn (Basingstoke/New York: Palgrave Macmillan).

Scheuerman, W. (2008) 'Realism and the Left: The Case of Hans J. Morgenthau', *Review of International Studies* (34) 29–51.

Schroeder, P. (1994) 'Historical Reality vs. Neo-Realist Theory', *International Security* (19) 108–48; and collected in M. E. Brown, Lynn-Jones and Miller, *The Perils of Anarchy* (1995).

Schweller, R. (1998) *Deadly Imbalances: Tripolarity and Hitler's Strategy of World Conquest* (New York: Columbia University Press).

Scott, S. V. and O. Ambler, (2007) 'Does Legality Really Matter? Accounting for the Decline in US Foreign Policy Legitimacy Following the 2003 Invasion of Iraq', *European Journal of International Relations* (13) 67–87.

Scruton, R. (2003) *The West and the Rest: Globalization and the Terrorist Threat* (London: Continuum).

Searle, J. (1995) *The Construction of Social Reality* (London: Allen Lane).

Sen, A. (1982) *Poverty and Famine* (Oxford: Clarendon Press).

Sen, A. (2000) *Development and Freedom* (Cambridge: Cambridge University Press).

Sending, O. J. and I. B. Neumann (2006) 'Governance to Governmentality: Analyzing NGOs, States, and Power', *International Studies Quarterly* (50) 651–672.

Sewell, J. P. (1966) *Functionalism and World Politics* (Princeton, NJ: Princeton University Press).

Shaikh, N. (ed) (2007) *The Present as History: Critical Perspective on Global Power* (New York: University of Columbia Press).

Shannon, V. P. (2005) 'Wendt's Violation of the Constructivist Project: Agency and Why a World State is Not Inevitable', *European Journal of International Relations* (11) 581–7.

Shapiro, I. and L. Brilmayer (eds) (1999) *Global Justice* (New York: New York University Press).

Shapiro, M. and H. R. Alker (eds) (1996) *Challenging Boundaries: Global Flows, Territorial Identities* (Minneapolis, MN: University of Minnesota Press).

Shaw, M. (ed.) (1999) *Politics and Globalization: Knowledge, Ethics and Agency* (London: Routledge).

Shawcross, W. (2000) *Deliver Us from Evil: Warlords and Peacekeepers in a World of Endless Conflict* (London: Bloomsbury).

Shawcross, W. (2004) *Allies at War* (London: Atlantic Books).

Shiller, R. J. (2008) *The Subprime Solution: How Today's Global Financial Crisis Happened and What to Do about It* (Princeton, NJ: Princeton University Press).

Shilliam, R. (2007) 'Morgenthau in Context: German Backwardness, German Intellectuals and the Rise and Fall of a Liberal Project', *European Journal of International Relations* (13) 299–327.

Shonfield, A. (ed.) (1976) *International Economic Relations of the Western World 1959–1971,* Vol. I, *Politics and Trade* (Shonfield *et al.*), Vol. II, *International Monetary Relations* (Susan Strange) (Oxford: Oxford University Press).

Shue, H. (1980) *Basic Rights: Subsistence, Affluence and U.S. Foreign Policy* (Princeton, NJ: Princeton University Press).

Shute, S. and S. Hurley (eds) (1993) *On Human Rights* (New York: Basic Books).

Singer, J. D. (1961) 'The Levels of Analysis Problem in International Relations', in K. Knorr and S. Verba (eds), *The International System: Theoretical Essays* (Princeton, NJ: Princeton University Press).

Singer, J. D. (1979) *Explaining War* (London: Sage).

Sklair, L. (1995) *The Sociology of the Global System* (Hemel Hempstead: Harvester Wheatsheaf).

Slaughter, A.-M. (2004) *A New World Order* (Princeton, NJ: Princeton University Press).

Smith, A. D. (1998) *Nationalism and Modernity* (London: Routledge).

Smith, H. (1994) 'Marxism and International Relations', in Groom and Light, *Contemporary International Relations.*

Smith, K. E. and M. M. Light (eds) (2001) *Ethics and Foreign Policy* (Cambridge: Cambridge University Press).

Smith, M. J. (1986) *Realist Thought from Weber to Kissinger* (Baton Rouge: University of Louisiana Press).

Smith, S. (1986) 'Theories of Foreign Policy: An Historical Overview', *Review of International Studies* (12) 13–29.

Smith, S. (1997) 'Power and Truth: A Reply to William Wallace', *Review of International Studies* (23) 507–16.

Smith, S. and M. Clarke (eds) (1985) *Foreign Policy Implementation* (London: Allen & Unwin).

Smith, S., K. Booth and M. Zalewski (eds) (1996) *International Theory: Post-Positivism and Beyond* (Cambridge: Cambridge University Press).

Smythe, E. and P. J. Smith, (2006) 'Legitimacy, Transparency, and Information Technology: The World Trade Organization in an Era of Contentious Trade Politics', *Global Governance* (12) 31–54.

Snyder, J. (1991) *Myths of Empire: Domestic Politics and International Ambition* (Ithaca, NY: Cornell University Press).

Snyder, R., H. W. Bruck, B. Sapin and V. Hudson, D. Chollet and J. Goldgeier (2003) *Foreign Policy Decision Making Revisited* (Basingstoke: Palgrave Macmillan).

Soederberg, S., G. Menz and P. Cerny, P. (eds) (2005) *Internalizing Globalization: The Rise of Neoliberalism and the Erosion of National Models of Capitalism* (Basingstoke: Palgrave Macmillan).

Sørenson, G. (2003) *The Transformation of the State: Beyond the Myth of Retreat* (Basingstoke/New York: Palgrave Macmillan).

Sørensen, G. (2006) 'What Kind of World Order? The International System in the New Millennium', *Cooperation and Conflict* (41) 343–63.

Soros, G. (2008) *The New Paradigm for Financial Markets: The Credit Crisis of 2008 and What It Means* (Jackson, TN: Public Affairs)

Spero, J. and J. Hart (2003) *The Politics of International Economic Relations,* 6th edn (Belmont, CA: Wadsworth).

Spiro, P. J. (2000) 'The New Sovereigntists', *Foreign Affairs* (79) 9–15.

Spykman, N. (1942) *America's Strategy in World Politics* (New York: Harcourt Brace).

Steans, J. (1998) *Gender and International Relations: An Introduction* (Cambridge: Polity Press).

Stein, A. (1982) 'Coordination and Collaboration: Regimes in an Anarchic World', *International Organization* (36) 294–324.

Steiner, H. J. and P. Alston (eds) (2007) *International Human Rights in Context: Law, Politics, Morals*, 3rd edn (Oxford: Clarendon Press).

Sterling-Folker, J. (2006) *Making Sense of IR Theory* (Boulder, CO: Lynne Reiner).

Stiglitz, J. (2004) *Globalization and its Discontents* (London: Penguin).

Stoessinger, J. G. (2005) *Why Nations Go to War*, 9th edn (Belmont, CA: Wadsworth).

Stopford, J. and S. Strange (1991) *Rival States, Rival Firms: Competition for World Market Shares* (Cambridge: Cambridge University Press).

Strange, S. (1970) 'International Economics and International Relations: A Case of Mutual Neglect', *International Affairs* (46) 304–15.

Strange, S. (1971) *Sterling and British Policy* (Oxford: Oxford University Press).

Strange, S. (1985) 'Protectionism and World Politics', *International Organization* (39) 233–59.

Strange, S. (1986) *Casino Capitalism* (Oxford: Basil Blackwell).

Strange, S. (1987) 'The Persistent Myth of Lost Hegemony', *International Organization* (41) 551–74.

Strange, S. (1988) *States and Markets* (London: Pinter).

Strange, S. (1992) 'States, Firms and Diplomacy', *International Affairs* (68) 1–15.

Strange, S. (1994) 'Wake up Krasner! The World *Has* Changed', *Review of International Political Economy* (1) 209–19.

Strange, S. (1996) *The Retreat of the State* (Cambridge: Cambridge University Press).

Strange, S. (1998a) 'Globaloney', *Review of International Political Economy* (5) 704–11.

Strange, S. (1998b) *Mad Money* (Manchester: Manchester University Press).

Strange, S. (1999) 'The Westfailure System', *Review of International Studies* (25) 345–54.

Stritzel, H. (2007) 'Towards a Theory of Securitization: Copenhagen and Beyond', *European Journal of International Relations* (13) 357–83.

Stubbs, R. and G. Underhill (eds) (1999) *Political Economy and the Changing Global Order*, 2nd edn (Toronto: Oxford University Press).

Suganami, H. (1989) *The Domestic Analogy and World Order Proposals* (Cambridge: Cambridge University Press).

Suganami, H. (1990) 'Bringing Order to the Causes of War Debate', *Millennium* (19) 19–35.

Suganami, H. (1996) *On the Causes of War* (Oxford: Clarendon Press).

Suganami, H. (1999) 'Agents, Structures, Narratives', *European Journal of International Relations* (5) 365–86.

Sunstein, C. R. and R. H. Thaler (2008) *Nudge: Improving Decisions About Health, Wealth, and Happiness* (New Haven, CT: Yale University Press).

Sylvester, C. (1994) *Feminist Theory and International Relations in a Post-Modern Era* (Cambridge: Cambridge University Press).

Sylvester, C. (2001) *Feminist International Relations: An Unfinished Journey* (Cambridge: Cambridge University Press).

Taleb, N. N. (2007) *The Black Swan: The Impact of the Highly Improbable* (New York: Random House).

Taliaferro, J. (2000/01) 'Security Seeking under Anarchy: Defensive Realism Revisited', *International Security* (25) 128–61.

Taylor, A. J. P. (1961) *The Origins of the Second World War* (London: Hamish Hamilton).

Taylor, C. (1971) 'Interpretation and the Sciences of Man', *Review of Metaphysics* (25) 3–51.

Taylor, C. (2007) *A Secular Age* (Cambridge, MA: Harvard University Press).

Taylor, P. (1993) *International Organization in the Modern World* (London: Pinter).

Taylor, P. and A. J. R. Groom (eds) (1978) *International Organization: A Conceptual Approach* (London: Pinter).

Taylor, P. and A. J. R. Groom (eds) (1989) *Global Issues in the United Nations Framework* (London: Macmillan).

Taylor, P. and A. J. R. Groom (1992) *The UN and the Gulf War, 1990–1991: Back to the Future* (London: Royal Institute of International Affairs).

Taylor, P. and A. J. R. Groom (2000) *The United Nations at the Millennium* (London: Continuum).

Thayer, B. (2000) 'Bringing in Darwin: Evolutionary Theory, Realism and International Politics', *International Security* (25) 124–51.

Thayer, B. (2004) *Darwin and International Relations* (Lexington: The University Press of Kentucky).

Thomas, C. (1987) *In Search of Security: The Third World in International Relations* (Brighton: Wheatsheaf).

Thomas, C. (1992) *The Environment in International Relations* (London: Royal Institute of International Affairs).

Thomas, C. (ed.) (1994) 'Rio: Unravelling the Consequences', Special Issue, *Environmental Politics* (2) 1–241.

Thomas, C. and P. Wilkin (eds) (1999) *Globalization and the South* (Basingstoke/New York: Palgrave Macmillan).

Thompson, H. (2006) 'The Case for External Sovereignty', *European Journal of International Relations* (12) 251–74.

Thompson, W. R. (2006) 'Systemic Leadership, Evolutionary Processes, and International Relations Theory: The Unipolarity Question', *International Studies Review* (8) 1–22.

Tickner, A. (2003) 'Seeing International Relations Differently: Notes from the Third World', *Millennium: Journal of International Studies* (32) 295–324.

Tickner, J. A. (1989) 'Hans Morgenthau's Principles of Political Realism: A Feminist Reformulation', *Millennium* (17) 429–40.

Tickner, J. A. (1992) *Gender in International Relations* (New York: Columbia University Press).

Tickner, J. A. (2001) *Gendering World Politics* (New York: Columbia University Press).

Tilly, C. (ed.) (1975) *The Formation of National States in Western Europe* (Princeton, NJ: Princeton University Press).

Tilly, C. (1990) *Coercion, Capital and European States AD 990–1990* (Oxford: Basil Blackwell).

Toffler, A. and H. Toffler (1993) *War and Anti-War* (Boston, MA: Little, Brown).

Tomlinson, J. (1999) *Globalization and Culture* (Cambridge: Polity Press).

Treitschke, H. von (1916/1963) *Politics* (abridged and ed. by Hans Kohn) (New York: Harcourt, Brace & World).

Tucker, R. W. and D. C. Hendrickson (1992) *The Imperial Temptation: The New World Order and America's Purpose* (New York: Council on Foreign Relations).

Turner, L. and M. Hodges (1992) *Global Shakeout* (London: Century Business).

United Nations (1995) *Our Global Neighborhood: Report of the Commission on Global Governance* (New York: United Nations).

United Nations (1999) *Human Development Report* (New York: UN Publications).

Van Evera, S. (1998) 'Offense, Defense and the Causes of War', *International Security* (22) 5–43.

Van Evera, S. (1999) *Causes of War: Power and the Roots of Conflict* (Ithaca, NY: Cornell University Press).

Vernon, R. (1971) *Sovereignty at Bay* (New York: Basic Books).

Veseth, M. (1998) *Selling Globalization: The Myth of the Global Economy* (Boulder, CO: Lynne Rienner).

Vincent, R. J. (1986) *Human Rights and International Relations: Issues and Responses* (Cambridge: Cambridge University Press).

Viotti, P. and M. Kauppi (1999) *International Relations Theory*, 3rd edn (New York: Prentice Hall).

Vogler, J. (2000) *The Global Commons: Environmental and Technological Governance* (New York: John Wiley).

Vogler, J. and M. Imber (eds) (1995) *The Environment and International Relations* (London: Routledge).

Waever, O. (1996) 'The Rise and Fall of the Inter-paradigm Debate', in Smith, Booth and Zalewski, *International Theory*.

Walker, R. B. J. (1993) *Inside/Outside: International Relations as Political Theory* (Cambridge: Cambridge University Press).

Wallace, W. (1994) *Regional Integration: The West European Experience* (Washington, DC: Brookings Institute).

Wallace, W. (1996) 'Truth and Power, Monks and Technocrats: Theory and Practice in International Relations', *Review of International Studies* (22) 301–21.

Wallace, W. (1999a) 'Europe after the Cold War: Interstate Order or Post-Sovereign Regional System', *Review of International Studies* (25) 201–33.

Wallace, W. (1999b) 'The Sharing of Sovereignty: The European Paradox', *Political Studies* (47) 503–21.

Wallerstein, I. (1974/1980/1989) *The Modern World System*, Vols I, II and III (London: Academic Press).

Wallerstein, I. (1991a) *Geopolitics and Geoculture: Essays on the Changing World System* (Cambridge: Cambridge University Press).

Wallerstein, I. (1991b) *Unthinking Social Science: The Limits of Nineteenth-Century Paradigms* (Cambridge: Polity Press).

Walt, S. (1985) 'Alliance Formation and the Balance of World Power', *International Security* (9) 3–43; and collected in M. E. Brown, Lynn-Jones and Miller, *The Perils of Anarchy* (1995).

Walt, S. (1987) *The Origin of Alliances* (Ithaca, NY: Cornell University Press).

Walt, S. (1991) 'The Renaissance of Security Studies', *International Studies Quarterly* (35) 211–39.

Walt, S. (2002) 'The Enduring Relevance of the Realist Tradition', in Katznelson and Milner, *Political Science*.

Walt, S. (2005) *Taming American Power: The Global Response to U.S. Primacy* (New York: W. W. Norton).

Walton, C. D. (2007) *Geopolitics and the Great Powers in the Twenty-first Century: Multipolarity and the Revolution in Strategic Perspective* (London: Routledge).

Waltz, K. (1959) *Man, the State and War* (New York: Columbia University Press).

Waltz, K. (1979) *Theory of International Politics* (Reading, MA: Addison-Wesley).

Waltz, K. (1990) 'Realist Thought and Neorealist Theory', *Journal of International Affairs* (44) 21–37.

Waltz, K. (1993) 'The Emerging Structure of International Politics', *International Security* (18) 44–79; and collected in M. E. Brown, Lynn-Jones and Miller, *The Perils of Anarchy* (1995).

Waltz, K. (1997) 'Evaluating Theories', *American Political Science Review* (91) 913–18.

Waltz, K. (1998) 'An Interview with Kenneth Waltz' (conducted by Fred Halliday and Justin Rosenberg), *Review of International Studies* (24) 371–86.

Waltz, K. (2000) 'Structural Realism after the Cold War', *International Security* (25) (1) 5–41.

Walzer, M. (ed.) (1997) *Toward a Global Civil Society* (New York: Berghahn Books).

Walzer, M. (2000) *Just and Unjust Wars,* 3rd edn (New York: Perseus).

Walzer, M. (2004) *Arguing about War* (New Haven, CT: Yale University Press).

Warleigh, A. (2006) 'Learning from Europe? EU Studies and the Re-thinking of "International Relations"', *European Journal of International Relations* (12) 1, 31–51.

Warren, B. (1980) *Imperialism: Pioneer of Capitalism* (London: New Left Books).

Watson, A. (1982) *Diplomacy: The Dialogue of States* (London: Methuen).

Watson, A. (1992) *The Evolution of International Society: A Comparative Historical Analysis* (London: Routledge).

Watt, D. C. (1989) *How War Came* (London: Heinemann).

Webber, M. and M. Smith (2002) *Foreign Policy in a Transformed World* (London: Longman).

Weber, C. (1999) *Faking It: US Hegemony in a 'Post-Phallic' Era* (Minneapolis, MN: University of Minnesota Press).

Wee, H. Van der (1986) *Prosperity and Upheaval 1945–1980* (Harmondsworth: Penguin).

Weinberg, G. L. (1994) *A World at Arms: A Global History of World War II* (Cambridge: Cambridge University Press).

Weiss, T. G. (1999) *Military–Civil Interactions: Intervening in Humanitarian Crises* (Lanham, MD: Rowman & Littlefield).

Welch, D. A. (1992) 'The Organizational Process and Bureaucratic Politics Paradigm', *International Security* (17) 112–46.

Weller, M. (1999) 'On the Hazards of Foreign Travel for Dictators and Other Criminals', *International Affairs* (75) 599–618.

Wendt, A. (1987) 'The Agent/Structure Problem in International Relations Theory', *International Organization* (41) 335–70.

Wendt, A. (1991) 'Bridging the Theory/Metatheory Gap in International Relations' *Review of International Studies* (17), 383–92.

Wendt, A. (1992) 'Anarchy Is What States Make of It: The Social Construction of Power Politics', *International Organization* (46) 391–426.

Wendt, A. (1999) *Social Theory of International Politics* (Cambridge: Cambridge University Press).

Wendt, A. (2003) 'Why a World State Is Inevitable', *European Journal of International Relations* (9) 491–542.

Wendt, A. (2004) 'The State as Person in IR Theory', *Review of International Studies* (30) 289–316.

Wendt, A. (2005a) 'Agency, Teleology and the World State: A Reply to Shannon', *European Journal of International Relations* (11) 589–98.

Wendt, A. (2005b) 'How Not to Argue against State Personhood: A Reply to Lomas', *Review of International Studies* (31) 357–60.

Wheeler, N. J. (1992) 'Pluralist and Solidarist Conceptions of International Society: Bull and Vincent on Humanitarian Intervention', *Millennium* (21) 463–87.

Wheeler, N. J. (2000) *Saving Strangers* (Oxford: Oxford University Press).

Wheeler, N. J. (2000/1) 'Reflections on the Legality and Legitimacy of NATO's Intervention in Kosovo', in Booth (ed.), *The Kosovo Tragedy*.

White, B. (1999) 'The European Challenge to Foreign Policy Analysis', *European Journal of International Relations* (5) 37–66.

White, S. (1991) *Political Theory and Postmodernism* (Cambridge: Cambridge University Press).

Wibbels, E. (2006) 'Dependency Revisited: International Markets, Business Cycles, and Social Spending in the Developing World', *International Organization* (60) 433–68.

Wiener, A. and T. Diez (eds) (2004) *European Integration Theory* (Oxford: Oxford University Press).

Wiener, J. (1995) 'Hegemonic Leadership: Naked Emperor or the Worship of False Gods', *European Journal of International Relations* (1) 219–43.

Wight, C. (1999) '"They Shoot Dead Horses Don't They?" Locating Agency in the Agent–Structure Problematique', *European Journal of International Relations* (5) 109–42.

Wight, C. (2004) 'Social Action without Human Activity', *Review of International Studies* (30) 269–80.

Wight, C. (2006) *Agents, Structures and International Relations* (Cambridge: Cambridge University Press).

Wight, M. (1946/1978) *Power Politics*, 2nd edn (Leicester: Leicester University Press).

Wight, M. (1977) *Systems of States* (Leicester: Leicester University Press).

Willetts, P. (ed.) (1983) *Pressure Groups in the International System* (London: Pinter).

Williamson, J. (1990) 'What Washington Means by Policy Reform', in Williamson (ed.), *Latin American Adjustment: How Much Has Changed* (Washington, DC: Institute for International Economics).

Williamson, J. and C. Milner (1991) *The World Economy* (Hemel Hempstead: Harvester Wheatsheaf).

Williams, M. C. (2005) *The Realist Tradition and the Limits of International Relations* (Cambridge: Cambridge University Press).

Williams, M. C. (2007) *Realism Reconsidered: The Legacy of Hans Morgenthau in International Relations* (Oxford: Oxford University Press).

Wilson, P. (2001) 'Radicalism for a Conservative Purpose: The Peculiar Realism of E. H. Carr', *Millennium: Journal of International Studies* (30) 123–36.

Wilson, P. (2003) *The International Theory of Leonard Woolf* (Basingstoke/New York: Palgrave Macmillan).

Wohlforth, W. (1993) *Elusive Balance: Power and Perception during the Cold War* (Ithaca, NY: Cornell University Press).

Wohlforth, W. (1994/5) 'Realism and the End of the Cold War', *International Security* (19) 91–129.

Wohlforth, W. C. (1999) 'The Stability of a Unipolar World', *International Security* (24) 5–41.

Wohlforth, W., R. Little, S. Kaufman, D. Kang, C. Jones, V. T. Hui, A Eckstein, D. Deudney and W. Brenner (2007) 'Testing Balance-of-Power Theory in World History', *European Journal of International Relations* (13) 155–85.

Woodward, B. (2002) *Bush at War* (New York: Pocket Books).

Woodward, B. (2004) *Plan of Attack: The Road to War* (New York: Pocket Books).

Woolsey, R. J. (ed.) (2003) *The* National Interest *on International Law and Order* (London: Transaction).

World Bank – China Quarterly Update http://web.worldbank.org/WBSITE/EXTER-NAL/COUNTRIES/EASTASIAPACIFICEXT/CHINAEXTN

World Politics (forthcoming 2009) Special Issue: 'International Relations Theory and the Consequences of Unipolarity' (62).

Wright, M. (ed.) (1989) 'The Balance of Power', Special Issue, *Review of International Studies* (15) 77–214.

Young, O., G. Demko and K. Ramakrisna (eds) (1996) *Global Environmental Change and International Governance* (Hanover, NH: University Press of New England).

Zacher, M. with B. A. Sutton (1996) *Governing Global Networks: International Regimes for Transport and Communication* (Cambridge: Cambridge University Press).

Zakaria, F. (1992) 'Realism and Domestic Politics: A Review Essay', *International Security* (17) 177–98.

Zakaria, F. (1994) 'Culture is Destiny: A Conversation with Lee Kwan Yew', *Foreign Affairs* (73) 109–26.

Zakaria, F. (1998) *From Wealth to Power* (Princeton, NJ: Princeton University Press).

Zakaria, F. (2008a) *The Post-American World* (New York: W. W. Norton).

Zakaria, F. (2008b) 'The Future of American Power', *Foreign Affairs* (87), 3.

Zalewski, M. and J. Papart (eds) (1997) *The 'Man' Question in International Relations* (Boulder, CO: Westview Press).

Zehfuss, M. (2007) *Wounds of Memory: The Politics of War in Germany* (Cambridge: Cambridge University Press).

Index